Alabama Women

Alabama Women

THEIR LIVES AND TIMES

EDITED BY

Susan Youngblood Ashmore and

Lisa Lindquist Dorr

The University of Georgia Press   *Athens*

This publication is made possible in part through a grant
from the Bradley Hale Fund for Southern Studies.

Most University of Georgia Press titles are
available from popular e-book vendors.

Printed digitally

Library of Congress Cataloging-in-Publication Data

Names: Ashmore, Susan Youngblood, 1961– editor. |
Dorr, Lisa Lindquist, editor.
Title: Alabama women : their lives and times /
edited by Susan Youngblood Ashmore and Lisa Lindquist Dorr.
Other titles: Southern women (Athens, Ga.)
Description: Athens : University of Georgia Press, [2017] |
Series: Southern women: their lives and times |
Includes bibliographical references and index.
Identifiers: LCCN 2016051435 | ISBN 9780820350783 (hardback : alk. paper) |
ISBN 9780820350790 (pbk. : alk. paper) | ISBN 9780820350776 (ebook)
Subjects: LCSH: Women—Alabama—History. | Alabama—Social
conditions—19th century. | Alabama—Social conditions—20th century.
Classification: LCC HQ1438.A2 A43 2017 | DDC 305.409761—dc23
LC record available at https://lccn.loc.gov/2016051435

To all Alabama women, past and present,
whose lives may as yet be invisible to history
but who shaped their world in large and small ways.

Contents

Acknowledgments

We start by thanking Nancy Grayson, whose vision made this series possible and enabled us to meet each other as well as the wonderful scholars whose work fills this volume. It has been a long but rewarding process. We also thank the Alabama Department of Archives and History. Their support allowed us to host an early presentation of essay drafts and to reach out to local social studies teachers. The department's collections made much of this research possible, and the stories of countless other unsung Alabama women no doubt await discovery on the department's shelves. We also thank the College of Arts and Sciences at the University of Alabama and the Academic Dean of Oxford College at Emory University for supporting this project.

Susan Youngblood Ashmore and Lisa Lindquist Dorr

Alabama Women

Introduction

LISA LINDQUIST DORR

When Alabama midwife Margaret Charles Smith declared in 1992, "I want a book about me," she voiced a larger truth about women's place not only in the history of Alabama but in history in general. In that statement, Smith acknowledged that women's contribution to the lives and experiences of Alabama, while critical to the maintenance of communities, culture, and social relations, remained largely invisible. Smith's experiences attested to that truth—she had worked for decades as a midwife for poor black women in the Black Belt. Women did the work that allowed families to keep body and soul together and thus allowed society to continue, but for many years, the seclusion of those efforts within the walls of the household rendered those efforts and the women who made them invisible to history. Smith ultimately took matters into her own hands, and in 1996 her memoir, *Listen to Me Good*, was published.[1] In her eyes, the story of a woman who birthed future generations was too important to disappear into the undocumented past.

For too many years, all of women's activities disappeared with time. Much of the life-giving work that comprised their days was consumed, worn out, and consigned to the trash heap of daily life. The mundane details of the everyday not only left little evidence in the archives but were deemed of little import in the larger scheme of history. Not until the late 1960s and the 1970s did a new generation of historians begin to argue that histories that ignored half the population were hopelessly incomplete. The first generation of women's historians began to use the techniques developed by social historians to unearth the lives of women in the past. Their first efforts added women to the larger story of men's history, looking to document women's contribution to the established events and trends that historians had accepted as the important aspects of the past. Those early efforts were followed by women's historians who put women at the center of the past. Their efforts opened new areas of study, putting the seemingly insignificant aspects of women's lives under historical scrutiny. What previous historians had viewed as the irrelevant aspects of the private world became the fodder for a new generation of historical investigation. Historians of women argued that topics such as the history of courtship, women's economic contributions, and the development of birth control, to name just a few, carried larger historical significance. Only at this juncture did historians come to attribute historical significance to the world of women. This new generation of historians argued that issues of family life and the home carried relevance for historical understanding. They soon showed that while the women's world seemed circumscribed by domestic boundaries, it nonetheless expanded outward to shape much of social life and indeed the wider world. Lives like that of Margaret Charles Smith took on added significance as historians of women argued that no aspect of the past was complete without incorporating some understanding of the roles of women and the private world of the home. Perhaps more important, the work of women's historians challenged ideas that the roles of men and women were timeless, divinely ordained, and/or determined by biology. Exploring the lives of women in the past revealed that understandings of men and women had changed dramatically over the centuries and that what contemporaries viewed as unchangeable aspects of social organization in fact evolved. Women's and men's roles were created by culture as a product of history. For women involved in struggles to improve their position in society, such realizations were invaluable. If gender roles had changed in the past, they could change again or even be changed as a result of organized agitation.[2]

Contrasting the public world of men with the private world of women brought women's lives and experiences out of historical obscurity but nevertheless had its limits. It privileged the experiences of women whose economic circumstances enabled them to confine their lives to a domestic world, eliding over the experiences of women whose race and class forced them into the "male" world of work. It suggested that the lives of white, middle-class women represented the norm while the experiences of other women were somehow exceptional and therefore less significant. A bit more time would pass before the day-to-day struggles of African American women such as Smith would move to center stage. But the developing idea of separate spheres—that men operated in the public world of work while women confined themselves to the private world of the home—proved to have other shortcomings as well. The ideology of separate spheres helped to elucidate the ideology that structured women's lives and became the standard by which women were often judged but suggested a clearer boundary between the public and private world than often existed in reality.[3] Indeed, as women's historians looked more deeply into the lived experiences of women and men in the past, it became clear that despite women's seeming ideological confinement in the domestic realm, myriad women crossed their thresholds to influence the public world of work and politics. Indeed, many of these women used the ideology about women's unique nature as leverage to demand a greater role in public life. Women—and men—increasingly realized that the boundary between public and private was in fact permeable, that ideas about gender, what men and women were supposed to be and do, were quite fluid. The lives, experiences, and influence of women of all kinds were indeed woven into the larger fabric of the American story.[4]

Much of the earliest research into the lives and experiences of women focused on women in the Northeast—yet another shortcoming in the efforts to recover women's history. Anne Firor Scott's *The Southern Lady: From Pedestal to Politics* (1970) began calling attention to the role of women in the southern past.[5] Nevertheless, in the southern context, the public/private frameworks that seemed sufficient to hold an understanding of women's lives again seemed inadequate. Southern historians grappled with the implications of a society fundamentally structured around distinctions between the free and the unfree. Divisions of class, at least initially, seemed inconsequential compared to the power of whiteness to shape the social order. In addition, the seemingly timeless divisions of home and work appeared to have less sway in the South. In a society based on plantation agriculture and cash crop production, work and home were often the same place, even for men, meaning that the domestic realm was not women's domain. The patriarchal order of the plantation master at least for a while inhibited women's efforts to bring their influence to the public world. The plantation economy shifted idealized roles for mistresses and masters and almost entirely erased the experiences of enslaved women and poorer women of all races. As explorations into the lives of southern women expanded, historians realized that no "universal woman" existed. Women's experiences were always a function of their race, their class, where they lived, their family structure, and many other factors.[6]

After more than forty years of expansion, the field of American women's history is clearly no fad. Indeed, as one of my advisers said in the 1990s, during my first class in women's history, writing history without including a consideration of the role of gender is simply *wrong*.[7] Events over the past two decades have made this statement even more true. Ideas of gender inflect all aspects of American life and can no longer be compartmentalized as the part of history dealing with the insignificant private aspects of women and family life. Indeed, the experiences of women inflect and shape our overall understanding of the past. Women contributed not only to the private world but also to events on the global stage. And yet there is still so much we do not know about all the ways in which American women, southern women, and even Alabama women played crucial roles in shaping history.

This volume of essays contributes to that process of recovery, bringing the efforts of Alabama's women to center stage and situating them within the larger sweep of events that we have come to understand as the narrative of Alabama history, southern history, and American history, as well as the history of women in the American South. This collection illuminates the efforts of both the famous and the seemingly insignificant, in the process demonstrating that all lives contribute to the larger historical narrative of the state.

The eighteen essays included in this volume of course make no pretense at being comprehensive, at incorporating all of the most interesting lives, the most significant, the most publicly acclaimed, or the most important. Such an effort would require essays on many thousands of women and would fill countless volumes. Instead, we sought to present women who represented a variety of experiences across the state. We selected women who exemplify different aspects of the state's history from the Creek women in the state's earliest years through the Civil War era, Reconstruction, segregation, and the civil rights movement. We also sought broad geographical representation, from Mobile on the Gulf Coast to Huntsville in the northern part of the state and from the rural Black Belt to the industrial landscape of Birmingham. We included women from different races and different ethnicities whose experiences suggested the range of efforts of women across more than two centuries of Alabama's past. We would have liked to include many additional women, most of whom might arguably be considered essential to a book of this sort, but doing so was just not possible. Whatever its flaws or omissions, this collection of essays clearly demonstrates that Alabama women may have been invisible in the works of historians but were never invisible in the worlds they inhabited. Their efforts were not insignificant and were rarely confined by the boundaries of their domestic worlds. Indeed, Alabama women, like women everywhere, actively engaged with the world around them. Whether or not they were frustrated by the limits on their opportunities, they creatively found ways to carve out room to maneuver in the wider world and expand the scope of activity for succeeding generations of women. Indeed, that subtle—and not-so-subtle—pressure on the constraints they faced ensured that while women could not always accomplish all they wanted, they were never bound completely by ideologies that sought to limit their influence.

Yet the lives of women in this volume make plain that women's experiences depended on their circumstances and that circumstances depended not only on when but on where they lived. Alabama's history encompasses the larger

American story. It witnessed the thriving Mississippian culture before becoming a frontier representing opportunity to whites and a bitter site of conflict and exile for Native Americans. Like other Deep South states, it hosted a plantation cotton economy made possible by the work of enslaved African Americans. It witnessed the upheaval of civil war and was home to the first capital of the Confederacy. Like the South as a whole, Alabama convulsed with change and resistance during Reconstruction, only to fall to a Redeemer government committed to white supremacy. Decades of Jim Crow segregation were finally overcome by soaring voices of protest and activism in the civil rights movement. Alabama's history in many ways paralleled that of its southern neighbors but also reflected the history of the larger United States. Like much of the nation, Alabama experienced significant industrial development after the Civil War, yet its insistence on a segregated society and the persistence of a rural economy based on sharecropping and tenant farming allowed too many of its inhabitants to live in dire poverty well into the present day. Like much of the country, Alabama was transformed by the mobilization for World War II and the consumer society of the postwar period. And Alabama's history of Jim Crow segregation and the civil rights movement reflects the problems of race that have bedeviled the nation as a whole. Over the twentieth century, Alabama held the federal government at arm's length while simultaneously benefiting from Uncle Sam's largesse in the form of the New Deal, military spending, and social programs. Alabama's history is simultaneously unique and emblematic of the larger trends that shaped and at times convulsed the region and the nation.

Throughout it all, women—black and white, native-born and immigrant, rich and poor—struggled to live their lives and occasionally even remake the world they knew. Though these women lived in Alabama, they were not isolated from larger historical currents. Some, like Bess Bolden Walcott, came to the South from elsewhere, stepping in to meet local needs in times of crisis. Other women, such as Slovak women during Birmingham's industrial heyday, had experiences that echo those of immigrant women around the nation. Julia Tutwiler and Pattie Ruffner Jacobs, like many white women of means in the South and around the country, used their privilege to center their lives on reform, whether for the benefit of the less fortunate or in pursuit of their own interest in suffrage. Similarly, Margaret Murray Washington used her education and position to work for the betterment of African-descended peoples locally, nationally, and around the world. Still other women were nationally recognized, though their origins in Alabama were or perhaps are unfamiliar. Author Harper Lee's ties to Alabama are well recognized; however, few modern-day Americans know that one of the most widely read novelists of the nineteenth century,

Augusta Evans Wilson, made her home in Mobile—if they have even heard of Wilson. And many today may not realize that the quintessential flapper of the 1920s, Zelda Sayre Fitzgerald, was a wild child of Montgomery. These women's lives show the ongoing ebb and flow of the state's and region's relationship to the larger nation. But exploring the lives of these women also reveals the limitations of our understandings of that relationship. The 1955 Montgomery Bus Boycott, for example, represented a moment of singularity, in which Alabama's experience was like that of no other state, but Rosa Parks's later life showed that Alabama was in many ways unique only in the particulars. Parks did not leave racial exclusion and oppression behind in the South but found it waiting for her in Michigan when she arrived there. At the same time, Lurleen Wallace's election as governor shows that those particulars might be everything. She was only the third woman elected to a governorship, but her achievement did not represent unalloyed progress for American or southern women. While in some ways she was her own governor, in others she followed the lead of her husband, George, resisting federal encroachments into traditional southern values. Indeed, the interplay among local, state, regional, and national currents adds an appealing texture to this volume.

How each of these women negotiated the limits that she faced is perhaps one of the book's most intellectually intriguing themes. Social constraints in the South were never merely a function of gender. Ida Mathis capitalized on that understanding, using her status as "just a farmer" to move outside of women's traditional roles and become a prominent advocate for agricultural reform. Maria Fearing did not allow her former enslavement and her gender to prevent her from obtaining an education and living as a missionary in the Congo. Southern historians of women have shown that race and gender as well as class always intersected in defining identity and experience. What was expected of and acceptable for white women was very different from racialized gender identities for black women, just as ideas about black men's nature varied considerably from those ascribed to white men.

These intertwined ideologies not only shaped the opportunities men and women of both races experienced but also justified their social and legal privileges and disabilities. Indeed, understandings of racialized gender were a cornerstone of the ideology of segregation in the Jim Crow South. Beliefs, stereotypes, and attitudes about the alleged superiority of white women and men justified and supported their privileges, while the opposing stereotypes of other races justified their circumscribed place in southern society and the specific indignities they endured. Nevertheless, those seemingly intractable rules of interracial interaction could be strangely malleable in particular circumstances, allowing women of color to leverage them in unexpected ways. Creek women used the tensions between their community's ideas of gender roles and those of whites to assert, with some success, independent power and influence. The young, mixed-race Townsend women and others like them used their close relationships with white men to obtain benefits. Disempowered in no way meant entirely powerless.

The essays in this volume place understandings of Alabama women's lives within the context of a racialized and gendered world. They show how women's efforts were understood through the prism of race and class position. Yet the lives of many of these women suggest that while they were products of a social order structured for many years by strict rules of race, different kinds of relationships could develop in the interactions among individuals. Many readers will already be familiar with Virginia Durr, a steadfast participant in Alabama's civil rights movement. Others, however, are less well known: Ruby Pickens Tartt, for example, collected the folk songs of African Americans as a result of her personal relationships with them. These complicated interactions become most conflicted perhaps in the relationship among Dr. J. Marion Sims and the enslaved women who sought his help for their unbearable maladies. Were these women exploited by their enslaved status or willing participants in finding treatments for a condition many described as "loathsome"? There is no easy answer to this question. But at the very least, the women in this collection suggest that individual lives complicated the operations of slavery and segregation, not necessarily mitigating its injustice but providing some necessary flexibility—some wiggle room—in their everyday lives.

The essays in this volume not only present some of the best new scholarship of the women of Alabama but also bring knowledge about the role of women in Alabama to a wider audience. While historians have argued about the need to include the experiences of women in understandings of the past, the resources needed to do so have not always trickled into the classrooms in which students first encounter both Alabama and American history. These essays are written with a broad audience in mind and seek to provide new understandings for historians, to entertain and enlighten readers interested in the history of the state, and finally to provide knowledge about the lives and efforts of women across the state that teachers can bring into their classrooms. There can never be too many examples of people in the past, especially women, who found ways to move around the obstacles they faced and change the world around them. And this project in our view does not end with this book of essays. We hope to follow up with a collection of lesson plans that busy teachers can readily incorporate and adapt for their own use. We want to provide not only a predigested narrative of these women's lives but also a sense of the primary sources the historians used to craft the essays. The study of history is not merely the amassing of a collection of facts or the mastering of an established narrative of what happened long ago. Instead, the study of history is the process of critical analysis in which a wide collection of information and sources from the past—letters, newspaper articles, archival collections, photographs, recordings, and whatever else—are synthesized into an interpretive narrative that presents an explanation, though not always the only one, for why history unfolded the way it did. This process requires the development of habits of mind that go far beyond mere memorization of names and dates. And while historians' intellectual skills require considerable practice, they are also useful well beyond the study of history. Their mastery contributes to the development of thoughtful citizens who bear some understanding of how we got to where we are and who can critically assess the mass of information they encounter in their daily lives. The primary sources embedded in the lessons associated with this volume will provide young citizens the opportunity to practice those analytical skills as well as to develop a fuller understanding of the complicated texture of the past. Perhaps then they will have the tools needed to understand and shape the complex world around them and maybe even use that understanding to expand the boundaries of their lives and those who come after them.

NOTES

1. Margaret Charles Smith, *Listen to Me Good: The Life Story of an Alabama Midwife* (Columbus: Ohio State University Press, 1996).

2. For an excellent overview of the development of women's history, see Linda Gordon, "U.S. Women's History," in Eric Foner, ed., *The New American History*, rev. and exp. ed. (Philadelphia: Temple University Press, 1997), 257–84. For more recent trends in the field, see Rebecca Edwards, "Women's and Gender History," in Eric Foner and Lisa McGirr, eds., *American History Now* (Philadelphia: Temple University Press, 2011), 336–57. Gerda Lerner first outlined the stages of incorporating women into understandings of the American past in "Placing Women in History: Definitions and Challenges," *Feminist Studies* 3 (1975): 8–15, reprinted in Lerner, *The Majority Finds Its Past: Placing Women in History* (New York: Oxford University Press, 1979), 115–26. A very brief selection of foundational works includes Nancy F. Cott and Elizabeth H. Pleck, eds., *A Heritage of Her Own: Toward a New Social History of American Women* (New York: Simon and Schuster, 1979); Joan Wallach Scott, *Gender and the Politics of History* (New York: Columbia University Press, 1988); Nancy F. Cott, *The Bonds of Womanhood: "Women's Sphere" in New England, 1780–1835* (New Haven: Yale University Press, 1977); Linda K. Kerber, *Women of the Republic: Intellect and Ideology in Revolutionary America* (Chapel Hill: University of North Carolina Press, 1980); Carroll Smith-Rosenberg, *Disorderly Conduct: Visions of Gender in Victorian America* (New York: Knopf, 1985); Linda Gordon, *Women's Body, Women's Right: Birth Control in America* (New York: Viking, 1976); Sara Evans, *Per-*

sonal Politics: The Roots of Women's Liberation in the Civil Rights Movement and the New Left (New York: Vintage, 1979); John D'Emilio and Estelle Freedman, *Intimate Matters: A History of Sexuality in America* (New York: Harper and Row, 1988).

3. For a discussion of the evolving role of separate spheres as a framework for understanding women in the past, see Kim Warren, "Separate Spheres: Analytical Persistence in United States Women's History," *History Compass* 5 (2007): 262–77.

4. The many fine works of women's historians contributing to this discussion are too numerous to list here in their entirety. A few notable participants include Alice Kessler-Harris, *Out to Work: A History of Wage-Earning Women in the United States* (New York: Oxford University Press, 1982); Christine Stansell, *City of Women: Sex and Class in New York, 1789–1860* (New York: Knopf, 1986); Kathy Peiss, *Cheap Amusements: Working Women and Leisure in Turn-of-the-Century New York* (Philadelphia: Temple University Press, 1989); Paula Giddings, *When and Where I Enter: The Impact of Black Women on Race and Sex in America* (New York: Bantam, 1984); Jacqueline Jones, *Labor of Love, Labor of Sorrow: Black Women, Work, and Family from Slavery to the Present* (New York: Basic Books, 1985); Deborah Gray White, *Ar'n't I a Woman: Female Slaves in the Plantation South* (New York: Norton, 1985); Ramón A. Gutiérrez, *When Jesus Came, the Corn Mothers Went Away: Marriage, Sexuality, and Power in New Mexico, 1500–1846* (Stanford: Stanford University Press, 1991); Vicki L. Ruiz, *From Out of the Shadows: Mexican Women in Twentieth-Century America* (New York: Oxford University Press, 1998); Theda Perdue, *Cherokee Women: Gender and Culture Change, 1700–1835* (Lincoln: University of Nebraska Press, 1998); Lillian Faderman, *Odd Girls and Twilight Lovers: A History of Lesbian Life in Twentieth-Century America* (New York: Columbia University Press, 1991).

5. Anne Firor Scott, *The Southern Lady: From Pedestal to Politics* (Chicago: University of Chicago Press, 1970). Scott is credited with creating the field of southern women's history, though she recognizes the foundational efforts of Julia Cherry Spruill, who wrote *Women's Life and Work in the Southern Colonies* (Chapel Hill: University of North Carolina Press, 1938).

6. In addition to Scott, *Southern Lady*, some foundational works of southern women's history are Kathleen Brown, *Good Wives, Nasty Wenches, and Anxious Patriarchs: Gender, Race, and Power in Colonial Virginia* (Chapel Hill: University of North Carolina Press, 1996); Elizabeth Fox-Genovese, *Within the Plantation Household: Black and White Women of the Old South* (Chapel Hill: University of North Carolina Press, 1988); Leslie Schwalm, *A Hard Fight for We: Women's Transition from Slavery to Freedom in South Carolina* (Urbana: University of Illinois Press, 1997); Laura F. Edwards, *Scarlett Doesn't Live Here Anymore: Southern Women in the Civil War Era* (Urbana: University of Illinois Press, 2000); Glenda Elizabeth Gilmore, *Gender and Jim Crow: Women and the Politics of White Supremacy in North Carolina, 1886–1920* (Chapel Hill: University of North Carolina Press, 1996); Marjorie Spruill Wheeler, *Women of the New South: The Leaders of the Woman's Suffrage Movement in the Southern States* (New York: Oxford University Press, 1993); Vicki L. Crawford and Jacqueline Anne Rouse, *Women in the Civil Rights Movement: Trailblazers and Torchbearers, 1941–1965* (Bloomington: University of Indiana Press, 1993).

7. Cindy Sondik Aron may very well have been paraphrasing another women's historian, but I heard the idea first from her. She, along with Ann J. Lane at the University of Virginia, nurtured my commitment to studying the history of women and gender.

The Indomitable Women of the Creek Removal Era

"Some One Must Have Told Her That I Meant to Run Away With Her"

CHRISTOPHER D. HAVEMAN

❀ ❀ ❀

Sometime in the spring of 1827, a Creek woman entered the Asbury Mission, a Methodist school established at Coweta (one mile north of Fort Mitchell) in the Creek Nation in 1821, and forcibly removed her seventeen-year-old daughter, Mary Ann Battis, from the compound. Battis's mother and uncle were associated with the McIntosh party, a faction of the Creek Nation comprising primarily friends, followers, and family members of the late William McIntosh, a Coweta headman who in 1825 illegally ceded a large portion of the Creek domain to the federal government in exchange ("acre for acre") for land in the Indian Territory.[1] Throughout the early nineteenth century, federal officials had encouraged the Creeks and many other Indian nations to voluntarily emigrate westward in an attempt to extinguish Indian title east of the Mississippi River. McIntosh was executed for his treason, but many of his allies followed through on their promise to resettle in the West. Although her family was intent on moving to Indian Territory with the first McIntosh party in the fall of 1827, Battis had rebuffed repeated overtures and threats made by her mother and uncle and refused to move with them. She declared that she would go west only if "she was bound & carried of[f]," a pronouncement that may well have led to her abduction. Battis anticipated being taken captive and had repeatedly threatened to "run away" from her family and return to Asbury if such an event occurred. Indeed, when the first voluntary emigrating party of Creeks left their rendezvous at Harpersville, Alabama, on November 8, 1827, Mary Ann Battis remained behind at Asbury.[2]

Mary Ann Battis has garnered scholarly attention primarily because of her

TCHOW-EE-PÚT-O-KAW, A [CREEK] WOMAN, 1838

George Catlin (1796–1872).

Gift of Mrs. Joseph Harrison Jr., Smithsonian American Art Museum, 1985.66.292.

ethnicity. She was a Cusseta woman of African, European, and Indian ancestry. She was also a Christian who considered her (no doubt unconverted) family members to be "so vile." Indeed, Andrew K. Frank has shown that Battis's fair complexion ("so light color'd as to have red hair"), Christian education, and matrilineal clan connections allowed her to move between two worlds. She was a Creek Indian but could just as easily integrate into white society (as illustrated by the fact that she lived in Georgia's capital, Milledgeville, for a time).[3] While issues of race and ethnicity feature prominently among observers of the time, in the growing Creek historiography, gender is often overlooked and misunderstood.[4] This is not by accident. Most Creek Indians did not understand English and even fewer had learned to read or write. As a result, documentation produced by Creek men is extremely scarce and that by Creek women virtually nonexistent. And because federal officials (who produced most of the information we have on the Creeks during this period) dealt almost exclusively with Creek males and wrote about the Creeks from a patriarchal worldview, Indian women are almost entirely absent from the historical record. When they do appear—typically in accounts written by European or American travelers—Creek women are too often mischaracterized as passive bystanders, overworked drudges, or helpless victims. Trader James Adair, for example, believed southeastern women to be "of a mild, amiable, soft disposition: exceedingly modest in their behaviour, and very seldom noisy, either in the single, or married state." Adam Hodgson, a British traveler who visited the Creek Nation in 1820, saw Creek women as little more than servants to the whims of their husbands. Swiss traveler Carl David Arfwedson wrote that women were treated as "subordinate beings, slaves, with whom the husband may do what he pleases." Author and actor John Howard Payne, who visited the Creek country in 1835, watched as a young Creek woman brazenly walked up to a federal investigator and asserted that "she had been counterfeited by some knave." The episode probably surprised Payne if for no other reason than the accuser was a "fine, gentle, innocent-looking girl."[5]

If Payne had known Creek women better, he would not have been surprised. Creek women during emigration (1825–36), removal (1836), and relocation (1836–37) were far from passive bystanders.[6] Like Mary Ann Battis and that "innocent-looking girl," Creek females were assertive and in many cases fearless about protecting their rights. Despite being threatened with "tying & whipping" by her mother, Battis was unflinching in her determination to remain at Asbury. And Battis was not alone. Creek women exerted a significant degree of autonomy on both sides of the emigration debate. Some Creek women were on the front lines of resistance against federal attempts to move them westward, while others broke up families when they chose voluntarily to move to Indian Territory without their husbands and/or clans. Some Creek women defied the will of their chiefs, violated Creek law, and attempted to avoid punishment by moving west. A few flaunted social mores without any apparent concern of reprisals. And while the uninformed considered them "drudges," Creek women are best remembered as the glue that held families together even as starvation threatened to rip them apart. Creek women were also vital to the maintenance of domestic, religious, and ceremonial customs both on the home front and during the journey west. They continued their role as domestic providers even as starvation forced them to move to nontraditional forms of food acquisition and commerce. Women continued to feature prominently in the Busk, an annual renewal ceremony that celebrated the new harvest and the bounty of the land. They provided moral support during the ceremonial lead-up to the hunt, warfare, and ball plays. And while on the march west, Creek women cooked, washed clothing, and gathered food for their families.[7]

The 1825 Treaty of Indian Springs and its successor, the 1826 Treaty of Washington, ceded large tracts of the Creek domain, eroded the buffer between whites and the Creek people, and commenced the voluntary emigration program. As a result, starvation (from land loss) and white encroachment exponentially increased over the next decade. The treaties made life increasingly difficult for the Creeks but offered the promise of amelioration if they resettled west of the Mississippi River. The Creeks had to vacate the known borders of Georgia by January 1, 1827, and thousands of people were subsequently forced into the Creek Nation within Alabama.[8]

Creek women adapted to the loss of their Georgia domain to varying degrees. Upper Creek women, far removed from the limits of Georgia, were the least affected, while the refugees from Georgia were the hardest hit. Many of the refugees were unable or unwilling to rebuild their lives in Alabama and subsequently began a long period of transience and starvation. Indeed, English traveler Margaret Hall, who along with her husband, daughter, and family nurse visited Alabama in 1828, witnessed refugees "flocking" about Creek agent John Crowell's house "in eager expectation of supplies of food." Her husband, Basil, observed that the refugees seemed like "bees whose hive has been destroyed." From their Eurocentric perspective, the Halls viewed the situation as resulting from Creek idleness, but these Georgia Creeks were now interlopers on other towns' hunting grounds and gathering spots within Alabama. With their communal fields, home garden plots, and favorite wild plant locations expropriated by Georgians, these Lower Creeks modified their food-gathering techniques by taking government provisions to continue providing for their families.[9]

The Halls witnessed Creek women adapting to new realities while resolutely maintaining their domestic influence and cultural way of life. Creek women took these raw provisions and turned them into food, especially *sofkee*, a corn gruel left to age and thicken until it soured. *Sofkee* was not only a favorite dish but also a spiritual food, and as Amelia Rector Bell has noted among contemporary Creeks, preparing it reasserted the woman's femininity and authority within the family structure. Even after resettling in Indian Territory, *sofkee* preparation (by the women) and consumption (by the men) provided the symbolic vehicle for signaling a willingness to wed. Likewise, the end of *sofkee* production in a household portended the termination of matrimony. It is doubtful that there was a stigma attached to receiving provisions that had not been grown by Creek female labor. In fact, the origin of the raw food appears to have been of little concern, as Creeks routinely stole everything from green corn to beef from whites who had expropriated the land. Livestock that wandered onto Creek territory were historically considered fair game for hunting, and the same attitude may have prevailed with regard to produce among Creeks who did not consider the Treaty of Washington a legitimate transfer of their domain. Despite not growing the plants themselves, these women reaffirmed their role as providers by turning the rations into food. In the piazza section of a post office deep in the heart of the Alabama Creek country in 1835, Harriet Martineau watched as "miserable-looking squaws were about the dwellings, with their naked children, who were gobbling up their supper of hominy [probably *sofkee*] from a wooden bowl." It is plausible that this family was loitering about a government building because they had been there seeking rations.[10]

Creek women also maintained their important ceremonial and religious roles in the face of increasingly difficult circumstances. The Busk, or Green Corn Ceremony, was a days-long celebration of the new harvest, the new year, and the bounty of the land. Women played a central role in the festivities both independently (purifying themselves separately from the men) and as part of the communal whole. Women took embers from the sacred fire to light their homes. Female refugees from Georgia helped their town consecrate new land when they participated in their first Busk in Alabama after 1826. References to warfare also featured prominently in the ceremony. Creek women traditionally held considerable power in their ability to publicly persuade men, especially with regard to warfare. Women could call for a truce in hostilities or exhort men to declare war on enemies. During one of the 1835 Busks, Payne observed the song of "the wail of mothers, wives, and daughters at the departure of the warriors for the fight." Up to fifty women performed a long chant regularly interspersed by the "whoop" of male voices conveying "the resolution of the warriors not to be withheld, but to fight and conquer."[11]

Women were also important actors in the "little brother of war," the Creek ball game. The sport was played on a large field of one hundred yards or more, and the object was to get a deerskin-covered ball through goal posts (or strike the posts) using two wooden sticks. Hundreds of Creeks participated in a game, and the sport's speed and violence almost guaranteed injury and sometimes death and was considered adequate preparation for actual warfare. Because of women's influence in war, it is perhaps not surprising that they also participated in the ceremonial lead-up to the event. Female participation in the pregame ceremonies was so important that it constituted one of the few times they were allowed inside the public square ground. During his 1828 visit, Basil Hall observed twenty women dancing in front of the male audience next to one of the open-air council houses. Creek women also participated in a lesser-known, coed version of the ballgame where the object was to throw a ball and hit a spot a few feet from the top of a pole that was between twenty-five and fifty feet tall. The game pitted men against women, although a few men often aided the female team. Although John Swanton was told that the men generally let the women win (and it no doubt was an exhibition), this did not mean that the sport lacked competitiveness. One observer of the game in Indian Territory saw a woman throw "herself at length on the ground" while chasing the ball. Moreover, the game began with a headman throwing the ball in the air: "all rush to seize" it, and "men and women pell mell together."[12]

The Busk and ball plays continued even as many Creeks suffered from starvation and material want. The distribution of federal provisions (like that witnessed by the Halls) was irregular and often only of limited duration because officials feared promoting "idleness" among the Creek people and disrupting the government's emigration program. As a result, many refugees continued to suffer as a consequence of the loss of their Georgia land, while an increasing number of Alabama Creeks saw their harvests diminished by a severe 1830–31 drought. The drought notwithstanding, Creek agent John Crowell observed that "there are hundreds of families who seldom plant as much, as would subsist them a fourth part of the year"—the result perhaps of a dearth of quality land or of livestock-raising practices that diverted laborers from the fields. And even when harvests abounded, many Creeks sold their last bit of produce for alcohol, leaving the women and children "in the most misrable state of starvation." By the late 1820s, alcohol could easily be purchased in Columbus, Georgia, a boomtown platted soon after the Treaty of Washington, or at grog shops operating illegally within the Creek limits. Some Creeks were also driven from their homes and fields by white squatters. In 1830 the Alabama General Assembly incorporated the town of Irwinton on the site of the Lower Creek *talwa* of Eufaula. Whites subsequently drove the Eufaulas from their homes and fields before burning or removing their homes. As landlessness increased, so did starvation. Some Creeks, for example, were seen eating the diseased carcass of a hog, in defiance of their deeply held sense of purity. In another case, an observer noticed Creeks hasten to a discarded hogshead barrel "as bees to the honey comb, to lick off the few remaining particles" of sugar. But even in the bleakest of times, women appear to have maintained their roles as household providers and food makers even if they had no food to produce. Witnesses noted that in some cases the inner bark was stripped off of trees, boiled, and consumed as "a substitute for bread"—a process that, if tradition holds, would have been done by women. Other people wrote that the Creeks consumed roots, berries, and the bark off of trees, although bystanders may have mistaken food for Creek medicine, which females also gathered for their families.[13]

Columbus and its environs were the source of many problems for the Creek people—the area housed large numbers of traders, speculators, and would-be squatters—but also offered expanded opportunities for Creek women looking to trade, find work, steal, or receive provisions. As traffic increased through the Creek Nation, women could be found selling melons, produce, and prepared food such as cold flour (a sugary corn mush) at stands along the roads. Conversely, "hundreds" and "sometimes thousands" of Creeks, both men and women, typically traveled into Columbus by day, and many loitered around shops, looking for food or begging door to door. As a trading town, Columbus begrudgingly welcomed these Creeks, but whites ordered them back across the Chattahoochee River each night. Indeed, Tyrone Power, an Irish actor who visited the Creek country in 1834, saw large numbers of women returning from Columbus after a long day of trade. During her visit in 1835, Harriet Martineau watched from her window as a parade of Creek women marched single file down one of Columbus's streets outside her inn. The women, "with their hair, growing low on the forehead, loose, or tied at the back of the head," were barefoot and carried large Indian baskets on their backs while following a train of mounted and walking Creek men. Perhaps driven by economic necessity, other women were compelled to work in more nontraditional occupations. Anne Royall, who passed through Georgia and Alabama in 1830, encountered two Creek female servants, one employed as a chambermaid and the other a cook, in a tavern near Fort Mitchell. Creek women also continued their long tradition of engaging in what whites considered "illicit" commerce. George William Featherstonhaugh, a British geologist living in the United States, visited Alabama in 1835 and noticed Creek women at crude log tables along the roads through the Creek country, selling glasses of whiskey for money or bartering for "anything to give in return, if it were only the skin of an animal." The sight of women selling alcohol along the roadside was extremely common. Indeed, in many cases female whiskey sellers relied on sex appeal (and male weakness) to attract customers. One Indian Territory observer, for example, saw a "rather young and good looking" woman selling alcohol along a road while her sly merchant boss, an "older and uglier squaw," hid in the nearby bushes.[14]

Columbus was also a magnet for Creek prostitution. Indeed, Featherston-haugh observed the town's streets "swarming" with intoxicated Creeks and young Indian and white prostitutes working side by side. Sex for money was common, and unmarried women lost no virtue by having many suitors, in-cluding paying ones. Because white men were so often smitten by the beauty of young Creek females, they likely had little trouble finding customers. And like the whiskey sellers, women often used their beauty and feigned modesty to attract and take advantage of white men. Naturalist William Bartram saw the ways in which a Creek woman's physical appearance and personality could be mistaken for "modesty, diffidence, and bashfulness" but nevertheless warned that "these charms are their defensive and offensive weapons, and they know very well how to play them off, and under cover of these alluring graces, are concealed the most subtile artifice." Some Creek women reduced grown men to adolescent giddiness. John Howard Payne, for example, was taken by the beauty and coquettishness of the eighteen-year-old daughter of headman Opothle Yo-holo, quipping, "Some one must have told her that I meant to run away with her, for I had said so before I saw her to many of her friends."[15]

Adultery, however, was socially unacceptable and punished accordingly. Clan members of the aggrieved beat the accused and her lover then cut off or muti-lated their ears or noses. Once a woman "had the law," however, all was forgiven. Indeed, one observer noted that "a woman who has been cropped may lead off the very next dance dressed up in all her finery." Although divorce was common, easy, and socially acceptable in Creek society (Christian unions, for example, were known as "long marriage"), adultery was obviously prevalent enough that the Creeks created a systematized method for dealing with the offense. Adultery in and of itself was a brazen act, but it was common for adulteresses and their lovers to flout social laws by escaping into the woods to wait for the arrival of the approaching Busk, when all grievances except murder were forgiven. Emigra-tion, however, gave women new opportunities to defy punishment, especially if the Green Corn Ceremony was not on the immediate horizon. In the spring of 1829 Neah Emathla and a band of Hitchiti warriors under his charge traveled to Fort Bainbridge, thirty miles west of Fort Mitchell in the Creek Nation, and after "most barberously beating" a man and a woman, "wantonly took off their ears." Fort Bainbridge was the site of a federal emigration camp, a staging area where Creeks willing to move to the Indian Territory packed their belongings into wagons and waited to commence the journey westward. The two lovers were attempting to avoid punishment by securing refuge in the camp with the anticipation of making their escape to the Indian Territory and starting a new life. Neah Emathla knew as much and pithily quipped during the raid that "if the United States had promised them protection, he would see whether they would be protected or not." Some Creek women, perhaps undeterred by the threat of cropping, were even audaciously repeat offenders. Creek headman Jim Boy, for example, "lost" his wife—reputed to be one of the "virtuousest women in the Nation"—only to remarry the "outrageousest woman in the world," someone known throughout Indian Territory as "having been a common slut on the Arkansas."[16]

Despite the differences in marital norms, many white men married Creek women. When Richard Augustus Blount (a member of a team surveying the border of Georgia in accordance with the Treaty of Washington) stopped by Asbury in July 1826, he observed Mary Ann Battis and other female students engaged in sewing and other domestic activities. Marveling at their "civiliz'd style," he had little doubt but that "intermarriages with the white people will be the result." From Blount's ethnocentric (and condescending) perspective, such intermarriages constituted reason to celebrate, as he no doubt believed an American husband would only further solidify the females' place in "civilized" society. But white husbands living in the Creek country were bound by the rules and mores of their wives' culture, and most white men fully embraced those practices. In fact, ten days after seeing Battis at Asbury, Blount passed by the homestead of "an old white man of about 40 years residence among those poor ignorant benighted people—who has become Indianiz'd."[17]

Wealth transcended race and gender in the Creek Nation. There were many wealthy women of mixed Creek and white parentage, just as there were wealthy women of full Indian ancestry. Jane Hawkins was the Creek daughter of William McIntosh and the widow of Samuel Hawkins (who was also executed for signing the Treaty of Indian Springs). When she voluntarily moved to Indian Territory in the late 1820s or early 1830s, Hawkins claimed one two-story hewed-log house and one double hewed-log house (fifty feet by twenty feet); both had piazzas with "good floors." She also claimed another smaller hewed-log house, a kitchen, a smokehouse, nine corn cribs, four horse stables, and one dairy.

Her estate was surrounded by two hundred acres of cleared land, a garden, and five slave quarters. A small number of rich white women, like the daughter of a Georgia planter who married William McIntosh's son, Chilly, resided in the Creek Nation. There were also wealthy Creek women who were black. When Royall traveled through the Creek Nation in 1830, she passed the abandoned home and farm of Sukey Randall, a wealthy Creek woman of African ancestry, whom Royall described as "rich" and married to a white man. The family moved to Indian Territory in the late 1820s. Some women married to white men ran inns, taverns, or public houses with their husbands and worked as hostesses. In doing so, they maintained the historic Creek female tradition of welcoming foreigners into the village with food but also adapted to market forces. Kendall Lewis, a Marylander who arrived in the Creek Nation sometime around 1808 after fleeing a murder charge in Georgia, married one of the daughters of Creek headman Big Warrior. Lewis and his Creek wife (who was known to be a fine cook) hosted travelers on their plantation. Some of the wealthiest Creek women owned black slaves, and they performed most domestic jobs. In 1835, Featherstonhaugh observed "breakfast cooked for some Indian women by a negress who was their slave."[18]

Many of the wealthy Creek families who voluntarily emigrated west accompanied the 1827 and 1828 parties to Indian Territory. Kendall Lewis and his family, for example, moved west with the second McIntosh detachment in 1828. In a few cases, wealthy women contributed provisions such as food, wagons, and teamsters to the government's voluntary emigrating parties. Delilah Stidham, for example, a member of a prominent Sawokli family, sold five thousand pounds of beef and 217 bushels of corn to the government in support of the Creek emigrants during the third voluntary party in 1829. Nelly Perryman, wife of William, sold three hundred pounds of beef and five bushels of rice. Other wealthy Creeks, among them McIntosh's widow, Susannah, self-emigrated by traveling separately from a federally sponsored emigrating party and paying for their transportation and provision costs out of pocket before being reimbursed by the United States. Most of these early emigrants had some connection to McIntosh. By 1829, however, disease, starvation, and white encroachment had resulted in a significant deterioration of the quality of life in the Creek Nation. Aside from a handful of McIntosh party members who accompanied the 1829, 1833, 1834, and 1835 emigrations, most of the Creeks who moved west after 1828 had no connection to the Coweta headman but were desperate enough that they chose to abandon the eastern Creek Nation.[19]

As was the case with Mary Ann Battis, family breakups were not uncommon as women exerted their independence in the emigration debate. Some left their families for a new life in the West, while others refused to emigrate although their spouses or relatives moved on without them. William Wills, for example, had a Thlakatchka wife and in 1828 entered his name on the second McIntosh party roll in anticipation of moving to Indian Territory. Wills's life had previously been threatened by Tuskenehaw, a prominent yet unpredictable Tuckabatchee headman and Jim Boy, a former Red Stick in the First Creek War (1813–14). Tuskenehaw, in fact, drew a sword and vowed to kill Wills for emigrating: Wills followed through with his plans to move west, and Tuskenehaw did not make good on his promise. Before leaving the Creek Nation, however, Wills's wife got cold feet, and she does not appear to have emigrated with her husband in 1828. Her reasons for her change of heart are unknown: she may have taken seriously Tuskenehaw's threats, been pressured by her clan to stay behind, decided to rendezvous with Wills at a later date, or consciously determined to live and die on the land of her ancestors. According to Thomas S. Woodward, Jane Carr (formerly Hawkins), the daughter of William McIntosh, left her husband, Paddy Carr (a prominent Cusseta man who was raised by Creek agent John Crowell) when she moved to the Indian Territory in the late 1820s or early 1830s. Jane Carr self-emigrated and paid for the transportation and rations of forty-nine members of her family, while Paddy Carr did not reach the Creek Nation in the west until 1847.[20]

The most high-profile divorces typically involved Creek women and men of European ancestry (called Indian countrymen). George Stinson, for example, married a Coweta woman and settled in the Creek Nation. The partnership, however, appears to have been little more than a business arrangement, with the two parties signing an unusual prenuptial agreement in which Stinson promised not to take any property from the marriage if they divorced "as he brought none with him" into the union. This stipulation was unnecessary under Creek tradition. Agent Benjamin Hawkins noted that marriage gave a husband no rights over his wife's property, and if a divorce occurred, the woman kept custody of the children and the "property belonging to them." Stinson was later arrested for violating trade laws and hauled off to Savannah at least once for trial. Sometime after that incident, the Indian countryman abandoned his wife, married a white woman, and resettled in Georgia. In hindsight, the prenuptial agreement appears to have been a savvy move by an assertive woman (or her family) to take precautions to protect what was rightfully theirs. For her part, "Mrs. Stinson" is listed on the second McIntosh party emigration roll, moving west in 1828.[21]

Creek headmen tried to prevent Creeks from leaving the eastern Creek country, fearing that a massive demographic shift would effectively break up the

Creek Nation and force all of its inhabitants west of the Mississippi River. In the 1820s the Creeks enacted laws that criminalized moving west, prescribing threats and in some cases physical violence to intimidate would-be emigrants. While most threats were directed at the men, Creek women could also be targeted. In 1828 Creek warriors visited an emigration camp at Fort Bainbridge and kidnapped the child of an emigrating woman as punishment for leaving. In other instances, women were caught up in the drawn-out battle between pro- and anti-emigration factions. James Moore, a fifty-six-year-old white man who married a woman from the Creek town of Weogufka, was threatened over his decision to voluntarily emigrate with the second McIntosh party in 1828. Moore was especially targeted because he not only vowed to emigrate but tried to induce others to go along with him. One emigration opponent named Red Mouth tried to physically prevent Moore's wife and children from accompanying him west. The threats seem to have worked: after "Red Mouth came to Mrs Moore & prevented her from going," James Moore appears to have had a change of heart. Although the 1828 muster roll shows him emigrating alone with his eight slaves, documentation places Moore in Alabama in the 1830s and 1840s.[22]

Many more women, however, were resolute in their decision to remain and die on the land of their ancestors. More than thirty-five hundred people (including Indian countrymen and the Creeks' black slaves) voluntarily emigrated to Indian Territory. But life for those who stayed in the east became increasingly difficult, as disease, starvation, and unabated white encroachment disrupted their daily routine. Creek delegates made many trips to Washington requesting assistance, and on one occasion, Andrew Jackson gave them an option: emigrate west or cede the Creek Nation and take individual land reserves (guaranteed to family heads in a fee-simple patent after five years). The 1832 Treaty of Washington turned out to be a monumental disaster for the Creek people and hastened their forced removal and relocation to Indian Territory. Moreover, the treaty contravened the matrilocal tradition in Creek society and threatened matrilineage control over cropland, as federal locating agents, operating within their patriarchal worldview, assigned the 320-acre plots to the husbands. But just because women were not assigned land in their own name did not necessarily mean that they suddenly lost influence when it came to land use. Most Creeks no doubt continued to abide by matrilineal tradition even under increasingly difficult circumstances. Although communal lands were subsumed by private ownership, garden plots, tilled primarily by the women, would theoretically continue on fertile soil. And federal agents noticed that many Creek men allowed their wives to enter their names on the land location register, although the agents often mistook this action for "indifference" on the part of the husbands. Lucy Locko of Broken Arrow was assigned a half section despite the fact that she was the "wife of R. Royster, a white man." Similarly, Polly of Coweta (Koochkalecha Town) was listed as "half negro & having a negro slave for her husband, named John." She also retained legal control of her family's land. And five years after refusing to emigrate to the Indian Territory with her family, Mary Ann Battis Rogers returned to Alabama with her Cherokee missionary husband to claim a reserve. Within days of the treaty signing, Rogers proactively petitioned both Creek agent John Crowell and secretary of war Lewis Cass for a reserve. She succeeded, although the half section was ultimately listed under the name of her spouse, Robert, despite his appeal that the land be allotted in Mary Ann's name, in keeping with Creek custom.[23]

When it came to legal control of the half sections, however, women not located on the land register were at the legal mercy of their husbands, a circumstance that affected all women but in a variety of ways. Indian countrymen (whites married to Indian women) such as land speculator Nimrod Doyle of Horse Path Town and Barent Dubois, an Albany, New York, native, who aided the government's emigration program, were no longer "tenants at will" on land belonging to their wives' families; these men could theoretically sell their reserves, and their wives or wives' families had no power to prevent such sales. Some headmen consequently complained that the treaty allowed "the white man to dispose of the land & leave his wife." Indeed, many whites sought to marry Creek women for precisely this purpose. One white man with no apparent connection to the Creek people, for example, claimed a twelve-year-old Creek girl as his wife in an attempt to procure a half section. The man abandoned the young girl shortly after receiving the land but likely was not actually married to her. At Tallassee, Payne visited one white woman who was angry because "her husband is continually marrying Indian wives,—probably to entitle himself to their lands." This practice was so common that it was lampooned by Johnson Jones Hooper, an author and satirist who moved to Chambers County, Alabama, in 1835 at the height of the land frauds. In his most famous work, *Some Adventures of Captain Simon Suggs, Late of the Tallapoosa Volunteers*, Hooper devises a character, Eggleston, who marries Litka, the fifteen-year-old daughter of Sudo Micco, to gain ownership of the family's land reserve. Once the land is signed over, Eggleston abandons the woman and her father. More insidious was the practice of "wife stealing," in which whites enticed married Creek women with money or alcohol to leave their husbands and marry speculators.[24]

The 1832 treaty did not initially grant Creek women, who were not heads of family, rights to land even after the death of their husbands or brothers. Traditionally, when a Creek man died, his property went to his sisters. But if a man died prior to selling his reserve, the case fell under Alabama law, and such cases often were assigned to administrative courts, where administrators were notorious for simply pocketing the purchase money rather than seeking out widows or other heirs, especially if they had already moved to Indian Territory. Jackson declined to deal with this issue despite repeated complaints, instead deferring to Congress. Not until March 3, 1837, did Congress pass a bill authorizing sales by Creek widows.[25]

All Creek women were vulnerable to fraud perpetrated by unscrupulous white land buyers. In most cases, women were victims by proxy: their husbands were cheated out of their land, leading the women to become landless. Would-be purchasers relentlessly pursued Creek men, who in most cases had the legal authority to transfer reserves to white ownership. Female heads of families, however, suffered the same types of fraud. One of the most common approaches, "personation," involved bribing an Indian with money, food, or alcohol to impersonate the true owner of the reserve and then "sell" the land to the speculator for a fraction of its value; another involved white buyers who would pay fair prices for land but then physically steal back some of the purchase money once the government certifying agent departed. Some women sold after white men threatened physical violence. Regardless of how allotments were stolen, their loss undermined Creek women's ability to tend to crops and maintain their role as food providers. Indeed, Alfred Balch, a federal commissioner appointed by President Jackson to investigate the causes of the Second Creek War, noted that the cropland that had been "cultivated in former years by the Indian women, now belonged to the new comers; and thus the means of subsistence of the tribe were lessened."[26]

Creek women were not shrinking violets, however. Some, like the women who took part in personation schemes, participated in the frauds, while others purchased reserves for themselves. Elizabeth Grayson, a member of a prominent Hillabee family, bought (or perhaps speculated on) two of her neighbors' reserves for $905. Still others took advantage of Creek cultural norms to procure half sections of land federal officials never intended to allot. Leonard Tarrant, a locating agent charged with assigning the reserves, complained that the ease with which Creek marriages could be dissolved allowed women to quickly divorce their husbands and receive land as family heads. Tallasseehatchee residents Marhoille and Tefulgar, for example, received a half section each despite claims that they were married. Multiple wives of polygamous Creeks could also have taken advantage of this loophole. Polygyny was accepted in the Creek country, though it was traditionally practiced by wealthier men and only with the consent of their first wives. First wives typically exerted control over subsequent wives and could whip them or drive them from the family for various offenses. Indeed, Chilly McIntosh married a white woman along with a Creek Indian woman from the town of Thlakatchka. He wanted more wives, but his white wife drove the other women out of the home "with scolding and disgrace" and said that "she would only submit to one Indian rival." Creek women who were driven from or voluntarily left their homes could have shrewdly petitioned for reserves. Some Creek girls who lived with their families and were not eligible for land deceived federal agents by claiming that they were in fact family heads. Other married Creek women lied and claimed to be single to obtain personal reserves.[27]

And like that "fine, gentle, innocent-looking girl," Creek women went after the speculators with an aggressiveness not seen in their male counterparts. Balch, for example, wrote in his report that the Creek women "uttered their complaints with the greater freedom because they could do so with impunity. They were active and clamorous, and appealed for redress to their chiefs, as well as to the agents of the United States, with persevering importunity." Marhoille was relocated west in 1836 and used her time in camp near Memphis to confront a white man who had purchased her land in Alabama for thirty-five hundred dollars but had taken back twenty-one hundred dollars, claiming that he had paid too much for the reserve. After numerous depositions and affidavits, Marhoille's persistence was rewarded, and the money was ordered returned to her in 1841.[28]

The 1832 Treaty of Washington also exacerbated starvation in the Creek country. In addition to the loss of crop production through land fraud, many allotments were located on uncultivable soil. Sinkawhe, a "very old Blind woman," was one of many who petitioned the federal government for new land because the reserve assigned to her was "of no account it was Hilley & Rockey & [too poor] for any use such as neither white nor Red people could make a living on." Sinkawhe and her townspeople pleaded for aid, claiming that they were in "grait need of Sustanance & Clothing." Balch noted that because of the land frauds, women were reduced to asking white planters living on what was once Creek land if they could "glean up the small potatoes which were left after removing the main crop, and regarded this permission as an inestimable favor." Gleaning was another strategy Creek women employed to provide for themselves and their families, both in Alabama and in Indian Territory.[29]

The outbreak of the Second Creek War represented the culmination of decades of suffering from white encroachment, starvation, emigration, land fraud, and disease. Despite doing their best to maintain their way of life under increasingly difficult circumstances, many Creeks were pushed to the breaking point. In May 1836 a small band of Creeks, primarily those from the lower towns, rose up in an attempt to cleanse the Creek country of its worst evils. The war, however, gave Jackson and Cass, his secretary of war, the excuse they needed to forcibly remove the Creeks west without a treaty. John T. Ellisor, who has written thoroughly on the war, notes that many women accompanied their rebel menfolk on military offensives, while others were sent away for their own protection. Some women fought alongside the men, and many were killed or taken prisoner as enemy combatants. Others acted as spies. And in keeping with their traditional role in persuading men to start or stop warfare, Creek women almost certainly provided moral support for the uprising. Indeed, locals noticed an unusually high number of dances and ball plays in the weeks and months leading up to the outbreak of war.[30]

Creek women, like those in other southeastern Indian tribes, also served as public mourners in times of loss. While native men typically prided themselves on stoicism, having been taught from an early age to endure physical and mental discomfort with little emotion, women bore responsibility for displaying sadness or anger on behalf of their clans or families. Trader James Adair relayed a story of the killing of a Chickasaw hunter by a group of Choctaws in the mid-eighteenth century. After discovering the corpse of their kinsman in a hollow tree, one of the Chickasaws declared that "as they were men and warriors, it belonged to the female relations to weep for the dead, and to them to revenge it." Creeks certainly grieved the loss of family members to disease or starvation or in battle during the Second Creek War, although one Indian Territory observer noted years later that Creek women "do not weep and cry with such clamorous vehemence as the Choctaws and others." During forced removal, however, Creek women were especially demonstrative. Jacob Rhett Motte, an army surgeon with a company of soldiers fighting the Creeks and Seminoles, observed the stark contrast between the sexes as they began their journey in chains. According to Motte, neither the physical or mental sufferings of the men "could elicit from them the least indication of distress," but the women, who followed behind, were "drowned in tears, and giving utterance to most distressing cries." These displays were nothing new and had been exhibited by Creek women who had voluntarily emigrated prior to 1836 but later regretted their decision. Visiting the western Creeks in 1829 to survey the frontier for a possible migration, a delegation of Chickasaws observed Creek women "in continual sorrow." Public mourning could take many forms and included the performance of gender-specific leave-taking rituals. Creek women "erected piles of light wood over the remains of their relatives and friends, and burnt them in honor of their memories." Others used what little money they had to purchase jewelry—a highly portable form of personal wealth—to mark their departure from Alabama. Both men and women danced all night just prior to leaving, as was customary before a long journey.[31]

Some Creek women were also demonstrative and aggressive in showing frustration or anger over their forced removal. Just before departing from Montgomery, Alabama, in July 1836, Lieutenant John Waller Barry, the military agent overseeing the twenty-three hundred prisoners captured during the Second Creek War, felt compelled to divide the party on the steamboats as "it was found next to impossible to prevent strife between the Creek & Uchee women." The source of the strife is unclear, although the Creeks and Yuchis (who belonged to the Creek Nation but did not speak the Muskogean language) had a complex relationship dotted with periods of friendship and hostility. Approximately fifteen hundred Creeks rode the *Meridian*, while the remainder of the prisoners traveled on the steamboat *Lewis Cass*. Both vessels towed barges "freighted with Indians."[32]

Removal and relocation also served as a litmus test for white men's commitment to their native wives. George Shirley, for example, was relocated to Indian Territory with his Creek wife and two children in 1836. For others, removal offered an opportunity to start a new life. Married to a Tuckabatchee woman, Milly, Barent Dubois was a prominent figure in Creek affairs and a close confidante of Opothle Yoholo, often appearing as a witness to the headman's letters. Dubois, whose allegiance to the Creek people was dubious at best, used his marriage connections to profit by aiding federal officials in forcing Creeks westward in the 1820s and 1830s, even serving as a subagent for the 1829 voluntary emigrating party and accompanying the first detachment of relocated Creeks west beginning in late August 1836. Rather than following Milly to Indian Territory, Dubois abandoned his wife and reentered white American society.[33]

Women provided a stabilizing presence on the journey westward, continuing to tend to their previous domestic responsibilities. Even the combined pressures of maintaining control over their domestic sphere and juggling the daily grind of travel were no doubt eased by the fact that women were accustomed to accompanying their menfolk on long journeys to hunt or trade. Creek women helped establish camp, gather and prepare food, and wash clothes. During the forced removals, Creek men marched through Alabama in chains, while Major Sylvester Churchill employed the Creek women in "cooking and supplying [the men] with food, water, bushes for shade and covering." Months later, white Alabama residents observed women kindling fires and cooking food while the men loitered "about or stretched upon a blanket" with "scores of playful children scattered around" as a detachment passed near Huntsville, Alabama. Creek women sometimes made food from provisions supplied by federal agents and at other times brazenly reasserted their role as gatherers by stealing corn and fruit from the fields and orchards of whites along the route. Most women traveled by water along portions of the journey. Keel-, flat-, or steamboats allowed women, children, and elderly men to avoid treacherous roads and swamps. In a number of cases, cooking hearths enabled women to prepare meals while on the water.[34]

One of the best descriptions of camp life comes from the autobiography of John Hewitt Jones, a part owner of the steamboat *Alpha*, which transported a party of Creek emigrants from Waterloo, Alabama, to Fort Gibson, Indian Territory, in 1835–36. Jones, who accompanied the party as a clerk, took notes on Creek manners and customs. In accordance with the Creeks' wishes, the boats came to shore most evenings to allow the party to rest and the women to prepare food. When the boats reached shore,

> It was a fine sight to see the camping of the Indians on the trip. As soon as the Boat was tied to the shore and a plank out the first to leave was the squaws, who gathered up their kit, which was usually tied up by the corners in a blanket in which was their tents, blankets, cook articles &c. They would throw it over their backs and let the tie come across their forheads, resting on their backs and in one hand take an axe and in the other and under their arm a little papoose and run ashore and up the bank. They would chop trees and make a fire and prepare supper.

Jones also noted that supper included *sofkee*. *Sofkee* production was tedious, and some compared it to blacksmithing with a ten-pound pestle. Nevertheless, the women "parched corn in a kettle and then would pound it in a mortar or deep cut trough in a log and then boil it up and make a very fine dish."[35]

Women also aggressively managed men's consumption of alcohol. During the 1835 emigration, conductors and agents did their best to prevent whiskey from reaching camp, even anchoring the boats in the middle of the river near cities so that Creeks could not purchase spirits in town, for example. Still, some men obtained alcohol. When intoxication occurred, Jones noted that "there was a tear round among the Indians. The women (squaws) would down a fellow and tie his legs and tie his arms and let him lay till he got sober." This was not an isolated incident. While in the Creek country in 1832, Carl David Arfwedson observed a drunken fray between men around a campfire. The Swiss traveler feared that the men "would kill each other, and this would probably have happened had not the women interfered, and succeeded in parting the combatants." The "howling and gesticulating" continued until morning, when, Arfwedson noted, "one after another departed under the guidance of the females." Alcohol abuse likely affected both sexes, although documentary evidence suggests that it was predominantly a male vice.[36]

In addition to serving in a domestic capacity, Creek women also performed purification rituals during the trip west. On May 25, 1837, a child died of exposure as the steamboat *Black Hawk* (with a keel and flat in tow) passed Paducah, Kentucky, near the confluence of the Tennessee and Ohio Rivers. The 543 Creeks who had commenced the journey had been captured in the Cherokee country while attempting to elude forced removal. Most were discovered living in abject poverty. Although Lieutenant Edward Deas, the military agent overseeing the party, scornfully asserted that the death was likely caused by "the folly of its mother, in putting it in cold water," he likely misread the episode. The mother was guided not by foolishness but by the Creeks' firmly held views on purity and strength. She was either trying to cleanse the child or make the child strong by exposing her progeny to the elements. Many southeastern Indians preferred cold water, and infants were submerged to give them strength. In fact, Lieutenant Henry Timberlake believed that the Cherokee practice of bathing babies daily in cold water gave them strength and prevented deformities. The Creeks also valued the practice of "going to water" and would ritually bathe in nearby streams. Dutch botanist and writer Bernard Romans noted that Creek children were submerged in cold water immediately after birth. Once in the Indian Territory, Creek women rolled their offspring in the snow "to make them hardy." During the coerced relocations of 1836, days of rest were budgeted into the itinerary at the behest of the headmen, and the Creeks washed and purified themselves whenever the opportunity afforded it. Indeed, in September 1836 Susanna Claiborne Clay, wife of governor Clement Clay, noted that Tuscaloosans gathered on the banks of the Black Warrior River and its tributaries and watched as Creek women "tossed their young children into the stream." Because the Creeks on the *Black Hawk* had been captured as runaways and were therefore likely to escape, they were not permitted to camp and wash, and the mother acted accordingly.[37]

At no point was the Creeks' sense of purity and balance more compromised than on the route westward. In Creek culture, menstruating women were considered a source of pollution and traditionally took up residence in an isolation hut to avoid contact with men and thus threatening their well-being. To avoid contamination, the male Creeks who carried their *talwa*'s fire embers from Alabama to their new town's public square in Indian Territory were careful not to mingle with women or drink from a cup used by a woman during their travels. In many instances, however, the forced march probably meant that men could not avoid "pollution" from contact with women. Isolating menstruating women would have been very difficult on the march west and entirely impossible on a steamboat or keelboat. Similarly, pregnant women traditionally followed various rituals and taboos, including giving birth some distance from the men, either in the menstrual hut or in a river or stream, that would have posed great challenges during the move west. Lieutenant Richard B. Screven, the U.S. military agent overseeing the approximately three thousand people in the second detachment, reported eighteen births during the three-and-a-half-month journey from Wetumpka, Alabama, to Fort Gibson, Indian Territory, in 1836. Deas reported one birth aboard the steamboat *Alpha* (or the barges it towed) and two on the march during early 1836. Women who remained in camp for extended periods of time, like the women of detachment 6, who waited along the Gulf of Mexico for their menfolk to return from fighting the Seminoles in Florida, would have been afforded more opportunities to observe the isolation rituals. Dozens of Creek children were born on the Gulf over the spring, summer, and fall of 1837.[38]

Creek women were among those who suffered the most during the forced removals and coerced relocations. Five detachments of Creeks left Alabama in August and September 1836 and experienced extreme heat and torrential rainfall in Alabama, a lack of potable water in Tennessee, and up to eight inches of snow in Arkansas and Indian Territory. As detachment 1 passed by Moscow, Tennessee, the military agent in charge, Lieutenant Mark W. Bateman, wrote that "number of deaths increasing, old men & women & children dropping off." Near Fort Gibson, a witness observed that "the snow for five days, has been from 4 to 8 Inches deep—and during the first and second days of the Storm, women and children were seen bending their way Onward, with most Piteous and heart rending Cries, from Cold."[39]

No one, however, suffered more than the women of detachment 6. As the mass relocation of the Creek Indians commenced, federal agents tried to recruit as many Creek men as possible to aid the American forces in the Second Seminole War. Most Creeks refused, although some agreed, enticed by, among other things, a promise to allow family members to remain in Alabama until the tours of duty ended. But local militias nevertheless demanded that all Creeks be removed from the state's borders. One fifteen-year-old Creek girl was shot in the leg as she tried to elude some white men who had attempted to rape her and indeed "accomplished their diabolical views upon [some other] frightened women." Traveling through Alabama in 1837, ornithologist and painter John James Audubon observed "half clad females and . . . naked babes, trudging through the mire" as they made their way to Mobile Point. While on the Gulf, large numbers of Creeks, including women, died of yellow fever. And when they finally commenced their journey west in earnest in October 1837, approximately three hundred people, including dozens of women, were killed when the *Monmouth* collided with another steamboat on the Mississippi River near present-day Baton Rouge, Louisiana.[40]

Still, Creek women fought removal and relocation and suffered greatly because of it. While some participated in the Second Creek War, many others fled the Creek country altogether and sought refuge among the Cherokees, Seminoles, or to a lesser degree the Chickasaws. Others remained secreted in the swamps of Alabama, Georgia, and Florida. Most of these women lived on the edge of survival while caring for their children. In the Cherokee country, agents discovered a number of impoverished Creeks hiding in mountain camps as far away as North Carolina. One woman, the daughter of Chinnabee, a Nauchee headman and ally of Andrew Jackson during the First Creek War (1813–14), was discovered wearing only "part of an old blanket, not a yard square." Witnesses reported that "blood was runing out of her and her children's legs; they had parched them so by the fire, to keep warm, that where the twigs, touched them, as they came in the blood ran freely." After being enticed out of her hiding spot with food and clothing, the woman just as quickly fled with her children before they could be arrested and taken west. And even after capture, some women brazenly deserted the forced removal parties during the journey west. At about the same time agents were searching for Creeks in the Cherokee country, Creeks who had escaped to Florida were being captured and sent to Mobile Point (and later Pass Christian, Mississippi) to join detachment 6. While scouring the region near LaGrange, Florida, Lieutenant John G. Reynolds and his men arrived at a small patch of ground on the edge of a swamp where a party of refugees had been murdered by American soldiers. Reynolds reported that "the poor women with children upon their backs were inhumanly butchered the cries of the children were distinctly heard at a house distant a quarter of a mile, after their mothers were shot down the children's brains were deliberately knocked out—the women's Ears cut off, for the purpose of obtaining their Ear Rings."[41]

The major operations of Creek deportation ended in late 1837 or early 1838 as the last of the victims of the *Monmouth* disaster belatedly arrived at Fort Gibson. More than seven hundred people died during the forced removals and coerced relocations. Approximately thirty-five hundred (and possibly thousands more), however, perished during the first year of resettlement in Indian Territory. Like their ancestors generations earlier, Creek women were once again called on to help build a new nation and a new way of life for their families. In most cases, they relied on what they knew. Communal farming, which had been significantly curtailed by the Treaty of Washington, resumed for segments of the population in the Indian Territory. And just as they had in the east, many of the wealthiest Creek women lived on southern-style plantations run almost entirely by black slaves. Women also helped those Creeks who had avoided removal to rebuild the Creek Nation in Alabama's Tensaw region. Those who had managed to escape being forced west petitioned federal officials for land patents guaranteed under article 1 of the 1814 Treaty of Fort Jackson. Hettie Semoice and Betsy Elliot played important roles in founding what would become the Poarch Band of Creek Indians. In the late twentieth century, other Creek women, among them Nina Gail Thrower, played an integral part in the Poarch Creeks' bid to receive federal recognition, which they did in 1984.[42]

Twenty years after Mary Ann Battis refused to move west with her family, the name *Marianne Rogers* appears on an 1847 voluntary emigration muster roll. She was one of a nineteen-member party conducted by Paddy Carr. If, in fact, she is the same Mary Ann Rogers, she traveled with other members of her family, although her husband, Robert, did not accompany her west. A handful of Creeks remained in the east in the years after the forced removals and coerced relocations of 1836–37, although their status remains unclear. Some were tied to the land in some way—either as sharecroppers or as slaves on white men's plantations. Others hid in the swamps and continued to evade detection. A few, like Paddy Carr, remained behind to dispose of their sizable property. For her part, Mary Ann's fair complexion and "civiliz'd style" would have allowed her access to the privileges that came with white society in Alabama or Georgia. Why this woman chose to move across the Mississippi River is a mystery, but like most Creek women, she probably did it for her own reasons and on her own terms.[43]

NOTES

1. Hill to McKenney, May 29, 1828, Letters Received by the Office of Indian Affairs, 1824–81, Creek Agency, 1824–76, Microcopy 234, Roll 221, 821–25 (hereafter LR, CA); Charles J. Kappler, *Indian Affairs: Laws and Treaties*, vol. 2, *Treaties* (Washington, D.C.: U.S. Government Printing Office, 1904), 214–17; Michael D. Green, *The Politics of Indian Removal: Creek Government and Society in Crisis* (Lincoln: University of Nebraska Press, 1982). For the Asbury Mission, see *Report of the Select Committee of the House of Representatives, to Which Were Referred the Messages of the President U.S. of the 5th and 8th February, and 2d March, 1827, with Accompanying Documents and a Report and Resolutions of the Legislature of Georgia*, 19th Cong., 2nd sess., 1827, H.R. 98, Serial Set 161, 1–84.

2. Hill to McKenney, May 29, 1828, LR, CA, 821–25; Andrew K. Frank, *Creeks and Southerners: Biculturalism on the Early American Frontier* (Lincoln: University of Nebraska Press, 2005), 124. Battis's family may have emigrated with the second McIntosh party in 1828. For David Brearley's rebuttal and his version of the Battis controversy, see Brearley to Porter, June 27, 1828, Letters Received by the Office of Indian Affairs, 1824–81, Creek Agency West, 1826–36, Microcopy 234, Roll 236, 25–28.

3. Frank, *Creeks and Southerners*, 72, 124; Hill to McKenney, May 29, 1828, LR, CA, 821–25; Rich-

ard Blount Journal, June 26–September 18, 1826, Alabama Department of Archives and History, Montgomery. See also Tiya Miles, "The Lost Letter of Mary Ann Battis: A Troubling Case of Gender and Race in Creek Country," *Journal of the Native American and Indigenous Studies Association* 1 (2014): 88–98; *The Methodist Magazine, Designed as a Compend of Useful Knowledge, and of Religious and Missionary Intelligence, for the Year of Our Lord 1826* 9 (1826): 436. Battis's life has even entered the larger popular culture. See Tiya Miles, *The Cherokee Rose: A Novel of Gardens and Ghosts* (Winston-Salem, N.C.: Blair, 2015).

4. For more on Creek women, see Kathryn E. Holland Braund, "Guardians of Tradition and Handmaidens to Change: Women's Roles in Creek Economic and Social Life during the Eighteenth Century," *American Indian Quarterly* 14 (1990): 239–58; Kathryn E. Holland Braund, "Reflections on 'Shee Coocys' and the Motherless Child: Creek Women in a Time of War," *Alabama Review* 64 (2011): 255–84; Joshua Piker, *Okfuskee: A Creek Indian Town in Colonial America* (Cambridge: Harvard University Press, 2004), 162–95. Mary Musgrove, who like Battis could operate in two worlds, receives the lion's share of the attention to Creek women. See Michael Morris, "The Peculiar Case of Mary Musgrove Matthews Bosomworth: Colonial Georgia's Forgotten Leader, 1733–1759," *International Social Science Review* 71 (1996): 14–23; Michele Gillespie, "The Sexual Politics of Race and Gender: Mary Musgrove and the Georgia Trustees," in Catherine Clinton and Michele Gillespie, eds., *The Devil's Lane: Sex and Race in the Early South* (New York: Oxford University Press, 1997), 187–201; Michael D. Green, "Mary Musgrove: Creating a New World," in Theda Perdue, ed., *Sifters: Native American Women's Lives* (New York: Oxford University Press, 2001), 29–47; Michael Morris, "Emerging Gender Roles for Southeastern Indian Women: The Mary Musgrove Story Reconsidered," *Georgia Historical Quarterly* 89 (2005): 1–24; Angela Pulley Hudson, "Imagining Mary Musgrove: 'Georgia's Creek Indian Princess' and Southern Identity," in Mary C. Carruth, ed., *Feminist Interventions in Early American Studies* (Tuscaloosa: University of Alabama Press, 2006), 112–25; Steven C. Hahn, *The Life and Times of Mary Musgrove* (Gainesville: University Press of Florida, 2012). There is a sizable and growing historiography on southeastern Indian women and their adaptation to cultural change through contact, the civilization program, and removal. A sampling includes Theda Perdue, "The Traditional Status of Cherokee Women," *Furman Studies* 26 (1980): 19–25; Mary Elizabeth Young, "Women, Civilization, and the Indian Question," in Mabel E. Deutrich and Virginia C. Purdy, eds., *Clio Was a Woman: Studies in the History of American Women* (Washington, D.C.: Howard University Press, 1980), 98–110; Theda Perdue, "Cherokee Women and the Trail of Tears," *Journal of Women's History* 1 (1989): 14–30; Theda Perdue, "Southern Indians and the Cult of True Womanhood," in Catherine Clinton, ed., *Half Sisters of History: Southern Women and the American Past* (Durham: Duke University Press, 1994), 36–55; Theda Perdue, "Women, Men, and American Indian Policy: The Cherokee Response to 'Civilization,'" in Nancy Shoemaker, ed., *Negotiators of Change: Historical Perspectives on Native American Women* (New York: Routledge, 1995), 90–114; Clara Sue Kidwell, "Choctaw Women and Cultural Persistence in Mississippi," in Shoemaker, ed., *Negotiators of Change*, 115–34; James Taylor Carson, "From Corn Mothers to Cotton Spinners: Continuity in Choctaw Women's Economic Life, A.D. 950–1830," in Christie Anne Farnham, ed., *Women of the American South: A Multicultural Reader* (New York: New York University Press, 1997), 8–25; Alice Taylor-Colbert, "Cherokee Women and Cultural Change," in Farnham, ed., *Women of the American South*, 43–55; Carolyn Ross Johnston, *Cherokee Women in Crisis: Trail of Tears, Civil War, and Allotment, 1838–1907* (Tuscaloosa: University of Alabama Press, 2003); Theda Perdue, *"Mixed Blood" Indians: Racial Construction in the Early South* (Athens: University of Georgia Press, 2003). Earlier works can be found in Rayna Green, ed., *Native American Women: A Contextual Bibliography* (Bloomington: Indiana University Press, 1983).

5. James Adair, *The History of the American Indians*, ed. Kathryn E. Holland Braund (Tuscaloosa: University of Alabama Press, 2005), 68; Adam Hodgson, *Letters from North America, Written during a Tour in the United States and Canada* (London: Hurst, Robinson, 1824), 1:135–36; C. D. Arfwedson, *The United States and Canada, in 1832, 1833, and 1834* (London: Bentley, 1834), 2:29; John Howard Payne, "The Green-Corn Dance," *Continental Monthly* 1 (1862): 18. See also Harriet Martineau, *Harriet Martineau on Women*, ed. Gayle Graham Yates (New Brunswick: Rutgers University Press, 1985), 61; Albert S. Gatschet, *A Migration Legend of the Creek Indians, with a Linguistic, Historic and Ethnographic Introduction* (Philadelphia: Brinton, 1884), 1:183–84. For historians who view Creek women with limited self-determination, see Richard A. Sattler, "Women's Status among the Muskogee and Cherokee," in Laura F. Klein and Lillian A. Ackerman, eds., *Women and Power in Native North America* (Norman: University of Oklahoma Press, 1995), 214–29. For the changing relationship between men and women during the "plan of civilization," see Claudio Saunt, *A New Order of Things: Property, Power, and the Transformation of the Creek Indians, 1733–1816* (Cambridge: Cambridge University Press, 1999), 139–63. Conversely, Jean Chaudhuri and Joyotpaul Chaudhuri, *A Sacred Path: The Way of the Muscogee Creeks* (Los Angeles: UCLA American Indian Studies Center, 2001), 43–51, emphasizes Creek women's "authoritative" role in family and community.

6. I refer to the 1825–38 period as the *removal era* but differentiate among *emigration*, when Creeks "voluntarily" moved to Indian Territory; *removal*, July–August 1836, when they were shackled and placed on steamboats; and *relocation*, when the majority of the population were coerced west without a removal treaty. See Christopher D. Haveman, *Rivers of Sand: Creek Indian Emigration, Relocation, and Ethnic Cleansing in the American South* (Lincoln: University of Nebraska Press, 2016).

7. Hill to McKenney, May 29, 1828, LR, CA, 821–25.

8. Michael D. Green, *Politics of Indian Removal*, 141–42; Haveman, *Rivers of Sand*, 11–41. A small strip of Georgia land was excluded from the 1826 treaty and ceded in the 1827 Treaty of the Creek Agency. See Kappler, *Indian Affairs*, 264–68, 284–86; Richard J. Hryniewicki, "The Creek Treaty of Washington, 1826," *Georgia Historical Quarterly* 48 (1964): 425–41; Richard J. Hryniewicki, "The Creek Treaty of November 15, 1827," *Georgia Historical Quarterly* 52 (1968): 1–15.

9. Margaret Hunter Hall, *The Aristocratic Journey: Being the Outspoken Letters of Mrs. Basil Hall Written during a Fourteen Months' Sojourn in America, 1827–1828*, ed. Una Pope-Hennessy (New York: Putnam's, 1931), 239; Basil Hall, *Travels in North America, in the Years 1827 and 1828* (Edinburgh: Cadell, 1830), 3:288–89. Field locations were controlled by *talwas* and allotted by lineage (Robbie Ethridge, *Creek Country: The Creek Indians and Their World* [Chapel Hill: University of North Carolina Press, 2003], 141–43). Creek hunters tended to hunt in well-defined ranges (Kathryn E. Holland Braund, *Deerskins and Duffels: The Creek Indian Trade with Anglo-America, 1685–1815* [Lincoln: University of Nebraska Press, 1993], 62).

10. Amelia Rector Bell, "Separate People: Speaking of Creek Men and Women," *American Anthropologist* 92 (1990): 335–36; Ethan Allen Hitchcock, *A Traveler in Indian Territory: The Journal of Ethan Allen Hitchcock, Late Major-General in the United States Army*, ed. Grant Foreman (1930; Norman: University of Oklahoma Press, 1996), 131; Braund, *Deerskins and Duffels*, 149; Harriet Martineau, *Society in America* (Paris: Baudry's European Library, 1837), 1:150.

11. Payne, "Green-Corn Dance," 25–26; Braund, "Guardians of Tradition," 242; Braund, "Reflections on 'Shee Coocys,'" 255–84; William L. Anderson, Jane L. Brown, and Anne F. Rogers, eds., *The Payne-Butrick Papers* (Lincoln: University of Nebraska Press, 2010), 4:69–72.

12. Charles Hudson, *The Southeastern Indians* (Knoxville: University of Tennessee Press, 1976), 408–21; Basil Hall, *Travels*, 3:291–92; John R. Swanton, "Social Organization and Social Usages of

the Indians of the Creek Confederacy," in *Forty-Second Annual Report of the Bureau of American Ethnology to the Secretary of the Smithsonian Institution, 1924–1925* (Washington, D.C.: U.S. Government Printing Office, 1928), 467; Hitchcock, *Traveler in Indian Territory*, 157–58; James H. Howard, *The Southeastern Ceremonial Complex and Its Interpretation* (Columbia: Missouri Archaeological Society, 1968), 62–63, 92–93, 144–48.

13. Crowell to Randolph, July 7, 1831, LR, CA, Roll 222, 520–22; Crowell to McKenney, February 4, 1830, LR, CA, Roll 222, 303–6; Hamilton to Crowell, June 11, 1831, Letters Sent by the Office of Indian Affairs, Roll 7, 272–73; Eaton to Gilmer, June 17, 1831, Hamilton to Crowell, July 25, 1831, Records of the Office of Indian Affairs, Letters Sent, Microcopy 21, Roll 7, August 1, 1830–December 31, 1831, 279–81; Michael D. Green, *Politics of Indian Removal*, 175–77; Boykin and Thomas to Gilmer, June 1, 1831, Governor's Subject Files, Gov. George Rockingham Gilmer, Record Group 1-1-5, Box 13, Georgia Archives; Salli to Cass, May 13, 1836, LR, CA, Roll 225, 151–52; "Report of A. Balch, Commissioner, on the Causes of the Creek Hostilities, January 1837," in U.S. Congress, *The New American State Papers: Indian Affairs* (Wilmington, Del.: Scholarly Resources, 1972), 9:505; John T. Ellisor, *The Second Creek War: Interethnic Conflict and Collusion on a Collapsing Frontier* (Lincoln: University of Nebraska Press, 2010), 139. For the effects of livestock raising on Creek matrilineage field production, see Gregory A. Waselkov, "Changing Strategies of Indian Field Location in the Early Historic Southeast," in Kristen J. Gremillion, ed., *People, Plants, and Landscapes: Studies in Paleoethnobotany* (Tuscaloosa: University of Alabama Press, 1997), 190–91.

14. John H. Martin, comp., *Columbus, Geo., from Its Selection as a "Trading Town" in 1827, to Its Partial Destruction by Wilson's Raid, in 1865* (1874; Easley, S.C.: Georgia Genealogical Reprints, 1972), 1:10; Tyrone Power, *Impressions of America, during the Years 1833, 1834, and 1835* (London: Bentley, 1836), 2:135; Martineau, *Society in America*, 1:147–48; Anne Royall, *Mrs. Royall's Southern Tour; or, Second Series of the Black Book* (Washington, D.C.: n.p., 1831), 2:142; G. W. Featherstonhaugh, *Excursion through the Slave States, from Washington on the Potomac to the Frontier of Mexico* (New York: Harper, 1844), 152; Angela Pulley Hudson, *Creek Paths and Federal Roads: Indians, Settlers, and Slaves and the Making of the American South* (Chapel Hill: University of North Carolina Press, 2010), 158, 165; Hitchcock, *Traveler in Indian Territory*, 96–97; James Taylor Carson, "Dollars Never Fail to Melt Their Hearts: Native Women and the Market Revolution," in Susanna Delfino and Michele Gillespie, eds., *Neither Lady nor Slave: Working Women of the Old South* (Chapel Hill: University of North Carolina Press, 2002), 15–33.

15. Featherstonhaugh, *Excursion*, 153; William Bartram, *The Travels of William Bartram*, ed. Mark van Doren (New York: Dover, 1928), 380–81; Braund, "Guardians of Tradition," 249; Payne, "Green-Corn Dance," 28.

16. Charles Hudson, *Southeastern Indians*, 200–201; Hitchcock, *Traveler in Indian Territory*, 163; Letter from Robertson, September 24, 1849, American Indian Correspondence, Collection of Missionaries' Letters, 1833–93, Presbyterian Historical Society, Box 9, Roll 1, Letter 154; Swanton, "Social Organization," 349; Creeks to Eaton, April 12, 1829, Letters Received by the Office of Indian Affairs, 1824–81, Creek Agency Emigration, 1826–49, Microcopy 234, Roll 237, 263–64 (hereafter LR, CAE). Divorce was much less common after the birth of children (Braund, "Guardians of Tradition," 241).

17. Blount Journal.

18. "A List of Improvements Abandoned," Miscellaneous Creek Removal Records, c. 1827–59, Record Group 75, Entry 300, Box 11, National Archives and Records Administration, Washington, D.C. (hereafter CRR-Misc.); U.S. Indian Department to Rebecca Bruner, Record Group 75, Special Files of the Office of Indian Affairs, 1807–1904, Microcopy 574 (hereafter SFOIA), Special File 207,

Roll 61, 685; Royall, *Mrs. Royall's Southern Tour*, 2:179; Robert P. Collins, "A Swiss Traveler in the Creek Nation: The Diary of Lukas Vischer, March 1824," *Alabama Review* 59 (2006): 269 n. 73; Frank, *Creeks and Southerners*, 43; Karl Bernhard, Duke of Saxe-Weimar-Eisenach, *Travels through North America, during the Years 1825 and 1826* (Philadelphia: Carey, Lea, and Carey, 1828), 2:27–28; Kathryn E. Holland Braund, "The Creek Indians, Blacks, and Slavery," *Journal of Southern History* 57 (1991): 601–36; Power, *Impressions of America*, 2:134; Featherstonhaugh, *Excursion*, 151.

19. Muster Roll (2nd McIntosh Party), Record Group 217 (Records of the Accounting Officers of the Department of the Treasury), Entry 525 (Settled Indian Accounts and Claims), Agent (Brearley), Account (14,487), Year (1830), National Archives and Records Administration (hereafter, SIAC); U.S. Indian Department to Delilah Stidham, CRR-Misc., Entry 300, Box 5, Receipt 14; United States to Perryman, SFOIA, File 207, Roll 61, 785; Haveman, *Rivers of Sand*, 42–81, 114–48.

20. Muster Roll (2nd McIntosh Party and Duplicate), SIAC, Agent (Brearley), Account (14,487), Year (1830); Copy of a Certificate, John Reed, May 18, 1828, LR, CA, Roll 221, 750; Thomas S. Woodward, *Woodward's Reminiscences of the Creek, or Muscogee Indians, Contained in Letters to Friends in Georgia and Alabama* (Montgomery, Ala.: Barrett and Wimbish, 1859), 114; Muster Roll (Paddy Carr), LR, CAE, Roll 240, 428; Thomas L. McKenney and James Hall, *History of the Indian Tribes of North America, with Biographical Sketches and Anecdotes of the Principal Chiefs* (Philadelphia: Rice and Clark, 1842), 2:23–24.

21. Crowell to Barbour, September 10, 1827, LR, CA, Roll 221, 248–49; Remarks, SIAC, Record Group 217, Entry 525, Agent (Crowell), Account (15,814-G), Year (1831); Michael D. Green, *Politics of Indian Removal*, 61; Letter from Crowell, n.d., SIAC, Record Group 217, Entry 525, Agent (Crowell), Account (15,814-B), Year (1831); Benjamin Hawkins, *The Collected Works of Benjamin Hawkins, 1796–1810*, ed. H. Thomas Foster II (Tuscaloosa: University of Alabama Press, 2003), 74s; Frank, *Creeks and Southerners*, 118–19; Muster Roll (2nd McIntosh Party), SIAC, Agent (Brearley), Account (14,487), Year (1830). See also Theda Perdue, "'A Sprightly Lover Is the Most Prevailing Missionary': Intermarriage between Europeans and Indians in the Eighteenth-Century South," in Thomas J. Pluckhahn and Robbie Ethridge, eds., *Light on the Path: The Anthropology and History of the Southeastern Indians* (Tuscaloosa: University of Alabama Press, 2006), 165–78.

22. Haveman, *Rivers of Sand*, 61–64; Creeks to Brearley, June 3, 1828, LR, CAE, Roll 237, 154–56; Deposition of Moore, August 24, 1826, SFOIA, File 136, Roll 27, 802–3; Deposition of Moore, August 22, 1826, SFOIA, File 136, Roll 27, 805; Mitchell to Crawford, June 1, 1842, LR, CA, Roll 226, 652–54; Muster Roll (2nd McIntosh Party and Duplicate), SIAC, Agent (Brearley), Account (14,487), Year (1830).

23. Christopher D. Haveman, "'Last Evening I Saw the Sun Set for the Last Time': The 1832 Treaty of Washington and the Transfer of the Creeks' Alabama Land to White Ownership," *Native South* 5 (2012): 61–94; Abert to Herring, March 4, 1834, Letters Received by the Office of Indian Affairs, 1824–81, Creek Agency Reserves, 1832–50, Microcopy 234, Roll 241, 727–30 (hereafter LR, CAR); 1832 Census of Creek Indians Taken by Parsons and Abbott, Record Group 75, Microcopy 275, Roll 1; Map of Russell County (Map 238), Record Group 75, Entry 163, Central Map Files, National Archives and Records Administration II; Rogers to Cass, March 31, 1832, in *Correspondence on the Subject of the Emigration of Indians, between the 30th November, 1831, and 27th December, 1833*, 23rd Cong., 2nd sess., 1835, S. Doc. 512, vol. 3, Serial Set 246, 278; Rogers to Cass, November 23, 1833, LR, CAR, Roll 241, 327–28.

24. Haveman, *Rivers of Sand*, 82–113; Haveman, "Last Evening I Saw the Sun Set," 65, 87 n. 10, 88 n. 11; Letter from Creeks, November 7, 1832, LR, CAR, Roll 223, 174–76; Payne, "Green-Corn Dance,"

23; Johnson Jones Hooper, *Some Adventures of Captain Simon Suggs, Late of the Tallapoosa Volunteers; Together with "Taking the Census," and Other Alabama Sketches* (Philadelphia: Carey and Hart, 1845), 70–72; Ellisor, *Second Creek War*, 134; Perdue, "Sprightly Lover," 169.

25. *Documents Relating to the Sale of Creek Reservations, under the Treaty of March 24, 1832*, 24th Cong., 2nd sess., 1837, S. Doc. 180, Serial 298, 2–5; Creek Treaty of 1832, CRR-Misc., Record Group 75, Entry 300, Box 1; Act of March 3, 1837, in *The Public Statutes at Large of the United States of America, from the Organization of the Government in 1789, to March 3, 1845* (Boston: Little, Brown, 1856), 5:186; Saunt, *New Order of Things*, 89; *Estill, et al., vs. the Heirs of Towhallosskee* (no. 42 and 251), CRR-Misc., Box 12. For Alabama dower laws, see John G. Aikin, ed., *A Digest of the Laws of the State of Alabama: Containing All the Statutes of a Public and General Nature, in Force at the Close of the Session of the General Assembly, in January, 1833* (Philadelphia: Towar, 1833), 132–33; David I. Durham and Paul M. Pruitt Jr., "Early Alabama Law and Chancery Practice," in J. Anthony Paredes and Judith Knight, eds., *Red Eagle's Children: Weatherford vs. Weatherford et al.* (Tuscaloosa: University of Alabama Press, 2012), 50–51.

26. Haveman, "Last Evening I Saw the Sun Set," 66–68; Mary Elizabeth Young, *Redskins, Ruffleshirts, and Rednecks: Indian Allotments in Alabama and Mississippi, 1830–1860* (Norman: University of Oklahoma Press, 1961), 73–113; *Nokagey vs. McDougald, Howell, & Co.*, No. 447, CRR-Misc., Entry 300, Box 6; Testimony Taken at Green's, January 3, 1837, CRR-Misc., Entry 300, Box 2; "Report of A. Balch," 9:504. See also William W. Winn, *The Triumph of the Ecunnau-Nuxulgee: Land Speculators, George M. Troup, State Rights, and the Removal of the Creek Indians from Georgia and Alabama, 1825–38* (Macon, Ga.: Mercer University Press, 2015).

27. Claudio Saunt, *Black, White, and Indian: Race and the Unmaking of an American Family* (Oxford: Oxford University Press, 2005), 42–43; Tarrant to Herring, May 15, 1833, LR, CAR, Roll 241, 344–47; Charles Hudson, *Southeastern Indians*, 199–200; Bernhard, *Travels*, 2:27; George Stiggins, *Creek Indian History: A Historical Narrative of the Genealogy, Traditions, and Downfall of the Ispocoga or Creek Indian Tribe of Indians* (Birmingham, Ala.: Birmingham Public Library, 1989), 58–59; Ellisor, *Second Creek War*, 52. Relations between wives of polygamous husbands could often be tense. While being hosted for the evening by an elderly Creek headman, Carl David Arfwedson reported that "in the course of the night, a violent contest arose between two of the [wives], which for a while threatened the most serious consequences" (*United States and Canada*, 2:19–20). Conversely, some, like William McIntosh's wives, Peggy (a Cherokee woman) and Susannah Coe, got along well even though they had very different personalities. Richard A. Blount reported that "upstairs in [McIntosh's] two story house he had two curtain bedsteads quite in flaming style and in the same room, and that he lodg'd in one with Peggy—and in the other with Susanna, and strange to tell that in this singular copartnership they agreed like sisters and members of the same [household]— This circumstance strongly demonstrates the powerful influence of custom and habit—They yet live together in apparent harmony" even after McIntosh's death (Blount Journal). See also John Bartlett Meserve, "The MacIntoshes," *Chronicles of Oklahoma* 10 (1932): 310–25.

28. "Report of A. Balch," 9:503–4; *Marhoille vs. Hall, Winslett, and Genl. W. Griffin*, LR, CAR, Roll 247, 156–76; "Decision in the Case of Marho-e-il-le," December 7, 1841, LR, CAR, Roll 247, 977–78; Testimony, CRR-Misc., Entry 300, Box 1.

29. Hall to Cass, March 21, 1835, LR, CAR, Roll 242, 154–55; Statement of Thomason, March 17, 1835, LR, CAR, Roll 242, 156; "Report of A. Balch," 9:505; Augustus Ward Loomis, *Scenes in the Indian Country* (Philadelphia: Presbyterian Board of Publication, 1859), 257–58.

30. Ellisor, *Second Creek War*, 192, 220, 254, 273, 292–93; Braund, "Guardians of Tradition," 242;

Hogan to Cass, March 8, 1836, *American State Papers: Documents, Legislative and Executive, of the Congress of the United States, for the First and Second Sessions of the Twenty-Fourth Congress, Commencing January 12, 1836, and Ending February 25, 1837,* vol. 6, *Military Affairs* (Washington, D.C.: Gales and Seaton, 1861), 751–53; Diary of Thomas Sidney Jesup, 1836, Ethan Allen Hitchcock Collection on Indian Removal, Box 2, Folder 6, Beinecke Rare Book and Manuscript Library, Yale University. For women and the First Creek War, see Joel W. Martin, *Sacred Revolt: The Muskogees' Struggle for a New World* (Boston: Beacon, 1991), 139–45.

31. Charles Hudson, *Southeastern Indians,* 201–2; Adair, *History of the American Indians,* 329; Josiah Gregg, *Commerce of the Prairies* (1844; Philadelphia: Lippincott, 1962), 2:325; *Niles' Weekly Register,* July 25, 1829; Jacob Rhett Motte, *Journey into Wilderness: An Army Surgeon's Account of Life in Camp and Field during the Creek and Seminole Wars 1836–1838,* ed. James F. Sunderman (Gainesville: University of Florida Press, 1953), 20; Haveman, "Last Evening I Saw the Sun Set," 74–75, 77; "Report of A. Balch," 9:507.

32. Barry to Jesup, July 16, 1836, Records of the Adjutant General's Office, 1780s–1917, Record Group 94, Entry 159, Thomas S. Jesup, Box 11, Folder "Letters Received from Officers of the Army, 1836–37, Names beginning with '"B'"; Steven C. Hahn, "'They Look upon the Yuchis as Their Vassals': An Early History of Yuchi-Creek Political Relations," in Jason Baird Jackson, ed., *Yuchi Indian Histories before the Removal Era* (Lincoln: University of Nebraska Press, 2012), 123–53; Grant Foreman, *Indian Removal: The Emigration of the Five Civilized Tribes of Indians* (1932; Norman: University of Oklahoma Press, 1972), 152–56; Haveman, *Rivers of Sand,* 187. Yuchi men and women and their Creek counterparts also had different gender relations. Agent Benjamin Hawkins noted that "the [Yuchi] men take part in the labors of the women, and are more constant in their attachment to their women, than is usual among red people" (Hawkins, *Collected Works,* 62s). Auguste Levasseur echoed this assessment, noting while accompanying the Marquis de Lafayette that the women on Uchee Creek (where the Yuchis lived) "did not appear to me as unhappy as I was led to expect. I saw before almost all the houses the women sitting in circles, engaged in weaving baskets or mats, and amusing themselves with the games and exercises of the young men, and I never remarked any signs of harshness on the part of the men, or of servile dependence on the part of the women" (Auguste Levasseur, *Lafayette in America in 1824 and 1825; or, Journal of a Voyage to the United States* [Philadelphia: Carey and Lea, 1829], 2:78–79).

33. Testimony of Shirley, January 30, 1842, in U.S. Congress, *New American State Papers,* 10:529–30; Payne, "Green-Corn Dance," 25; Frank, *Creeks and Southerners,* 124; 1832 Census of Creek Indians Taken by Parsons and Abbott, Record Group 75, Microcopy 275, Roll 1. A white man named Alexander (probably James Alexander) also was forced west with Opothle Yoholo's detachment; see Hitchcock, *Traveler in Indian Territory,* 110.

34. Braund, *Deerskins and Duffels,* 67–68; *National Intelligencer,* October 10, 1836; Franklin Hunter Churchill, *Sketch of the Life of Bvt. Brig. Gen. Sylvester Churchill, Inspector General U.S. Army, with Notes and Appendices* (New York: McDonald, 1888), 35; Sprague to Harris, April 1, 1837, LR, CAE, Roll 238, 739–56; Abadie to Gibson, October 20, 1836, Indian Removal to the West, 1832–40, Files of the Office of the Commissary General of Subsistence (Bethesda, Md.: University Publications of America), Roll 5, 800–802.

35. John H. Jones, "The Autobiography of John H. Jones, 1814–1882," Indiana History Mss. Manuscripts Department, Lilly Library, Indiana University, Bloomington; R. E. Banta, *The Ohio* (New York: Rinehart, 1949), 294–95; Bell, "Separate People," 335; W. O. Tuggle, *Shem, Ham, and Japheth: The Papers of W. O. Tuggle Comprising His Indian Diary, Sketches and Observations, Myths and*

Washington Journal in the Territory and at the Capital, 1879–1882, ed. Eugene Current-Garcia and Dorothy B. Hatfield (Athens: University of Georgia Press, 1973), 96; Gaston Litton, "The Journal of a Party of Emigrating Creek Indians, 1835–1836," *Journal of Southern History* 7 (1941): 225–42.

36. Jones, "Autobiography"; Arfwedson, *United States and Canada*, 2:33–34. For more on women, men, and alcohol, see Saunt, *New Order of Things*, 145–48.

37. Journal (Deas), LR, CAE, Roll 238, 251–81; Muster Roll (Deas), SIAC, Agent (Reynolds), Account (1687), Year (1838); Theda Perdue, *Cherokee Women: Gender and Culture Change, 1700–1835* (Lincoln: University of Nebraska Press, 1998), 33; Hitchcock, *Traveler in Indian Territory*, 130; Bernard Romans, *A Concise Natural History of East and West Florida*, ed. Kathryn E. Holland Braund (Tuscaloosa: University of Alabama Press, 1999), 148; Matthew William Clinton, *Tuscaloosa, Alabama: Its Early Days, 1816–1865* (Tuscaloosa: Zonta Club, 1958), 66. Another, albeit less likely, possibility was that the mother killed her child to spare the infant from the horrors of removal. This was not unusual during times of extreme desperation. In fact, during the Second Creek War, American soldiers reported that Creek women had killed six of their children "who were unable to keep up with them in their flight" (McIntosh to Jesup, August 13, 1836, Records of the Adjutant General's Office, Jesup, Box 12, Folder "Letters Received from Officers of the Army"). Creek women poisoned some children and suffocated others by stuffing their mouths with dry grass and moss to prevent them from making sounds that American soldiers would hear (Ellisor, *Second Creek War*, 293–94).

38. Charles Hudson, *Southeastern Indians*, 319–22; Simon Johnson interview, September 22, 1937, Indian Pioneer History Collection, Works Progress Administration Project s-149, Roll 11, Vol. 31, 299–302, Oklahoma Historical Society, Oklahoma City; Journal (Deas), Indian Removal to the West, 1832–40, Files of the Office of the Commissary General of Subsistence, Roll 6, 33–55; Journal (Screven), SIAC, Agent (Reynolds), Account (1687), Year (1838).

39. Journal (Bateman), SIAC, Agent (Reynolds), Account (1687), Year (1838); Stuart to Jones, January 15, 1838, LR, CAE, Roll 238, 19–22; *Arkansas State Gazette*, January 3, 1837; Haveman, *Rivers of Sand*, 200–233.

40. John James Audubon, *Letters of John James Audubon 1826–1840*, ed. Howard Corning (Boston: Club of Odd Volumes, 1930), 2:145–46; Muster Roll (Felton), SIAC, Agent (Reynolds), Account (1687), Year (1838), Box (238); Reynolds to Wilson, March 31, 1837, "Lieut. Jno. G. Reynolds Journal of a Party of Creek Indians, about to Emegrate to the West of the Mississippi, Commencing 19th February and Ending 19th October 1837," Box 1, Folder 3, Manuscripts Division, Department of Rare Books and Special Collections, Princeton University Library; *Arkansas State Gazette*, September 26, 1837; Muster Rolls, SIAC, Agent (Reynolds), Account (1687), Year (1838).

41. Smith to Harris, May 29, 1837, LR, CAE, Roll 238, 792–94; Muster Roll (Clements), Record Group 75, Entry 299, (Creeks), Emigration Lists, 1836–38, Vol. 7, Box 2, National Archives and Records Administration; Muster Roll (Deas), SIAC, Agent (Reynolds), Account (1687), Year (1838), Box (239); Reynolds to Wilson, June 4, 1837, in "Liet. Jno. G. Reynolds Journal"; "List of Creek Indians who Came in from the Seminoles, & Joined the Friendly Indians in the Spring of 1837," Records of the Adjutant General's Office, Jesup, Box 4, Folder "Major Freeman." See also John T. Ellisor, "'Like So Many Wolves': Creek Removal in the Cherokee Country, 1835–1838," *Journal of East Tennessee History* 71 (1999): 1–24.

42. Haveman, *Rivers of Sand*, 299; "The U.S. in Account Current with the Alabama Emigrating Company," SIAC, Agent (Reynolds), Account (1687), Year (1838); Isaac McCoy, *The Annual Register of Indian Affairs: In the Western (or Indian) Territory, 1835–1838* (Springfield: Particular Baptist Press, 2000), 276; Gregg, *Commerce of the Prairies*, 317; J. Anthony Paredes, "Back from Disappear-

ance: The Alabama Creek Indian Community, in Walter L. Williams, ed., *Southeastern Indians since the Removal Era* (Athens: University of Georgia Press, 1979), 123–41; Nina Gail Thrower (recorded and transcribed by Robert Thrower), "A Modern Creek Indian Reflection on *Weatherford vs. Weatherford et al.*," in Paredes and Knight, eds., *Red Eagle's Children*, 166–79.

43. Muster Roll (Paddy Carr), LR, CAE, Roll 240, 428; Testimony of Stidham, Exhibit AA, SFOIA, File 285, Roll 77, 145; Stidham Roll, SFOIA, File 285, Roll 77, 32.

Augusta Evans Wilson

America's Forgotten Best-Selling Author

SUSAN E. REYNOLDS

Although few people know the name *Augusta Evans Wilson* today, her books ranked among the most popular American novels during the nineteenth century. In fact, her most famous novel, *St. Elmo,* "is believed to have sold more widely than any other single woman's fiction, and is ranked among the most successful works published in the nineteenth century." Most of what we know of her today results from the efforts of William Perry Fidler, author of the first biography about her, but many scholars are rediscovering her work and exposing her writing to a new audience. They have recognized her particular importance in the genre of domestic fiction, which critic Nina Baym explains "in essence, . . . is the story of a young girl who is deprived of the supports she had rightly or wrongly depended on to sustain her throughout life and is faced with the necessity of winning her own way in the world." Indeed, Wilson spent her life writing stories about women. Some of her heroines marry; some do not. But all of her female lead characters share an unflinching drive to discover the truth about themselves and the world they inhabit. Wilson's female heroines, according to Baym, "are the strongest, most brilliant, and most accomplished in the long line of woman's heroines," yet scholars have for decades barely noticed her fiction.[1]

Augusta Jane Evans was born in Georgia into privileged circumstances. Her father, Matthew Ryan Evans, met Sarah Skrine Howard, a young woman from a prosperous family, during the early 1830s. According to Fidler, Howard was both "modest and brilliant," and she proved a successful match for the young entrepreneur. The couple married on July 15, 1834, and on May 8, 1835, the Evanses welcomed into the world a daughter they named Augusta Jane. Few records exist regarding Augusta's infancy, and scholars can only speculate about her earliest years. Fidler imagines her spending time at relatives' rural

AUGUSTA EVANS WILSON, C. 1900

Alabama Department of Archives and History, Montgomery.

homes in Alabama and elsewhere. However, Augusta's idyllic childhood days ended when Matthew Evans began to have serious financial problems by the late 1830s. Banks foreclosed on his estate by 1839, and the Evanses had to sell not only the estate but also most of their belongings, including the furniture, silver, and slaves.[2]

It is hard to say what the young Augusta felt about her family's troubles, but if her later writing can be taken as evidence, she obsessed about finding economic security as a result of her experiences in childhood. While the family struggled, however, Augusta's education was not neglected. Sarah Evans tutored her daughter and encouraged her to read widely. As Fidler notes, Augusta Evans's "early craving for books was fairly well satisfied while the family remained near Columbus," where any books that her immediate family did not own "were usually to be found in one of the libraries of her wealthy relatives."[3]

In 1845, finding no respite from his financial problems, Matthew Evans decided to pack up his family, which now included four additional children, and move west to San Antonio, Texas. In later years, Augusta proudly recalled that her mother entertained her with stories and poetry and taught her lessons during the long journey.[4]

The Evans family arrived in Texas at the end of the summer of 1845, stopping in Houston so that Sarah could give birth to her sixth child. By January 1846, the family had settled in San Antonio, where Augusta would get the inspiration to write her first novel, *Inez: A Tale of the Alamo*. Augusta later wrote in a letter, "I remember rambling about the crumbling walls of the Alamo, recalling all its bloody horrors; and as I climbed the moldering, melancholy pile, to watch the last rays of the setting sun gild the hill-tops, creep down the sides, and slowly sink into the blue waves of the San Antonio River: as I looked over the quietly beautiful valley, with its once noble Alameda of stately cottonwoods, my heart throbbed, and I wondered if I should be able some day to write about it for those who had never looked upon a scene so fair." That calm lasted only a few months, however, because the United States declared war against Mexico the following May. Augusta saw the small town of San Antonio grow to include "hundreds of troops." She also witnessed the tensions between the Catholic Mexicans and the largely Protestant American community in which she lived, tensions that subsequently formed an important theme in her first novel.[5]

In 1849, likely as a result of the harsh conditions of life on the Texas frontier and the fact that Matthew Evans continued to struggle financially, the family moved back east, settling in Mobile, Alabama, where Augusta spent the rest of her life. The booming town was home to the Mobile and Ohio Railroad, and Matthew hoped—again in vain—to find his fortune there. The move not only brought the Evanses closer to extended family but also meant that Augusta could receive formal education at a school with experienced teachers, a prospect that excited her. However, Augusta attended school only briefly before being "forced to withdraw because of poor health."[6]

Sometime in late 1849, just months after their arrival in Mobile, the Evanses' home caught fire, resulting in the loss not only of their residence but also of most of their possessions. Matthew's health soon began to decline, and in the absence of a steady income, the family, which had grown to include eight children, struggled to make ends meet. Augusta spent time as a volunteer nurse and was not afraid to work, but her status in society would not allow her to take a paying job. As Fidler notes, "Southern traditions placed a strict limitation upon the kinds of work which a daughter of 'quality folks' could accept."[7] Augusta Evans decided, however, that she could try to write.

She began to work in secret on her first novel, laboring so diligently on the project that she made herself ill with exhaustion. Sarah Evans discovered Augusta's work, but the young woman was afraid to tell her father about her aspirations. Augusta persuaded her mother to keep the secret, and on Christmas Day 1854, Augusta presented her father with the manuscript of *Inez: A Tale of the Alamo*.[8]

Although Harper published the novel, a family member (perhaps Augusta's uncle, Augustus Howard) supplied a generous amount of money to provide for a printing, making *Inez* almost the equivalent of a self-published novel. *Inez* was not a commercial success and today is often described as "religious propaganda" because of its relentless anti-Catholicism.[9] *Inez*, however, also marks an important first step in Evans's attempt at writing fiction about women.

The plot of *Inez* centers on two young female cousins, Mary Irving and Florence Hamilton, and the story opens in New Orleans sometime in the 1830s, before the Battle of the Alamo has taken place. Mary is an orphan dependent on her uncle Hamilton's charity and is the paragon of virtue, while Florence is impetuous and selfish. Florence becomes the subject of Mary's guidance throughout the novel, and, typical of the domestic plot, Florence's transformation must be ensured.[10]

The reformation of Florence's character is typical of domestic fiction, and at first glance, the novel appears to model itself on the popular genre. In domestic plots, before a woman can become a proper wife and mother, she must conform to accepted norms of morality and gender. Evans often sets up two female characters (sometimes dual heroines), with one emotional and frivolous and the other serious and vehemently attached to her ideals. Particularly in Evans's earlier novels, these virtuous women convert others to their sense of faith and commitment to morality. But even within this familiar story line, Evans crafts the novels slightly differently from other popular nineteenth-century domestic novels. Unlike some authors in this genre, she allows her female characters to be fiercely outspoken. Even the most virtuous is not afraid of speaking her mind or being independent and supporting herself. Never meek, Evans's heroines do not bow to the belief that men are superior simply as a consequence of their sex. In addition, Evans's heroines do not prevail through emotion. Though they may feel passionately about what they believe, they succeed based on arguments grounded in intellect, study, and logic.

But *Inez* also contains more than the typical domestic storyline, and a closer look shows Evans transforming the domestic novel in other ways. *Inez* can also be seen as a manipulation of Gothic fiction, and Evans uses familiar Gothic tropes to turn the story into a uniquely American religious statement. The villain and threat to Florence's fate is not merely a man (as in so many domestic plots) but instead an entire belief system: Catholicism. To Evans, the Catholic faith is not only wrong but also completely anti-American. She takes the familiar Gothic plot device of the corrupt priest and uses it to advocate the idea that American Protestant belief can easily overpower the foreign corrupt Catholic faith.

After the death of Florence's father, the girls are left without male protection and guidance (another typical threat to women found in many Gothic and domestic plots), but Mary remains the steadfast rock of morality. The novel's titular character, Inez, a young and virtuous Mexican girl who refuses to be ensnared by the chief villain, Mazzolin, a Catholic priest, tells Mary that he has converted the impressionable and emotional Florence. Mary confronts Florence, pleading with her to give up "Romanism" and telling her, "I fear the extension of papal doctrines, because liberty of conscience was never yet allowed where sufficient power was vested in the Roman Catholic clergy to compel submission. To preserve the balance of power in ecclesiastical affairs is the only aim of Protestants. We but contend for the privilege of placing the Bible in the hands of the masses—of flashing the glorious flambeau of truth into the dark recesses of ignorance and superstition—into the abysmal depths of papal iniquity."[11] At first glance, this passage appears to be the typical Protestant outcry against Catholicism, but a closer look reveals distinctly American values. For example, Mary emphasizes the importance of "liberty of conscience" and the idea that Protestantism "preserve[s] the balance of power." Protestantism is also a great equalizer, "placing the Bible in the hands of the masses."

Evans's argument is emphatically American as well as fascinating because the words come from a female character. Evans insists that it is false to believe that faith can come solely via a male gatekeeper and emphasizes that any kind of knowledge is freely accessible to and can be understood by women—especially American women.

Mary persuades Florence that she has been wrong to convert to the Catholic faith, and the girls flee San Antonio. Though both Mary and Inez die, Florence makes a complete change and becomes the proper embodiment of the nineteenth-century American woman.

Evans's bias against Catholicism aligned with nineteenth-century American popular opinion. In *Fire and Fiction: Augusta Jane Evans in Context*, critic Anne Sophie Riepma explains,

> The great waves of Irish and other European Catholic immigrants to the United States in the 1830s and 1840s struck American Protestants with a great fear. . . . The fact is that in 1850 Roman Catholicism had become the largest religious denomination in America [and, consequently], between 1834 and 1850 a number of often lurid anti-Catholic novels were written by American Protestants who attributed every sin in the book to priests and nuns. Convents were described not only as prisons and as a threat to democracy, but also as places where prostitution, child murder, torture, and alcoholism were rampant. Priests were portrayed as ambitious and corrupt, and as seducers of young women.

Mary acts as the voice of Protestantism in the book (and, indeed, as Evans's personal voice), and "like a minister, Mary tries to influence and convert others." According to Riepma, as "the titular heroine, [Inez's role] is to help the American settlers. Inez is a Protestant [and] is presented as good, and serves as a foil for Mazzolin."[12] Riepma's opinion of the novel is seconded by critic Suzanne Bost, who notes that *Inez* is "notably not about the Alamo or the minor character Inez. [It] invoke[s] a symbol of the 1850s U.S. national and racial anxieties (including anti-Catholicism and disdain for the Mexican residents of the nation's most recent territorial acquisition)"; "Evans encodes her celebration of white Protestant femininity through a representation of Anglo-Texans' sacrifice at the Alamo."[13] Evans's damning of Catholicism seems to have evolved out of a need to prove to herself that her own faith was superior. Living among devout Catholics in San Antonio brought Evans into contact, perhaps for the first time, with a belief system that was both as strong as her own and opposed to her religious worldview, forcing her to confront and define her definition of herself as an American and as a woman.

Inez did not become a best seller, but it was crucial to Augusta's development as a novelist and opened new doors of intellectual exploration for Augusta Evans. Once *Inez* was published and out in the world for everyone to see, Evans, perhaps because she had made her religious views so public, began to experience a religious crisis and felt the need to be absolutely certain about her Methodist faith. She befriended Methodist minister Walter Harriss, who offered to help her find theological scholarship and materials to examine. Evans also read philosophy and history to aid her quest to find answers and return to belief. Though she had moments of security in her religious beliefs, her faith continued to wane at times. She wrote to Harriss,

> There are seasons when my soul plumes itself for the lofty regions of speculation, and for a time I flutter among the bald cliffs and crags of a so-called "philosophic spiritualism" of intuitionalism, but I seem to freeze in those Artic heights, and my numb soul gladly warms itself in the sunny realms of God's holy revelation. Verily I am a mystery unto myself. Like a dazzled moth I hover round and round a brilliant spark that may one day consume me. I have not struggled through the morasses of skepticism without inhaling some of its deadly vapors. I mean that when my soul is serenely, happily basking in the light of an eternal God and his equally eternal word, a grim gaunt spectre stands by me as my shadow and makes me doubt the reasonable certainty and absolute proof of the faith that consoles me, and herein lies the curse of skepticism—that its ghostly battles have to be continually fought over and over. Blessed the soul that never began to question and debate regarding its arcana.

Evans returned to her faith in God, but her quest for truth led her also to believe that art and writing could be "a teacher of moral truths."[14] Much of mid-nineteenth-century literature is didactic in tone and purpose, and Evans's conclusions on this point allowed her to fit in with mainstream Victorian literary culture.

Out of this time of spiritual searching came Evans's first best seller, *Beulah*. The story chronicles Beulah Benton, a young orphan who is taken in by a local doctor, Guy Hartwell. Beulah diligently studies philosophy and history, much as Evans did, and struggles with religious faith. Her benefactor is a skeptic who cannot change his mind, even when Beulah appears to reach a peace with her Christian beliefs. Hartwell eventually declares his love for Beulah, and the narrator implies that Beulah's influence brings Hartwell back to faith.

The novel's plot, like that of *Inez*, "followed the conventions of the domestic novel." In addition, the emphasis on Protestant Christianity is just as strong in *Beulah* as in *Inez*. As Riepma acknowledges, "*Beulah* received many favorable reviews, most of which stressed the novel's great moral value." But *Beulah* parts company with other contemporary domestic novels in important ways. Evans's heroines are rarely simplistic in how they approach their lives and goals, and though Beulah might marry and assume a traditional female role by the end of the novel, she certainly expresses her opinions about the autonomy of women throughout the story. Beulah believes that women should be able to "stand up" alone, and she abhors women who depend on men for happiness or a sense of self. Beulah says, "I feel humbled when I hear a woman bemoaning the weakness of her sex, instead of showing that she has a soul and a mind of her own, inferior to none." Although faith and domesticity are important in the novel, "Evans's message to her readers is clearly that it is of vital importance for a woman to have skills allowing her to be independent, if necessary."[15] Beulah is intellectually autonomous, and she supports herself by moving out of her benefactor's home and securing employment. This emphasis on self-sufficiency is likely a product of Evans's situation: her father had proved that men are not always capable of supporting families, and Evans's attempts to provide security for her family yet remain respectable become her characters' goals as well.

Evans finished writing *Beulah* in 1859 but could not find a publisher. After receiving one rejection, she decided to travel to New York to pitch *Beulah* to publishers. In the summer of 1859, she and her cousin and traveling companion, Col. John Jones, arrived in the city, and she made an appointment to see J. C. Derby of Derby and Jackson Publishers. He agreed to have his wife and children read the manuscript and to publish it if they liked it. They did, leading to one of the most important relationships of Evans's life. Derby not only published *Beulah* but became Evans's ally and introduced her to the New York literary world. He introduced Evans to Rachel Lyons, a young Jewish woman who soon became one of Evans's closest friends as her religious prejudices became a thing of the past.[16]

Beulah sold well and brought Evans considerable success. More than twenty-two thousand copies of the novel were printed in the first year alone, and the money Evans earned from it allowed her to purchase a permanent home for her family, Georgia Cottage.[17] But her financial and professional success was soon overshadowed by more pressing matters—the impending Civil War.

Though Evans publicly stated that women should not be involved in politics, she jumped directly into the political turmoil in the South. She always retained her loyalty to the region and believed that the real issue at hand was not slavery but state's rights. She wrote to Alabama papers, accusing northern writers of sensationalism and immorality by seeking to force the South to change its ways. She backed the idea of secession: "Prompt and separate state action I believe to be the only door of escape from the worse than Egyptian bondage of Black Republicanism. For fifteen years, we of the South have endured insult and aggression; have ironed down our just indignation, and suffered numberless encroachments, because of our devotion to the 'Union'; because we shuddered and shrank from laying hands on the magnificent Temple which our forefathers reared in proud triumph. . . . Northern fanaticism has grown on Southern endurance. . . . The 'Union' has become a misnomer, and rather than witness the desecration of our glorious Fane, we of the South will Sampson-like lay hold upon its pillars, and if need be, perish in its ruins."[18] She continued her impassioned support for the Confederacy throughout the war.

Evans witnessed firsthand Alabama's role in secession, visiting the new Confederate capital in Montgomery to observe Jefferson Davis "forming a new government." She also made sandbags for ramparts at Fort Morgan, gave speeches, and nursed soldiers. She found nursing particularly appealing and helped to establish an informal hospital, "Camp Beulah," near her home. She saw her duty to the sick and wounded as sacred, telling a friend, "I have been constantly engaged in nursing sick soldiers, keeping sleepless vigil by day and night, and this morning sitting beside one whose life has hung upon a slender thread for many days. . . . Many times since I began this [letter] I have laid down my pen to administer medicine, count pulse, dress blisters, and perform many offices which absent sisters and mothers would gladly relive me of if they could only be with their dear ones. God bless our noble army, and preserve them from the pestilence and suffering which have decimated their ranks during the past few months." Evans's zeal for nursing was prompted by her concern for male family members fighting in the war, including her brothers, Howard and Vivian, who saw combat and whom Evans visited on the battlefield.[19]

However, nursing was also a way for Evans to prove her femininity to a world that saw her as something of an anomaly. Considering that most women did not financially support their families as Evans did, she likely felt insecure in some ways when it came to her relationship with Victorian society and gender roles. Nursing provided her with a way to demonstrate that she was womanly in spite of being a professional writer. As George Rable explains, "Charity, tenderness, [and] mercy remained peculiarly feminine virtues. . . . When women nursed sick, wounded, and dying soldiers, they also nurtured conventional ideas about their own place and character."[20] Nursing allowed Evans to identify herself as feminine in a world in which she did not exactly fit the norm and that was changing for women day by day.

At one point during the war, Augusta and Sarah Evans traveled to Virginia to see Augusta's brothers before fighting intensified. While she was there, she visited other friends at Fort Monroe, and as she wrote, "While I stood looking at its savage portholes the immense Rifle Cannon at the Rip-Raps thundered angrily, and to our amazement, a heavy shell exploded a few yards from us." After she watched Union soldiers reloading, "a second flash sent its missile of death right at us. When a third ball whizzed over our heads and exploded in a field just beyond us, the officers insisted we should get out of sight, as they were evidently firing at us, and our lives were in danger." But Evans was not afraid; instead, she "longed for a secession flag to shake defiantly in their teeth at every fire; and my fingers fairly itched to touch off a red hot ball in answer to their chivalric civilities."[21]

In 1862, as the war continued, Evans undertook what she believed to be her most important contribution to the southern cause: a novel, *Macaria; or, Altars of Sacrifice*. She dedicated the work "To the Brave Soldiers of the Southern Army." The novel follows Irene Huntingdon and Electra Gray, women who embody both sides of Evans's personality. Irene is headstrong and vocal, while Electra reflects Augusta's artistic nature. Both are independent women who seek to support themselves on their own rather than marry for security. The wealthy Irene refuses to take a husband to secure her father's fortune, while Electra is poor and goes out into the world to become an artist. The Civil War brings the two women together, and the novel does not feature the stereotypical happy ending—marriage. Instead, the characters show that women surviving in the war-torn South have other options.

Evans proved that women could support the war effort and live satisfying lives without husbands, an important message for female readers in the Confederate states, which lost so many men in the war. According to Riepma, Evans sought "to create a new type of woman, strong, capable, useful, purposeful, and independent, as a role model for helpless and dependent Southern women whose new living conditions forced them to drastically change their lives."[22] Devotion to domesticity turned to devotion to southern nationalism, an important change since, as Rable points out, "the Confederates forced women to take on new and sometimes frightening tasks. Sexual confusion reigned as the course of the fighting seemed to make hash of traditional definitions of female propriety. . . . Adolescent girls and even older single women trying to live up to antebellum social ideals faced an especially cruel dilemma: they were still expected to marry even though the war had taken away most of the potential husbands."[23] Evans's novel gave women a new outlook and purpose.

In some respects, *Macaria* also follows the pattern of domestic novels. Instead of preparing women for marriage and family life, however, Evans prepares women for how to behave as patriots in wartime. The story advocates the idea that women could serve their country in a feminine capacity, much in the same way that they would serve their husbands or a home in a domestic novel. As

Riepma notes, "Evans presents her heroine Irene as an example for Confederate women. At first Irene and several other female characters in the novel are
involved in typically feminine wartime activities such as making flags, sewing
uniforms, rolling bandages, and preparing hospital stores and food supplies. . . .
These activities reflect reality." Irene believes in serving her country as long as
she can do so in keeping with her proper role as a woman. She says, "Practically,
women should have as little to do with politics as men with darning stockings or making puff-paste; but we should be unworthy of the high social *status*
which your chivalry accords us were we indifferent to the conduct of public
affairs." Evans took the contemporary view that "woman is above partisan politics [and] public participation in politics was unwomanly." But refraining from
public political involvement did not mean that women did not have very important roles in society; rather, those roles were situated within the private sphere.
Women would "help make a better world" by influencing men.[24]

For all of its emphasis on the autonomy of women and the Confederacy, *Macaria* neglects one significant aspect of southern life: slavery. Many scholars have
criticized the novel's lack of attention to enslaved African Americans, and this
gap is consistent with Evans's other writings, which rarely mentioned African
Americans except as one-dimensional domestic servants. One British reviewer
of *Macaria* noted, "The negro is judiciously kept out of sight, though from a passage here and there we find that the servants whose names are mentioned from
time to time are undoubtedly of the African race. The principal personages
are of pure European descent; and the author, who writes in the interest of the
South, is too skillful to bring the dark spot too prominently forward." Though
later reports claimed that Evans's African American servants were fond of her,
she clearly believed that African Americans were her inferiors.[25]

One instance in *Macaria* subtly displays Evans's racist views. Irene defends
Electra's aunt, the poor but dignified Mrs. Aubrey, by saying, "Is people's worth
to be determined only by the cost or the quality of their clothes? If I were to
give your cook a silk dress exactly like that one your uncle sent you from Paris,
and provide her with shawl and bonnet to match, would she be your equal, do
you think? I imagine you would not thank me or anybody else who insinuated
that Mrs. Harriss' negro cook was quite as genteel and elegant as Miss Grace
herself, because she wore exactly the same kind of clothes. I tell you, Grace,
it is all humbug! This everlasting talk about fashion, and dress, and gentility!
Pshaw! I am sick of it."[26] On the surface, the speech makes a statement about
fashion, vanity, and morality; however, the comparison between Mrs. Aubrey
and the "negro cook" shows a difference not only in position but also in racial
identification. When Irene states that dressing a slave in the clothing belonging

to a white woman would not make the slave her equal, Evans displays her core beliefs about the differences between African Americans and whites.

Evans refused to allow a northern publisher to have *Macaria*, instead submitting it to a Virginia publisher, West and Johnson (although after the book's initial printing, Evans "smuggled a copy to [Derby] by a blockade runner via Cuba, and he made arrangements with J. B. Lippincott to issue a Northern edition"). However, another copy had already ended up in the hands of another New York publisher, Michael Doolady, who tried to profit off of the novel without paying Evans a dime. She remained ignorant of the scandal, though Derby stepped in and secured royalties for her.[27]

When the Civil War ended, Evans continued to serve the ideals of the Confederacy, especially by working to erect monuments to fallen soldiers. But she, like many other southerners, struggled to deal with the aftermath of the conflict. Not only was she impoverished, but her brother, Howard, returned from the battlefield scarred in both mind and body.[28]

Evans took what little money she had and traveled with Howard from Mobile to New York to seek specialized medical attention. When she called on Derby, "she was so heavily veiled and her clothing was so worn and out-moded that he hardly recognized her." He then surprised her with the royalties for *Macaria*, much to her appreciative delight.[29]

After receiving treatment, Howard and Augusta returned to Mobile, and in 1866 she began working on what became her most famous novel, *St. Elmo*. The novel's heroine, Edna Earl, is an orphan under her grandfather's care until his death, when she vows to support herself. She boards a train, hoping to move to another city to find work and earn enough money to pay for an education. The train wrecks, and Edna is taken in by the wealthy Mrs. Murray, the mother of St. Elmo Murray. Edna and St. Elmo had met previously, when she witnessed him being unkind to her grandfather. St. Elmo resents Edna's presence in his mother's house, and she is uncomfortable taking charity from the well-to-do family. She eventually earns St. Elmo's trust, but she does not have faith in him. She moves to New York and becomes a writer, while St. Elmo pines for her. He then follows her to the city and again professes his love. He has reformed, and Edna finally trusts him. With his conversion to moral living firmly established, Edna agrees to marry St. Elmo and gives up her career to be a wife.

St. Elmo is more typically a domestic novel than Evans's earlier works. The novel appealed to Victorian tastes, and making the Christian Edna the vehicle for the rake St. Elmo's transformation and redemption into a proper hero accorded with nineteenth-century notions about gender. In addition, the novel's conventional happy ending gave war-weary Americans—particularly southerners—

hope for a brighter future. As Fidler explains, "Not only were the hero and heroine idealized in *St. Elmo*, but the setting was more elegant than life, and the style more refined than mere thinking."[30]

Many readers found the dark Byronic hero, St. Elmo, very attractive. According to Riepma, "Although characterized by a powerful intellect, he is dominated by his fiercely passionate nature, and his face shows an almost permanent savage sneer, and signs of dissipation." In addition, "From the beginning of the novel Evans develops a theme typical of the ideology of domesticity: woman's influence. From their first acquaintance, Edna's influence on St. Elmo is for the good." As a good nineteenth-century woman, Edna "brings about change in St. Elmo by the sole means of her exemplary behavior, her female influence."[31]

Of course, Edna also changes, forgoing her independent nature in favor of St. Elmo's patriarchal authority. But the novel reverses that characterization, presenting Edna as unshackled not when she is a writer but when she becomes a wife: before their wedding, St. Elmo proclaims, "To-day I snap the fetters of your literary bondage. There shall be no more books written! No more study, no more toil, no more anxiety, no more heart-aches! And that dear public you love so well, must even help itself, and whistle for a new pet. You belong solely to me now, and I shall take care of the life you have nearly destroyed, in your inordinate ambition."[32] Exhausted and faltering, Edna willingly surrenders her life of independence.

While Edna's actions seem a stark contrast from those of Evans's earlier heroines, this plot device not only fits the domestic plot but also aligns with the author's beliefs about the role of women. According to Riepma, "Although Evans wanted to stimulate her Southern countrywomen to become more active and independent, she advocated a strict demarcation of woman's sphere. . . . Evans feared that equality would entail a male loss of chivalry towards women." Edna is lauded for her decision and ability to support herself rather than to give herself to a less-than-worthy man, but when St. Elmo accepts God and religion, he can unite completely with Edna and becomes worthy of her. Under those circumstances, she can take up the coveted and highest female role: wife and mother. "The hero after whom the novel has been named is reformed as a result of Edna's influence. Edna's greatest achievement is the hero's transformation from a dissipated, blasphemous cynic into a man who has found peace as a minister, and who is now, like the heroine, ruled by his heart. St. Elmo has been regenerated by fire; his passion for Edna has allowed him to burn his old bad life and become a better man. From now on Edna will rule the heart of St. Elmo," as a proper domestic heroine should.[33]

But the novel may also have spoken to the war-torn South in other ways, offering more than domestic escapism. The Civil War had complicated or destroyed lives, and *St. Elmo* may also be seen as an early example of southern Gothic fiction, albeit with a happy ending. In this light, the novel's events can offer hope to white southerners who felt that they had lost everything. Southern women must be independent because so many men have been lost in the war and because so many of those who remain are so damaged that, like St. Elmo, they cannot be proper husbands or leaders. St. Elmo's darkness in the early parts of the novel seems impenetrable, and though he is attracted by Edna's goodness and light, she remains incomprehensible to him, and he knows he cannot have her. He is also associated with foreignness, so clearly separated from all identifiable marks of the southern gentleman that he continually has a "darkening countenance"; his study is described as an "Egyptian Museum."[34] Southern soldiers, too, might be seen as having returned from their "foreign" travels with a darkened emotional state, changed by the war. Evans may well have been telling her readers that faith would enable all southern men to mirror St. Elmo's transformation.

Edna agrees to marry St. Elmo only because he has regained control of his life and emotions, becoming a strong authority figure capable of providing the lifestyle and security of the past. When he shows he has reformed, Edna faints, symbolizing her ability to let go of her need to support herself. So unlike many more recent southern Gothic novels, *St. Elmo* offered its contemporary readers a glimpse of hope, arguing for the possibility that white southern men and their society could be rehabilitated and that white southern women could return to their perfect and beautiful antebellum lifestyle. Evans offered an idealized ending and perhaps a wishful rewriting of the Civil War's destruction of the South that falsely romanticized prewar life, in large part by neglecting the cruelties of slavery.

St. Elmo was a phenomenal success by any standards, and scholars estimate that "one million people had read the book four months after it appeared."[35] As Fidler notes, "The absence of reliable records and indexes of sales before the year 1895 makes it impossible to establish the exact place of *St. Elmo* among all-time best selling novels, but it is safe to say that before the advent of book-of-the-month clubs, *St. Elmo* ran a close third to *Uncle Tom's Cabin* and *Ben-Hur*. . . . It was judged to be more popular in [1867] than such works as *Oliver Twist*, *The Spy*, *Henry Esmond*, *Tom Sawyer*, and *Huckleberry Finn*."[36] People across the United States named children, towns, and consumer products after its hero. The novel also inspired a parody, and many people harshly criticized the novel's verbosity and unrealistic characterizations. Nevertheless, the book remained popular for the remainder of the century.

The publication of *St. Elmo* brought Evans financial security. Within three years, she also had the security of a marriage that she had advocated in the novel. Despite her father's opposition, she became engaged to her family's neighbor, the widowed Col. Lorenzo Wilson. Matthew Evans died on August 27, 1868, and Augusta married Wilson, who was nearly thirty years her senior, at Georgia Cottage a few months later.[37]

Augusta Wilson settled into a life befitting the married heroines of domestic novels. Like her heroine Edna, she abandoned her previous independence in favor of domestic bliss, but unlike Edna, Augusta continued to write. She sent her fifth novel, *Vashti, or, "Until Death Do Us Part,"* to the publisher scarcely six months after her marriage. However, she only wrote after she had finished her daily domestic duties: "When arrangements for dinner were complete, Mrs. Wilson opened her writing desk. Before taking up the manuscript of her latest novel, she answered all business and personal letters, usually on the day that each was received." Despite Augusta Evans's strong-willed nature, Augusta Wilson lavished attention on her husband and household duties.[38]

Augusta Wilson also filled her time with daily visits to her mother and frequent attendance at Mobile theatrical productions. She engaged with the moral and political debates of the day, though she did not always approve of women doing so. She did not support Prohibition (and even made wine for her guests), and she deplored the arguments in favor of woman suffrage, declaring in 1896, "I believe . . . that the day which endows women with elective franchise will be the blackest in the annals of this country, and will ring the death-knell of modern civilization, national prosperity, social morality, and domestic happiness. Every exciting political election will then witness the revolting deeds perpetrated by the furies who assisted in the storming of the Tuilleries, and a repetition of the scenes enacted during the reign of the Paris commune will mournfully attest how terrible is the female nature when perverted."[39] The contrast between her views and the outspoken and independent characters she created (as well as her personal outspokenness) may seem strange, but many domestic novelists shared these sentiments.[40]

Wilson did not publish her next novel, the melodramatic *Infelice*, until 1875, and another dozen years passed before the release of *At the Mercy of Tiberius*, a mystery that she considered her best novel. It chronicles the story of wrongfully imprisoned Beryl Brentano, a young New Yorker who must travel to the South to try to obtain money from her grandfather to help with her mother's medical treatment. Though the grandfather disinherited Beryl's mother when she married a northern man, he is moved by Beryl's pleas and gives her the money. Beryl boards a train to return home but is arrested: her grandfather has been found dead. Through many twists and turns, the community discovers that Beryl is innocent, but not before she spends more than a year in prison. The novel ends with Beryl married to the lawyer who originally accused her and providing a shining example of womanhood.

At the Mercy of Tiberius represents a bit of a departure for Wilson in that it was a detective story with elements of the domestic novel and it was more realistic than her previous works. By the late nineteenth century, Riepma notes, "sentimental domestic fiction was slowly losing its appeal, possibly because women writers as well as readers were losing faith in what they had earlier believed to be the pervasiveness of their moral influence exercised from the home." Critics applauded the novel, perhaps because the book speaks to many later nineteenth-century ideas that concerned Wilson, including an argument against Darwinism and a call to reinstate chivalry.[41]

On October 7, 1891, Lorenzo Wilson died, and Augusta decided to move from their home to another residence in Mobile. She remained in mourning for quite some time and did not release another book for more than a decade after his death. Published in 1902, *A Speckled Bird* had an initial print run of thirty-five thousand copies, all of which were "sold in advance of publication."[42] Wilson returned to the plotlines of her previous works, again telling the story of two women—in this case, Eglah Kent and Nona Dane. Wilson used the novel to express her disapproval of the "New Woman." Eglah is Wilson's ideal heroine, a more conventional woman who is flawed in interesting ways but still shares qualities with other domestic novel heroines and experiences a happy ending. Nona, however, does not: she personifies the New Woman and is degraded, humiliated, and destroyed. According to Riepma, *A Speckled Bird* "contrasts 'new womanhood' whose adherents lived primarily in the North, to 'true womanhood' which continued to prevail in the south."[43] The contrasting fates of the two main characters—Eglah is happily married, while Nona's future is bleak—demonstrate Wilson's approbation for the southern way of life and for the ideals presented in domestic novels.

Nona has been a rebel all of her life. She marries a man under bad circumstances, and believing that he has abandoned her, she sets out to raise her son alone and vows a hatred of men. When she is reunited with her husband (who has not abandoned her), he notices her unwavering dislike of all men, and says, "The circumstances coloring your life have destroyed every vestige of confidence in man's honor." While Nona's husband acknowledges his role in her unhappy fate, Wilson emphasizes Nona's inability to accept his help or apologies and capitulate, as Edna did in *St. Elmo*, to her proper and natural state as a woman. She is too far degraded as a result of her drive to live as an independent woman and as a political figure (almost as a man) that she has lost all ability to think and act as a woman should. She is beyond saving, and when her husband offers his hand, "she seemed not to see it," oblivious to her position as a woman and his as a savior.[44] As a New Woman, asserting herself and her ideas aggressively in public, Nona becomes impoverished and provides for a child alone, and she finally dies in a bombing related to a labor strike she has organized. Wilson clearly sees this end as fitting for a woman who insists on participating in affairs meant for men.[45]

Wilson wrote only one more story, *Devota*. Written when she was seventy-two years old and with the help of her niece, Lily Bragg, the novella is a fairly bland tale with a predictable outcome. Young Devota Lindsay has been charged to plead with the governor to spare a prisoner's life. Unlike the heroines in Wilson's other novels, Devota is not outspoken and appears fairly one-dimensional—she was previously engaged to the governor but has not seen him for many years, but they reconcile at the end of the story. The plot leaves most modern readers cold, and the book received mixed reviews when it was published in 1907. According to Riepma, by the time of the publication of *A Speckled Bird*, "critics turned increasingly condescending towards Evans's novels, or they discussed them in terms of nostalgia, as they supposedly reflected an ideology from the past."[46] But Wilson still had a strong fan base, and some readers gushed about *Devota*: "Her books are of the kind which are always in fashion, for they are, above everything else, love stories, and love stories of a very high order."[47]

On May 9, 1909, the day after her seventy-fourth birthday, Augusta Evans Wilson died of a heart attack at her home.[48] The public mourned her death, and her novels remained popular for years, not only in reprintings but also as stage and eventually movie adaptations.

Though the popularity of the domestic novel faded in the twentieth century, these books and their authors had tremendous influence. "When we look at the context from which woman's fiction emerged," Nina Baym states, "and recognize its role in the struggle against time-honored but destructive images of women as permanent children, toys, sexual animals, mindless drudges, or painted shells, then we may see it . . . properly."[49] For all of her complicated opinions about gender and politics, Augusta Evans Wilson played a crucial part in advancing American literature, and her writings reflected the events that occurred in the lives of nineteenth-century Alabamians.

NOTES

1. Nina Baym, *Woman's Fiction: A Guide to Novels by and about Women in America, 1820–1870* (Ithaca: Cornell University Press, 1978), 276, 11–12, 278.

2. William Perry Fidler, *Augusta Evans Wilson, 1835–1909: A Biography* (Tuscaloosa: University of Alabama Press, 1951), 12, 16, 19.

3. Ibid., 21.

4. Ibid., 22–23, 25.

5. Ibid., 26–29, 31.

6. Ibid., 32–33, 37.

7. Ibid., 38, 40.

8. Ibid., 41.

9. Ibid., 44–45, 42.

10. Anne Sophie Riepma, *Fire and Fiction: Augusta Jane Evans in Context* (Amsterdam: Rodopi, 2000), 29.

11. Augusta Jane Evans, *Inez: A Tale of the Alamo* (New York: Dillingham, 1887), 168.

12. Riepma, *Fire and Fiction*, 24, 25, 29.

13. Suzanne Bost, "Women and Chile at the Alamo: Feeding U.S. Colonial Mythology," *Nepantla: Views from South* 4 (2003): 503.

14. Fidler, *Augusta Evans Wilson*, 48, 49, 52, 54.

15. Riepma, *Fire and Fiction*, 33, 31, 36; Augusta Jane Evans, *Beulah* (New York: Dillingham, 1898), 137.

16. Fidler, *Augusta Evans Wilson*, 68–69, 73.

17. Ibid., 74–75.

18. Ibid., 71, 86.

19. Ibid., 89, 90, 91.

20. George Rable, *Civil Wars: Women and the Crisis of Southern Nationalism* (Urbana: University of Illinois Press, 1991), 121.

21. Fidler, *Augusta Evans Wilson*, 97.

22. Riepma, *Fire and Fiction*, 95.

23. Rable, *Civil Wars*, 50–51.

24. Riepma, *Fire and Fiction*, 94, 79, 85; Augusta Evans Wilson, *Macaria: The Works of Augusta Evans Wilson in Eight Volumes* (New York: Co-operative Publication Society, 1896), 314.

25. Review of *Macaria*, *The Athenaeum*, December 24, 1864, 859; Mrs. George C. Ball, "Mrs. Wilson, the South's Oldest Woman Writer," *Atlanta Constitution*, September 15, 1902, 9.

26. Augusta Jane Evans, *Macaria; or, Altars of Sacrifice* (London: Nicholson, 1883), 23.

27. Fidler, *Augusta Evans Wilson*, 106–7.

28. Ibid., 122.

29. Ibid.

30. Ibid., 133.

31. Riepma, *Fire and Fiction*, 110, 125, 140.

32. Augusta Jane Evans, *St. Elmo: A Novel* (New York: Dillingham, 1866), 562.

33. Riepma, *Fire and Fiction*, 144, 145–46.

34. Evans, *St. Elmo*, 92, 95.

35. Riepma, *Fire and Fiction*, 109.

36. Fidler, *Augusta Evans Wilson*, 129–30.

37. Ibid., 149–50.

38. Ibid., 150, 156–60.

39. Ibid., 163–64; "One of Our Own: Mrs. Augusta Evans Wilson, the Novelist, a Native Georgian," *Atlanta Constitution*, November 1, 1896.

40. Riepma, *Fire and Fiction*.

41. Riepma, *Fire and Fiction*, 173, 170.

42. Fidler, *Augusta Evans Wilson*, 197–98, 204–5.

43. Riepma, *Fire and Fiction*, 176.

44. Augusta Evans Wilson, *A Speckled Bird* (New York: Dillingham, 1902), 115, 116.

45. Riepma, *Fire and Fiction*, 179; Fidler, *Augusta Evans Wilson*, 206.

46. Riepma, *Fire and Fiction*, 174.

47. Review of *Devota*, *Nashville American*, August 11, 1907.

48. Fidler, *Augusta Evans Wilson*, 214.

49. Baym, *Woman's Fiction*, 299.

The Townsend Family

African American Female "Voice" and Interracial Ties

SHARONY GREEN

It was August 1890. Carrie Leontee Townsend, a young African American woman, began a letter from her home in Brookhaven, Mississippi, not far from the Gulf Coast, where she lived with her family when she was not at New Orleans University. Possibly because she would soon be returning to school, Townsend was writing to her Uncle Thomas, who lived one state over in Huntsville, Alabama. Townsend shared the latest news about her household, noting that "Cousin Alice" was visiting from New Richmond, Ohio. She also had news of her own: "I am not bragging but you ought to see me play piano. I tell you I make ours sing." Before closing, Carrie Townsend wondered if her uncle could send her something: "A nice winter dress would be accepted," she wrote.[1]

It is tempting to read Townsend's request for a winter dress as proof of the number of late nineteenth-century Americans, both black and white, who longed to acquire material possessions, especially given the rise of department stores and mail-order catalogs. But her assertiveness also stemmed from her status as the descendant of an influential white slaveholder who went to great lengths to provide for his children, including her uncle and her father.[2] Because he did, Carrie Townsend and her relatives were well-positioned African Americans. Her uncle, a lawyer, resided on Adams Street, one of Huntsville's "choice spots," where his neighbors included John David Weeden, a white man who had been a colonel in the Confederate army and was a lawyer himself.[3]

Though well positioned, the members of Carrie's family still felt the strain that other African Americans experienced. Her uncle was among the black southern men who were initially able to vote after the Civil War only to discover that their newfound freedom arrived in fits and starts following a failed Reconstruction.[4] While he was prominent enough that his marriage was announced in a local newspaper, that newspaper's audience was largely African American.[5]

every day when you writ let
us know what have be corn of Mr Sam
& Townsend people and how tends to
ion. um now. I expect to go out to Kansas
law this summer if I can hear from
Mr Caveness. pleas tell Frances.
He. she must ancer my letter
give my love to all my inquiring
friends. Sister is well and sends
her best love to you. you must
excuse bad writing as I am in a
hery I want to writ another letter to
Brother in Kansas. your absant
Sister Elizabeth Townsend

Still, the Townsend family and other African Americans in similar circumstances were better prepared than others to deal with white postwar hostility. Ironically, this ability to cope resulted not only from their own determination but also from the fact that they were descendants of a wealthy white American.[6] Such blacks enjoyed advantages that sometimes included the chance to obtain an education and the refinement to know how to request not just a dress but a *winter* dress. This essay explores the lives of such individuals using the Townsend family as a case study. Specifically, it looks at surviving letters from the mixed-race descendants of Samuel Townsend, an antebellum Huntsville planter, to explore how ties to a powerful white man enabled some freedpeople to enhance their lives amid oppression.[7]

Before his death in 1856, the never-married Townsend made provisions for the emancipation and manumission of his ten enslaved children by five enslaved women: Carrie's father, Wesley; her Uncle Thomas; and Bradford, Caroline, Willis, Osborne, Parthenia, Susanna, Milcha, and Elvira.[8] Townsend also sought to leave his children and their immediate enslaved relatives, whom he also freed, the bulk of his fortune—approximately $200,000 (equivalent to approximately $5.5 million today).[9] As these children and their offspring built their lives as freedpeople, they wrote to each other and to Septimus Cabaniss, Townsend's lawyer, to share both their accomplishments and their struggles. When studied closely, their lives as revealed via these letters provide a new perspective on the power African Americans held even in unjust relationships. The letters demonstrate that these people had a clear sense of purpose and forcefulness as they maneuvered through their daily lives. These traits were particularly visible among the Townsend women and girls.

Assertive behavior by African American women and girls is visible in numerous encounters with whites. For example, one enslaved woman chastised a Union soldier by asking why he was stealing her quilts if he was fighting for African Americans.[10] Though an imbalance of power clearly existed between this woman and the soldier, they were allies, generally speaking, since he was part of an army whose goal of preserving the Union meant the demise of the slave society that held her in bondage. But this unspoken affiliation did not prevent the soldier from stealing her quilts or the enslaved woman from speaking her mind. Her actions reveal that she had some understanding of how much she could get away with in the presence of an authoritative figure. She had almost certainly worked under the surveillance of whites, perhaps in a home where she heard and experienced much. Such proximity offered some African American women and girls a "distinct view of the contradictions" between what whites said and what they actually did.[11]

Indeed, the woman probably knew how far to go with this soldier.[12] Depending on their level of closeness and experience with such white men, other nineteenth-century African Americans—men and women, girls and boys—also had such knowledge. Some, among them the Townsends, eventually learned the degree to which some men would go to protect or provide for African Americans. Samuel Townsend owned sixty-three enslaved people, ten of whom were his children. After the death of his brother, Edmund, and the failure of his plan to free and provide for his daughters, Samuel Townsend developed "a great dread of his children becoming the slaves" of his white relatives. In 1854, he revised his will to leave the bulk of his estate to his enslaved children and his two nieces.[13] His actions reveal the inconsistencies in American society. Writing to Stephen A. Douglas, a prominent Democratic U.S. senator who lost to Abraham Lincoln in the 1860 presidential election, Cabaniss, who went on to serve in the Alabama legislature between 1861 and 1863, later explained that Samuel Townsend had asked for options that would secure the "ultimate improvement and happiness of his servants."[14] Townsend's use of the word *servant* demonstrates that he was aware of his powerful position in relation to his children and their kind. Nevertheless, he wanted to see them not only free and financially stable but also *happy*.

Samuel Townsend's regard for his offspring may have been reciprocated. Many years later, another of Carrie Townsend's relatives, Uncle Osborne, chastised Uncle Thomas for failing to "send me the inscription on our father's tombstone," a reaction that seems to suggest some degree of affection for his father—and former owner.[15] Because of the lack of surviving evidence, it is unknown how often enslaved or freedpeople used the word *father* rather than *master* while referring to southern men who acknowledged them as kin. Still, as historian Stephanie M. H. Camp has written, we can closely read archival documents and make guesses about their meanings if they reflect wider practices.[16] We may even infer from fragments of evidence that some intimate acts between blacks and whites may not have always represented mistreatment.

Sexual relations across the color line unquestionably occurred from the earliest days of European and African settlement in the New World.[17] In many cases, those encounters occurred without the woman's consent—that is, they involved rape. But in other instances, genuine mutual affection must have existed between the two parties. In 1749, an enslaved woman, Kate, and another black woman informed a South Carolina community about a planned slave revolt. Colonial authorities were alarmed not only by the news but also by Kate's closeness to a white man, who allegedly cared for her more than "his own Wife and Children." Outraged either by his behavior or by his failure to prevent his affection from becoming public knowledge, other whites took action, apparently banishing Kate from the community, for she never appears in any subsequent Carolina slave inventory.[18]

Kate's experience may have been unusual, but it is likely that similar incidents were simply not recorded. Interracial relations were a taboo subject despite the abundant legal evidence that they occurred. The Townsend family therefore provides an opportunity to investigate the dynamics in one mixed-race family in the Deep South with obvious intimate ties to a powerful white man. In fact, given the prohibitions on teaching enslaved African Americans how to read or write, the Townsend letters are a valuable resource because of the paucity of sources with information on the actions and especially the thoughts of enslaved people and former slaves. In learning about the Townsends, we are able to even move the story of enslaved "mistresses" from port cities such as New Orleans, Mobile, and Charleston, with which they are typically associated, inland to one northern Alabama town.[19]

Like such women in port cities, some of the enslaved women on Samuel Townsend's plantation benefited from his interest in them and their children. In fact, his interest in them seems to have contributed to these women's strong sense of self. For example, in 1860 Cabaniss hired a Huntsville man, D. L. Lakin, to escort these women and twenty-five of their immediate relatives to Kansas. Lakin reported to Cabaniss that three of the children's mothers caused "the greatest trouble" on the journey north to freedom on a Mississippi steamboat. Lakin was "forced Several times to Speak to them in tones of unmistakable command."[20] Emancipated and on their way out of the slave states, the women may have seen no reason to treat Lakin with the deference he expected as a white man. Lakin apparently had no need to speak forcefully to the male relatives who were accompanying him—it was the women whose behavior was troublesome. When the letters from the women and girls in the Townsend family are considered together, they reveal sturdy black female voices that may have been enabled by their emotional and physical ties to their now-dead master. While they may appear unusual, it is more likely that their experiences are simply better documented.

Prior to his death in 1856, Samuel Townsend lived on a seventeen-hundred-acre property in Huntsville, the Home Plantation. Some of his fortune, much of which apparently arrived as inheritance, was built here. He and his brothers, Edmund and Parks, had been among many Virginians fleeing failing farms in the 1820s. To them, the fertile land of Huntsville, which benefited from being in the drainage basin of the Tennessee River, held great promise. Surrounded by hills, the area's creeks fed into the river, the largest branch of the Ohio, enabling the movement of cotton and other merchandise to New Orleans, a key commercial hub. The area's promise and position in a rising Cotton Kingdom was reflected in the growing number of the town's main labor source: enslaved people. In 1816, some 4,200 slaves made up about a third of the 14,200 residents of Madison County, in which Huntsville sits. By 1850, 14,765 slaves comprised well over half of the county's total population of 26,451.[21]

Samuel Townsend's children tested the waters of autonomy in ways that most African Americans would not do until the postbellum period and that may very well have worried whites. Historian Mary Niall Mitchell has studied the public interest in such children before the Civil War. Photographs of them were sold by northern abolitionists, who unwittingly worried some whites about what life would soon be like if slavery ended and racially ambiguous children chose to pass as whites.[22] Lakin, who escorted some of the Townsends away from Huntsville, once told Cabaniss that in his best estimation the mixed-race Townsend children would be "more happy . . . back on an Alabama plantation than in any free condition."[23] One Freedmen's Bureau agent in Kansas described Milcha, one of Townsend's daughters, as "nearly white[.] [W]ould hardly be taken for an African away from them."[24] In looking at such African Americans, whites around them in the North and South perceived a future that would be vastly different from the past.

Even before the Townsends were freed, whites in Huntsville could see the children's privilege. On one occasion, two of the siblings were searching for chestnuts when one of them strayed onto a neighbor's property, prompting a scolding from the neighbor. The commotion got so out of hand that the neighbor's wife intervened.[25] The woman may simply have had a more tolerant attitude, but she may also have recognized that the child was no ordinary enslaved person. Perhaps there was some resemblance to Samuel Townsend. Perhaps she had previously seen the child receive preferential treatment. She may well have put two and two together and surmised that the boy was Townsend's child and knew that he was concerned for his offspring.

Edmund Townsend also expressed concern for his mixed-race children. Edmund never married and fathered enslaved children with a woman of color—in his case, two daughters, Elizabeth and Virginia. He, too, sought to free and provide for his mixed-race children. Upon his death, Edmund left instructions to give his estate, worth approximately a half million dollars, to these two girls. Though Edmund had made legal arrangements to manumit Elizabeth and Virginia and took precautions before his death to ensure that they received their inheritance, a court voided his will and divided his estate among his white relatives, who distributed the proceeds among themselves. They then made Elizabeth and Virginia the joint property of Samuel and John E. Townsend, another white relative.[26]

After witnessing this proceeding, Samuel apparently worried for his own children.[27] In 1854, two years prior to his death, he secured the services of Cabaniss to revise a previous will, expressing his wish to leave the bulk of his estate to ten enslaved children. In 1860, just before the start of the Civil War, the children were freed and relocated along with their two cousins (who were also freed following Samuel's death) to Ohio. Ohio's strong abolitionist presence, its location on the Ohio-Mississippi River network, the availability of wage work, and, as the war approached, the existence of boarding schools and colleges catering to people of African descent made it a popular destination for people of mixed race, recently freed people of color and runaways alike. White men planning to free blacks for whom they cared apparently wanted them to have a good head start. Cincinnati, which was the most important city in southern Ohio and had the country's highest per capita proportion of people of mixed race outside the South, offered freedpeople more opportunities than did most places.[28]

While their mothers and other relatives largely settled in Kansas, the Townsend children were initially relocated to Xenia, Ohio, about fifty-five miles northeast of Cincinnati. Several attended nearby Wilberforce University, at that time just a boarding school. After the war began, the school closed temporarily, and the Townsends scattered to Kansas, Illinois, Colorado, Alabama, Mississippi, Mexico, and elsewhere. Some later returned to Ohio, settling in Cincinnati or nearby New Richmond.

Meanwhile, their father's lawyer spent several years paying Townsend's debts, suing his debtors, foreclosing mortgages, and finally liquidating the estate. The outbreak of the Civil War brought a temporary halt to his labors, as the Confederacy refused to allow any financial settlement to be disbursed to individuals living in a "foreign country." With the end of the war, he once again took up the Townsend will, which still faced challenges from Townsend's white relatives. So persistent were they that Cabaniss died in 1889 without seeing the case settled, although he periodically disbursed sums to the Townsend children and grandchildren. The will was finally settled in 1896. Despite Townsend's desire that his mixed-race children inherit his estate, the children received a total of only $33,719.57, about a sixth of the original behest. Some died before "reaping the full benefit from their inheritance."[29]

While building their lives as freedpeople in the late nineteenth and twentieth centuries, the Townsends encountered many whites who had conflicted or genuinely hostile feelings about the former slaves' aspirations to enjoy the promise of freedom. Cabaniss, despite his service to the Confederacy, was not one of them. His rapport with the Townsends, particularly with the younger women, who sometimes addressed him almost as if *he* were their father, was nothing short of remarkable. His willingness to fulfill his dead client's wishes was evident in the more than thirty years he spent working on their behalf. In this way, he was one of a network of white men who shepherded black and mixed-race people to freedom.

The efforts of men such as Cabaniss seem odd when viewed beside the actions of northern white abolitionists and those of other white southerners. In the years surrounding the war, members of the legal profession, particularly judges, had an "unusual view of mixed-race sexual relations."[30] White slaveholders left money to black women and children so frequently that such transfers of property were often affirmed, "especially when precedents under the common law could be easily used to do so." In some instances, the legal community responded favorably because southern white men demonstrated a sense of moral obligation to care for their black children as they did for their white ones.[31] Such care was not unnoticed by black Americans, whose confidence was boosted. This was especially true of black women and girls.

Edmund's daughter, Elizabeth Townsend, was initially relocated to Ohio and attended Wilberforce. In an 1861 letter, she described her social activities: "All the young men and the young ladys had a social and we enjoyed ourselves indeed." She then relayed a bit of gossip. "And a few week ago we had a revival here[.] [A] good many of my school mats profess religion. Sister has profess religion. Thomas & Milcha & Bradford all these have profess religion."[32] Such revivals were a common feature of the American landscape during the antebellum Second Great Awakening. However, Elizabeth's commentary also reveals her independence, her unwillingness to simply follow the crowd. Elvira, one of Samuel Townsend's freed children, demonstrated similar independence and assertiveness. Writing to Cabaniss from her new home in Leavenworth, Kansas, just months after the war ended, she bluntly demanded, "It is necessary that I should know the condition of our affairs; of what has been done with Samuel Townsend estate, and our interest therein. The new state of affairs gives us the power to enforce remedies and we shall do it. Either through the military commanders, or the Freedmen's Bureau we can obtain our just rights, and call any and all parties to a strict account."[33] Elvira appears the have been the most assertive of the Townsends. Five years earlier, shortly after their arrival in Ohio, Wesley, Samuel Townsend's eldest child, had written to Cabaniss that Elvira was threatening to return to Huntsville.[34] Elvira's outspokenness may have resulted from the fact that she had been Samuel Townsend's housekeeper, a position that enabled her to live in close proximity to her father, who at times treated her indulgently.[35] That familiarity, in turn, might have led her to take a more assertive tone with other white men, including Cabaniss, who had been hired to ensure her financial future and whom she apparently viewed as working for her. That an African American woman of this time would address a white man in this tone is quite unusual and perhaps even shocking, since it completely upends the expected racial and gender norms of the time. She may have been testing his patience unnecessarily, but such directness appears to have been shared by other Townsend descendants, especially females.

More than twenty years later, in 1884, Nettie Caldwell, the teenaged daughter of Milcha Townsend, wrote to remind Cabaniss that he had promised to send her some money when she was old enough to select her own guardian. Echoing the sort of self-determination earlier expressed by her Aunt Elvira, Nettie wrote, "I am old enough now to choose one. Please let me know if I choose one, will you send me some money? I don't want to choose a guardian unless you send some money." Nettie, apparently in school at the time, added, "My books this session cost me eight dollars," and if Cabaniss had "any feeling for a motherless and fatherless child," she concluded, he would respond.[36] The direct and even manipulative tone of this letter may have been a function of Nettie's youth, but it also reflects what her relatives had taught her about the appropriate way to interact with the man charged with carrying out her grandfather's wishes.

The Townsends were not the only southern women and girls of color who addressed white men in this fashion. During the summer of 1847, Lucile Tucker, an enslaved woman, sent a letter to Rice Ballard, her master. She had been allowed to earn "good" money in Bainbridge, Georgia, far from Ballard's plantations in Mississippi, Louisiana, and Arkansas. Having been permitted to live far from her master and earn money, Tucker now demanded her freedom, writing, "I wish you could have emancipated me when you was last in New Orleans for that is a matter I deserve to have arranged as early as possible and if you could do it without putting me to the expense of returning to New Orleans, I should much prefer it for life you know is very uncertain and you might die before I can see you."[37] Avenia White, another woman of color whom Ballard freed, displayed a similar sense of having earned certain things from her former master. Living in Cincinnati in 1838, White and another woman freed with her together had four children, and they were likely Ballard's progeny. Two years later, as they sought to build new lives in Ohio, White wrote to Ballard of their need for money: "[If] you have forgotten me I hope you have not forgotten the children."[38]

These two letters, like the correspondence from the Townsend women, reveal the deep bonds between some southern white men and black women and girls. Though such ties may now seem surprising and may often have been overlooked in historians' accounts of the era, they provided some African American females with a basis from which to act boldly despite their ongoing oppression.

Their strong voices were not unique. Cora Gillam, a freedwoman from Arkansas who watched her siblings go off to school in Ohio because of their white father's financial generosity but could not do so herself, still declared, "My father was not a slave. Can't you tell by me that he was white?"[39]

While some African Americans drew strength from their bonds with whites or demanded benefits from those relationships, not all former enslaved people viewed them so favorably. Robert Smalls, a former enslaved man from South Carolina who became a boat pilot for the U.S. government and later a congressman, maintained that African American women, because of their relationships with white men, were inherently immoral.[40] Sarah Fitzpatrick, an ex-slave interviewed in Alabama, said, "The reason our race is so mixed up is by fooling with these white men."[41] They likely were not alone in their views.

The diary of the childless Mary Chesnut, a Charleston white woman, makes clear the degree to which white plantation mistresses struggled to contain their anger over their husbands' dalliances with female slaves. Mixed-race enslaved women, including ones who were sold as "fancy girls," or mistresses to white men, seemed to have especially bothered Chesnut. In one bitter diary entry, she wrote, "So I have seen a negro woman sold. [She] overtopped the crowd. . . . She was a bright mulatto with a pleasant face. She was magnificently gotten up in silks and satins. She seemed so delighted by it all—sometimes ogling the bidders, sometimes looking quite coy and modest, but her mouth never relaxed from its expanded grin of excitement. I daresay the poor thing knew who would buy her."[42] To Chesnut, this enslaved woman seemed well aware of white men's desires and how to play them to her advantage. Chesnut's rage stemmed not just from such relationships but from her inability to do anything about them beyond recording it in her diary.[43]

The sense of agency expressed by the Townsend women and others like them contrasts sharply with the standard of behavior that white southern women were expected to follow. In November 1847, Louise Ballard, the wife of Rice Ballard, wrote plaintively to her "Dearest Husband" from their Louisville home to ask about his whereabouts: "It is several days or three weeks since you left and we have not heard from you yet. Are you sick or have you so much to attend to that you have not had time to write?"[44] Louise Ballard clearly did not write to her husband with the same sense of power and entitlement possessed by the formerly enslaved mothers of his children.

Of course, many African American women and girls who received privileges and attempted to assert themselves were rebuffed. While touring the United States between 1849 and 1851, Swedish reformer Fredrika Bremer described seeing an enslaved girl whose owners decided she had grown too assertive and sold her.[45] Many other enslaved women considered "insubordinate" were also sold or received whippings and other punishments. In other cases, even unusual degrees of caring and regard that whites carried for African Americans had definite limits.

Carrie Townsend's Uncle Thomas was a neighbor of former Confederate colonel John Weeden, whose sister, Maria Howard Weeden, was an artist. Maria attended the 1893 World's Fair in Chicago and returned to Huntsville angered by the demeaning way African Americans were depicted at the fair. She reportedly set out to restore their dignity through her watercolor paintings. However, Weeden was a woman of her time, and she admitted to peering through a fence to observe a black woman who was unaware that she was being painted. Weeden had not asked permission to paint the woman and thus violated her privacy. And despite her wish to restore some dignity to African Americans' lives via painting, Weeden once said that the "southern slave-servant is better preserved" in a small town such as Huntsville than in the "strain and bustle" of a big city.[46] Dignity apparently did not mean independence or autonomy.

The Townsends' access to money and education could not protect them from the increasingly harsh laws targeting African Americans in the wake of Reconstruction.[47] Samuel Townsend's son Osborne attended school at Wilberforce and fought for the Union during the Civil War before settling in Georgetown, Colorado, and working as a barber and silver miner. In 1888, he wrote to his half-brother Thomas in Huntsville, "I read gloomy reports of the condition of the colored man in the South." And the following year, he vowed, "I never expect to come South again until I can travel like other people."[48] Osborne's comments reveal how discrimination affected even the most well-situated African Americans, but they also show that the Townsend men could be pointedly vocal about their dissatisfaction both to each other and to white men. In fact, after learning that Cabaniss had traveled to Kansas in September 1866, Willis, one of the freed children, wrote seeking news regarding the "estate of our Father."[49] His cousin Woodson, who quietly accompanied Lakin on that initial journey from Huntsville in 1860, later accused Cabaniss of failing to protect Woodson's share of the family's inheritance: "You did not try to do anything for me."[50]

In some ways, Cabaniss operated as a wishing well around which the Townsend family gathered as they awaited their inheritance. But he was also a white man toward whom the Townsends felt empowered to direct their demands. While the men insisted on what they saw as their just due, the voices of the Townsend girls and women are especially noteworthy. Their words convey the extent to which they resisted the racist idea that they deserved nothing. And any success they enjoyed in their entreaties to Cabaniss may indeed represent the fulfillment of the hopes of their enslaved mothers, who had shared a bed with a white man years earlier.

Access to money and white support could not protect some members of the Townsend family from the consequences of their actions, but their relationship with Cabaniss offered options that might allow them to sidestep familial constraints. Susanna Townsend left Wilberforce in the wake of the Civil War and resided with her older brother Wesley and his family in New Richmond, Ohio, where she attended school. She was not happy living with her brother and at times apparently did not stay at his house. In June 1868, when she was about fifteen, Susanna wrote an urgent letter to Cabaniss explaining that she needed money immediately so that she could marry and move to Kansas. Pregnant, she told the lawyer that Wesley apparently believed she had disgraced herself and the family and treated her "like I was a dog or some kind of . . . animal." Her intended husband, she told him, was "the nicest young man I ever did see"—and he was white. Five months later, apparently still living with her brother, Susanna gave birth to a baby, who seems to have died. Susanna herself died the following year. Susanna cast Cabaniss in the role of father or guardian, calling him "uncle."[51] She also did not hesitate to seek his assistance in the face of her brother's recalcitrance.

Susanna's strong tone and bold confidence in Cabaniss, the white man hired to arrange for her future, fits into a long history of black-white interactions that seem to contradict the accepted roles of whites and blacks, women and men. Such relations complicate our understanding of the past. Historian Emily West has looked at freed black women who petitioned to be allowed to remain in the South prior to the Civil War. That one-fifth of the ninety-eight enslavement requests came from single free women who may very well have been involved in intimate relations with white men—the women's petitions did not mention other common motives such as spouses or families, poverty, or debt—affirm again the degree to which such relationships existed and allowed certain freedpeople to access support from southern white men that enabled them to enhance their lives.[52] Indeed, that these women desired to remain in the South despite their free status suggests how powerful those relationships could be.[53]

The Townsend women used their inheritance and their other skills to build lives for themselves. Nettie Caldwell eventually received nearly three thousand dollars from the Townsend estate. She used some of the money on her education and may have invested some in land: when she died in Topeka, Kansas, she owned property. Her mother, Milcha, also purchased land with proceeds from the Townsend estate. Elvira eventually married Edmund Townsend's son, Woodson, though she left him after he was arrested during the war; relocated to St. Joseph, Missouri; and married a "good" but "poor" man. By the time of her death in 1868, she had received a little over seven hundred dollars from the Townsend estate. However, her two daughters eventually received more than two thousand dollars.[54]

After living in Ohio and Illinois, Edmund Townsend's daughter, Elizabeth, returned to Alabama. She continued to act boldly. In 1870, she and several other Townsends hired their own lawyer to collect money from her uncle's estate, and she received $3,418.96.[55] Carrie Townsend's father, Wesley, received $3,368.35 from Samuel Townsend's estate. He eventually returned from the Midwest to Alabama and worked briefly as a teacher in Huntsville before purchasing a farm in Brookhaven, Mississippi—the same farm from which Carrie wrote to her uncle. As for Carrie, after briefly working as a teacher in Huntsville, the twentieth century found her, the girl who knew how to ask for a winter dress, educated but unmarried.[56] She was undoubtedly helped by the $3,368.35 from Samuel Townsend's estate. As Samuel Townsend had hoped, his legacy had helped at least some of his children and grandchildren build successful lives for themselves. In the end, evaluating the experiences of her life and the other Townsends is the work of the modern researcher. Focused on living their lives and on surviving in a hostile world, Carrie Townsend and her aunts, uncles, and cousins may never have reflected on the part that capital and a relationship with an unlikely source—a white slave owner who had died half a century earlier—played in that success.

NOTES

I thank Lisa Dorr and Susan Youngblood Ashmore; John Beeler; Tim Barnes; Marie Bostick; Linda Riley; Lynne Williams of the Weeden House Museum; Amy Chen; Christa Vogelius; Craig Remington; my undergraduate research assistants, Ola Gerald and Alexandria Gilbert; the University of Alabama's Department of History and University of Alabama Libraries; David Roediger; Augusto Espiritu; Clarence Lang; Bruce Levine; Jennifer Hamer; Siobhan Somerville; and Kari Frederickson. This essay draws on material previously published in Sharony Green, "'Mr Ballard I Am Compelled to Write Again': Beyond Bedrooms and Brothels, a Fancy Girl Speaks," *Black Women, Gender and Families* 5 (2011): 17–40; Sharony Green, *Remember Me to Miss Louisa: Hidden Black-White Intimacies in Antebellum America* (DeKalb: Northern Illinois University Press, 2015).

1. Frances Cabaniss Roberts, "An Experiment in Emancipation of Slaves by an Alabama Planter" (master's thesis, University of Alabama, 1940), 8–10, 108–9; Carrie Leontee Townsend to Thomas Townsend, August 19, 1890, MSS 252, Box 252.054, Folder 01, Septimus Douglas Cabaniss Papers, William Stanley Hoole Special Collections Library, University of Alabama.

2. William R. Leach, *Land of Desire: Merchants, Power, and the Rise of a New American Culture* (New York: Vintage, 1994); Elaine Abelson, *When Ladies Go A-Thieving: Middle Class Shoplifters in a Victorian Department Store* (New York: Oxford University Press, 1992).

3. Bernice Fearn Young, "Howard Weeden, a Rose of Yesterday," n.d., A. S. Williams III Americana Collection, Gorgas Library, University of Alabama; "John David Weeden, 1840–1908," *Rootsweb*, http://www.rootsweb.ancestry.com/~allauder/bio-weeden.htm (accessed April 27, 2014); *Huntsville, Alabama, City Directory, 1908*.

4. W. E. B. Du Bois, *Black Reconstruction* (1935; New York: Harcourt Brace, 1976); Eric Foner, *Reconstruction: America's Unfinished Revolution, 1863–1877* (New York: Harper Perennial, 2002).

5. See Osborne Townsend to Thomas Townsend, February 14, 1888, MSS 252, Box 252.054, Folder 01, Cabaniss Papers.

6. See Joshua D. Rothman, *Notorious in the Neighborhood: Sex and Families across the Color Line in Virginia, 1787–1861* (Chapel Hill: University of North Carolina Press, 2003); Bernie D. Jones, *Fathers of Conscience: Mixed-Race Inheritance in the Antebellum South* (Athens: University of Georgia Press, 2009).

7. Dozens of such letters are among hundreds more pieces of correspondence in Septimus Douglas Cabaniss's papers, which were donated to the University of Alabama by Cabaniss's great-granddaughter, Frances Cabaniss Roberts, a historian at the University of Alabama at Huntsville.

8. Deposition of S. D. Cabaniss, MSS 252, Box 251.056, Folder 04, Cabaniss Papers.

9. Roberts, "Experiment in Emancipation," 105.

10. DoVeanna S. Fulton Minor and Reginald H. Pitts, *Speaking Lives, Authoring Texts: Three African American Women's Oral Slave Narratives* (Albany: State University of New York Press, 2010), 3. See also Deborah Gray White, *Ar'n't I a Woman: Female Slaves in the Plantation South* (1985; New York: Norton, 1999), 164.

11. Patricia Hill Collins, *Black Feminist Thought: Knowledge, Consciousness, and the Politics of Empowerment* (New York: Routledge, 1991), 11.

12. Eugene D. Genovese, *Roll, Jordan, Roll: The World the Slaves Made* (New York: Pantheon, 1974). For more recent studies addressing the issue of antebellum black resistance, see Stephanie M. H. Camp, *Closer to Freedom: Enslaved Women and Everyday Resistance in the Plantation South* (Chapel Hill: University of North Carolina Press, 2004); Walter Johnson, "On Agency," *Journal of Social History* 37 (2003): 113–24.

13. Deposition of S. D. Cabaniss, MSS 252, Box 251.056, Folder 04, Cabaniss Papers.

14. S. D. Cabaniss to Stephen A. Douglas, January 21, 1858, Box 13, Stephen A. Douglas Papers, 1764–1908, Special Collections Research Center, University of Chicago; Green, *Remember Me to Miss Louisa*, 176.

15. Osborne Townsend to Thomas Townsend, December 12, 1882, MSS 252, Box 252.054, Folder 01, Cabaniss Papers.

16. Camp, *Closer to Freedom*, 95.

17. Among many works on this subject, see Lisa Ze Winters, *The Mulatta Concubine: Terror, Intimacy, Freedom, and Desire in the Black Transatlantic* (Athens: University of Georgia Press, 2016).

18. Jennifer L. Morgan, *Laboring Women: Reproduction and Gender in New World Slavery* (Philadelphia: University of Pennsylvania Press, 2004), 191–95.

19. See Edward E. Baptist, "'Cuffy,' 'Fancy Maids,' and 'One-Eyed Men': Rape, Commodification, and the Domestic Slave Trade in the United States," *American Historical Review* 106 (2001): 1619–50; Green, *Remember Me to Miss Louisa*.

20. D. L. Lakin to S. D. Cabaniss, February 29, 1860, MSS 252, Box 251.056, Folder 03, Cabaniss Papers; Roberts, "Experiment in Emancipation," 25.

21. Roberts, "Experiment in Emancipation," 5, 7; *Williams' Huntsville Directory, City Guide, and Business Mirror, Vol. 1—1859–60*; Victor B. Haagen, *The Pictorial History of Huntsville, 1805–1865*

(Huntsville, Ala.: Haagen, 1963), 37; Joshua D. Rothman, *Flush Times and Fever Dreams: A Story of Capitalism and Slavery in the Age of Jackson* (Athens: University of Georgia Press, 2012); Thomas W. Owen, *History of Alabama and Dictionary of Alabama Biography* (Chicago: Clarke, 1921), 2:926.

22. Mary Niall Mitchell, *Raising Freedom's Child: Black Children and Visions of Freedom after Slavery* (New York: New York University Press, 2011), 9.

23. D. L. Lakin to S. D. Cabaniss, February 29, 1860, MSS 252, Box 251.056, Folder 03, Cabaniss Papers.

24. Freedmen's Bureau statement on behalf of Milcha Townsend, April 17, 1867, MSS 252, Box 252.054, Folder 01, Cabaniss Papers.

25. [Osborne Townsend?] to Thomas Townsend, December 3, 1872, MSS 252, Box 252.05, Folder 01, Cabaniss Papers.

26. Roberts, "Experiment in Emancipation," 9.

27. Deposition of S. D. Cabaniss, MSS 252, Box 251.056, Folder 04, Cabaniss Papers.

28. Green, *Remember Me to Miss Louisa*; James Oliver Horton and Stacy Flaherty, "Black Leadership in Antebellum Cincinnati," in *Race and the City: Work, Community, and Protest in Cincinnati, 1820–1970*, ed. Henry Louis Taylor Jr. (Urbana: University of Illinois Press, 1993), 81.

29. Roberts, "Experiment in Emancipation," 11, 102, 105–6; "Guide to the S. D. Cabaniss Papers," *University of Alabama University Libraries*, http://acumen.lib.ua.edu/u0003/0000252 (accessed October 8, 2012).

30. Jones, *Fathers of Conscience*, 22.

31. Ibid., 24, 42.

32. Elizabeth Townsend to Brother, May 18, 1861, MSS 252, Box 252.054, Folder 01, Cabaniss Papers; Paul Boyer, *Urban Masses and Moral Order in America, 1820–1920* (Cambridge: Harvard University Press, 1978), 12.

33. Elvira Townsend to S. D. Cabaniss, September 10, 1865, Box 252.009, Folder 5, Cabaniss Papers.

34. Wesley Townsend to S. D. Cabaniss, January 18, 1860, Box 252.009, Folder 6, Cabaniss Papers.

35. For more, see Isabela Morales, "The Townsends: Reconstructing the Lives of Seven Enslaved Women, 1830–1856," *University of Alabama University Libraries*, http://purl.lib.ua.edu/49504 (accessed July 28, 2016).

36. Nettie Caldwell to S. D. Cabaniss, October 11, 1884, MSS 252, Box 252.054, Folder 01, Cabaniss Papers. In 1865, Milcha Townsend married John Caldwell, a carpenter whom Milcha called "sober [and] industrious." In the wake of John Caldwell's death in 1872, Nettie ended up living with her father's sister, Nellie Bibb, in Louisville, Kentucky. See Milcha Townsend Caldwell Statement, April 17, 1867, Item 17, MSS 252, Box 252.054, Folder 01, Cabaniss Papers; Nellie Bibb to S. D. Cabaniss, August 3, 1880, MSS 252, Box 252.054, Folder 01, Cabaniss Papers; Roberts, "Experiment in Emancipation," 87. See also U.S. Census, 1880.

37. Lucile Tucker to R. C. Ballard, June 25, 1847, Folder 113, Rice C. Ballard Papers, Southern Historical Collection, Wilson Library, University of North Carolina at Chapel Hill. See also "Collection Overview," Ballard Papers; U.S. Census, 1850, 1860; Saidiya Hartman, *Scenes of Subjection: Terror, Slavery, and Self-Making in Nineteenth-Century America* (New York: Oxford University Press, 1997).

38. Avenia White to Ballard, February 2, 1840, Folder 31, Ballard Papers; Green, *Remember Me to Miss Louisa*.

39. George P. Rawick, ed., *The American Slave: A Composite Autobiography* (Westport, Conn.: Greenwood, 1972), 1:68.

40. Robert Smalls, American Freedmen's Inquiry Commission Interview, 1863, 8, in John W.

Blassingame, *The Slave Community: Plantation Life in the Antebellum South* (1972; New York: Oxford University Press, 1979), 373.

41. Sarah Fitzpatrick, Interview, 1938, in Blassingame, *Slave Community*, 639.

42. Elizabeth Fox-Genovese, *Within the Plantation Household: Black and White Women of the Old South* (Chapel Hill: University of North Carolina Press, 1988), 348–49. For more, see Mary Boykin Miller Chesnut, *The Private Mary Chestnut: The Unpublished Civil War Diaries*, ed. C. Vann Woodward and Elisabeth Muhlenfeld (New York: Oxford University Press, 1984).

43. Thavolia Glymph, *Out of the House of Bondage: The Transformation of the Plantation Household* (New York: Cambridge University Press, 2008), 3.

44. Louise Ballard to Rice Ballard, November 18, 1847, Folder 120, Ballard Papers.

45. Frederic Bancroft, *Slave-Trading in the Old South* (Baltimore: Furst, 1931), 57.

46. Frances C. Roberts and Sarah Huff Fisk, *Shadows on the Wall: The Life and Words of Howard Weeden* (Northport, Ala.: Colonial, 1962), 19–20; Sarah Huff Fisk and Linda Wright Riley, *Lost Writings of Howard Weeden as "Flake White"* (Huntsville, Ala.: Big Springs, 2005); *Atlanta Journal*, 1899.

47. Du Bois, *Black Reconstruction*; Siobhan B. Somerville, *Queering the Color Line: Race and the Invention of Homosexuality in American Culture* (Durham: Duke University Press, 2000).

48. Osborne Townsend to Thomas Townsend, February 14, 1888, July 27, 1889, MSS 252, Box 252.054, Folder 01, Cabaniss Papers.

49. Willis Townsend to S. D. Cabaniss, September 7, 1866, MSS 252, Box 252.009, Folder 6, Cabaniss Papers.

50. Woodson Townsend to S. D. Cabaniss, February 16, [?], MSS 252, Box 252.009, Folder 5, Cabaniss Papers

51. Roberts, "Experiment in Emancipation," 48–50; Susanna Townsend to S. D. Cabaniss, June 4, 1868, Adelaide Townsend to S. D. Cabaniss, May 10, 1869, both in MSS 252, Box 252.009, Folder 5, Cabaniss Papers. For more, see Isabela Morales, "Letters from a Planter's Daughter: Understanding Freedom and Independence in the Life of Susanna Townsend (1853–1869)," *University of Alabama McNair Journal* 12 (2012): 145–74.

52. Emily West, *Family or Freedom: People of Color in the Antebellum South* (Lexington: University Press of Kentucky, 2012), 130.

53. For more on the tenuousness of freedom for African American women in the North and South, particularly in the years surrounding the Civil War, see Harriet Jacobs, *Incidents in the Life of a Slave Girl* (New York: Oxford University Press, 1988); Erica Armstrong Dunbar, *Fragile Freedom: African American Women and Emancipation in the Antebellum City* (New Haven: Yale University Press, 2008); Stephanie Li, *Something Akin to Freedom: The Choice of Bondage in Narratives by African American Women* (Albany: State University of New York Press, 2010); Judith Kelleher Schafer, *Becoming Free, Remaining Free: Manumission and Enslavement in New Orleans, 1846–1862* (Baton Rouge: Louisiana State University Press, 2003); West, *Family or Freedom*.

54. Roberts, "Experiment in Emancipation," 86–87, 58, 75; Elvira Townsend to S. D. Cabaniss, November 8, 1866, MSS 252, Box 252.009, Folder 5, Cabaniss Papers.

55. Roberts, "Experiment in Emancipation," 51.

56. Adelaide Townsend to Thomas Townsend, November 16, 1900, MSS 252, Box 252.054, Folder 01, Cabaniss Papers; Roberts, "Experiment in Emancipation," 94.

The Enslaved Women Surgical Patients of J. Marion Sims in Antebellum Alabama

Sisterhood of Shared Suffering

HARRIET E. AMOS DOSS

❁ ❁ ❁

"Poor wretches!" exclaimed English naturalist Phillip Henry Gosse on a visit to Alabama cotton fields during harvest time in 1838 when he observed enslaved "women in this laborious occupation" of picking cotton while wearing ragged "clothing . . . barely sufficient for the claims of decency." He believed the enslaved women's "lot is harder than their brute companions in labour! For they have to perform an equal amount of toil, with the additional hardships of more whippings and less food."[1] As cotton production soared in central Alabama in the 1840s, plantation owners placed high expectations on their enslaved men and women, many of whom had assignments to pick hundreds of pounds of cotton each day. For example, in the Canebrake region, records for four plantations in the mid-1840s to mid-1850s indicate that the average field hand, male or female, picked between 194 and 270 pounds of cotton daily. Totals could be affected by weather, type of cotton under cultivation, and the picking skills of the enslaved laborer. Focusing on getting their crop to market, owners imposed labor demands on enslaved women regardless of their recovery from childbirth or gynecological problems.[2] Enslaved women had few and limited choices about their health, but as they gave birth to the babies who would augment their masters' wealth, some found opportunities to participate in medical experiments to cure life-limiting afflictions from obstructed childbirth. Contrary to scholarship portraying victimization and even abuse of slave women in medical experiments, historians analyzing patients who found their way to one surgeon in Montgomery, Alabama, have noted remarkable cooperation to reach a shared goal.[3]

SKETCH BY GEORGE FULLER (1822–
84), MASSACHUSETTS ARTIST

On a trip to Montgomery in 1853.
Courtesy of Pocumtuck Valley Memorial Association,
Memorial Hall Museum, Deerfield, Mass.

Cotton planters organized labor with duties for children as well as men and women. Both men and women worked as field hands, with men generally acting as plow hands and women doing the hoeing. A children's squad supervised by a woman might work in a field to learn the expected tasks. Some women handled heavier tasks. For example, Martha Bradley, who lived on the Dr. Lucas plantation in Mount Meigs, close to Montgomery, recalled that she always worked in the field and had to carry big logs in straps on her arms from the field to a pile. On one rainy morning when she did not want to go to the field the overseer whipped her until she jumped on him and bit and kicked him. He finally released her, and she continued living on the plantation until emancipation. During the cotton harvest, she recalled, enslaved people remained in the fields until after dark, picking by candlelight before finally carrying their sacks to the weigh station. Failure to meet picking quotas brought whippings. Even decades after emancipation, Adeline Hodges hated "to weigh anything" because she remembered how slaves who failed to meet their quotas received whippings.[4]

In some cases, pregnant women—especially those with a track record of giving birth to healthy babies—received favored treatment on plantations because these children increased their masters' assets. However, owners' provision of food, clothing, and medical care during pregnancy and childbirth varied widely. Martha Jackson recalled the overseer on the plantation where she grew up using a wide stiff leather strap with big holes in it to beat slaves' naked buttocks. But Jackson's aunt rarely received whippings because, in her aunt's words, she was a "breeder woman" who delivered a baby about every twelve months "jus' lack a cow bringin' in a calf." Her regular birthing of healthy children made her more valuable, and her master ordered overseers to avoid straining her. Martha's aunt praised her master for that protection on a plantation where other slaves worked night and day, seven days a week. While "breeders" usually received favored treatment, some pregnant women did not. One pregnant enslaved woman on a plantation in Chambers County was tied "up under a hack-a-berry tree, an' whipped . . . until she died," recalled an ex-slave. Her death would have represented a significant financial loss to her master. Evidence indicates that many other masters provided some health care for their slave investments, a common-sense practice since ill health led to lost work time and even death. Some planters employed doctors to come every two weeks to check on slaves' health and give them any needed medicine. This type of plantation practice proved quite lucrative for physicians, who charged fees for each mile traveled to the site, prescription drugs, and treatment as well as for each plantation visit. Masters who were doctors treated their slaves and called in other physicians as needed. In the slave quarters older women sometimes combined roles as midwives, root doctors, healers, and conjurers, treating other slaves, including pregnant women, with herbs and plants. Some enslaved women appeared on plantation sick lists for only one day before giving birth or worked until they went into labor.[5]

For some enslaved women, particularly young ones experiencing their first pregnancies, prolonged and obstructed labor in childbirth could result in a horrific complication, vesicovaginal fistula, in which a hole developed between the vagina and bladder, leading to constant and uncontrollable urinary incontinence.[6] In some cases, a hole developed between the vagina and the rectum, resulting in fecal incontinence. No viable therapy existed in the early 1840s, forcing many sufferers, both free and enslaved, to remain isolated in the country, ostracized and living in misery with an apparently incurable condition. Though the condition was not fatal, some women would have preferred death, and a few even committed suicide.[7]

In 1845, on the Wescott plantation, about one mile from Montgomery, Alabama, a town of more than two thousand people on the Alabama River, Anarcha, a seventeen-year-old enslaved woman, endured a labor of more than seventy-two hours and suffered gynecological damage following a forceps delivery of her child. Five days after the delivery, Anarcha lost control of her bladder and rectum. As the consulting surgeon on her case, J. Marion Sims, commented, "Of course, aside from death, this was about the worst accident that could have happened to the poor girl. The case was hopelessly incurable." About the same time, in Lowndes County, Betsey, a "servant girl" aged seventeen or eighteen, had a baby and subsequently suffered urinary incontinence resulting from destruction of the base of her bladder. And in Montgomery County on the Tom Zimmerman plantation, an eighteen-year-old enslaved woman, Lucy, gave birth and then developed "a fistula in the bladder—a hole in it. It may be no larger than a pipe-stem, or it may be as large as two or three inches in diameter; but whether big or little, the urine runs all the time; it makes no odds what position she is in, whether asleep or awake, walking or standing, sitting or lying down." Medical literature and physicians' beliefs at the time considered all three women's conditions "absolutely incurable."[8]

But the owners of Anarcha, Betsey, and Lucy nonetheless sought treatment from Sims, a Montgomery surgeon who had developed a reputation for curing cases that seemed hopeless. Soon after Sims, born in 1813 in South Carolina, settled in Montgomery in 1840, he studied and perfected surgeries for both clubfoot and crossed eyes, enjoying successes "until within one or two years he had about finished up and straightened all the cross-eyes and club-feet within forty or fifty miles of Montgomery," according to another physician. His surgical skills and captivating personality encouraged patients and other physicians to seek his counsel and services, and he soon had perhaps the largest surgical practice in central Alabama.[9]

Through Sims, the three enslaved women met each other and shared their suffering and hope for relief from their affliction. Anarcha was one of about two dozen slaves owned by wealthy Montgomery County planter Samuel T. Wescott and had probably worked in his cotton fields prior to her injury. She had the services of two physicians during some of her labor: the Wescotts' regular physician, Dr. H. W. Henry, had called in Dr. Sims after realizing that surgery might be necessary. When Henry subsequently reported to Sims that Anarcha had lost control of both her bladder and rectum, the surgeon researched the medical literature fully and advised Wescott that her condition made her unfit "for the duties required of a servant." Sims added, "She will not die, but will never get well, and all you have to do is to take good care of her as long as she lives." Thus, she would no longer benefit her master financially but instead would be a constant drain on his resources. Nevertheless, Wescott, whom Sims considered "a kindhearted man, a good master," accepted the situation and decided that "Anarcha should have an easy time in this world as long as she lived."[10] She remained on the Wescott plantation and tried to adjust to her medical problems.

Betsey was one of five slaves living in the household of Dr. James C. Harris, a Wetumpka physician. In 1844, at age seventeen or eighteen, Betsey married a slave from another household. After she gave birth the following year, Harris sent her to Sims, who examined her injuries and declared that "the base of the bladder was destroyed, and her case was certainly a miserable one." Sims considered her, too, incurable.[11]

Lucy was one of about thirty-five slaves owned by Montgomery County planter Tom Zimmerman. After she gave birth and suffered urinary incontinence for two months, Zimmerman sent her for examination by Sims, who had been the Zimmerman family's physician when both they and Sims had lived in Cubahatchee, Alabama, in the 1830s. When Lucy arrived in Sims's office, he recalled, "I had a little hospital of eight beds, built in the corner of my yard, for taking care of my negro patients and for negro surgical cases; and so when Lucy came I gave her a bed." After examining Lucy, Sims told her that he could do nothing for her: "She was very much disappointed," Sims noted, "for her condition was loathsome, and she was in hopes that she could be cured."[12] With her life already circumscribed by servitude, she faced the prospect of enduring further limitations as a consequence of her condition.

Soon after his examinations of the three enslaved women, Sims received an emergency case—a white female who had suffered a pelvic injury in a fall from her pony—that prompted Sims to consider new approaches to treating other cases. The animal had been startled by a hog and had thrown the woman, a heavyset washerwoman and seamstress in her mid-forties, so that she landed with all of her weight on her pelvis. Called to examine her, Sims discovered that she had suffered no broken bones; instead, she had a "retroversion of the uterus"—that is, it was bent backward from its usual position. He had attended a lecture at Charleston Medical College at which the speaker had advised placing patients with such complaints on their knees and elbows and using the position and air pressure to restore the organ to its normal place, thereby relieving the patient's pain. Sims realized that placing the women with fistulas in this position should allow him to examine and treat them, too. Perhaps their condition was in fact curable.[13]

This potential breakthrough so interested Sims that he skipped his morning visits to his patients and went to the store operated by Hall, Mores, and Roberts to buy a pewter spoon that would serve as the base for a new instrument he visualized that would enable him to conduct vaginal examinations. He then returned to his office, picked up his two medical students, and took them to his hospital, also called his negro infirmary, to reexamine Betsey. With a medical student on each side of her pelvis and her "willing consent," he had her kneel on her hands and elbows while he used the handle of the pewter spoon and light reflected by a mirror to examine her fistula. With a clear view of the affected area, he asked himself why the fistula could not be cured by surgically paring its edges, stitching it closed, and then placing a catheter in the neck of the bladder to drain off urine. Over the next three months, he devised and prepared the instruments he would need to perform the operation—most notably, a speculum or retractor—expanded his infirmary to twelve patient beds, and located additional patients for the experimental surgery.[14]

In their current condition, women with vesicovaginal fistulas were useless as laborers, meaning that owners might be willing to pay for the costly surgery as a means of recouping some of their investment. At this time the customary charge for keeping an African American surgical patient in a private infirmary ran approximately five dollars a week or fifteen dollars a month, a "very moderate" expense to return a slave to a condition in which she could work. Sims told Wescott and Harris, "If you will give me Anarcha and Betsey for experiment, I agree to perform no experiment or operation on either of them to endanger their lives, and will not charge a cent for keeping them, but you must pay their taxes and clothe them. I will keep them at my expense." Those two owners, along with Zimmerman, agreed to allow Sims to operate and to keep the women in his infirmary until they recovered. Other physicians referred six or seven other cases "that had been hidden away for years in the country because they had been pronounced incurable." He felt "very enthusiastic, and expected to cure them, every one, in six months." He "never dreamed of failure, and could see how accurately and how nicely the operation could be performed."[15]

Some local residents considered Sims's prospective patients "free niggers" because they had so much more freedom than other enslaved women in the area. Though still enslaved, "free niggers" were exempted by their owners from whippings, could readily get passes, and "had plenty to eat and milk to drink," as ex-slaves recalled years later.[16] The women in Sims's infirmary cared for themselves as much as they could, but the doctor also had additional enslaved women to care for the patients, particularly after procedures. Sims's household thus was home to as many as a dozen enslaved women at a time, and they helped to care for each other physically and emotionally, forming a sisterhood of shared suffering.

Lucy, the last of the three original fistula cases brought to Sims, became his first surgical patient because of the severity of her condition. According to the physician, "The whole base of the bladder was gone and destroyed, and a piece had fallen out, leaving an opening between the vagina and bladder, at least two inches in diameter or more." Sims invited about a dozen other physicians to observe the operation, and some of them assisted him. The operation was "tedious and difficult," he reported. The instruments he had designed reflected the right principles but required further refinement. Chloroform and ether did not come into general use until a year or two after Sims began his experiments, so Lucy remained unsedated and on her elbows and knees for the duration of the surgery: she "bore the operation with great heroism and bravery," Sims recorded. He closed Lucy's fistula in one hour and put his patient in bed to recover in his infirmary.[17]

Five days later, Lucy became "very ill" from complications that developed when a sponge placed in the neck of the bladder to act as a catheter caused inflammation. "She had frequent pulse, and real blood poisoning," Sims observed. To relieve his patient, he cut his sutures loose and removed the sponge. "Lucy's agony was extreme," he noted, and he "thought that she was going to die." But she recovered rapidly, "and in the course of a week or ten days was as well as ever." Lucy's "enormous fistula had disappeared," and only two small openings remained. Based on these positive results, Sims decided to operate again after he had developed a more successful catheter.[18]

While Lucy was still recovering from the effects of the operation (a process that took two to three months), Sims operated on Betsey, using a self-retaining catheter (made from a curved tube so that it remained in the bladder and urethra to drain urine until it was removed) rather than a sponge. Betsey did not develop chills or fever, and after seven days, Sims removed the sutures, only to see that three small openings remained. He considered "the operation . . . a failure."[19]

Next came Anarcha, who "had not only an enormous fistula in the base of the bladder, but . . . extensive destruction of the posterior wall of the vagina, opening into the rectum." With "the very worst form of vesico-vaginal fistula," Anarcha's urine ran "day and night, saturating the bedding and clothing" and causing "constant pain and burning" of her skin. Bad odor "from this saturation permeated everything, and every corner of the room; and, of course, her life was one of suffering and disgust." Because of the rectal opening, "intestinal gas escaped involuntarily . . . and continually, so that her person was not only loathsome and disgusting to herself, but to everyone who came near her." Sims's surgery provided a partial cure, though she continued to have involuntary loss of urine.[20]

Over the next four years, Anarcha, Betsey, Lucy, and three or four other women lived in Sims's private infirmary while he improved his procedures. His physician friends considered his efforts to have failed and refused to continue assisting him in the surgeries. Sims, however, took a different perspective: "I had succeeded in inspiring my patients with confidence that they would be cured eventually," and they were "perfectly satisfied with what I am doing for them." Consequently, he continued to perform "operations only with the assistance of the patients themselves." One held the speculum in place, another handed him other instruments, another restrained the patient on the operating table, another shifted the reflecting mirror where he directed. In short, the members of this sisterhood worked as a team with their surgeon. And when Sims halted surgery for several weeks until he could find an improved suture technique, the half dozen patients in his infirmary "were clamorous" for him to continue the operations to find a cure. After six weeks, he noted, "my devoted patients were begging me from day to day, to 'try only one more time.'"[21]

Several aspects of this situation are noteworthy. First, in contrast to popular beliefs about African Americans' lack of intelligence, Sims recognized that these women had the capacity to learn medical techniques. Second, though Sims may have overstated their eagerness, these women were in such misery that they were willing to submit themselves to repeated and no doubt painful surgical procedures in hopes of ending their suffering. In the words of modern gynecologist L. L. Wall, "As a matter of surgical practicality, considering the delicate and tedious requirements of performing surgery inside the vagina and the exceedingly difficult circumstances of exposure and inadequate lighting under which he was forced to operate, Sims could not have carried out these operations successfully without the cooperation of the women involved." Slight movement, much less active resistance, would have ruined any operation.[22] Moreover, according to twentieth-century physician Seale Harris, these women bore repeated surgeries with "a grim stoicism [that] possibly had been bred into them through several generations of enforced submission." Later in the 1840s, when anesthesia became available, many surgeons did not consider it necessary for fistula surgery during the first decade of the procedures, and white patients complained so much of the pain that the procedures failed.[23] Sims's patients must truly have been desperate for a cure.

While Sims's patients lacked anesthesia during the surgical procedures, which lasted between twenty minutes and an hour, they could have pain relief medications during their two- to four-week recuperation period. Each patient was restricted to her bed with a self-retaining catheter in place. She might lie on her back or on either side, but she could not sit up to avoid disrupting the healing of the sutured skin. The patient was fed a diet "of a constipating character" — "tea and crackers, allowing coffee if preferred, and prohibiting meats, fruits, saccharine substances, and all articles of food made of Indian, or common corn meal." Moreover, "to assist the diet in producing constipation," Sims administered a large dose of a painkiller—morphine, laudanum (opium), or "whatever we may know will best agree with the patient"—to keep the woman constipated "till the success or failure of the operation is ascertained." Sims generally ordered "some form of opium in as large doses as can be borne, at least twice in the twenty-four hours." Aside from constipation, Sims believed that opium had a variety of other "beneficial effects" for his patients: "It calms the nerves, inspires hope . . . prevents a craving for food, . . . subdues inflammatory action, and assists the patient . . . to pass the time with pleasant dreams, and delightful sensations, instead of painful forebodings, and intolerable sufferings." If recovery proceeded normally, patients had their sutures removed on the ninth or tenth day following surgery and continued to rest in bed for about five more days.[24]

In the summer of 1849, after nearly four years of experimentation, Sims decided to try using silver wire to suture close the fistulas. Sims had Swan's jewelry store at 108 Dexter Avenue, between Perry and Lawrence Streets, draw the first silver wire for his surgeries. Unlike silk, silver did not cause inflammation that compromised healing. Sims tried the silver sutures first on Anarcha, perhaps because she had "never murmured at the preceding failures." A week after the June 21 surgery, the sutures were removed, and Sims saw that she had no inflammation. She was cured—after her thirtieth operation. Within the next two weeks, both Lucy and Betsey underwent the same surgery with silver sutures and experienced the same results.[25]

Sims subsequently sought a few more fistula cases "to settle some doubtful points" before publishing a report on his experiments.[26] Lowndesboro physician Hardy Vickers Wooten, a longtime acquaintance of Sims, referred a slave owned by one of his patients. "Mrs. Hall's girl," as she was identified, was sent to Montgomery and stayed in Sims's infirmary for the surgery before returning home to her mistress. And in late 1849 or early 1850, Sims "came across a case in New Orleans, which I was forced to buy, because the owner was unwilling to run any risks about the cure, although I told him 'no cure, no pay.'" Sims thus purchased a slave specifically to perform surgery on her, explaining that he considered it "one of the most difficult cases to treat" that he had yet seen, though he had "not the least doubt about curing it eventually."[27] His use of depersonalized language when referring to this human being—*which* rather than *who*, *it* rather than *her*—and the fact that he did not identify either of these women by her name, indicates that he saw them as medical cases rather than people. And after curing the woman he purchased, he may well have put her to work in his infirmary, helping to care for others in the sisterhood. Its membership would have changed as those who had been cured returned to their owners and new sufferers arrived. In late 1849, at least three or four women remained at his hospital, awaiting the procedure.

But about six weeks after finally succeeding with the silver sutures, Sims "completely collapsed," suffering a breakdown accompanied by the return of his chronic diarrhea, an ailment from which he had intermittently suffered since his arrival in Alabama. "An exacting practice and the extreme mental tension of the past four years had produced a collapse, long foreseen by friends without my consciousness of its approach," Sims admitted. In hopes that a change of scenery would help, he took his family—and a handful of his uncured patients—to Butler Springs, planning to resume the surgeries at the resort. "But I was too ill to do anything. I was utterly prostrated," he lamented. In the summers of 1849, 1850, and 1852 he took extended trips to the North in an effort to recover his health, but his weight dropped as low as ninety pounds. Too weak to care for even himself, much less anyone else, he did not take his patients with him to the North.[28]

Sims returned to Montgomery at Christmastime in 1852 but remained plagued by illness, and by early February 1853 he concluded that he would die unless he sold everything and moved with his family to New York, where the climate seemed to suit him better. However, he lacked the strength and patience to make the preparations, leaving his wife, Theresa, to oversee the move. She said, "The whole question can be arranged as you would have it, without giving you one bit of trouble," and over the next two weeks, she sold all of her husband's property except a dozen enslaved people who "were house negroes and town negroes—cooks, waiters, and body-servants only." Marion and Theresa Sims explained that they were permanently leaving Montgomery and advised the slaves to select other masters "with whom you are willing to live." The Simses would then negotiate with the new masters regarding compensation. Marion Sims remembered the slaves weeping at the news and saying that they did not want to be sold. They proposed that they be allowed to stay in Montgomery and hire themselves out under the supervision of an agent, who would look out for them; in exchange, they would "pay him the same wage we would pay you." According to Sims, they hoped that his health would improve and that he and his family would return to Montgomery. Sims "told the negroes to do exactly as they pleased": he "consented to their plan, and wished them to be happy, and well taken care of."[29] However, Sims sold twenty-two-year-old Amanda and her two children, Edward and Haile, to a family friend, Henry Lucas, for one dollar. They would serve as collateral against a one-thousand-dollar loan Sims had obtained from J. W. McQueen of Montgomery. At the end of a year, if Sims had not repaid the loan, Lucas had authority to sell the slaves to pay the note.[30]

The feelings of the Simses' slaves are impossible to assess. The sale to Lucas enabled a mother to remain with her children, at least for a year. However, there is no record of what happened to them after that time. And the sale might have separated Amanda and her children from their father. Similarly, the slaves' sadness at the Simses' impending departure might reflect genuine emotion, or it might reflect their calculation that appearing to be sad would increase their chances of influencing their fate. And it is possible that by the time Sims began composing his autobiography, the passage of more than three decades had dimmed his memory of events or that he wanted to use his memoirs to present himself in the most favorable light, especially given that he had long resided in the North and might have been embarrassed by his previous ownership of slaves.

In one sense, there is less ambiguity about Anarcha, Betsey, Lucy, and the other women whose fistulas Sims repaired: the surgeon cured them of a horrific condition that not only caused them tremendous pain but very nearly made them unable to live in human society. Even if Sims's memoir exaggerated their eagerness to undergo more surgeries and his confidence in his ability to find a cure, those procedures would not have been possible without their acquiescence. However, after as long as four years living as "free niggers" in the Sims household, they presumably returned to their owners—that is, to bondage (although it is quite possible that some of them lived long enough to experience emancipation in the wake of the Civil War). It is not clear whether the patients who had been awaiting surgery at the time of Sims's breakdown were ever cured, but it is likely that they experienced anxiety and perhaps disappointment as they realized that his illness might mean the end of their hopes for a cure.

The enslaved women benefited personally from Sims's medical advances, and their willingness to participate in medical science opened the way to therapeutic surgery that improved the lives of thousands of women who came after them.[31] But they certainly did not give what the medical profession today would consider informed consent, and their participation can hardly be considered voluntary in the sense that they could not simply leave Sims's hospital. At least one—the woman he purchased in New Orleans—was actually his property. Nevertheless, as gynecologist Irwin Kaiser has pointed out, "One must . . . be skeptical of judging 1850 decisions" by modern norms.[32]

While Sims's patients returned to obscurity, the doctor recovered his health, published numerous accounts of his surgical experiments in medical journals, helped to found the New York Woman's Hospital, and enjoyed a flourishing international gynecological practice. In his writings and speeches he generally said little about the women patients who had made his illustrious career possible. His first publication about the pioneering surgery, "On the Treatment of Vesico-Vaginal Fistula," which appeared in January 1852, neglected to mention that his patients were enslaved women.[33] He dictated the article in October 1851 while bedridden and fearing that he was near death. He wanted his fellow physicians to know of his work, both to help other women and to secure his reputation. As he pondered relocating to the North for health reasons, he might have sought to distance himself from the South's slaveholding society. In 1857, after he had regained his health and helped to found the Woman's Hospital, the New York Academy of Medicine invited him to give its "Anniversary Discourse" on his pioneering surgery with silver sutures. On that occasion, he described Anarcha simply as "a young colored woman." With the issue of abolition tearing the nation apart and a thriving private practice and surgery at the Woman's Hospital, he likely sought to avoid mentioning anything that might provoke controversy. The details of the cases of the three enslaved women whose fistulas he cured did not appear in print until 1884, a year after his death, when his son completed and published the autobiography that Sims had begun writing.

Although Sims may have been less than forthcoming about the fact that Anarcha, Betsey, and Lucy were enslaved, he nevertheless praised their contributions to his medical breakthrough, declaring in his 1857 speech, "To the indomitable courage of these long-suffering women, more than to any one other single circumstance, is the world indebted for the results of these persevering efforts. Had they faltered, then would woman have continued to suffer from the dreadful injuries produced by protracted parturition, and then should the broad domain of surgery not have known one of the most useful improvements that shall forever grace its annals."[34]

NOTES

This research project received funding from a University of Alabama at Birmingham College of Arts and Sciences Dean's Humanities Grant for 2014–15. I am grateful for that support as well as for help in locating sources from Michael Flannery and Margaret Balch of the Reynolds-Finley Historical Library and Tim Pennycuff of the University of Alabama at Birmingham Archives. I also thank Norwood Kerr and the rest of the reference archivists at the Alabama Department of Archives and History in Montgomery. Part of an earlier version of this essay was presented at the March 2015 meeting of the Southern Association for the History of Medicine and Science in Jackson, Mississippi.

1. Phillip Henry Gosse, *Letters from Alabama, Chiefly Relating to Natural History* (1859; Tuscaloosa: University of Alabama Press, 1993), quoted in Herbert James Lewis, *Clearing the Thickets: A History of Antebellum Alabama* (New Orleans: Quid Pro Books, 2013), 40. Women received a fraction of men's rations even when pregnant and doing comparable labor.

2. James Benson Sellers, *Slavery in Alabama* (1950; Tuscaloosa: University of Alabama Press, 1994), 68; Edward E. Baptist, *The Half Has Never Been Told: Slavery and the Making of American Capitalism* (New York: Basic Books, 2014), 133–34.

3. Critics of Sims include Deborah Kuhn McGregor, *Sexual Surgery and the Origins of Gynecology: J. Marion Sims, His Hospital and His Patients* (New York: Garland, 1990); David Gonzalez, "Sculpture of Paradox: Doctor as Hero and Villain," *New York Times*, March 2, 2014; Durrenda Ojanuga, "The Medical Ethics of the Father of Gynecology, Dr. J. Marion Sims," *Journal of Medical Ethics* 19 (1993): 28–31; Jeffrey S. Sartin, "J. Marion Sims, the Father of Gynecology: Hero or Villain?" *Southern Medical Journal* 97 (May 2004): 500–504. More positive assessments of Sims appear in Barron J. Lerner, "Scholars Argue over Legacy of Surgeon Who Was Lionized, Then Vilified," *New York Times*, October 28, 2003; Irwin H. Kaiser, "Reappraisals of J. Marion Sims," *American Journal of Obstetrics and Gynecology* 132 (1978): 878–84; S. Buford Word, "The Father of Gynecology," *American Association for the History of Medicine* 9 (1972): 33–39.

4. Sellers, *Slavery in Alabama*, 66–67; George P. Rawick, ed., *The American Slave: A Composite Autobiography*, vol. 6, *Alabama and Indiana Narratives* (Westport, Conn.: Greenwood, 1972), 46–47, 182–83.

5. Sellers, *Slavery in Alabama*, 116, 109, 113–15, 163–64; Jacqueline Jones, *Labor of Love, Labor of Sorrow: Black Women, Work, and the Family from Slavery to the Present* (New York: Vintage, 1986), 40; Rawick, *American Slave*, 91, 115, 239, 222. Regarding slaves' folk medicine practices and their relationship to whites' treatment, see Eugene Genovese, *Roll, Jordan, Roll: The World the Slaves Made* (New York: Pantheon, 1972), 226; Steven M. Stowe, *Doctoring the South: Southern Physicians and Everyday Medicine in the Mid-Nineteenth Century* (Chapel Hill: University of North Carolina Press, 2004), 170.

6. L. L. Wall, "The Medical Ethics of Dr. J. Marion Sims: A Fresh Look at the Historical Record," *Journal of Medical Ethics* 32 (2006): 346–50. The modern term for the condition is *obstetric fistula*; see Mulu Muleta, "Obstetric Fistula in Developing Countries: A Review Article," *Journal of Obstetrics and Gynaecology Canada* 28 (2006): 962–66.

7. Seale Harris, *Woman's Surgeon: The Life Story of J. Marion Sims* (New York: Macmillan, 1950), 87. According to Kaiser, in urban areas, women with fistulas became social outcasts and "suicides among them were not unusual" ("Reappraisals of J. Marion Sims," 879).

8. J. Marion Sims, *The Story of My Life*, ed. H. Marion Sims (New York: Appleton, 1884), 226–29.

9. W. O. Baldwin, *Tribute to the Late James Marion Sims, M.D., L.D. by W. O. Baldwin, M.D., of Montgomery, Alabama* (Montgomery, Ala.: Brown, 1884), 6–8. This tribute by one of Sims's long-time friends in the profession was delivered at a memorial for Sims held in Montgomery shortly after his death in New York. Josiah C. Nott maintained perhaps Mobile's largest surgical practice, followed closely by Richard Lee Fearn. For biographical information about Sims, see "James Marion Sims," in Thomas McAdory Owen, ed., *History of Alabama and Dictionary of Alabama Biography* (1921; Spartanburg, S.C.: Broadfoot, 1978), 4:1564; Deborah Kuhn McGregor, "J. Marion Sims," *Encyclopedia of Alabama*, http://www.encyclopediaofalabama.org/article/h-1099 (accessed July 28, 2016); Sims, *Story of My Life*; Harris, *Woman's Surgeon*. Sims died before completing his autobiography, but his son completed it with the aid of Sims's notes as well as additional research. Owen and Harris laud Sims, while McGregor takes a critical position.

10. U.S. Census, 1850, District 1, Montgomery, Alabama, Roll: M432 12, p. 70B; U.S. Census, 1850, Slave Schedule; Sims, *Story of My Life*, 226–28.

11. U.S. Census, 1850, Wetumpka Ward 1, Coosa County, Alabama, Roll: M432 4, p. 2B; Owen, *History of Alabama*, 3:752, 755; Sims, *Story of My Life*, 227–28. Harris may have known Sims in the late 1830s when both men lived in Mount Meigs, Alabama.

12. Sims, *Story of My Life*, 228–30.

13. Ibid., 230–34.

14. Ibid., 230, 234–35, 236–37; Baldwin, *Tribute*, 27–28.

15. Sims, *Story of My Life*, 236; Minnie Clare Boyd, *Alabama in the Fifties: A Social Study* (New York: Columbia University Press, 1931), 193–94.

16. Edmond Souchon, "Places Rendered Famous by Dr. J. Marion Sims, in Montgomery, Ala.," reprint from the *New Orleans Medical and Surgical Journal*, February 1896, n.p., Reynolds-Finley Historical Library, University of Alabama at Birmingham; Rawick, *American Slave*, 63–64, 90. Statements using the term *free niggers* were recorded from Mandy McCullough Crosby and Emma Chapman in 1937.

17. Souchon, "Places Rendered Famous"; Sims, *Story of My Life*, 236–37.

18. Sims, *Story of My Life*, 238–39.

19. Ibid., 240.

20. Ibid., 240–41.

21. Sims, *Story of My Life*, 242, 243; Harris, *Woman's Surgeon*, 92; J. Marion Sims, *Silver Sutures in Surgery* (New York: Wood, 1858), 56–57. This address was delivered about a year after Sims became a member of the Academy. His paper includes drawings prepared by Dr. Thomas Addis Emmet, assistant surgeon at the New York Woman's Hospital.

22. Wall, "Medical Ethics," 4.

23. Ibid., 5–6; Harris, *Woman's Surgeon*, 99.

24. J. Marion Sims, *On the Treatment of Vesico-Vaginal Fistula* (Philadelphia: Blanchard and Lea, 1853), 80–81. In this account Sims includes woodcuts of his instruments and techniques for using them.

25. Sims, *Story of My Life*, 245–46; Souchon, "Places Rendered Famous," [5]; Sims, *Silver Sutures*, 60. The available records do not indicate whether the other women who had been Sims's patients between 1845 and 1849 had their fistulas cured by his procedure.

26. Sims, *Silver Sutures*, 61.

27. J. Marion Sims to Hardy Vickers Wooten, January 23, 1850, Hardy Vickers Wooten Papers, Box PR 325, Folder 1, Alabama Department of Archives and History, Montgomery. See also Boyd, *Alabama in the Fifties*, 178, 193–94; Harris, *Woman's Surgeon*, 107–8. Physicians bought and sold enslaved people for various reasons in the slave society of the Cotton Kingdom. Sims occasionally bought a surgical case to confirm his ability to cure the condition of the patient. When he needed cash assets he sold some of his enslaved men, women, and children and arranged for self-hiring of others under the supervision of a white agent. His acquaintance, Hardy Vickers Wooten, purchased enslaved men and boys as a financial investment to hire out, as he did in April 1850 when he bought from Watson and Brown in Montgomery "three negro boys . . . Barnett aged sixteen years, and Jim and William, each aged ten years" for $1,800.00. Four days later he hired the boys to Wooten and Sinclair for $120 for the balance of the year. See Hardy Vickers Wooten Diary, April 11, 15, 1850, Transcription, vol. 3, Wooten Papers, Box PR 325, Folder 10.

28. Sims, *Story of My Life*, 248; Sims, *Silver Sutures*, 61.

29. Sims, *Story of My Life*, ch. 15, esp. 264–66.

30. J. M. Sims to Nathan Bozeman, May 12, 1853, Montgomery County Deed Record Book, 4:608, Local Government Records Microfilm 083, Roll 10, Alabama Department of Archives and History, Montgomery; J. Marion Sims to Henry Lucas, May 16, 1853, Montgomery County Deed Record Book, 4:693, Local Government Records Microfilm, 083, Roll 10. For more information on Nathan Bozeman (1825–1905), see Howard A. Kelly and Walter L. Burrage, eds., *Dictionary of Medical Biography: Lives of Eminent Physicians of the United States and Canada, from the Earliest Times* (New York: Appleton, 1928), 135–36.

31. Muleta, "Obstetric Fistula." Her particular focus is Ethiopia.

32. Kaiser, "Reappraisals of J. Marion Sims," 882.

33. J. Marion Sims, "On the Treatment of Vesico-Vaginal Fistula," *American Journal of the Medical Sciences* 45 (1852): 226–46.

34. Sims, *Silver Sutures*, 55.

Maria Fearing

Domestic Adventurer

KIMBERLY D. HILL

❀ ❀ ❀

One sunny day about 120 years ago, a group of four friends spent a leisurely afternoon playing croquet. Their bright linen blouses and pith helmets looked genteel against the backdrop of thatched-roof houses, palm trees, and gaping fence posts. Two of the women—Lilian Thomas and Lucy Gantt Sheppard of Alabama—bent over their mallets, while Sheppard's husband, the Reverend William H. Sheppard, looked down to contemplate his next play. Only the most petite lady in the group, Maria Fearing, looked up toward her colleagues and the photographer. Her gaze seemed to acknowledge that this portrait represented more than just recreation. For Fearing and the other missionaries, every activity was an opportunity for education and community building.[1]

Leisure time—and the choice of how to spend it—could not be taken for granted in Maria Fearing's life. Born into slavery, she worked the first thirty years of her life as a nanny and a live-in domestic servant for a white Alabama family. The script of forced servitude offered precious little room for her interests or opinions. Yet Fearing expressed herself when no platform was offered and traveled thousands of miles through doors that had never been opened to her. Through tenacity and resourcefulness, she built a fulfilling career within the American Presbyterian Congo Mission.

Beyond the croquet field, the mission station consisted of a mud-walled church, a school, a medical station, planted fields, homes, and Maria Fearing's Pantops Home for Girls. She assembled a "family" of girls by redeeming them from the local slave trade, then educating them in Presbyterian doctrine and domestic science. These actions seemed straightforward as a mission plan but were enmeshed in complicated negotiations over women's activism in Protestant churches, European colonialism, and American Jim Crow politics. How

MARIA FEARING, C. 1880S

Alabama Department of Archives and History, Montgomery.

did a relatively unknown woman from Alabama become so involved in social justice campaigns by acting maternal?

Fearing designed her Congolese foster home based on the domestic ambitions of the women's missionary movement and through support from one of the oldest historically black colleges in the United States. Her long tenure in the Belgian Congo suggests that involvement in Alabama women's initiatives helped prepare her for public service on a global scale. Some authors have already explored her subtle power as a southern mammy turned slave liberator.[2] This essay delves further into Fearing's authority as a professional woman from the South and as a black leader in a rare setting. By observing how she used female domesticity to empower marginalized women (including herself), we gain further appreciation for the significance of Alabama women's activism within and beyond the United States.

Maria Fearing did not gain all of her notable housekeeping and child care skills by choice. Her training in domestic work started in her early childhood, when she was taken from her parents and sent to live with the family that enslaved them near Gainesville, Alabama. William Winston separated Maria from her parents shortly after her birth in 1838, ostensibly to protect the frail baby from difficult agricultural work.[3] In the main plantation house, she was called *Maria Winston* or just *Aunt Maria*, and she became the nanny who raised six of the eight Winston children.[4] According to the youngest Winston children, Maria acquired an interest in Africa and church activities because of her child care duties: she was expected to watch the toddlers during family story time and "attend" services with the baby by staying in the front yard or back row of Gainesville Presbyterian Church.[5]

The Winstons' account does not mention how the defeat of the Confederacy influenced Fearing's life, but she clearly shouldered the burden of becoming someone other than a babysitter, maid, and ostracized church attendee. Fearing left the Winston plantation as soon as she heard about emancipation and relocated to the city of Gainesville.[6] The fact that Fearing left alone suggests that her parents did not survive through the end of the war. Fearing did not discuss their passing in later writings or interviews, but she honored them by adopting their surname after she left Oak Hill Plantation.

Fearing worked as a live-in maid with a white family in Gainesville for five years before she made the next major change in her life. After learning that Talladega College, an American Missionary Association school, offered literacy classes for African American adults, she quit her job in 1871 and started the arduous 150-mile journey across the state. Though she could have traveled by rail, she lacked the money to do so, so she made her way by wagon or on foot. She may have also hoped to avoid the risks of segregated train travel: during this time, black women were increasingly relegated to the vulgar conditions of the smoking car and denied waiting room access.[7]

The pedagogical theory for Fearing's ministry was shaped by her work as a student and staff member at Talladega College between 1871 and 1894. In keeping with other black universities of the era, Talladega was a "college" in the broad sense of providing teacher training, basic education, and a moral environment on a residential campus.[8] The small faculty juggled multiple courses, dormitory supervision, and maintenance duties. Mainly because of the constant need to stretch inadequate donations, Talladega faculty and staff valued students who persevered against considerable odds to enroll.[9] Like Fearing, most incoming students were unable to pay tuition in cash or even afford train fare from their homes. Even those who had funds could face harassment and violence from whites who feared any change in former slaves' social status.[10] What became the cornerstone of the college industrial education program emerged as a cost-effective way to keep the campus operational. By the 1870s nearly all of the students at Talladega College worked on campus to cover tuition and board and spent the summers teaching elsewhere for wages or food.[11]

The residents of Talladega's female dormitory were expected to provide housekeeping and culinary services for the college while completing their coursework. By working more than thirty hours a week in the kitchen, dining hall, and sewing rooms, they provided support to the male students who worked half days at farming and construction.[12] The workload made it difficult to focus on studies, but college boarding director Lucy A. Alford and other administrators argued that manual labor training was an integral part of "working for our sex, our country, and our Lord."[13]

Fearing balanced campus work and studies at Talladega, eventually gaining employment in the college boarding department. With no previous formal schooling, she was directed to the elementary classes on campus. Of the 247 students enrolled during her second-grade year, she was the oldest student at the primary level. She mentioned in later interviews the awkwardness of attending classes with young children who sometimes mocked her illiteracy.[14] Yet she distinguished herself by completing her ninth-grade coursework, teaching lower grades, and contributing to campus initiatives. In 1877, Fearing was the only student to give livestock (three of her chickens) at a dedication ceremony for the new campus farm.[15] It was a valuable gift in light of the fact that the dining hall could not often afford to serve eggs or meat. In exchange for public recognition as a partner in the institution, she sacrificed part of her newfound financial independence.

Though Fearing did not advance to the normal school for teacher training, she still followed the precedent of earlier students by teaching basic classes at an Anniston school. She also worked as an assistant housing matron in the 1880s, monitoring activities in the women's dormitory and sometimes sharing a room with female students. Two of her most enduring friendships grew during her twenty-three years at Talladega: for at least one school year, she roomed with Lilian Thomas and Lucy Gantt, who later became her missions colleagues.

Supervising female students in the Foster Hall dormitory placed Fearing at the epicenter of a major confrontation between white college administrators and student protesters. In 1887, the Foster Hall residents started a prolonged protest against cuts to the campus dining budget, refusing to accept inferior rations while faculty received different food options. Though Fearing's statements during the dining hall protest were not recorded, her actions in the integrated Congo mission station echoed the black students' efforts to promote equality and professionalism. By the following semester, the students won recognition of their practical needs against the prerogatives of white teachers, administrators, and donors.[16] By the early 1890s, Fearing had established a steady career, financial stability, and a strong professional and personal network.

In 1894, Fearing's friend and former roommate, Lucy Gantt, returned to Talladega from Virginia, accompanied by her new husband, the Reverend William Henry Sheppard. In 1890, Sheppard had become one of the first missionaries from the Presbyterian Church (U.S.) (also known as the Southern Presbyterian Church) to the Congo Free State. What had started as a cautious attempt by the church to commission a young white minister with a Negro "assistant" had blossomed into a thriving mission station controlled by a renowned black missionary explorer and sponsored by mostly white congregations. Sheppard received international honors as the first westerner granted access to the "forbidden city" of the Bakuba kingdom in central Congo.[17] In 1894, he returned to the United States; married Gantt, his longtime fiancée; and traveled throughout the Northeast and the southern states to lecture about his expeditions, raise money, and recruit new missionaries.

Sheppard's speech made such an impression on Fearing that she decided immediately to volunteer for missions in Congo. She and Lilian Thomas planned to live together as the only single females accompanying the Sheppards and another male minister on the long journey by steamship. Fearing was fifty-six years old and weighed little more than ninety pounds.[18] Friends and coworkers noted a youthful, determined spark in her eyes, yet her appearance did not mask the fact that she had worked hard for decades. Could she withstand the hazards of rural living, riverboat transportation, food shortages, exotic animals, and malaria? The state-sponsored torture and genocide within the Belgian Congo had not yet been publicized to the missionaries, but it added to the many factors that made an American's successful return unlikely. The Foreign Mission Committee of the Presbyterian Church (U.S.) denied her application based on her age, health, and relative lack of education.[19]

Nevertheless, she sold her house in Anniston and purchased a one-way ticket across the Atlantic. As someone who had spent most of her first thirty years in slavery, the privacy and security provided by home ownership must have been extremely important to her, yet Fearing apparently was confident that she would devote the rest of her life to Congo and never return to Alabama: as an elderly woman without a home, she might be forced to resume live-in domestic servitude. She may have also considered the hazards of life in Alabama comparable to the risks of overseas travel. In addition to the drudgery and poverty of African American life in the turn-of-the-century South, violent racism had become more prevalent as whites came to consider educating former slaves to be a social and economic hazard, and her time at Talladega had included campus arson and a teacher's lynching.[20]

Fearing financed her voyage to Congo with the proceeds from the sale of her house and one hundred dollars in pledges from a women's group at Talladega College. As a further sign of her commitment, she did not purchase or request return fare. After spending several weeks sailing across the Atlantic, she and the rest of the Sheppards' party spent a short sojourn in London. While she was riding on a streetcar, a British gentleman apparently made a rude remark, and she surprised him by replying kindly in formal English.[21] This response foreshadowed her later mission strategy—specifically her decision to act as a professional minister long before she had denominational authority.

After the ship from London docked at the mouth of the Congo River, the missionaries traveled over land about two hundred miles to catch a steamer at Stanley Pool. The American missionaries attracted a great deal of official attention as they embarked in canoes and transported hammocks toward central Congo. A larger missionary population would mean more demand for railroad construction through the Kasai region. The activities of Protestant and Catholic missionaries in the region also became instrumental to the economic goals of King Leopold's administration in the Congo Free State. From 1890 to 1910, the king oversaw a network of rubber companies that divided the nation into industrial districts. Belgian officials required Congolese people to pay taxes to maintain this system and utilized a mercenary army to seize villagers when tax payments fell short. Prisoners were sent to other regions to harvest rubber or carry construction boxes under brutal conditions, usually with no hope of returning home.[22]

Though the Kasai region around Fearing's mission station was sheltered from state exploitation until 1898, forced laborers were marched through Kasai so frequently that the Presbyterian mission statement policies included provisions for dealing with the marches.[23] Fearing saw firsthand how state-sponsored violence jeopardized the mission's goals and destabilized local communities. To succeed in her ministry, Fearing had to connect her work to three of the most pressing issues for the Southern Presbyterian Church and the United States at large: slavery, segregation, and imperialism.

Fearing arrived in Congo in 1894 and settled into a mud-walled hut that she soon shared with Thomas and five homeless Congolese girls.[24] Within a year of her arrival, Fearing started using her savings to purchase girls enslaved during local conflicts. Specifically, she rescued child captives from the Zappo Zap people, a group of Congolese traders who formed a close alliance with the Free State government. After the Angolan slave trade through Congo declined in the mid-1890s, Zappo Zaps continued managing a similar labor system on behalf of King Leopold. The state rubber companies maximized their profits by sending Zappo Zap soldiers to extract taxes and laborers, while the Zappo Zaps maintained their livelihood as a landless tribe.[25]

Over the next several decades, Presbyterian missionaries watched this cycle unfold many times. Belgian officials often released child slaves to Protestant and Catholic mission stations but discouraged the missionaries from purchasing slaves directly "to fill up [their] ranks."[26] The missionaries kept these children and a group of local adults as live-in workers in exchange for room and board.[27] Four months before Fearing's arrival, the mission station sheltered forty-four children, including some "house children" retained for manual labor.[28] In William Sheppard's absence, the remaining missionary families, the Snyders and the Adamsons, struggled to support the mission station's occupants and nearly "had to refuse those who came to us, unless we were prepared to free and care for half of the natives of this district."[29] The local population of Baluba refugees and Bakete farmers only grew more desperate for support and protection when official demands for rubber laborers increased around the turn of the twentieth century. William Sheppard's hopes of starting a mission inside the nearby Bakuba kingdom dwindled when the Zappo Zaps decimated it in 1908, killing hundreds and taking some Bakuba hostage.[30]

Fearing came into this situation as an answer to D. W. Snyder's prayers for support. She and Thomas cared for the "house children" when Snyder's wife, Heginbotham, fell ill and after her death in 1896. After Snyder went back to the United States to grieve, Fearing, Thomas, the Sheppards, and a black minister, Henry Philip Hawkins, occupied the mission station, with Sheppard managing its affairs until another white male minister arrived later that year.[31]

In 1908, Lucy Sheppard published an article in which she described how the first girl was adopted into Fearing's home in 1894: "Little Ntumba came trudging up the path toward the station between two stalwart Zappo Zapps, [and] the Missionaries decided to redeem her, as the price was very small."[32] In March 1895, Fearing wrote to supporters at Talladega College that "Lilian and I have four little native girls to train" and "I have one special girl that the doctor [Snyder] gave me for my own. I am trying to teach her to sew and do housework of which she knows nothing." Fearing continued, "Pray for her conversion. Kapinga is her name."[33] Fearing and the other missionaries placed the highest priority on sharing their faith in Christ with the Congolese people, hoping to teach them to read a translated version of the Bible, sing Christian hymns, and memorize Presbyterian doctrine.[34] To assist her in these efforts, Fearing studied the local languages, eventually speaking a creolized combination of Baluba and Bakete with English. She also served as a traveling evangelist to neighboring villages, wrote two articles for the mission newsletter, and sent updates to her financial supporters at Talladega College. But Fearing's unique contribution to the mission was training Congolese girls to adopt a Christian lifestyle through domestic skills.

As a foster mother, Fearing helped to reconcile the Southern Presbyterian Church's ministry goals with the practical needs of the Luebo mission station, which was just one of many Christian missions in the Congo that sought to minister to growing numbers of refugees with inadequate funding from their denominations. The need to maintain and expand their infrastructure created a constant need for local cheap labor, but during the Luebo mission's first three years, prior to Fearing's arrival, none of these workers transformed into the converts that mission sponsors desired.[35] And people who were not involved in the rubber industry and the slave raids (such as the Bakuba nation) showed less patience for Presbyterian preaching.[36] Because Fearing emphasized domestic training and acculturation, she connected the Presbyterian mission to the industrial education movement at the height of its influence in Congolese mission work. Missionaries of various denominations started to report both spiritual conversions and industrial training as signs of success in the region.[37] And though the American Presbyterian Congo Mission had relied on local labor since its founding, Fearing's home was the first part of the mission station to adopt a work-based pedagogy.

Fearing's ministry focused on changing ideas of proper dress and family life-styles. Her house soon became known throughout the region as a place where young women would learn to sew clothing and blankets, cook meals with local fruits and vegetables, maintain a kitchen, wash and iron dresses, and keep new habits of sanitation.[38] Fearing chose a simple dress pattern, taught the girls to sew the dress, and then had them wear it as a substitute for their more revealing traditional clothing.

Each girl attended the mission church and daily classes with Fearing, Thomas, or Lucy Sheppard. The lessons included literacy, domestic skills, and the same "fundamental principles of Christianity" that adults needed to join the mission church—that is, memorizing the translated Westminster Shorter Catechism and learning Presbyterian hymns in the Baluba language.[39] Some came to class from their homes in the village of Luebo, but most lived together in Congolese-style houses built behind the house that Fearing and Thomas shared.[40] Many older girls continued working at the mission in a service role, sought employment at other missions, or chose to marry other Congolese Christians. During Fearing's twenty years in the Congo, she cared for between thirty and one hundred residents at a time.[41]

The girls in Luebo preferred to call Fearing *Mamu*, the Baluba word for "mother," or *Mama wa Mputu* (mother from far away). This honorary title was in keeping with Congolese tradition regarding relationships across different age groups and suggests that the local people found her missions work uniquely personal. Before Fearing's arrival, girls working for the mission received lessons only when their workload allowed and during weekly meetings designed to at-tract local villagers. But the black missionaries did not make spiritual training secondary to domestic training. And though the local people still referred to the African American missionaries as *Bakalinge* (white men), the children may have appreciated Fearing's efforts to teach grooming habits by example: she kept her hair in a short afro similar to local styles and made her dresses out of cloth similar to that supplied within the home.[42]

By 1903, the school enrolled 237 students and employed some Christian teachers from the local area. Fearing and Thomas improvised when they had "no books, charts, black-boards or anything to teach with." One of the white missionaries helped by publishing a Baluba-language reader.[43] Similar to the pedagogy at Talladega College, domestic labor took on a wider social and reli-gious purpose in the Congolese mission field. Published images of the Pantops Home girls in their self-made Western-style dresses gave American supporters visual confirmation of Fearing's success converting the girls' lifestyles and possibly their souls.

Writing to her supporters at Talladega in 1896, Fearing criticized the domestic habits she observed in the villages around the Congo mission station:

> Their homes are not what we call homes. They live in very small houses made of mud and sticks, with a very small door; no window, no chimney, nor fire place. . . . Their blankets are straw mats. They have no quilts. But we are teaching the girls in the home to make quilts. Some of them . . . are learning to sew quite nicely, which they like very much indeed. For it is the custom out here, for the men and the boys to do the sewing and light work, and the girls and women work in the peanut and chumby fields, carry heavy burdens and do other laborious things, while the men nurse the baby, smoke, sew, and such things. This people have nothing elevating nor uplifting to appeal to. They have no home training, know nothing of a parent's love nor of anything good, but all bad.[44]

Fearing equated "goodness" with American and British gender roles and social norms. Her sewing classes provided tangible sources of warmth, subverted the male-dominated tapestry art of the region, and defended her unofficial authority to "elevate" and "uplift" the students.[45] Fearing's extended criticism of Congolese culture echoed the types of concerns expressed in typical "Woman's Work for Woman" missions publications of the late nineteenth century. She and most other women relied on broad interpretations of domesticity to explain why they should lead within church organizations that forbade female ordination. The female missions movement justified its activism by emphasizing the weakness, filth, ignorance, or spiritual darkness of mothers in impoverished or undeveloped regions.[46] The sewing machine was marketed in the 1890s as a crucial symbol of female leaders' abilities to spread "civilization."[47] Indeed, Fearing and Thomas posed for a portrait with the foster home's sewing machine, disregarding the renowned artistry of the traditional handmade tapestries from the Kasai region.[48] Fearing's contributions to the Woman's Work for Woman movement are remarkable not because she altered the pattern but because she embraced it years before the denomination granted her official missionary status.

Fearing proved her skills by embracing the terminology of her chosen profession, and the Presbyterian Mission Board responded by supporting her as a full missionary starting in 1896. The board renamed the foster home Pantops Home for Girls after an elite Presbyterian school in Virginia, and it gained prestige and reached its enrollment capacity within ten years.[49] The American Presbyterian

Congo Mission also gained recognition among church organizations as a rare Jim Crow–era institution where "all sense of color difference [was] absolutely banished in their common purpose."[50] Missionaries of both races and genders often sat together during committee meetings and shared meals and lodging during their evangelistic travels.[51]

White Southern Presbyterian officials in the United States adjusted their racial traditions by honoring the black missionaries with equal pay and respectful titles, but the mission board continued to seek "capable and sympathetic white men" to oversee the Congo project.[52] Though William Sheppard had managed the mission alone before 1896, a mission station managed almost entirely by black ministers and teachers—one of them a former slave—was a clear aberration from the original plans to model the Luebo station after a prosperous Alabama plantation.[53] The segregated management of the Congo mission occurred simultaneously with the forced segregation of black Southern Presbyterians into a short-lived, underfunded Afro-American Synod.[54]

Between 1892 and 1916, the mission supported forty-five missionaries, ten of them black Americans.[55] William Sheppard reacted to the arrival of new white supervisor William Morrison by relocating to work with a different Congolese ethnic group, and most of the newer black missionaries joined him at Ibanche by 1909. But Fearing and Thomas remained at Luebo, adjusting their personal ministry goals to the interests of the white leadership. To the extent that the American Congo Presbyterian Mission promoted interracialism, that effect grew from these female ministers' cooperative efforts. By attending regular staff meetings with increasing numbers of white colleagues and writing articles for the *Kasai Herald*, Fearing participated in the official affairs of the Luebo mission and offered assistance as a midwife, nurse, cook, treasurer, and undertaker.[56] When the station needed to replace its steamship, she pledged twenty-five dollars of her meager personal funds.[57] She was one of the few black missionaries who interacted with Morrison and the other white missionaries on a daily basis, and she continued to do so for almost fifteen years.

Yet Fearing also balanced collegiality with strict boundaries around her own sphere of influence. She and Thomas ran the Pantops Home without managerial assistance from the white missionaries, and after Thomas married Lucius DeYampert, a fellow black missionary, Fearing ran the home alone. Despite her independence, Morrison and the Foreign Mission Board remained satisfied with the home's operation. The success of the Pantops Home also provided a substitute family for the teacher and the many children under her care. Beginning in 1914, the missionaries allowed children to leave at any time and specified that "all must be done to make the children and parents satisfied."[58] A single, elderly woman with no biological children must have gained a significant sense of fulfillment from teaching two generations of girls, particularly since she viewed them as desperately in need of the "civilizing" she could provide.

By 1919, the Congolese church had around twenty thousand members and had become the largest in the Southern Presbyterian denomination.[59] Other missionaries often commended Fearing for her frugal, thorough management of the Pantops Home despite overcrowding and local crises.[60] In 1898, several Zappo Zap soldiers marched into Fearing and Thomas's bedroom seeking a female refugee. The two American women not only were unintimidated but also served as witnesses against the intruders.[61]

The black missionaries' involvement in a legal case against the colonial government contrasted sharply with the status of black Southern Presbyterian ministers within the United States, where the denomination's rules limiting black ministers mimicked contemporary American legal precedents that banned black people from serving as jurors or witnesses.[62] Sheppard and his colleagues in Congo took on state-sponsored atrocities and won reforms after 1909 based on American citizenship rights and international treaties.[63] Laws against slavery were enforced, and the practice of terrorizing villages with piles of prisoners' amputated hands became less common.[64]

Fearing's status as a missionary enabled her to join in the legal effort against King Leopold, but she rarely addressed legal and political issues in her written statements, possibly because she doubted that her observations regarding colonial abuses would carry weight against the word of the Belgian ruler.[65] Instead, her published reports focused on her aid to the refugee children and to elide the reasons for their displacement. After redeeming the first group of four girls from slavery, she wrote, "When these girls came to us they were naked, with the exception of a piece of cloth pinned around their waists. They know nothing of purity."[66] Likewise, the group of sixteen children given as "a present" by government officials had inadequate clothing until the mission's Talladega supporters sent a package of supplies. Thanking her Alabama benefactors, Fearing wished that "you all could only see the ten boys stepping around in the nice new shirts, your hearts would also rejoice with ours."[67] In addition to such tangible support, Fearing also relied on protection from above: in June 1896, when the students clung to her skirts in fear of an imminent slave raid, Fearing suggested Psalm 91 instead of an escape route. Thomas was shocked to tears when she later saw all of the girls safe in the front yard following Fearing's advice to "walomba Nzambi" (pray to God).[68]

In proclaiming her ability to help ensure Congolese children's spiritual and material welfare, Fearing aligned herself with African American leaders' racial uplift endeavors in the United States. Women's organizations such as the National Baptist Women's Convention and the National Association of Colored Women mobilized local female leaders to teach other women how to fight crime, disease, promiscuity, alcoholism, unemployment, and poverty within their families.[69] Though other black missionaries (including William Sheppard) were prominent in the racial uplift movement, Fearing was unusual in claiming the mantle of uplift because she did not share these leaders' elite status through higher education or family heritage.[70] But she did share the black clubwomen's commitment to "Lifting as We Climb." Fearing funded one female student's tuition at Talladega College and subsequently devoted most of her personal funds to the Pantops Home girls and other projects in Luebo.[71]

In 1915, Fearing, Lilian Thomas DeYampert, and Lucius DeYampert left Congo for a yearlong sabbatical in Selma, Alabama. As they had during their 1908 respite, the ministers probably devoted their time in the United States to visiting relatives and seeking donations.[72] The DeYamperts announced their plans to return to work and renewed their passports, while the eighty-year-old Fearing wrote to the mission board, "I am having a little [medical] treatment so as to be already for the Congo." She paid the medical bills with her savings.[73] But the board refused to send Fearing and the DeYamperts back to Africa.

The denomination forced the retirements of six black missionaries between 1910 and 1916, a decision that went against the interests of their white colleagues but fit the overall trend in mostly white American Protestant denominations.[74] As legal and social restrictions on black individuals in the United States increased, white church leaders showed more willingness to enforce and accept new colonial restrictions on blacks serving in western and southern Africa.[75] Except for one Jamaican woman hired to work in Congo in 1923, the Southern Presbyterian denomination hired no new black missionaries until 1958.[76]

Fearing lived with the DeYamperts in Selma until Lilian's death in 1930 and then returned to Gainesville to live with a nephew. She continued volunteering with a local Presbyterian church, possibly helped establish a Congolese art exhibit in Mobile, and corresponded with the Presbyterian Negro Women's Conference of Jackson, Mississippi.[77] Despite the Great Depression, Fearing continued to send money to support the Congolese mission.[78] She died on May 23, 1937, at almost one hundred years old.

Her network of missions supporters at Talladega College helped maintain a thriving missions program and international connections. The college avoided the Southern Presbyterians' ban on new black missionaries by nominating two students for service with the Congregational Church in 1917. A student from

Luebo enrolled in the Talladega primary school in 1913.[79] The memory of the Congo Mission's temporary racial integration lives on through the Presbytery of Sheppards and Lapsley, which was founded in Selma, Alabama, in 1988. And Fearing has been honored posthumously by the Alabama Women's Hall of Fame and an Atlanta-based memorial fund that supports partnerships between African American and African humanitarian projects. In so doing, the Maria Fearing Memorial Fund embodies her dedication to training "strong Christian women" through "so many little deeds of kindness."[80]

NOTES

1. The croquet photograph is archived as "Missionaries Taking Recreation," William H. Sheppard Papers, Record Group 457, Box 3, 835.02.12d, Presbyterian Historical Society, Philadelphia.

2. Althea Brown Edmiston, "Maria Fearing: A Mother to African Girls," in Hallie Paxson Winsborough, ed., *Glorious Living: Informal Sketches of Seven Women Missionaries of the Presbyterian Church, U.S.* (Atlanta: Committee on Women's Work, Presbyterian Church, U.S., 1937); Patricia Sammon, *Maria Fearing: A Woman Whose Dream Crossed an Ocean* (Huntsville, Ala.: Writers Consortium, 1989); Darius L. Swann and Vera Poe Swann, *Maria: Born Enslaved . . . Freed to Serve* (Washington, D.C.: A.P. Foundation Press, 2007); Kimberly DeJoie Hill, "Careers across Color Lines: American Women Missionaries and Race Relations, 1870–1920" (PhD diss., University of North Carolina at Chapel Hill, 2008).

3. The exact date of Maria Fearing's birth is uncertain, but her mission colleagues and most historical accounts list her birth year as 1838.

4. Edmiston, "Maria Fearing," 291; Nellie Winston Peterson, "An Old Woman Reminisces," n.d., 1, Maria Fearing Foreign Missionary Vertical File, Record Group 360, Series 3, 4, Presbyterian Historical Society.

5. Peterson, "Old Woman Reminisces," 1.

6. Robert D. Bedinger, "Maria Fearing: 1838–1937," July 19, 1937, Maria Fearing Foreign Missionary Vertical File; Edmiston, "Maria Fearing," 293–94; Sammon, *Maria Fearing*, 39–52. This short biography is based on Althea Brown Edmiston's 1902 interviews with Fearing in Congo and on background information and memories from Fearing's grandniece, Lucille Perkins Nesbitt.

7. Charles Reagan Wilson, *The New Encyclopedia of Southern Culture* (Chapel Hill: University of North Carolina Press, 2014), 3:330–32; Howard N. Rabinowitz, "From Exclusion to Segregation: Southern Race Relations, 1865–1890," *Journal of American History* 63 (1976): 327–30, 342–43.

8. Stephanie J. Shaw, *What a Woman Ought to Be and to Do: Black Professional Women Workers during the Jim Crow Era* (Chicago: University of Chicago Press, 1996), 42–43.

9. Maxine D. Jones and Joe M. Richardson, *Talladega College: The First Century* (Tuscaloosa: University of Alabama Press, 1990), 6–8, 24, 34–35, 53–54.

10. Ibid., 12–13.

11. Heather Williams, *Self-Taught: African American Education in Slavery and Freedom* (Chapel Hill: University of North Carolina Press, 2005), 177–78.

12. Jones and Richardson, *Talladega College*, 36–37, 55.

13. Ibid., 36.

14. Bedinger, "Maria Fearing," 1.

15. Jones and Richardson, *Talladega College*, 35.

16. Ibid., 57–58.

17. Pagan Kennedy, *Black Livingstone: A True Tale of Adventure in the Nineteenth-Century Congo* (New York: Viking, 2002), 14–17, 81, 90–94.

18. Bedinger, "Maria Fearing," 1.

19. Sammon, *Maria Fearing*, 62–65.

20. Jones and Richardson, *Talladega College*, 12–16.

21. Sammon, *Maria Fearing*, 71–74.

22. Jan Vansina, *Being Colonized: The Kuba Experience in Rural Congo, 1880–1960* (Madison: University of Wisconsin Press, 2010), 59–61, 86–125, 67, 73–75; Adam Hochschild, *King Leopold's Ghost* (Boston: Houghton Mifflin, 1999), 109–12.

23. Vansina, *Being Colonized*, 60–61; William E. Phipps, *William Sheppard: Congo's African American Livingstone* (Louisville, Ky.: Geneva, 2002), 108–9.

24. Photographs of Fearing and Thomas with residents of the Pantops Home for Girls are available in Sheppard Papers, Boxes 3, 4.

25. Vansina, *Being Colonized*, 24–30; George D. Adamson, "A Diary Kept in Congo Land" [July 28, 1894], *The Missionary* (Nashville) 28 (June 1895): 266–67.

26. D. W. Snyder, "Letters from the Field: Africa" [June 3, 1894], *The Missionary* (Nashville) 27 (November 1894): 484.

27. Maggie Waugh Adamson, "Woman's Work on the Congo" [October 1893], *The Missionary* (Nashville) 27 (March 1894): 101–2.

28. D. W. Snyder, "Letters from the Field: Africa" [June 3, 1894], *The Missionary* (Nashville) 27 (November 1894): 483–84.

29. Ibid., 483.

30. William M. Morrison, "Statement to His Majesty's Government on Conditions in the Congo," May 4, 1903, in Robert Benedetto, ed., *Presbyterian Reformers in Central Africa: A Documentary Account of the American Presbyterian Congo Mission and the Human Rights Struggle in the Congo, 1890–1918* (New York: Brill, 1996), 154.

31. For details of Fearing's traveling evangelism, Tshiluba language acquisition, and writing, see Althea Brown Edmiston, "Maria Fearing: A Mother to African Girls," in *Four Presbyterian Pioneers in Congo: Samuel N. Lapsley, William H. Sheppard, Maria Fearing, Lucy Gantt Sheppard*, edited by J. Phillips Noble (Anniston, Ala.: First Presbyterian Church of Anniston, 1965); Maria Fearing, "Children's Page," *Kasai Herald*, July 1904, Congo Mission Records, Presbyterian Historical Society; Maria Fearing, "Visiting," *Kasai Herald*, July 1901, Congo Mission Records; Maria Fearing to Mrs. Andres, October 8, 1896, *Talladega College Record*, March 1897, Maria Fearing to Talladega College Mission Band, *Talladegan*, March 1895, both in Maria Fearing Biographical File, Presbyterian Historical Society.

32. Mrs. W. H. Sheppard, "The Girls' Homes," *Kasai Herald*, January 1, 1908, 17, Sheppard Papers.

33. Maria Fearing to Talladega College Mission Band, *Talladegan*, March 1895, Maria Fearing Foreign Missionary Vertical File.

34. "Admittance to Church Membership," *Kasai Herald*, January 1, 1904, Congo Mission Records.

35. Kennedy, *Black Livingstone*, 77.

36. D. W. Snyder, "Letters from the Field: Africa" [October 17, 1893], *The Missionary* (Nashville) 27 (June 1894): 234; "Six Months among the Bakete" [based on George Adamson's diaries, June 1893–January 1894], *The Missionary* (Nashville) 27 (June 1894): 240–42.

37. Barbara Ann Yates, "The Missions and Educational Development in Belgian Africa, 1876–1908" (PhD diss., Columbia University, 1967), 182–87.

38. Edmiston, "Maria Fearing," 304–8.

39. "Admittance to Church Membership," *Kasai Herald*, January 1, 1904, Congo Mission Records.

40. Edmiston, "Maria Fearing," 304.

41. Sylvia Jacobs, "Their 'Special Mission': Afro-American Women as Missionaries in the Congo, 1894–1937," in Sylvia M. Jacobs, ed., *Black Americans and the Missionary Movement in Africa* (Westport, Conn.: Greenwood, 1982), 157–58.

42. D. W. Snyder, "Letters from the Field: Africa" [June 3, 1894], *The Missionary* (Nashville) 27 (November 1894): 483; D. W. Snyder, "Letters from the Field: Africa" [October 25, 1894], *The Missionary* (Nashville) 33 (June 1895): 264. For an example, see the photograph "Children of the Pantops Home," Sheppard Papers, Box 2, 835.01.16b.

43. Lilian Thomas, "Our Schools," *Kasai Herald*, April 1, 1903, Congo Mission Records.

44. Maria Fearing to Mrs. Andrews, October 8, 1896, *Talladega College Record*, March 1897, Maria Fearing Foreign Missionary Vertical File.

45. Fearing continued to use the language of racial uplift throughout her missions career. See Maria Fearing, "Visiting," *Kasai Herald*, July 1901, Congo Mission Records.

46. Dana Robert, *American Women in Mission: A Social History of Their Thought and Practice* (Macon, Ga.: Mercer University Press, 1996), 130–35.

47. Louise Michele Newman, *White Women's Rights: The Racial Origins of Feminism* (New York: Oxford University Press, 1999), 44.

48. See the photograph "Saturday Afternoon Mending," Sheppard Papers, Box 3, 835.02.17e.

49. Edmiston, "Maria Fearing," 308. Virginia's Pantops Academy offered secondary education to Presbyterian teenagers from the United States and abroad. The school probably hosted missionary children, which is why missionaries gave its name to Fearing's Congolese orphanage; see "Local Mission News," *Kasai Herald*, October 1905, Congo Mission Records.

50. Ernest Trice Thompson, *Presbyterians in the South* (Richmond: Knox, 1973), 3:124.

51. Benedetto, introduction to *Presbyterian Reformers*, 34–35.

52. Phipps, *William Sheppard*, 107; Benedetto, introduction to *Presbyterian Reformers*, 34, 32; H. R. Lamberth to Lucius DeYampert, December 24, 1911, Lucius DeYampert Foreign Missionary Vertical File, Record Group 360, Series 3, 4, Presbyterian Historical Society; Robert D. Bedinger to Lucius A. DeYampert, March 3, 1916, Lucius DeYampert Foreign Missionary Vertical File; Samuel Verner, "The Evangelization of Africa by the American Negro," *The Missionary* (Nashville), March 1897, 114–16.

53. Kennedy, *Black Livingstone*, 65–66.

54. Andrew E. Murray, *Presbyterians and the Negro: A History* (Philadelphia: Presbyterian Historical Society, 1966), 150–52.

55. A group of Presbyterian churches in Alabama still calls itself the Presbytery of Sheppards and Lapsley because "the name represents the inclusiveness of all God's people—black and white, male and female—working together for the furtherance of God's Kingdom" ("History," *Presbytery of Sheppards and Lapsley*, http://pslpcusa.org/history/ [accessed February 2, 2016]).

56. Edmiston, "Maria Fearing," 309.

57. "Thy Will Be Done," *Kasai Herald*, April 1, 1904, Congo Mission Records. In addition to their regular salaries, after 1912 the missionaries earned pay for their additional work improving the mission station. Fearing would have received the single rate of twenty-eight francs per month (Luebo Station Minutes, June 6, 1912, Congo Mission Records).

58. "Rules for Luebo Homes," 1914, Minutes of the American Presbyterian Congo Mission, Congo Mission Records.

59. Benedetto, introduction to *Presbyterian Reformers*, 44–45.

60. "Local Mission News," *Kasai Herald*, January 1905, Congo Mission Records.

61. Morrison, "Statement to His Majesty's Government," 153.

62. Eric Foner, *Reconstruction: America's Unfinished Revolution* (New York: Harper and Row, 1988), 595.

63. William M. Morrison, "Treatment of the Native People by the Government of the Congo Independent State" (address to Boston Peace Congress, October 1904), in Benedetto, ed., *Presbyterian Reformers*, 207.

64. See "Three Boys with Hands Cut Off," photograph from the Sheppard Papers, Box 4, 835.03.18b.

65. Kennedy, *Black Livingstone*, 161.

66. Maria Fearing to Talladega College Mission Band, *Talladegan*, March 1895, Maria Fearing Biological File, Presbyterian Historical Society.

67. Maria Fearing to Mrs. Andrews, October 8, 1896, *Talladega College Record*, March 1897, Maria Fearing Biographical File.

68. Lilian Thomas, "Six Months without Mail," *The Missionary* (Nashville), April 1897, 174.

69. Deborah Gray White, *Too Heavy a Load: Black Women in Defense of Themselves, 1894–1994* (New York: Norton, 1999), 69–72; Evelyn Brooks Higginbotham, *Righteous Discontent: The Women's Movement in the Black Baptist Church, 1880–1920* (Cambridge: Harvard University Press, 1993), 172–77.

70. Kevin K. Gaines, *Uplifting the Race: Black Leadership, Politics, and Culture in the Twentieth Century* (Chapel Hill: University of North Carolina Press, 1996), 2, 16–17; "W H Sheppard, FRGS: Missionary Spoke to Large Audiences Yesterday," *Lynchburg (Va.) Daily News and Advance*, January 30, 1905, Sheppard Papers; Walter L. Williams, *Black Americans and the Evangelization of Africa, 1877–1900* (Madison: University of Wisconsin Press, 1982), 96–101.

71. White, *Too Heavy a Load*, 70.

72. S. H. Chester, "Foreign Mission Committee," *Christian Observer*, February 12, 1908, 163.

73. Maria Fearing to Egbert W. Smith, January 29, 1917, Maria Fearing Foreign Missionary Vertical File.

74. William M. Morrison to Edwin F. Willis, January 5, 1918, Congo Mission Records, provided to the author by Dr. Robert Benedetto.

75. Jacobs, *Black Americans*, 20–22; Sylvia Jacobs, "Give a Thought to Africa: Black Women Missionaries in Southern Africa," in Darlene Clark Hine, Wilma King, and Linda Reed, eds., *"We Specialize in the Wholly Impossible": A Reader in Black Women's History* (Brooklyn, N.Y.: Carlson, 1995), 116–18.

76. Sammon, *Maria Fearing*, 121.

77. "Only Remembered by What We Have Done," *Presbyterian Survey*, [1934], Maria Fearing Foreign Missionary Vertical File.

78. "History," Presbytery of Sheppards and Lapsley, Presbyterian Church (USA) website, http://pslpcusa.org/history/ (accessed September 19, 2016); "Maria Fearing (1838–1937)," Alabama Women's Hall of Fame website, http://awhf.org/fearing.html (accessed September 19, 2016). For information on the founders of the Maria Fearing Memorial Fund, see the biographies of Darius L. Swann and Vera Poe Swann at Abena Productions website, http://www.abenaproductions.com/vAUTHOR.HTM (accessed September 19, 2016).

79. List of African Students enrolled at Talladega College since 1893, African Missions Collection, Folder TC/Afr. 1/1, Talladega College Archives; Edwin C. Silsby to Dr. Cornelius H. Patton of the American Board of Commissioners for Foreign Missions, February 22, 1917, African Missions Collection, Folder TC/Afr.3/2/1.

80. Maria Fearing, "Children's Page," *Kasai Herald*, July 1904, Congo Mission Records. For more information, see the Maria Fearing Fund website, http://www.mariafearingfund.com/ (accessed October 1, 2014).

Julia S. Tutwiler

The Burdens of Paternalism and Race

PAUL M. PRUITT JR.

Julia S. Tutwiler (1841–1916) was one of the ablest Alabamians of the New South era. The highly accomplished daughter of a famous schoolmaster, she dedicated herself to a life of service. She was so valiant and persistent that her name still lives—on university buildings, in the Julia Tutwiler State Prison for Women, and as author of the lyrics of "Alabama," the state song sung by schoolchildren.[1] Tutwiler taught at the Alabama Normal College in Livingston from 1881 to 1910, serving as principal for the last two decades of her tenure. A tireless proponent of vocational and collegiate education for women, she was responsible for the 1893 admission of women to the University of Alabama. As head of the prison department of the state's Woman's Christian Temperance Union beginning in 1883, Tutwiler was a leading critic of the convict lease system and an advocate on behalf of prisoners. In addition to her teaching, writing, lobbying, visiting, and temperance work, she found time to participate in the Chautauqua and peace movements.[2]

Julia Strudwick Tutwiler was born in Tuscaloosa on August 15, 1841, the third of eleven children of Julia Ashe Tutwiler and Henry Tutwiler, who in 1847 established the Greene Springs School for Boys in Hale County. Henry Tutwiler was a strong proponent of education for women, and his daughter received her earliest lessons at the Greene Springs School. She studied at Madame Maroteau's school in Philadelphia around 1859–60 and attended New York's Vassar College in 1865 before becoming a teacher at the Hale County's Greensboro Academy from roughly 1866 to 1869. She spent the next three years as a teacher at the Greene Springs school and then studied privately with faculty at Washington and Lee University in Virginia around 1872–73.[3]

In her early thirties, therefore, Tutwiler was well educated, an experienced teacher, and what one observer called "brilliantly accomplished."[4] Still, she was

JULIA S. TUTWILER, C. 1890S
William Stanley Hoole Special Collections
Library, University of Alabama, Tuscaloosa.

something of a late bloomer, and she did not really come into her own until the late 1870s. In August 1873, she dramatically abandoned a European tour group to enroll at Germany's Kaiserswerth Institute of Deaconesses, where Lutheran nuns taught the principles of primary education and practiced charity toward sinners, even "Magdalens" and prisoners. The Kaiserswerth atmosphere of sisterhood, service, and perseverance served Tutwiler as a model for the rest of her life.[5]

The foundation for Julia Strudwick Tutwiler's transformation and subsequent activism was laid by her parents. The son of a Harrisonburg, Virginia, postmaster of German-Swiss descent, Henry Tutwiler earned a master's degree in 1831 from the University of Virginia, where he sat at Thomas Jefferson's dinner table. Tutwiler's brilliance (he passed no fewer than six departmental examinations) attracted the attention of James G. Birney, best known for his future abolitionist work but in 1830 a faculty recruiter for the University of Alabama.[6] Tutwiler accepted an appointment as professor of ancient languages. Unlike many Virginians, he adapted readily to life in an unfinished community, and his love of learning and modest demeanor endeared him even to the ungovernable youths who were his students.[7]

As a result of problems at the university, Tutwiler and other unhappy faculty resigned their posts in 1837.[8] Two years earlier, he had married Julia Ashe, the daughter of Paoli Pascal Ashe, the university's business manager.[9] Intelligent and strong, Julia Ashe Tutwiler traveled with her husband and tended to their growing family as he spent the next decade teaching at various small Alabama colleges. After the Tutwilers opened the Greene Springs School, she managed an extended family that at times included dozens of her husband's students and as many as thirty slaves.[10]

The decision to settle at Greene Springs provided Henry Tutwiler with the opportunity to put into practice educational tactics that he had been turning over in his mind since his days at the University of Virginia.[11] It was no accident that the Tutwilers based their operations in the Black Belt, home of the state's political leadership and its wealthiest planters. Access to such families would make Greene Springs a successful business venture.[12]

Julia S. Tutwiler would have absorbed some significant pedagogical and personal ideas from watching her parents and an assortment of teachers.[13] First, education could be both stimulating and enjoyable. A former pupil wrote that Henry Tutwiler "could invest even the most abstract problems of mathematics with the interest of a novel."[14] Next, education should have some practical end. Greene Springs students applied their mathematics lessons by learning to use surveying tools. Science classes conducted experiments; foreign language classes emphasized usage. Each student completed a weekly composition because Henry Tutwiler believed that essay writing promoted complex thinking.[15] After morning chapel, Tutwiler often spoke to his students on current events. Whiggish in his refusal to accept tribal views of people, regions, and institutions, he used newspaper and journal articles to give his students a sense of the world's broad horizons and to foster "a taste for reading in all classes of students."[16] Third, education should be individualized: each student progressed at his own rate. Fourth, education should not involve violence. Greene Springs teachers did not inflict corporal punishment, and any student who rejected moral suasion was sent home. Finally, religious exercises should be intellectually satisfying. Henry Tutwiler was at his best during Sunday chapel meetings, giving brief talks and expecting (but not requiring) his students to recite Bible verses or appropriate quotations. On these occasions he exhibited "sweet, benign, tender" aspects of his personality, creating a familial atmosphere at the school.[17]

Julia Tutwiler also learned indirectly that women were intellectually equal to men and could operate in the world of men. The patriarchal doctrine of the time declared that women were fitted for a "separate sphere" of domesticity and should not be exposed to the wider world.[18] Young women often received superficial educations and were expected, as Tutwiler's Georgia counterpart Rebecca L. Felton put it, to go "back home for the domestic duties that were imperative."[19] A considerable number of the women's seminaries and colleges founded in the late antebellum South sought to promote both excellence in education and traditional gender roles, but such was not the case at the Tutwilers' school.[20] Despite its name, the Greene Springs School for Boys educated not only male students but also the Tutwilers' daughters and other young women from nearby families. The girls sat in class with the boys and were held to the same standards of recitation.[21] Greene Springs' teachers would likely have agreed with Alabama reformer Benjamin F. Porter that women "have intellects entirely equal to the most laborious tasks of the most masculine scholar."[22]

Greene Springs afforded Julia Tutwiler an opportunity to measure herself against intelligent boys and to make useful contacts. Throughout this early phase of her education, she benefited from her parents' open-minded approach to raising daughters and their belief in the then-modern notion of nurturing children rather than breaking their will.[23] Julia received opportunities to read and write prose and poetry and even to teach as well as to play boisterous games with her siblings.[24] Like her Mississippi contemporary, Belle Kearney, Tutwiler was raised "in a very liberal atmosphere concerning the intellectual and political status of women."[25] By her teenage years, Tutwiler was ready to join the growing ranks of southern women who participated in the world of public discourse.[26]

The Tutwilers had allowed some of their children to travel to the North as early as 1855, and later in the decade they sent Julia to Madame Maroteau's good French school in Philadelphia, where Henry Tutwiler had business interests, for "two winters." It was a cosmopolitan move for the teenager—living in a northern city, speaking French in class and at meals.[27]

Then, when she was seventeen, as Julia Tutwiler later wrote, she was expected "to come home for no better reason except that I was old enough to leave school." It is not clear whether her parents made this decision because they felt that she had enough education, because the family could no longer afford to send her to school, or because of increasing sectional tensions. But she was devastated at being summoned home: "I cried my eyes nearly out at the thought of being through life the same ignorant unfinished creature that I then felt myself."[28]

Like most southerners, the Tutwilers suffered during the war years. Not only did many former students as well as the fifth Tutwiler child, Hal, fight on behalf of the Confederacy, but the frantic temper of war was inimical to people whose lifework had been devoted to reason and toleration. And of course, the war ended slavery, an issue on which Henry and Julia Tutwiler (and probably most of the rest of the family) held complex and somewhat contradictory views. As a young disciple of Jefferson, Henry Tutwiler had believed that slavery was inherently wrong. In 1832 he told Birney, then an agent of the American Colonization Society, that "almost all of the moral and political evil in our Country may be traced to this fruitful source—it exhausts our soil, corrupts our morals and is the chief cause of that diversity of interest which is fast tending to rend asunder our political fabric."[29] As late as the 1850s, Tutwiler was a member of the society, which sought to promote gradual emancipation and send freed slaves to Africa as settlers and missionaries.[30] Unlike Birney, who became a radical abolitionist, Tutwiler praised the society's gradual approach.[31] But as sectional tensions worsened, this time-consuming moderation was unpopular in both the North and the South. As Alabama lawmakers made slavery increasingly oppressive in an attempt to ensure its continuation, Tutwiler fell back on what amounted to his own slave code.[32]

As he wrote in an 1868 "Address to the Freedmen of Alabama," Tutwiler had tried to base his conduct on the Golden Rule: "To do unto [slaves] as I would have them, under the same circumstances, to do unto me."[33] According to Hal Tutwiler, one slave, "Aunt Amy," confronted his father (probably not long before the war) and told him "that a good Christian man like he was ought to set her free" so that she could rejoin family members whom her former master had taken to Matagorda, Texas. In response, Henry Tutwiler promptly "sent her to

Mobile to our commission merchant, and he sent her to Matagorda on a schooner, her free papers all made out and recorded."[34] By his own account Henry Tutwiler never purchased a slave "except at [the slave's] request, to better his condition," and "*never* sold one."[35] After the war, former slave Legrand Tutwiler, who had been a "janitor and house boy" who tended the school's vegetable garden, recalled that Henry Tutwiler conducted a weekly "Sabbath school" and that the Tutwilers gave all their "servants" Bibles and books of "Bible Stories."[36]

Henry and Julia Ashe Tutwiler believed that education was a basic component of life. Though Henry uneasily accepted the existence of "mental as well as bodily differences among men," he saw no reason to cut off an entire race from the "happiness" of knowledge.[37] The Tutwilers consequently offered instruction to their slaves. "Those who wished to learn," Henry Tutwiler recalled in 1868, "were taught to read by myself and members of my family. All were encouraged to learn, and one was taught to write, and kept his own accounts."[38] The youthful Julia Tutwiler taught some of these classes, and over the years of her childhood and adolescence, she absorbed her parents' complex racial stance, blending paternalism and compassion with a capacity for self-criticism.[39] Having seen slavery at Greene Springs, Julia did not view the institution as uniformly wicked. She later described Alabama's convict lease system as having "all the evils of slavery without one of its ameliorating features—the pride of ownership, self-interest, and inherited affection."[40]

In the mid-nineteenth century, teaching slaves was nonconformist at best and was illegal in Alabama both prior to 1852 and after 1856. Those who violated the statute faced fines of up to one hundred dollars and/or imprisonment for three months.[41] Several notable Alabamians shared the Tutwilers' crypto-abolitionist views, but in the aftermath of John Brown's 1859 raid on Harpers Ferry, Virginia, pro-slavery vigilantes snuffed out public expressions of nonconformity.[42] When war broke out in 1860, the Tutwilers were almost certainly not ardent secessionists but they and many other such families came to support the Confederacy.[43]

Women were among the Confederacy's most loyal and diligent supporters, responding courageously to the challenges of the home front.[44] Henry Tutwiler wanted Julia to embrace those challenges by staying home, but she had other ideas: the young woman wanted to follow her classmates and kin to war as a nurse. By January 1862, when Julia was twenty, nursing would not necessarily have involved traveling far from home, since Confederate hospitals had begun operating near Mobile.[45] One morning, she left a short poem by her father's breakfast plate, "Let Me Go—The War Drum Soundeth," in which she evoked the landscape of combat: "See my countrymen lie bleeding; On the gory sands they lie, Messengers of Death still speeding, O'er their heads a burning sky."[46] But Julia's parents remained unmoved.

During the war years she took part in self-denying economies, joining the other women who worked, in the words of one local writer, "with willing hearts, if feeble hands" to ensure that "our soldiers lack nothing that can be provided."[47] Julia's good works also included horseback trips into the countryside to "help ambitious children learn to read and write." She also spent much time doing chores at Greene Springs, commenting on one occasion that "if she thought she'd have to do this kind of thing the rest of her life, she'd rather die."[48] Otherwise, she was hard at work envisioning her future life, filling up notebooks in an attempt to educate herself. Then "help came in a strange way," as she wrote to her sister Ida. "Providence threw on me the responsibility of assisting Father" and thus the "necessary work of preparing for the recitations." For three years, this process brought "some little order & system into my labors."[49]

The Tutwilers were known for their cosmopolitan appreciation of European writers and philosophers, especially brilliant Germans Johann Wolfgang von Goethe (1749–1832) and Friedrich von Schiller (1759–1805).[50] Julia was especially attracted to Schiller's *Maid of Orleans*, a poetic retelling of the story of Joan of Arc.[51] On one windy cloud-swept night, Julia's sister Katie recalled, Julia paraphrased lines from the *Maid*, saying "she never would marry, she knew— then she looked up at the moon and said, 'No slumbering babe shall rest upon this breast,' and went on about a lonely life and [one] given to great deeds." Katie also remembered Julia reading aloud, translating the *Maid* as she read "in a most dramatic way, with voice and hands," so that "everybody would feel thrilled with patriotism."[52] The patriotism involved was of the Confederate variety, and beyond peaceful Greene Springs, the war ground on.

Schiller envisions Joan of Arc's father as able neither to comprehend nor approve of her; indeed, he accuses her of witchcraft.[53] Henry Tutwiler was more understanding, even when she suffered some type of breakdown and "lost [her] health" at the end of the war.[54] In part to help her get well, her parents allowed her to return to Madame Maroteau's school almost as soon as the firing ceased, and in January 1866 she enrolled at the recently launched Vassar College. She took part in Vassar's first Founder's Day, composing a poem for the occasion.[55] She thus resumed her progress toward her goal of becoming well educated.

However, Tutwiler's year at Vassar was not happy, and she subsequently found herself haunted by "events [that had] occurred almost at the very beginning of my stay which caused me such great pain & sorrow besides wounded pride & self-respect." Writing to Ida, Julia continued, "The year was one of such intense wretchedness that I cannot bear to think of many events in it."[56] Awkward situations seemed to multiply around her. While at Vassar she met one of the Harper brothers, whose family published the strongly antisecession *Harper's Weekly* and startled him by asking why he published articles that inflamed sectional hatred. His reply revealed that he had little knowledge of what was published in the magazine, and she was further offended the next morning when he asked her for a goodbye kiss as if she were a child.[57] As she wrestled with powerful emotions, she captured some of them in poems, which she had begun submitting with some success to magazines and journals. Many of the feelings she recorded were simply those of a homesick young person who had learned "How sad to be quite, quite alone," as she wrote in a poem published in *Godey's Lady's Book* in June 1866.[58] She was—or believed she was—resigned as a Christian to the Confederacy's defeat. One August 1865 poem asks God, the "Ruler of nations," to teach her

> to sorrow with my land
> Yet not to hate her foe,
> To bow submissive to Thy hand,
> Which dealt the chastening blow.

Such sentiments reflect the feelings of sad bewilderment experienced by large numbers of white southerners in the aftermath of defeat.[59]

There was every reason for her to grieve. Fifty-two Greene Springs alumni had been killed in the war, including Lt. Ruffin Y. Ashe of Tuscaloosa, who was likely a relative of Julia Ashe Tutwiler.[60] In "Friendship," published in the *Saturday Evening Post* in January 1866, Julia Tutwiler recalled her childhood and her hopes for a life of "boundless good," noting that such memories now called forth "a smile, a sigh; / A smile to think how fair each dream, / A sigh how hopeless they now seem."[61] Despite her pain, continuing this internal dialogue in the pages of popular magazines may have helped her steel herself and provided hope for a productive future, as she wrote in another poem designed as a hymn:

> "Spend and be spent for others' sake!"
> When once this joy is known
> 'Twere hard its sweetness to forsake
> And live for self alone.[62]

In the summer or fall of 1866, Julia found a job as a teacher at the Greensboro Female Academy, a few miles from Greene Springs.[63] The following year, she was appointed principal, a post she held until 1869. In the spring of that year, she oversaw a spectacular May Day festival at which students performed songs that she had written. She taught languages and built up the school's library, but the work was exhausting, and both the facilities and the funds were insufficient.[64] By the fall of 1869, Julia had returned to the Greene Springs School, where she was teaching a range of subjects, including "special classes in ancient and modern languages."[65] She increasingly focused on the practical realities of teaching, but she also believed that she needed further language study and travel.

By the late 1860s or early 1870, Tutwiler saw her parents growing frailer and worried about them. In particular, she fretted to her sister Ida that the fact that her brothers were "averse to literature" surely was "a grief to Father." Moreover, Julia told Ida, who was studying at Hollins Institute in Virginia, that their father "seems so proud & pleased when your reports come, that I cannot help wishing sometimes that you could give a few of your good marks to" their brother Peyton who was enrolled at Washington and Lee. Julia feared that Peyton, who was ten years her junior, would not listen to the urgings of his older sister and suggested that Ida encourage him to stay at the school over the summer for extra work. According to Julia, Henry Tutwiler would be happy to think that Peyton cared about his studies. Julia also encouraged Ida to remain in school and take advantage of the opportunities that had been denied to Julia: though she "felt that I had powers which would enable me to learn as much & as well as most men," she had been summoned home and forced to discontinue her education. She continued, "There is no reason why your education should not be as thorough & complete as Father's is," and "were I in your place I would persevere until I attained it." If Ida did so, she might replace Julia at Greene Springs: "How pleasant it would be for Father in his advancing years to have a young companion to whom his mind would not be compelled to stoop to hold converse; who had studied the same subjects & read the same books," and who "could understand all his interests & appreciate every quotation & allusion."[66] This letter reveals an intriguing combination of traits and feelings — self-analysis, a degree of manipulativeness, ambition, and paternal hero worship.

In 1872–73 Julia Tutwiler's desire for further education was fulfilled, and she lived with a relative in Lexington, Virginia, while studying privately with professors at the all-male Washington and Lee. There she learned "the latest and most improved methods of language instruction and pronunciation."[67]

In 1873, with her parents' backing, Julia decided to further broaden her horizons by joining the ranks of the postwar American tourists who were exploring Europe. As part of a large group of teachers and ministers, Julia and one of her brothers sailed to England, where they witnessed debates in Parliament. From there they moved across the Continent, seeing sites including the "Universal Exposition" (World's Fair) in Vienna and traveling along the Rhine.[68] The German empire interested Tutwiler deeply as the font of her ancestors' culture. Most of all, she wanted to study languages, especially German, and to acquire a better accent in "that land of careful attention to details."[69]

After learning from one of her friends that the Order of Deaconesses at Kaiserswerth operated not only the nursing school for which they were famous but also a teacher-training school, Tutwiler instantly decided to enroll there.[70] With an ocean between her and all the things that had interfered with her dreams of knowledge, she took a train to Düsseldorf and endured a bumpy ride in a rented hack and found herself late at night in the village of Kaiserswerth. The sisters were astonished to find an emancipated American woman seeking to enroll but nevertheless admitted her.[71] Academically, the normal school posed no challenge. The curriculum included "no mathematics higher than arithmetic; no Latin; no Greek, . . . and hardly more of the natural sciences than might be taught in . . . an American kindergarten." But the students were immersed in the study of German language and literature as well as French and English, ideal for someone who wanted to speak—and not just read—modern languages. Tutwiler and the other women studied Goethe and Schiller "with earnestness and enthusiasm." To her delight, they also studied "hymnology," memorizing and analyzing German hymns. The sisters taught geography as Henry Tutwiler had taught it—that is, in combination with the study of history and culture.[72]

Kaiserswerth sought not to produce learned women but rather to encourage absorption of knowledge and a sense of community. Tutwiler thrived in an environment of "plain living and high thinking," and she was aware that the order had taken on broader responsibilities—"the Orphan Home, the Magdalen House, the hospital for insane ladies," as well as separate hospitals for men, women, and children—and all of these enterprises were run by women acting in a spirit of Christian devotion.[73] Thus her institute training reinforced the conviction, founded at Greene Springs, that a school should offer a community that was residential and religious as well as academic.[74] In short, the Kaiserswerth model convinced Tutwiler of the utility of an intense, practical education for women that would benefit a war-blighted Alabama in which few men and even fewer women could afford a classical education.

Julia Tutwiler remained abroad until 1876, studying in Berlin and other cities, publishing pieces in American periodicals, and trying without success to persuade Alabama relatives to visit her. During this time, Tutwiler also wrote a poem, "Alabama," whose words became the lyrics to the state song in 1931.[75] After returning to her home state, she found a teaching job at Tuscaloosa Female College, which was headed by Alonzo Hill, a former Greene Springs teacher. In 1878 she took a leave of absence and returned to Europe, covering the Paris

Exposition for the *National Journal of Education*. She also studied charitable, missionary, and vocational institutions for young women.[76] In 1881 Tutwiler was hired as coprincipal at the Livingston Female Academy, which became Alabama Normal College two years later. She initially worked with Carlos G. Smith, the husband of her mother's sister, Martha Ashe Smith, and a former Greene Springs teacher and University of Alabama president (1874–78). From 1888 to 1890 she served as coprincipal with J. W. A. Wright, the husband of Julia's oldest sister, Margaret Tutwiler Wright.[77] With Wright's departure, she became sole principal.[78]

Tutwiler's time in Europe confirmed her sense of what women could accomplish and provided her with better training to convey what she later described as "that indefinable essence called culture."[79] But she still seemed dependent on her father and his scholarly network—Hill, Smith, and Wright. By the late 1870s, however, she was moving in a different direction from them. Nearing the end of their careers, they had become fixed in their modes of thought. For all Henry Tutwiler's insistence that learning should have practical applications, he was high priest of a classical order that served a privileged population of young men and (very recently) women. Julia Tutwiler, however, arrived at Livingston and developed a bold program to combine cultural and vocational education for women. She presented her plan to the Alabama Educational Association, but in keeping with conventional notions of women's proper actions and to avoid provoking unnecessary confrontation, she allowed the paper she prepared to be read aloud by a man. She commenced with a hard fact: in most sections of the United States, women outnumbered men. Therefore, large numbers of women were unlikely to fill their conventional roles as wives and mothers and "must be either producers or consumers."[80] Alabama needed a way to prepare young women to be producers, and suggested adopting the model provided by the *écoles professionelles* of Paris, which combined craft training with "a good general education."[81] Many of her ideas were put into practice with the founding of the Alabama Girls' Industrial School at Montevallo in 1893. Tutwiler was offered the presidency of the new school but turned it down because she objected to the school's location.[82]

Tutwiler also strived to balance practical training and liberal education at Alabama Normal College. The college curriculum included instruction in literature, music, painting, German, and "mental and moral philosophy," as well as courses in pedagogy, some of which involved hands-on training with scientific instruments. By the late 1890s, she added vocational craft training.[83] In 1893–94, Alabama Normal had 131 students, all of them female and most from Sumter and nearby Black Belt counties. A few students came from Georgia and Mississippi, and one was from Michigan. The school's catalog listed special fields of study for only 12 students: 9 were musicians, 2 were painters, and Alice Roberts from Michigan was studying German and "Tonic Sol-Fa," a pedagogical system for teaching voice.[84] By 1904, Alabama Normal College enrolled students from forty of the state's sixty-seven counties, and between 1883 and 1904, the school graduated 210 students from the normal course and 74 from the literary course.[85] Most of the normal graduates became teachers, while some of the literary graduates took advantage of the unprecedented opportunities for further education available to women at the turn of the century.

In 1891 Julia Tutwiler presented another paper to the Alabama Educational Association. In "Coeducation and Character," Tutwiler contended that the state needed to provide educational opportunities not only to its young men but also to its young women. Basing her arguments on inductive reasoning, ancient and modern history, a comparison of family structures in Europe and America, and an appeal to the "Great Framer of the laws of the Universe," she made the case that coeducation benefited both sexes.[86] Her chief target was the University of Alabama, which since the Civil War had been an all-male military school. Penning an open letter to the university's faculty and administration "in the name of the women of Alabama," Tutwiler observed that several other southern states had already allowed women into their universities and urged the University of Alabama trustees to do likewise, though she conceded that an initial policy of "careful and prudent limitation" might be best. She pointed out that the state had spent significant sums on university education for men but had spent nothing for women, although Alabama Agricultural and Mechanical College (now Auburn University) had admitted a female student the preceding year, a move she applauded.[87] In the summer of 1892, after hearing Tutwiler's "strong and eloquent appeal" in person, the board of trustees took steps that would lead to the fall 1893 admission of the University of Alabama's first female students, as Tutwiler had "wished and hoped for 20 years."[88]

Julia Tutwiler not only had adapted to changing conditions but also had surpassed her father by demonstrating a willingness to engage in educational politics—and considerable skill at doing so.[89] She similarly adapted her views of the "race question," as it was known, in ways that were quite beyond what Henry Tutwiler had been willing to consider.

In 1898, the *Boston Woman's Journal* published an article on Tutwiler declaring that when she "was a little girl she used to beg to have the little pickaninnies to play with, as a sort of animated dolls." Her favorite game with the slave children was "playing school," and she taught many of them to read. The author of the article continued, "Miss Tutwiler never lost her interest in the colored race, nor did she forget that they were capable pupils."[90] As the child of conscientious slave owners, Tutwiler had grown up having daily interactions with African Americans, and though the Greene Springs of her youth was not egalitarian, it was emphatically biracial. When she returned from her European travels in 1876, southern racial mores were fluid and inconsistent but were not yet marked by automatic hostility or ostracism.[91] Tutwiler took a fresh look at the situations of African Americans and experienced a series of personal revelations.

In 1879 or 1880, Tutwiler visited a "servant girl" in the Tuscaloosa County Jail and was appalled at the misery and filth she saw. The building lacked heat, water, and proper ventilation. To remedy the problem, she enlisted the backing of the Tuscaloosa Female Benevolent Society and sent a questionnaire to jailers across the state. Then, armed with the results, she lobbied the legislature, resulting in the passage of a December 1880 law requiring that counties provide prisoners with healthy facilities, clean water, and access to religious services.[92] Upper-middle-class women across the nation were beginning to discover that they could organize and affect public policy on issues—for example, temperance, family security, or children's welfare—that fell within the "domestic" realm.[93]

Tutwiler next turned her attention to the largely African American inmates in the state prison camps. Alabama had been leasing its convicts to industrialists since 1866, with little effort to supervise conditions in mines or stockades. Reports of appalling conditions caused an outcry in the early 1880s.[94] Soon after the appointment of a board of inspectors headed by lawyer R. H. Dawson, Tutwiler asked whether she could send books and tracts to prisoners at the Pratt coal mines near Birmingham. One of the commissioners "kindly offered to take me in his buggy to see them." The experience, which probably occurred in 1883, Tutwiler wrote, "made an epoch in my life." Transfixed by "the full, hopeless misery in the eyes that met mine," she began to visit "as often as my time and means would allow," determined "to have an auger-hole in the roof of the darkest cavern in hell, and let in one ray of heavenly light."[95]

That same year, Tutwiler broadened her tactics when she joined the Woman's Christian Temperance Union (WCTU), one of the earliest women's reform organizations. Taking as its motto "Do everything," the WCTU sought to promote social reform based on religious principles.[96] Tutwiler joined the WCTU in 1883 after the group asked her to serve as superintendent of its prison work. Believing that her "suggestions might have more weight" if supported by "so many good women," Tutwiler agreed.[97] Efforts to alter or abolish the convict lease system were gaining strength at the time, and in 1883, 1885, and 1886 the legislature enacted measures giving Dawson and his fellow inspectors authority to enforce humane standards of treatment.[98]

With the backing of the WCTU, Tutwiler developed an agenda that persisted for two decades. She repeatedly pushed for separation of prisoners by gender, age, and degree of criminality. She argued for the establishment of reform schools, where trained attendants could teach morals and skills to children whom the state had condemned to "hard labor in the mines in the company of ruffians."[99] Her great triumph was the 1887 enactment of night schools for the mining camps. Tutwiler wrote the bill, suggested parliamentary maneuvers, and lobbied by holding a prayer vigil in the gallery. The legislature passed the measure but did not provide funding for schoolrooms, so Tutwiler persuaded the owners of the Pratt mines to provide facilities.[100] However, the battle was far from over, and Tutwiler spent many years working to prevent mine owners and legislators from rolling back these reforms.[101]

Despite her efforts to improve the conditions under which both African American and white prisoners were held, Tutwiler's reform efforts reflected the lines of segregation laid down in the turn-of-the-century South. A number of WCTU leaders had spoken approvingly of both segregation and disfranchisement, while organizations such as the National Prison Association accepted claims of African American criminality at face value.[102] From 1888 onward, Tutwiler spoke of segregation in the mine schools as benefiting both races, declaring in 1893, for example, "Only those who have labored in the prison mission work can imagine what an advantage it will derive from the separation of the races."[103] And Tutwiler shared in the casual racism that permeated southern white society: in 1890, she referred to "the stupid, dusky African faces" of black pupils.[104]

However, Tutwiler could also display compassion and a more complex racial worldview. In an 1883 essay, "Why the Wash Did Not Come Home," written from the point of view of an impatient white housewife, the narrator goes to her washerwoman's house to complain about her wash being late and intending to deliver "a straightforward, sensible speech about doing what one undertakes to do." But when she arrives, she sees the washerwoman's dead baby girl laid out in an unpainted crib, wearing a "white embroidered robe" and clasping a spray of violets. The essay concludes, "It came upon me as such a shock that 'my washerwoman' was not merely a personified wash-board and smoothing iron."[105]

Tutwiler's private writings also reflected a more complicated view of race. In 1891 she wrote to Booker T. Washington to suggest that he establish a reform school for African American children. Like her, Washington was a well-known educator identified with a marginalized group, and like her, he sought to avoid stirring up animosity. Tutwiler took a respectful tone in her letter to Washington, noting his "great executive ability and enthusiasm for the uplifting of the human race." She did not want to take a public role in this matter because black men and white women were not supposed to appear as equals.[106] However, on another occasion, Tutwiler outraged Livingston's whites by riding in a buggy with Washington.[107]

Alabama Normal College came under state control in 1907, resulting in the appointment of a new board of trustees and business manager. Long accustomed to running the school as she saw fit, Tutwiler chafed at the restrictions on her autonomy. She retired in 1910, at the age of seventy-one. Over the next five years, numerous Alabama organizations honored her contributions to the state, accolades that included the state legislature's formal recognition of her efforts in 1915. She died on March 24, 1916, leaving a fifteen-thousand-dollar scholarship fund and a much larger legacy of educational, prison, and other reforms that is still felt in Alabama today.[108]

NOTES

1. Marcia G. Synnott, "Julia S. Tutwiler," *Encyclopedia of Alabama*, http://www.encyclopediaofalabama.org/face/Article.jsp?id=h-1112 (accessed July 29, 2016).

2. Ibid. See also Anne Gary Pannell and Dorothea E. Wyatt, *Julia S. Tutwiler and Social Progress in Alabama* (1961; Tuscaloosa: University of Alabama Press, 2004); Clara L. Pitts, "Julia Strudwick Tutwiler" (EdD diss., George Washington University, 1942); Eoline Wallace Moore, "Julia Tutwiler, Teacher," *Birmingham Southern College Bulletin* 27 (1934): 2–35; Paul M. Pruitt Jr., *Taming Alabama: Lawyers and Reformers, 1804–1929* (Tuscaloosa: University of Alabama Press, 2010), 32–45.

3. Synnott, "Julia S. Tutwiler"; Pannell and Wyatt, *Julia S. Tutwiler*, 9–10, 12, 17–26; Pruitt, *Taming Alabama*, 34–35, 38–39.

4. William Russell Smith, *Reminiscences of a Long Life: Historical, Political, Personal, and Literary* (Washington, D.C.: Smith, 1889), 230.

5. Pannell and Wyatt, *Julia S. Tutwiler*, 30–34; Julia S. Tutwiler, "A Year in a German Model School," *Journal of Proceedings and Addresses* (National Educational Association) 30 (1891): 161–69. See also Paul M. Pruitt Jr., "Julia S. Tutwiler: Years of Innocence," *Alabama Heritage* 22 (1991): 37–44; Paul M. Pruitt Jr., "Julia S. Tutwiler: Years of Experience," *Alabama Heritage* 23 (1992): 31–39.

6. Thomas Chalmers McCorvey, "Henry Tutwiler and the Influence of the University of Virginia on Education in Alabama, 1904," in *Transactions of the Alabama Historical Society* (Montgomery: Alabama Historical Society, 1906), 5:85, 90–91, 92–93.

7. Joseph Glover Baldwin, *The Flush Times of Alabama and Mississippi: A Series of Sketches* (1851; Gloucester, Mass.: Smith, 1974), 52–76; McCorvey, "Henry Tutwiler," 88.

8. Ibid., 96–99. For an account of the university's problems from the perspective of Tutwiler's colleague, Henry W. Hilliard, see David I. Durham, *A Southern Moderate in Radical Times: Henry Washington Hilliard, 1808–1892* (Baton Rouge: Louisiana State University Press, 2008), 36–38. For

another view, see Sarah Haynsworth Gayle, *The Journal of Sarah Haynsworth Gayle, 1827–1835: A Substitute for Social Intercourse*, ed. Sarah Woolfolk Wiggins and Ruth Smith Truss (Tuscaloosa: University of Alabama Press, 2013), 306.

9. William Russell Smith, *Reminiscences*, 246–74; Gayle, *Journal*, 251.

10. Pannell and Wyatt, *Julia S. Tutwiler*, 4–5; G. Ward Hubbs, *Guarding Greensboro: A Confederate Company in the Making of a Southern Community* (Athens: University of Georgia Press, 2003), 63.

11. McCorvey, "Henry Tutwiler," 99.

12. William Russell Smith, *Reminiscences*, 228–30; McCorvey, "Henry Tutwiler," 100, 102; George Long, *Letters of George Long*, ed. Thomas Fitzhugh (Charlottesville: University of Virginia Library, 1917), 61.

13. For Henry Tutwiler's explanation of Greene Springs's philosophy and method, see his *Address Delivered before the Erosophic Society at the University of Alabama* (Tuscaloosa: Robinson and Davenport, 1834), 4–16. See also Pannell and Wyatt, *Julia S. Tutwiler*, 5–6, 10; McCorvey, "Henry Tutwiler," 100–101, 102–3, 106; Thomas McAdory Owen, *History of Alabama and the Dictionary of Alabama Biography* (Chicago: Clark, 1921), 1:671–72; advertisement, *Greensboro Beacon*, August 10, 1850.

14. McCorvey, "Henry Tutwiler," 103.

15. Ibid., 101; Henry Tutwiler, *Address*, 14.

16. Willis G. Clark, *A History of Education in Alabama, 1702–1889* (Washington, D.C.: U.S. Government Printing Office, 1889), 207, quoted in Owen, *History of Alabama*, 1:672; Pruitt, *Taming Alabama*, 34–35.

17. Clark, *History of Education*, quoted in Owen, *History of Alabama*, 1:672.

18. Pruitt, *Taming Alabama*, 33–34, 35–36; Anne Firor Scott, *The Southern Lady: From Pedestal to Politics, 1830–1930* (Chicago: University of Chicago Press, 1970), 4–7, 71. See also Michael O'Brien, *Conjectures of Order: Intellectual Life and the American South, 1810–1861* (Chapel Hill: University of North Carolina Press, 2004), 1:253–66.

19. Rebecca Latimer Felton, *Country Life in Georgia in the Days of My Youth* (Atlanta: Index, 1919), 58–62.

20. Christie Anne Farnham, *The Education of the Southern Belle: Higher Education and Student Socialization in the Antebellum South* (New York: New York University Press, 1994). For example, At Judson College, chartered in 1841 in nearby Perry County, young women received what would today be termed a thoroughgoing liberal arts education. Though many of the students no doubt were destined for marriage, the "Graduation Essay" (titled "Elevated Aims Essential to Success") and the "Valedictory Address" of 1841 graduate Caroline Frances Smith made no mention of education's role in suiting women for domesticity. Smith wished subsequent classes "success in climbing the rugged sides of the Hill of Science." See Frances Dew Hamilton and Elizabeth Crabtree Wells, *Daughters of the Dream: Judson College, 1838–1988* (Marion, Ala.: Judson College, 1989), 37, 40, 76–77, 262–66.

21. Pannell and Wyatt, *Julia S. Tutwiler*, 2–3, 9–10. During the latter years of the Greene Springs School, some girls may have boarded; see Pitts, "Julia Strudwick Tutwiler," 47–48.

22. Quoted in Pruitt, *Taming Alabama*, 34.

23. Sarah Wiggins, *Love and Duty: Amelia and Josiah Gorgas and Their Family* (Tuscaloosa: University of Alabama Press, 2005), 30.

24. Pannell and Wyatt, *Julia S. Tutwiler*, 7–9; Pruitt, *Taming Alabama*, 138 n. 13.

25. Belle Kearney, *A Slaveholder's Daughter* (New York: Abbey, 1900), 108–9.

26. Other Alabama women who fit this description on the eve of the Civil War included best-

selling novelists Caroline Lee Hentz (1800–1856) and Augusta Jane Evans Wilson (1835–1909); Octavia Walton Le Vert (1810–77), author of travel books and leader of a Mobile literary-artistic salon; Virginia Tunstall Clay (1825–1915), a socialite and political confidante in Washington, D.C.; and poet Zitella Cocke (1840–1929), whose career somewhat paralleled Tutwiler's. See Benjamin Buford Williams, *A Literary History of Alabama: The Nineteenth Century* (Rutherford, N.J.: Fairleigh Dickinson University Press, 1979), 170–75 (Hentz), 183–94 (Evans), 59–66 (Le Vert), 152–53 (Clay), 131–32 (Cocke).

27. Henry Tutwiler to John Hartwell Cocke, March 28, 1855, Cocke Papers, Box 148; Pannell and Wyatt, *Julia S. Tutwiler*, 12, 18–19.

28. Julia Tutwiler to Ida Tutwiler, n.d., Ida Tutwiler Letters [#2770z], Southern Historical Collection, Wilson Library, University of North Carolina at Chapel Hill. This letter definitely was written after the Civil War, and internal evidence indicates that it predates Julia Tutwiler's year of private study (1872–73) with Washington and Lee University faculty. See Pannell and Wyatt, *Julia S. Tutwiler*, 21–24.

29. James Gillespie Birney, *Letters of James Gillespie Birney, 1831–1857*, ed. Dwight L. Dumond (New York: Appleton-Century, 1938), 1:17–18, 19. For Jefferson's views on the moral corruptions engendered by slavery, see *Thomas Jefferson: Writings*, ed. Merrill D. Peterson (New York: Library of America, 1984), 264–70, 288–89.

30. O'Brien, *Conjectures of Order*, 1:181–86; Elizabeth Fox-Genovese and Eugene Genovese, *Mind of the Master Class: History and Faith in the Southern Slaveholders' Worldview* (New York: Cambridge University Press, 2005), 231–35; "Receipts of the American Colonization Society, from the 20th January, to the 20th February, 1852," *African Repository* 28 (March 1852): 96.

31. "A Letter from Professor Tutwiler, of Alabama," *African Repository and Colonial Journal* 23 (October 1847): 312–13.

32. Leah Rawls Atkins, "The Cotton Kingdom," in William Warren Rogers, Robert David Ward, Leah Rawls Atkins, and Wayne Flynt, *Alabama: The History of a Deep South State* (Tuscaloosa: University of Alabama Press, 1994), 93–112; John J. Ormond, Arthur P. Bagby, and George Goldthwaite, *The Code of Alabama* (Montgomery, Ala.: Brittan and De Wolf, 1852), 786 (index entries under "Slaves").

33. Henry Tutwiler, "Address to the Freedmen of Alabama," Henry Tutwiler Papers, Albert and Shirley Small Special Collections Library, University of Virginia; George Burke Johnston, *Thomas Chalmers McCorvey: Teacher, Poet, Historian* (Blacksburg, Va.: White Rhinoceros Press, 1985), 237.

34. Dr. H. A. Tutwiler to Margaret [T. Hazard], June 1 [1891?], Henry Tutwiler Papers. According to Hal Tutwiler, Aunt Amy reappeared some time after Emancipation and lived with the family until her death. See Pannell and Wyatt, *Julia S. Tutwiler*, 14–15.

35. Tutwiler, "Address," in Johnston, *Thomas Chalmers McCorvey*, 237. See also Dr. H. A. Tutwiler to Margaret [T. Hazard], June 1 [1891?], Henry Tutwiler Papers, for the story of how Tutwiler almost sold a slave named Amelia, at her request, but refused because the purchaser refused to take her child, too. For a critical view of such tales of slaveholding benevolence, see Mark Auslander, *The Accidental Slaveholder: Revisiting a Myth of Race and Finding an American Family* (Athens: University of Georgia Press, 2011).

36. "Some Recollections of Legrand Tutwiler, Former Slave of Dr. Henry Tutwiler, of Greene Springs, Alabama," 2, 4, Henry Tutwiler Papers.

37. Henry Tutwiler, *Address*, 10–11. Tutwiler added numerous qualifications to this statement, including the admission that "some philosophers, indeed, have even gone so far as to assert that

there are no *natural* differences between one man and another in point of intellectual character, but that all are born with an equal capacity of improvement."

38. Tutwiler, "Address," in Johnston, *Thomas Chalmers McCorvey*, 237–38. The slave who learned to write was probably Legrand Tutwiler, who remembered that Henry Tutwiler "had night school for the servants who wanted to learn to read and write" ("Some Recollections of Legrand Tutwiler," 1–2).

39. Pannell and Wyatt, *Julia S. Tutwiler*, 8.

40. Julia S. Tutwiler, "Our Brother in Stripes, in the School-Room," *Journal of Proceedings and Addresses of the National Educational Association, Session of the Year 1890* (1890), 601–2.

41. Acts of Alabama (1855–56), 50. The 1852 *Code of Alabama* (see secs. 1005–32, 2042–63, 3126–30, 3219, 3279, 3282–89) had not specifically forbidden the teaching of slaves; see Clement C. Clay, *A Digest of the Laws of the State of Alabama* (Tuscaloosa, Ala.: Slade, 1843), 543 sec. 24.

42. See [Paul M. Pruitt Jr.,] "Amicus Curiae: Henry W. Hilliard's View of Slavery," in David I. Durham and Paul M. Pruitt Jr., eds., *A Journey in Brazil: Henry W. Hilliard and the Brazilian Anti-Slavery Society* (Tuscaloosa: University of Alabama School of Law, 2008), 5–7.

43. Supporting the Confederacy was in some ways an inescapable business matter. By the summer of 1861, Tutwiler's advertisements for the Greene Springs School noted that "Confederate bonds or Treasury notes [will be] received as payment" (*Montgomery Weekly Advertiser*, August 31, 1861).

44. H. E. Sterkx, *Partners in Rebellion: Alabama Women in the Civil War* (Rutherford, N.J.: Fairleigh Dickinson University Press, 1970); Mary Jane Chadick, *Incidents of the War: The Civil War Journal of Mary Jane Chadick*, ed. Nancy M. Rohr (Huntsville, Ala.: SilverThreads, 2005); Scott, *Southern Lady*, 81–102.

45. Augusta Jane Evans, *A Southern Woman of Letters: The Correspondence of Augusta Jane Evans*, ed. Rebecca Grant Sexton (Columbia: University of South Carolina Press, 2002), 39, 39 n. 2, 43.

46. Pannell and Wyatt, *Julia S. Tutwiler*, 13.

47. "A Rebel Daughter of Alabama," *Greensboro Beacon*, April 22, 1862, quoted in William Edward Wadsworth Yerby, *History of Greensboro, Alabama, from Its Earliest Settlement* (Montgomery, Ala.: Paragon, 1908), 48. Julia Tutwiler may well have written this letter, which also promises to "assist in every way within the sphere of woman's influence."

48. Pannell and Wyatt, *Julia S. Tutwiler*, 13–14. Pannell and Wyatt note that Julia cared for two elderly slaves, including Aunt Amy. See also Pruitt, *Taming Alabama*, 140 n. 37.

49. Julia Tutwiler to Ida Tutwiler, n.d., Ida Tutwiler Letters; Pannell and Wyatt, *Julia S. Tutwiler*, 13–14, 94.

50. William Russell Smith, *Reminiscences*, 232.

51. Schiller's *Die Jungfrau von Orleans* (1801) was published in English as early as 1843, in an edition translated by British feminist Anna Swanwick (1813–99). Julia Tutwiler was familiar with the work in its original German. See K.T.M. to Netta, [ca. 1916], Julia S. Tutwiler Papers, Hoole Special Collections Library, University of Alabama.

52. Ibid. See also Pruitt, *Taming Alabama*, 35, 138 n. 17; Pannell and Wyatt, *Julia S. Tutwiler*, 8–9.

53. Schiller, *Maid of Orleans*, 142–45.

54. Julia Tutwiler to Ida Tutwiler, n.d., Ida Tutwiler Letters.

55. Pannell and Wyatt, *Julia S. Tutwiler*, 19–21. According to Pannell and Wyatt, the Vassar interlude was financed by sale of some Tutwiler investments. See also Pruitt, *Taming Alabama*, 38–39.

56. Julia Tutwiler to Ida Tutwiler, n.d., Ida Tutwiler Letters.

57. Pruitt, *Taming Alabama*, 39, 140 n. 36, citing K.T.M. to Netta, [ca. 1916], Julia S. Tutwiler Papers.

58. Julia S. Tutwiler, "Light after Darkness," *Godey's Lady's Book and Magazine*, June 1866, 517.

59. Pannell and Wyatt, *Julia S. Tutwiler*, 18–19; Gaines M. Foster, *Ghosts of the Confederacy: Defeat, the Lost Cause, and the Emergence of the New South* (New York: Oxford University Press, 1987), 11–15.

60. *Resolutions in Memoriam and Roll of Honor of the Hermathenian Society of Greene Springs School* (Columbus: Mississippi Index, 1867).

61. Julia S. Tutwiler, "Friendship," *Saturday Evening Post*, January 13, 1866, 5.

62. Quoted in Pannell and Wyatt, *Julia S. Tutwiler*, 19.

63. Ibid., 21.

64. Pannell and Wyatt, *Julia S. Tutwiler*, 22–23. Julia Tutwiler to Ida Tutwiler, n.d., Ida Tutwiler Letters. According to Julia's letter, her preparations for the festival included having work crews clearing brush and raking leaves, making a winding path, arranging rocks, mowing, building fifty seats, installing latticework, and trying to drain a "horrible sink between the three springs."

65. Pannell and Wyatt, *Julia S. Tutwiler*, 23.

66. Julia Tutwiler to Ida Tutwiler, n.d., Ida Tutwiler Letters. Julia may have been exaggerating her concerns, since Hal Tutwiler became a physician; Pascal Ashe Tutwiler became a "well-known member of the Greensboro bar" (McCorvey, "Henry Tutwiler," 105); and Peyton Tutwiler graduated from Washington and Lee in 1872 and became a planter (*Catalogue of the Officers and Alumni of Washington and Lee University, Lexington, Virginia, 1749–1888* [Baltimore: Murphy, 1888], 164). Her youngest brother was Carlos Smith Tutwiler. Ida Tutwiler indeed remained in school, graduating from Hollins in 1875.

67. Pannell and Wyatt, *Julia S. Tutwiler*, 24. According to the *Catalogue of the Officers and Alumni of Washington and Lee University*, 41, the language faculty present in 1872 were Carter J. Harris (Latin), Edward S. Joyner (modern languages), and James T. Whitney (Greek).

68. Julia Tutwiler to Ida Tutwiler, n.d., Ida Tutwiler Letters; Pannell and Wyatt, *Julia S. Tutwiler*, 26–32. See also Pruitt, "Julia S. Tutwiler: Years of Innocence," 37, 43.

69. Tutwiler, "Year in a German Model School," 161.

70. Ibid., 161–62. See also Fredrika Bremer, "A Visit to the Protestant Sisters of Mercy at Kaiserswerth," *Godey's Lady's Book*, June 1852, 488; "The Kaiserswerth Deaconesses," *Woman's Journal*, August 1, 1874, 250.

71. Tutwiler, "Year in a German Model School," 162–63.

72. Ibid., 164, 165–66, 167.

73. Ibid., 163.

74. Ibid., 168–69. Tutwiler concludes her article with a spirited defense of religion's place in education.

75. Pannell and Wyatt, *Julia S. Tutwiler*, 38–47; Julia Tutwiler to "Dearest Netta," March 27, 1875, Julia S. Tutwiler Papers; Synnott, "Julia S. Tutwiler."

76. Pannell and Wyatt, *Julia S. Tutwiler*, 49–58. For Tutwiler's appraisal of French female vocational schools, see Julia S. Tutweiler [sic], "The Technical Education of Women," *Education: An International Magazine* 3 (1882–83): 203–6.

77. Pannell and Wyatt, *Julia S. Tutwiler*, 58–59, 70.

78. See Pannell and Wyatt, *Julia S. Tutwiler*, 49–96.

79. Ibid., 82.

80. Pannell and Wyatt, *Julia S. Tutwiler*, 56; Tutwiler, "Technical Education," 201.

81. Tutwiler, "Technical Education," 203–5.

82. Pannell and Wyatt, *Julia S. Tutwiler*, 98–99, 139 n. 3.

83. Ibid., 64–66, 67–70, 77–78.

84. Judy Massey, comp., "Catalogue of Pupils for Alabama Normal College for Girls 1893–94," http://library.uwa.edu/finding_aids/pupils_rev.html (accessed July 29, 2016).

85. Pannell and Wyatt, *Julia S. Tutwiler*, 82.

86. Julia S. Tutwiler, "Co-Education and Character," in Alabama Educational Association, *Proceedings and Papers of the Tenth Annual Session* (Birmingham, Ala.: Siler, 1891), 73–77. Tutwiler ends by quoting the ideal of gender relations set forth in Alfred Tennyson's 1847 poem, "The Princess": "Not like to like, but like in difference . . . May these things be!" See also Pannell and Wyatt, *Julia S. Tutwiler*, 100–101.

87. "To the President, Faculty, and Trustees of the University of Alabama," enclosed in Julia S. Tutwiler to William Leroy Broun, July 11, 1892, Broun Papers, Special Collections, Ralph Brown Draughon Library, Auburn University.

88. University of Alabama Board of Trustee Minutes (1888–95), 352–53 (June 29, 1892), 439 (June 28, 1893); Pannell and Wyatt, *Julia S. Tutwiler*, 99–105; Julia S. Tutwiler to William Leroy Broun, July 11, 1892, Broun Papers.

89. In addition to refusing the presidency of the University of Alabama, Henry Tutwiler had backed out of the 1878 race for state secretary of education, which he was more or less assured of winning, when he realized that he would have to appear before a convention and solicit votes. Tutwiler wrote to a friend, "I do not think that the office of Superintendent of Education has anything more to do with politics than that of president or professor of college or university," and it would be "very repugnant to my feelings" to appear before a party convention (William Russell Smith, *Reminiscences*, 231).

90. "Miss Julia Tutwiler," *Woman's Journal*, November 26, 1898, 3–4. The article incorrectly states that Tutwiler's parents sent her to France at the outbreak of the Civil War, and *pickaninnies* may or may not have been the term Tutwiler used when she spoke to the reporter.

91. C. Vann Woodward, *The Strange Career of Jim Crow*, 2nd rev. ed. (New York: Oxford University Press, 1966), 31–47.

92. Pannell and Wyatt, *Julia S. Tutwiler*, 108–9; Pruitt, *Taming Alabama*, 42–43.

93. Mary Martha Thomas, *The New Woman in Alabama: Social Reforms and Suffrage, 1890–1920* (Tuscaloosa: University of Alabama Press, 1992).

94. See Paul M. Pruitt Jr., "Convict Lease System and Peonage," in *New Encyclopedia of Southern Culture*, 10:26–29; Robert David Ward and William Warren Rogers, *Convicts, Coal, and the Banner Mine Tragedy* (Tuscaloosa: University of Alabama Press, 1987), 26–39; Mary Ellen Curtin, *Black Prisoners and Their World: Alabama, 1865–1900* (Charlottesville: University Press of Virginia, 2000), 75–80.

95. Curtin, *Black Prisoners*, 81–85; Tutwiler, "Our Brother in Stripes," 603, 605.

96. Mary Martha Thomas, *New Woman in Alabama*, 12–15.

97. Tutwiler, "Our Brother in Stripes," 603; Julia Tutwiler to R. H. Dawson, August 11, 1889, Alabama State Board of Inspectors of Convicts, Administrative Correspondence, Alabama Department of Archives and History.

98. Curtin, *Black Prisoners*, 83–96, 106–9, 111–12; Paul M. Pruitt Jr., "The Trouble They Saw: Approaches to the History of the Convict Lease System," *Reviews in American History* 29 (2001): 399–400; Pannell and Wyatt, *Julia S. Tutwiler*, 110–17; Tutwiler, "Our Brother in Stripes," 603–4, 607.

99. Tutwiler, "Our Brother in Stripes," 603; Pitts, "Julia Strudwick Tutwiler," 196–98, 199–201, 203–6, 207–9, 209–11, 212–13, 213–16.

100. Tutwiler, "Our Brother in Stripes," 603–4; *Supplement to the Minutes of the Alabama Woman's Christian Temperance Union for 1887: Report of Superintendent of Prison and Jail Work* (Selma, Ala.: Mail Job, [1888]), 2–3.

101. See, e.g., Tutwiler to Captain Frank S. White, June 13, 1913, Alabama Department of Archives and History Digital Collections, digital.archives.Alabama.gov/cdm/ref/collection/voices/id/2601 (accessed July 29, 2016).

102. Edward J. Blum, *Reforging the White Republic: Race, Religion, and American Nationalism, 1865–1898* (Baton Rouge: Louisiana State University Press, 2005), 16, 178–79; Curtin, *Black Prisoners*, 169–73; Pruitt, "Trouble They Saw," 396.

103. Pitts, "Julia Strudwick Tutwiler," 199, 208.

104. Tutwiler, "Our Brother in Stripes," 607. For a 1900 description of "a band of colored boys locked up together in a room without even the oversight of an old prisoner," see Pitts, "Julia Strudwick Tutwiler," 215. Tutwiler notes how these young men leave prison "half devil and half beast," adding abruptly that "criminal assaults upon women will never cease so long as the State maintains these Universities for the education and graduation of criminals."

105. Julia S. Tutwiler, "Why the Wash Did Not Come Home: (A Southern Sketch)," *Christian Union*, March 8, 1883.

106. Julia S. Tutwiler to Booker T. Washington, March 7, 1891, in Louis R. Harlan, ed., *The Booker T. Washington Papers* (Urbana: University of Illinois Press, 1972–89), 2:135–36.

107. Kathryn Tucker Windham, *My Name Is Julia* (Birmingham: Birmingham Public Library Press, 1991), 17–18.

108. Synnott, "Julia S. Tutwiler."

Margaret Murray Washington

A Southern Reformer and the Black Women's Club Movement

SHEENA HARRIS

On October 4, 1972, on the campus of Judson College in Marion, Alabama, the Alabama Women's Hall of Fame inducted its first African American member, Margaret Murray Washington. Prior to her death nearly fifty years earlier, she had been an educator, a Pan-Africanist, and a clubwoman. The Hall of Fame referred to her as "one of the greatest women of her century. . . . A woman of great compassion, intelligence, and independence of judgment." Dr. Luther Hilton Foster Jr., the president of Tuskegee Institute, presented a short biographical sketch of Washington in which he asserted that she "dedicated her energies and her spirit toward the uplift of black women." He also described her work as "an inspiring example of the opportunities for leadership when the will is strong, the mind is keen, the cause is worthy, and the heart is deeply moved."[1] And while renowned as the third wife of Booker T. Washington, Margaret Washington merited recognition based on her own achievements.

These posthumous honors constituted a dramatic change from the realities of the South during Margaret Washington's life. However, the southern system of segregation formed an important context for her social activism and her pioneering endeavors in relation to educating blacks, particularly women.

Margaret James Murray was born in Macon, Mississippi, on March 9, 1861—just four days after President Abraham Lincoln delivered his first inaugural address. Her father, James Murray, had emigrated to Mississippi from Ireland; her mother, Lucy Murray, hailed from Georgia and may have been a slave. After emancipation, Lucy Murray became a washerwoman, an occupation that provided black women with a sense of more autonomy than domestic labor, the other primary avenue of employment open to them. According to Booker T. Washington's secretary, Emmett Scott, when Maggie, as she was affectionately

MARGARET MURRAY WASHINGTON, C. 1917

Tuskegee University Archives.

known, "grew old enough to count she found herself one of a family of ten, and, like nearly all children of Negro parentage at that time, very poor."[2]

As an African American girl living in extreme poverty during a time of war and great social unrest, Murray felt firsthand the South's significant racial inequalities. When she was seven, her father died, and she went to live with the Saunderses, a brother and sister who were members of the Society of Friends (commonly known as the Quakers). Prior to the Civil War, the Quakers had been ardent opponents of slavery, petitioning Congress on behalf of enslaved blacks and opening schools for African Americans. After the war, members of the Quaker community continued to work to eliminate injustice and commonly adopted black children and taught them Quaker doctrines and concepts of holiness. The Saunderses had come to the South in 1864 and were eager to help former slaves get an education. Murray likely received her early schooling from private institutions or tutors, since Macon did not offer public education even for whites until 1882.[3]

Between 1865 and about 1877, Congress and President Andrew Johnson implemented Reconstruction policies aimed at reorganizing the southern states, providing the foundation for their readmission to the Union and defining the means by which whites and blacks could live together in a nonslaveholding society. Despite the southern states' unwillingness to fund efforts to educate blacks; acts of terrorism, including the burning of African American schools and lynching; laws mandating racial segregation; and disenfranchisement, black and white teachers from both the North and South, missionary organizations, churches, and schools worked to provide educational opportunities to the emancipated population. Many believed that education would open the doors for first-class citizenship previously denied to blacks. Still, as Murray and other leaders learned, achieving citizenship proved an uphill battle.[4]

In 1875, when Murray was fourteen, the Saunderses sent her to Nashville, Tennessee, to further her schooling.[5] Nashville was only three hundred miles from Macon, but it was a world apart from what Murray had ever known. In 1870, Davidson County, which includes Nashville, had a population of 62,897, including 25,412 African Americans. Many members of Nashville's thriving urban black community were progressive, and the city featured a sizable Quaker community that understood the need for basic education. Educating future teachers of the race took priority.[6]

Murray performed extremely well in her subjects and was asked to teach soon after her arrival in Nashville. She passed the teacher's examination and began instructing her peers. Murray probably did not teach in Nashville's public school system, which had no African Americans among its seventy teachers in 1875. She likely joined other blacks teaching basic reading and writing in temporary school buildings. Having become a Quaker, Murray benefited from the society's resources as well as from the institutions of the black community, including Fisk Institute, which had opened its doors on January 9, 1866.[7]

In 1881, Murray enrolled at Fisk Institute's preparatory school, located on forty acres of land in the heart of Nashville. She attended Fisk part-time for eight years while teaching preparatory classes and working in the homes of Fisk faculty members during the summer months. She also collaborated with other blacks to create schools in less urban areas of Tennessee and Mississippi. She spent at least one summer in Pontotoc, Mississippi, where she and other teachers "opened [a] school with 21 pupils."[8]

While at Fisk, Murray met W. E. B. Du Bois, who in 1883 cofounded a school newspaper, the *Fisk Herald*, and became its editor in 1886, the same year that Murray joined the paper's staff. She, Du Bois, and other students used the publication to document African American progress across the country. In 1884, Murray visited the Colored Methodist Episcopal High School in Jackson, Tennessee, about 130 miles west of Nashville. Just two years after its founding, Murray rejoiced, "the school is conducted entirely by the colored people," and their advancement "moved steadily on." The paper suggested that the advancement of the black race was the responsibility of the best of the race, a philosophy that provided the basis for the concept that Du Bois later advanced and popularized as the "Talented Tenth" (a term coined by the Reverend Henry Lyman Morehouse in an 1896 essay).[9]

In June 1889, twenty-eight-year-old Margaret James Murray and another female student, Emma Jane Terry, graduated from Fisk with honors. Booker T. Washington, the founding president of Alabama's Tuskegee Normal and Industrial Institute, had come to give a "happy after dinner speech" to the graduates and was seated directly across from Murray at a table. Murray mustered up the courage to ask Washington for a position teaching English at Tuskegee. Though she had already written to inquire about a job at the school, she had received no response; however, when asked in person, Washington hired her on the spot. After just a year at Tuskegee, Murray was promoted to lady principal (later dean of women). In that position, she helped to educate the new generation of black women who were speaking out and making a difference.[10]

Washington knew all too well the barriers blacks faced. Born enslaved in rural Virginia on April 5, 1856, he took full advantage of the freedom that arrived when he was nine years old. In 1871 he made the nearly five-hundred-mile journey to Virginia's Hampton Normal and Industrial Institute. After graduating with honors in 1875, he entered Wayland Seminary in Washington, D.C. His mentor, General Samuel Armstrong, subsequently asked Washington to join the school's staff. In 1881, halfway through his first year, his ties to Armstrong helped win him an invitation to head the newly created Tuskegee Normal and Industrial Institute. Washington accepted.[11]

By June 1889, when he met Margaret Murray, Washington had twice been widowed: his second wife, Olivia Davidson Washington, whom he had met when he spoke at her 1879 graduation from Hampton Institute, had died just a month earlier. The possibilities of courtship among the educated classes had as much to do with location as with respectability. Young and attractive, Murray had come of age during a period that welcomed ideas of passionate love. She frequently read romantic novels that emphasized the pleasure and enjoyment associated with marriage rather than its reproductive component. She may have had at least one suitor while at Fisk. After her arrival at Tuskegee, Washington began to court her, though his name was linked to two other possible romantic interests, Hallie Tanner Dillon, also newly hired at Tuskegee and the first black female physician in Alabama, and Mary Moore, who had been a close friend of Olivia Washington. Murray worked with both women and at times was insecure about Washington's interest in her. In October 1891, after he had mentioned that Moore wrote more romantic letters than Murray did, she wrote to him, "Her letters are more like love letters than are mine? You would laugh if I were to tell you that I am jealous of her."[12]

On October 12, 1892, Murray and Washington exchanged vows, and the new Mrs. Washington immediately became the mother of three young children from her husband's previous marriages.[13] Margaret Washington's commitment to improving the Tuskegee community and to presenting a positive image of the black home life subsequently intensified, becoming the focus of many of her self-help outreach initiatives. "Where the homes of colored people are comfortable and clean, there is less disease, less sickness, less death, and less danger to others," she wrote. In addition to helping to counter notions that "black marriages [were] devoid of fidelity," this emphasis challenged notions of private and public spheres, which generally identified the proper place for women and men, and helped to extend women's influence beyond the home and into the community. Moreover, the Washingtons' very public domestic harmony solidified their position among other black elites.[14]

The prevailing Progressive Era emphasis on respectability combined with Booker Washington's vision for Alabama and the South to restrict Margaret Washington's activities to what was expected from women. Nevertheless, her position at Tuskegee enabled her to spread the school's gospel and to foster changes in women's education. As lady principal, her initial responsibilities included directly supervising the female students as well as their curriculum. She soon established undergraduate and postgraduate programs in making soap, basketry, laundering, millinery, sewing, table setting, cooking, and making brooms. She thus helped to expand the industrial training opportunities Tuskegee offered to its female students and to enhance their understanding of the importance and usefulness of both industrial and liberal arts education to the development of the larger community.[15]

Margaret Washington quickly began to identify herself as a race woman and sought not only to help blacks prepare themselves for the needs and demands of the New South but also to train African Americans to be self-sufficient. In addition, having witnessed firsthand white hostility toward African American education and the havoc wreaked by the Ku Klux Klan, she understood that blacks would have to tread carefully so that their educational efforts appeared nonthreatening. Many southern whites who objected to classical or higher education for African Americans "grasped eagerly at industrial education as a method of satisfying blacks' desire for learning while at the same time keeping them in their 'place.'" Washington also sought personal visibility to help spread her message of uplift and social reform.[16]

However, the Washingtons' focus on elites as models for the masses of African Americans and on racial uplift was also in some ways problematic. The idea of the Talented Tenth extended class differences created by capitalism and created divisions among African Americans, mimicking the split that white supremacists created between themselves and blacks. In the words of Kevin K. Gaines, "The term 'uplift' carried with it the assumption that those being lifted occupied inferior positions." Many of the problems that African Americans faced resulted from their economic status, a situation Margaret Washington blamed on white supremacy and the legacy of slavery rather than on African Americans' innate traits. However, she also believed that race women needed to elevate the lives of the poor, an approach that proposed Victorian ideas of appropriate behavior as solutions to America's race and gender problems.[17]

In February 1892, Booker T. Washington invited black farmers and their families to come from rural areas to attend the first Tuskegee Negro Conference, where they would discuss the problems they faced as well as possible solutions. However, Washington did not allow the farm women to present their concerns, and Margaret Murray decided that she needed to do something to help them. Women seemed to have no significant role in the important matters of life outside of the household. Moreover, both men and women seemed to view women's domestic duties as innate and unrelated to the skill set required of farmers, and the women at the conference did not seem to believe that they were affected by the daily affairs discussed by their sons and husbands. But Margaret Washington believed that women could improve their situations.[18]

In 1893, therefore, she began holding "Mothers' Meetings" at which she taught local women and children simple lessons of domesticity, thrift, and "proper character." Participants found the sessions so beneficial that women began traveling long distances to attend, leading organizations across Alabama and ultimately other states to begin holding similar meetings. By 1908, the *Tuskegee Student* praised the Mothers' Meetings for beautifying the city and for teaching children to behave in accordance with middle-class standards.[19]

Extending her work in this vein, Washington and twelve other women founded Tuskegee's first official black women's group, the Tuskegee Woman's Club (TWC), on March 2, 1895. Many of the founders were married to men who played prominent roles at Tuskegee Institute and in the city, while others included teachers and other upstanding members of the community—in other words, they were solidly middle class. Membership initially required a recommendation from one of the founders, further heightening the club's exclusivity.[20]

Stressing the "general intellectual development of women" and working in such areas as temperance, jail reform, women's suffrage, and the Mothers' Meetings, the TWC created a community where middle-class women could receive intellectual and social elevation through discussion panels and various lectures. Members would then devise ways to share practical lessons with the larger community—usually by working with local women in their homes.[21] This approach, too, began to spread to middle-class black women across the United States, and according to journalist and antilynching crusader Ida B. Wells, clubs became "the new power, the new molder of public sentiments, to accomplish the reforms that the pulpit and the law have failed to do."[22]

As the TWC gained strength and influence, Margaret Washington began to forge connections with women of the North. On July 29, 1895, more than one hundred delegates representing fifty-four black women's clubs convened in Boston to form the National Federation of African American Women. The federation ultimately brought together more than thirty-five black women's clubs from twelve states and included not only "fine, cultured women" but also domestic workers. Margaret Washington was elected the first president.[23]

Almost immediately after its founding, the federation was invited to demonstrate black women's culture, skills, and talents as part of the Woman's Congress at the Cotton States and International Exposition held in Atlanta in the fall of 1895. Booker T. Washington also received an invitation to speak at the exposition, and on September 18 he delivered an address in which he proposed a solution for the "Negro problem"—the abysmal social and economic conditions in which southern African Americans lived and black-white relations in a region that was undergoing significant economic changes. In what became known as the Atlanta Compromise Speech, Washington declared, "The wisest among my race understand that the agitation of questions of social equality is the extremest folly. . . . It is important and right that all privileges of the law be ours, but it is vastly more important that we be prepared for the exercise of these privileges. The opportunity to earn a dollar in a factory just now is worth infinitely more than the opportunity to spend a dollar in an opera-house." In short, Washington was offering "to trade black acquiescence in disfranchisement and some measure of segregation, at least for the time being, in return for a white promise to allow blacks to share" in the nation's economic growth. The speech quickly made national headlines and received an enthusiastic response in both the North and the South and among both whites—who approved of his conditional acceptance of black inferiority—and most African Americans. It made Washington the undisputed leader of the black community. And as his prestige rose, so did that of his wife.[24]

At the July 1896 National Association of Colored Women's Clubs, the National Federation of African American Women merged with the Colored Women's League of Washington, D.C., and the Women's Era Clubs of Boston to form the National Association of Colored Women's Clubs (NACWC). Attendees elected Mary Church Terrell president of the new organization, which sought to "furnish evidence of moral, mental and material progress made by our people." Addressing the gathering, Margaret Washington described her efforts over the preceding year: "We have formed chapters, or branches, in Charleston, S.C., Memphis, Tenn., Philadelphia, Penn., and Brooklyn, N.Y. Since our organization, we have called public meetings to our churches to discuss topics affecting the interests of the race in the Southland and in our own section, with beneficial results."[25]

In 1898, Margaret Washington drafted the blueprint for the Alabama Federation of Colored Women's Clubs. The state federation provided Alabama women with a way to convey their goals to the national organization. Washington headed the federation, with assistance from Tuskegee graduate Cornelia Brown and Jennie B. Moton, wife of Robert Moton and subsequent First Lady of Tuskegee Institute. The state federation solicited support from state institutions such as health and juvenile agencies, and white philanthropists and attracted a large number of members. The state federation implemented programs to build community awareness, sponsoring the state's first black history program celebrating the birthday of race leader Frederick Douglass and sponsoring an essay contest to highlight African American achievements. The state federation also created the Mount Meigs Reformatory for Juvenile Negro Law-Breakers. The success of these activities resulted in large part from Washington's national influence and provided a model for other clubs and state groups. In addition to serving as Tuskegee's lady principal and president of the Alabama Federation, she simultaneously held the posts of first vice president of the NACWC and president of the TWC.[26]

In 1899 Washington formed the Southern Federation of Colored Women's Clubs, adding a regional organization that provided additional political visibility and another avenue for racial uplift. She traveled to Mississippi to organize its middle- and upper-class black women, and by 1903 the state had an array of black women's clubs. A decade later, Mississippi clubwomen joined the NACWC.[27]

On October 16, 1901, President Theodore Roosevelt invited the Washington family to dinner at the White House. While Douglass and other individual black leaders had met with presidents, the occasion represented the first time that an African American family had dined with the president and his family. The event shocked the country and provoked a firestorm of controversy, particularly among white southerners, who were appalled at this demonstration of respect for African Americans. Among the African American community, however, the visit cemented the Washingtons' status as race leaders, as Roosevelt declared his admiration for the Tuskegee president's "character, his devotion to the cause, and for what he has accomplished." The heightened attention on Booker T. Washington also meant an increased focus on his wife and her work to educate African American women and children. Margaret Washington used this momentum to further advance industrial training for women at Tuskegee. Writing in the *Tuskegee Student* in 1905, she declared, "I see no reason why [the black woman] should not take her place as teacher, homemaker, and in industrial pursuits such as millinery and dressmaking, filling an important place in her community, especially the South."[28]

To provide a communication network, the NACWC began publishing *National Notes*, edited by Margaret Washington. This position gave her a highly visible role in the organization and in turn ensured the visibility of the South in general and Alabama in particular. However, Washington's editorship of the paper came in for criticism by Wells. At the NACWC's 1909 meeting, Wells stated that delegates had complained about "the irregularity of the *National Notes*, about its failure to publish matter sent, [and] about the dissatisfaction of subscribers who had never received the paper." Wells requested a formal election to choose "an editor who would be responsible to the body." Rising to Washington's defense, NACWC members "hissed" Wells from the floor and accused her of acting selfishly and capriciously out of a personal animosity toward Booker T. Washington.[29]

The controversy did not affect Margaret Washington's status in the NACWC, and three years later the group elected her its president. Speaking to members in 1913, Washington pronounced them "the best women of the race" and credited the efforts of clubwomen for numerous community advances. She pointed out the NACWC's pioneering role in placing Bibles in public facilities such as hotels and restaurants and in calling for the separation of black children from adults in prisons and in the court system. As a consequence of the clubwomen's efforts, Washington declared, "the world at large realizes that the child must be saved in order to have the women and men needed for . . . development." During her four years at the organization's helm, the NACWC added more than three hundred new clubs.[30]

In 1915, Booker T. Washington's health began to deteriorate, and he died on November 14. While the death of her husband affected the whole country, Margaret Washington suffered the most, losing her best friend, mentor, and mate. However, she gave herself very little time to mourn and continued her work with the NACWC or the TWC.[31] At around this time, World War I brought tremendous changes to the United States, including the start of the Great Migration of southern blacks to northern and western cities. After having fought on behalf of the United States abroad, African American veterans began to ask why they should settle for less than full equality at home. These changes helped to set the stage for what would later become known as the "New Negro," who sought to escape Jim Crow and was willing to fight for equality.[32] This New Negro ideology implicitly rejected Booker T. Washington's Atlanta Compromise.

Margaret Washington was fully aware of these changes. In 1919 she wrote that black soldiers "have had to develop themselves physically, mentally, and morally; they have traveled and had contact with culture." In her eyes, however, these experiences meant that the veterans "necessarily . . . are going to be superior to our girls." In keeping with her long-standing advocacy of racial uplift, she believed that race leaders needed to provide women with the tools they would need to thrive in the new era.[33]

Those tools encompassed more than just practical skills. In 1921 she wrote to Robert R. Moton, who had succeeded Booker T. Washington as Tuskegee's president, "I am . . . sending you some examination questions for all of those trades here so you will get an idea that we [women] do not just use our hands down here, but we also use our minds." Still serving as Tuskegee's lady principal, Washington wanted to make sure that the school's male administrators understood that the lessons and curriculum did more than provide proficiency in the domestic arts and prepare women to be effective mothers. Female graduates not only would practice proper nutrition, sanitation, and food preparation but also teach those skills to other southern women.[34]

With the resurgence of the Ku Klux Klan and racial terrorism in the United States in the early 1920s, Washington concluded that her present club affiliations could not meet the challenges provided by the state of the race and looked abroad for additional solutions. In 1922 she formed the International Council of Women of the Darker Races (ICWDR), headquartered in Richmond, Virginia. With the creation of this international organization of black women, Washington became in her own way a Pan-Africanist.[35]

The ICWDR marked the height of African American women's international activism, which arguably had begun as early as 1850. The council sought to accumulate information on women of color both within the United States and around the world and then to use that information to promote self-improvement among members as well as the broader public. Washington and the other middle- and upper-class women involved in the ICWDR, including Mary Church Terrell and Addie W. Hunton, declared "that the many handicaps, barriers and embarrassments from which the women of the dark races suffer because of color prejudice can and must be overcome by a powerful organization working intensively along definite lines."[36] On August 14, 1922, "representatives from Africa, Haiti, West Indies, Ceylon," and national organizations in the United States met in Washington, D.C., and officially formed the council, declaring their goal to be the "economic, social and political welfare of the women of all the dark races."[37]

Washington particularly advocated the study of black women's history throughout the world. ICWDR activists encouraged elementary and secondary schools as well as colleges to incorporate lessons about women of the African diaspora into their curricula. The women of the ICWDR insisted on defining themselves, seeking support from the international community, and publicly challenging white supremacy.[38] They contributed to a school in West Africa and worked to improve conditions in Cuba and Haiti. Closer to home, as early as 1921, the organization helped to incorporate African American history and literature into Alabama's school curriculum.[39]

In 1924, Washington devised a plan that eventually transformed the ICWDR. She suggested that the women take an active role in their own communities by forming local study groups, an approach that reflected many of the techniques that she had used in Alabama. The women of the ICWDR labeled the new groups "Washington's Committees of Seven."[40]

Margaret Murray Washington continued her work on behalf of racial uplift until her death on June 4, 1925, at her home in Tuskegee. Writing in the

Tuskegee Messenger, fellow activist Jennie Moton declared, "Mrs. Washington is asleep—not dead. 'Can a woman die whose ideals live?' Tuskegee and our country have lost a great character in her passing, but her memory and influence will live always."[41]

Though Margaret Washington did not originate the idea of uplifting women through education, she put the theory into practice at the local level with the TWC; expanded it with state, regional, and national women's organizations; and then took it to the international stage via the ICWDR. She pushed the concept of African American and women's history as part of the project of racial uplift. She devoted her life to bettering the black community, and although she worked on national and international platforms, her initiatives in Alabama and the rest of the South always remained at the heart of her outreach.

NOTES

1. Induction Ceremonies, Alabama Women's Hall of Fame, Judson College, October 4, 1972, Tuskegee University Archives.

2. Jacqueline Ann Rouse, "Out of the Shadow of Tuskegee: Margaret Murray Washington, Social Activism, and Race Vindication," *Journal of Negro History* 81 (1996): 31; Emmett Scott, "Mrs. Booker T. Washington's Work among Colored Women," in Louis R. Harlan and Raymond Smock, eds., *Booker T. Washington Papers* (Urbana: University of Illinois Press, 1972–89), 9:289 (hereafter *BTWP*); Bernadette Pruitt, "Margaret Murray Washington," in Henry Louis Gates Jr. and Evelyn Brooks Higginbotham, eds., *African American Lives* (New York: Oxford University Press, 2004), 855; Clement Richardson, *The National Cyclopedia of the Colored Race* (Montgomery, Tenn.: National Publishing, 1919), 63; Henry F. Kletzing and William Henry Crogman, *Progress of a Race; or, The Remarkable Advancement of the Afro-American* (Atlanta: Nichols, 1903), 446; "Margaret Murray Washington," Margaret Murray Washington Papers, Tuskegee University Archives; U.S. Census, 1870, 1880; Noralee Frankel, *Freedom's Women: Black Women and Families in Civil War Era Mississippi* (Bloomington: Indiana University Press, 1999), 56; "Born in Slavery: Slave Narratives from the Federal Writers' Project, 1936–1938," vol. 9, Mississippi Narratives, Library of Congress, https://memory.loc.gov/cgi-bin/ampage?collId=mesn&fileName=090/mesn090.db&recNum=0 (accessed August 17, 2016); Jacqueline Jones, *Labor of Love, Labor of Sorrow: Black Women, Work, and the Family, from Slavery to the Present* (New York: Basic Books, 1985), 52–57; Frank Lincoln Mather, ed., *Who's Who of the Colored Race: A General Biographical Dictionary of Men and Women of African Descent* (Chicago: n.p., 1915), 278; Scott, "Mrs. Booker T. Washington's Work," 9:290. Various sources give different years for Margaret Murray Washington's birth—most commonly 1861, 1864, and 1865. Both the 1870 and 1880 Censuses list her as being born in 1861, although the Fisk Institute published her birth year as 1864.

3. Hugh Barbour and J. William Frost, *The Quakers* (New York: Greenwood, 1988), 8–9; "Training Dusky Griseldas: Mrs. Booker T. Washington's Missionary Work among Negro House-Wives," *San Francisco Bulletin,* August 2, 1903, *BTWP,* 7:248; Pruitt, "Margaret Murray Washington," 855; Scott, "Mrs. Booker T. Washington's Work," 9:289.

4. Darlene Clark Hine and Kathleen Thompson, *A Shining Thread of Hope: The History of Black Women in America* (New York: Broadway, 1998), 154–57.

5. Charles Harris, *The History of the National Association of Colored Women's Clubs: A Legacy of Service* (Washington, D.C.: Mercury, 1984), 21.

6. Bobby L. Lovett, *The African American History of Nashville, Tennessee, 1780–1930* (Fayetteville: University of Arkansas Press, 1999), 57, 131; David H. Jackson Jr., *Booker T. Washington and the Struggle against White Supremacy: The Southern Educational Tours, 1908–1912* (New York: Palgrave MacMillan, 2008), 18, 123; U.S. Census, 1870.

7. Scott, "Mrs. Booker T. Washington's Work," 9:289; Kathleen Thompson, "Margaret Murray Washington (1865–1925)," in Darlene Clark Hine, Elsa Barkley Brown, and Rosalyn Terborg-Penn, eds., *Black Women in America: An Historical Encyclopedia* (Bloomington: Indiana University Press, 1993), 2:1233–34.

8. "Margaret J. Murray to the Fisk Herald, August, 1887," Fisk University Archives; Linda Lane, *A Documentary of Mrs. Booker T. Washington* (Lewiston, N.Y.: Mellen, 2001), 24–28.

9. W. E. B. Du Bois, *Dusk of Dawn: An Essay toward an Autobiography of a Race Concept* (1940; New York: Schocken, 1968), 31–32; *New York Times*, January 5, 1887; Joe M. Richardson, *A History of Fisk University, 1865–1946* (Tuscaloosa: University of Alabama Press, 1980), 48; Lane, *Documentary*, 99; *Fisk Herald*, May 1884. The Colored Methodist Episcopal High School later became Lane College.

10. Margaret Murray Washington, "The Negro Home: Address Made by Mrs. Booker T. Washington at the International Conference Held in Memphis, Tennessee, October 1920," in Margaret Murray Washington Papers; "On Visitors," *Fisk Herald*, July 1889; Joe M. Richardson, *History*, 48; William Jenkins to Booker T. Washington, March 3, 1889, *BTWP*, 2:514; Margaret James Murray to Booker T. Washington, May 5, 1889, *BTWP*, 3:3; "The New South," *Fisk Herald*, January 1889; Paula Giddings, *Ida: A Sword among Lions: Ida B. Wells and the Campaign against Lynching* (New York: HarperCollins, 2008), 364–65; Louis R. Harlan, *Booker T. Washington: Making of a Black Leader, 1856–1900* (Oxford: Oxford University Press, 1980), 161.

11. Booker T. Washington, *Up from Slavery: An Autobiography* (New York: Doubleday, 1901), 1–2, 19; Jackson, *Booker T. Washington*, 1–2, 15–18; Louis R. Harlan, *Booker T. Washington: The Wizard of Tuskegee, 1901–1915* (Oxford: Oxford University Press, 1983), 19–21; Robert J. Norrell, *Up from History: The Life of Booker T. Washington* (Cambridge: Belknap Press of Harvard University Press, 2009), 26–27, 30–31, 39–40, 209; Harlan, *Booker T. Washington: Making of a Black Leader*, vii; John Edgar Wideman, *My Soul Has Grown Deep: Classics of Early African American Literature* (Philadelphia: Running Press, 2001), 632–33; Robert Francis Engs, *Freedom's First Generation: Black Hampton, Virginia, 1861–1890* (Philadelphia: University of Pennsylvania Press, 1979), 142–44; Robert Francis Engs, *Educating the Disfranchised and Disinherited: Samuel Chapman Armstrong and Hampton Institute, 1839–1893* (Knoxville: University of Tennessee Press, 1899), 78.

12. Lawson Bush, "Davidson, Olivia A. (1854–1889)," Blackpast.org, http://www.blackpast.org/aah/davidson-olivia-1854-1889 (accessed August 16, 2016); Lane, *Documentary*, 32, 33; Giddings, *Ida*, 98, 100; Margaret James Murray to Booker T. Washington, October 1891, *BTWP*, 3:174–75; Norrell, *Up from History*, 100–101.

13. "The Certificate of Marriage of Washington and Margaret James Murray," Tuskegee, Alabama, October 12, 1892, *BTWP*, 3:268.

14. J. W. Gibson and W. H. Crogman, *The Colored American: From Slavery to Honorable Citizenship* (Atlanta: Nichols, 1901), 527; Paula Giddings, *When and Where I Enter: The Impact of Black*

Women on Race and Sex in America (New York: Morrow, 1984), 99, 112; Margaret Murray Washington, "The Negro Home: Address Made by Mrs. Booker T. Washington at the International Conference Held in Memphis, Tennessee, October 1920," 6, Margaret Murray Washington Papers; Student to Margaret Murray Washington, n.d., in Lane, *Documentary*, 25–26, 28, 33; Jon W. Gibson, *Progress of a Race* (Naperville, Ill.: Nichols, 1925), 179; Kletzing and Crogman, *Progress of a Race*, 446; Norrell, *Up from History*, 119; *BTWP*, 3:305; David H. Jackson Jr., *A Chief Lieutenant of the Tuskegee Machine: Charles Banks of Mississippi* (Gainesville: University Press of Florida, 2002), 13; Willard Gatewood, *Aristocrats of Color: The Black Elite, 1880–1920* (Bloomington: Indiana University Press, 1990), 347.

15. Emmett Scott to Margaret Murray Washington, April 15, 1916, Booker T. Washington Papers, Tuskegee University Archives; Giddings, *Ida*, 435–36.

16. Joe M. Richardson, *History*, 56.

17. Kevin K. Gaines, *Uplifting the Race: Black Leadership, Politics, and Culture in the Twentieth Century* (Chapel Hill: University of North Carolina Press, 1996), 20–28.

18. *BTWP*, 1:135; Charles Harris Wesley, *History of the National Association of Colored Women's Clubs: A Legacy of Service* (Washington, D.C.: Mercury, 1984), 21–23; Rouse, "Out of the Shadow," 33; Scott, "Mrs. Booker T. Washington's Work," 9:291–92; Milton C. Sernett, *Bound for the Promised Land: African American Religion and the Great Migration* (Durham: Duke University Press, 1997), 31; Norrell, *Up from History*, 106–7.

19. *Tuskegee Student*, December 5, 1908.

20. "The Tenth Annual Report of the Tuskegee Woman's Club," *BTWP*, 8:475.

21. Leon Litwack, *How Free Is Free?: The Long Death of Jim Crow* (Cambridge: Harvard University Press, 2009), 13; Norrell, *Up from History*, 39–40; Giddings, *Ida*, 165; Margaret Murray Washington, "The Gain in the Life of Negro Women," *Outlook Magazine*, January 1904.

22. Gibson and Crogman, *Colored American*, 527; Jacqueline Anne Rouse, *Lugenia Burns Hope, Black Southern Reformer* (Athens: University of Georgia Press, 1992), 89; Cynthia Neverdon-Morton, *Afro-American Women of the South and the Advancement of the Race, 1895–1925* (Knoxville: University of Tennessee Press, 1989), 133; Shirley J. Carlson, "Black Ideals of Womanhood in the Late Victorian Era," *Journal of Negro History* 77 (1992): 61–73; *Baltimore Afro-American Ledger*, January 17, 1903; Giddings, *Ida*, 440.

23. Pruitt, "Margaret Murray Washington," 856; Elizabeth Lindsay Davis, *Lifting as We Climb* (Washington, D.C.: National Association of Colored Women, 1933), 18; Giddings, *When and Where I Enter*, 98, 105; "Minutes of the First National Conference of Colored Women, 1896," Records of the National Association of Colored Women's Clubs, Part 1, Minutes of National Conventions, Publications, and President's Office Correspondence (Microfilm), Reel 1; Lane, *Documentary*, 165; Gerda Lerner, "Early Community Work of Black Women," *Journal of Negro History* 59 (1974): 161; Beverly W. Jones, "Mary Church Terrell and the National Association of Colored Women, 1896 to 1901," *Journal of Negro History* 67 (1982): 20–21; Nancy Woloch, *Women and the American Experience* (New York: McGraw Hill, 2006), 290; Darlene Clark Hine, *Black Women in United States History* (Brooklyn, N.Y.: Carlson, 1990), 2:320–21.

24. Lane, *Documentary*, 165; Louis R. Harlan, *Booker T. Washington: The Wizard of Tuskegee, 1901–1915* (New York: Oxford University Press, 1983), viii; Derrick P. Aldridge, "Atlanta Compromise Speech," *New Georgia Encyclopedia*, 2015, http://www.georgiaencyclopedia.org/articles/history-archaeology/atlanta-compromise-speech (accessed August 16, 2016).

25. "Minutes of the First National Conference of Colored Women, 1896"; Hine, *Black Women*

in United States History, 2:323; Lane, *Documentary*, 165–66; Linda O. McMurry, *To Keep the Waters Troubled: The Life of Ida B. Wells* (New York: Oxford University Press, 1998), 347–48; Margaret Murray Washington, "National Association of Colored Women's Clubs," June 1913, Margaret Murray Washington Papers; Wesley, *History*, 3–4; Lane, *Documentary*, 5, 171, 178; *NACWC Constitution*, Margaret Murray Washington Papers; Mary Church Terrell, *A Colored Woman in a White World* (Washington, D.C.: Ransdell, 1940), 192; Giddings, *When and Where I Enter*, 101; Daphne Spain, *How Women Saved the City* (Minneapolis: University of Minnesota Press, 2001), 98; Beverly W. Jones, "Mary Church Terrell," 20–21.

26. Neverdon-Morton, *Afro-American Women*, 137–38; Raymond W. Smock, *Booker T. Washington: Black Leadership in the Age of Jim Crow* (Chicago: Dee, 2009), 93–98; Addie Hunton, "The Southern Federation of Colored Women," *Voices of the Negro* 2 (1905): 850–51; Rouse, "Out of the Shadow," 31–46; David M. Oshinsky, *"Worse Than Slavery": Parchman Farm and the Ordeal of Jim Crow Justice* (New York: Free Press, 1996), 79; *Minutes of the Ninth Annual Session of the Alabama Federation of Colored Women's Clubs*, Salem, Alabama, July 3–6, 1907, Tuskegee University Archives.

27. Lane, *Documentary*, 216, 218, 223; Jackson, *Chief Lieutenant*, 23–24.

28. "Mr. Roosevelt Explains the Dinner Incident," *New York Times*, October 19, 1901; Jackson, *Booker T. Washington*, 3; Norrell, *Up from History*, 5–6; Harlan, *Booker T. Washington: The Wizard of Tuskegee*, vii–viii; Giddings, *Ida*, 436; *Tuskegee Student*, April 1, 1905.

29. McMurry, *To Keep the Waters Troubled*, 347–48; Thomas Holt, "The Lonely Warrior: Ida B. Wells-Barnett and the Struggle for Black Leadership," in John Hope Franklin and August Meier, eds., *Black Leaders of the Twentieth Century* (Urbana: University of Illinois Press, 1982), 48–60; Norrell, *Up from History*, 176–77; Rouse, "Out of the Shadow"; Giddings, *Ida*, 493.

30. Neverdon-Morton, *Afro-American Women*, 137–38; Wesley, *History*, 70, 467; Twenty-Fourth Conference Minutes, June 6, 1922, Margaret Murray Washington Papers; Lane, *Documentary*, 169–71; Rouse, "Out of the Shadow," 34; Davis, *Lifting as We Climb*, 171; Thompson, "Margaret Murray Washington," 1234; Pruitt, "Margaret Murray Washington," 856; Clement Richardson, *National Cyclopedia*, 63; Martha H. Patterson, *Beyond the Gibson Girl: Reimagining the American New Woman, 1895–1915* (Urbana: University of Illinois Press, 2010), 50–51, 58; "National Association of Colored Women's Clubs Speech Delivered in 1913," *Nashville Globe*, June 20, 1913.

31. Jackson, *Chief Lieutenant*, 187; Harlan, *Booker T. Washington: The Wizard of Tuskegee*, 452–54; Norrell, *Up from History*, 418–19.

32. Adriane Lentz-Smith, *Freedom Struggles: African Americans and World War I* (Cambridge: Harvard University Press, 2009), 1.

33. *Tuskegee Student*, March 1, 1919; Nell Irvin Painter, *Creating Black Americans: African American History and Its Meaning, 1619 to the Present* (New York: Oxford University Press, 2007), 189; Lane, *Documentary*, 54.

34. Margaret Murray Washington to Robert R. Moton, May 17, 1921, Margaret Murray Washington Papers, Tuskegee University Archives; Lane, *Documentary*, 131; Neverdon-Morton, *Afro-American Women*, 36–37.

35. Margaret Murray Washington, "We Must Have a Cleaner Social Morality," *Charleston News and Courier*, September 13, 1898; "National Organization of Colored Women Formed," [1922], Tuskegee Institute News Clippings File, 1899–1966 (Microfilm), Reel 17.

36. Lane, *Documentary*, 64, 218–19; "National Organization of Colored Women Formed."

37. "National Organization of Colored Women Formed."

38. Mary Jackson McCrorey to Margaret Murray Washington, May 16, 1924, Mary Church Terrell

Papers (Microfilm), Reel 5, Library of Congress; Michelle M. Rief, "'Banded Close Together': An Afrocentric Study of African American Women's International Activism, 1850–1940, and the International Council of Women of the Darker Races" (PhD diss., Temple University, 2003), 170.

39. Lane, *Documentary*, 218–19.

40. Margaret Murray Washington to Mary Church Terrell, October 4, 1924, Christine Smith to Margaret Murray Washington, December 3, 1924, both in Mary Church Terrell Papers (Microfilm), Reel 5.

41. Hallie Quinn Brown, *Homespun Heroines and Other Women of Distinction* (Xenia, Ohio: Aldine, 1926), 1233; Lane, *Documentary*, 7, 293–94; Wesley, *History*, 90–91; Rouse, "Out of the Shadow," 31; Hine and Thompson, *Shining Thread*, 226.

Pattie Ruffner Jacobs

Personal Anxiety / Political Triumph

WAYNE FLYNT AND MARLENE HUNT RIKARD

In July 1895, deep into one of her "blue" periods, nineteen-year-old Pattie Ruffner sat in the Birmingham home of her married sister and spilled her despair onto the pages of a well-worn diary. Although Pattie appeared gay and flirtatious to her circle of friends and suitors, her writing revealed an introspective and often insecure young woman frequently haunted by family traumas and thwarted ambitions. Unable to afford the college education she so desperately wanted, she agonized, "I so long to stretch my limbs before they are dwarfed and cripply [*sic*] by disuse."[1]

In her emotional and intellectual turmoil, however, is also evidence of the struggle and determination that one day would bring her to public prominence as Alabama's bold suffragist leader. Twenty years after she wrote those words, she led a brilliantly organized campaign challenging the Alabama legislature to allow voters to decide if the women of the state should have the right to vote. The legislature's intransigence propelled her to the national scene. In years to come she held offices in the National American Woman Suffrage Association, the League of Women Voters, the Democratic Party, and the federal government as part of the New Deal.

The path that led this bright young woman to such heights of public service was not an easy one. Society's limiting expectations for women of her generation as well as personal family circumstances caused her much suffering, but they also helped to forge a strong feminist philosophy that thrust her into numerous progressive causes.

Though Pattie's teenage angst often grew from difficult situations within her immediate family, the history of the Ruffners helped fuel her personal ambitions. Born in 1875 in Malden, West Virginia, Pattie had relatives who included

PATTIE RUFFNER JACOBS
Birmingham Public Library Archives.

successful businessmen, prosperous farmers, innovative and inventive entre-
preneurs, well-respected ministers, and college presidents.

Descended from German-speaking Swiss immigrants, the Ruffners migrated
in the eighteenth century from Pennsylvania to the Shenandoah Valley and
then to the wilderness of Kanawha County, Virginia. Beginning as farmers,
they ignored skeptical neighbors as they experimented with wells for brine,
constructed furnaces, and developed a prosperous salt manufacturing industry. From their location on the Kanawha River, family members used the river
system to build a salt trade in such developing cities as Cincinnati; Louisville;
St. Louis; Evansville, Indiana; and Nashville.[2]

Pattie Ruffner had an example of both political involvement and defying conventional thinking in the person of her grandfather, Lewis Ruffner Sr. After
receiving a fine education, he entered the salt trade in the 1820s. But his career
also included several terms in the Virginia state legislature, interrupted by time
in Louisville, Kentucky, as the sales agent for a salt trust. His service in the state
legislature included the crucial year of 1861. Despite the staunch Confederate
loyalty of many of his family and friends, he was a Union man who eventually
helped develop West Virginia's state constitution.[3]

Pattie's great-uncle, Henry Ruffner, provided her with a model of educational and academic achievement. A graduate of Washington College (now
Washington and Lee University) in Lexington, Virginia, Henry studied theology, preached, and did mission work before returning to his school to serve as
professor and president. His son, William Henry Ruffner, was a minister, state
superintendent of education, and president of Virginia's State Female Normal
School.[4]

Lewis Ruffner Jr., Pattie's father, entered the salt business as well, but his timing was unfortunate. He began just as the Kanawha salt industry started to decline: floods destroyed many of the wells, new competition developed along the
Ohio River, and the Civil War disrupted the river trade.[5] By the early 1880s Lewis
was in Nashville working as a broker for grain, flour, and general merchandise.
His wife, Virginia, and their four children joined him in 1883. Pattie, the youngest, enrolled at the Ward Seminary for Young Ladies. The family began to scat-
ter when the oldest sister, Julia, married and moved to Louisville. Sister Bertha
married and moved to Birmingham, followed by her brother, Lewis W. Ruffner.[6]

While Pattie was still in school in Nashville, she enjoyed summer visits to
Bertha's home, but her family circumstances became increasingly difficult. Her
father's lack of business success, undoubtedly worsened by the depression of
the 1890s, evidently led to excessive drinking and her parents' separation. After
her graduation in 1893, Pattie and her mother moved into Bertha's home in

Birmingham, and Pattie found herself living with a resentful older sister and attending a teacher training school instead of a university, as she desired: "I would give most anything to be able to go to college, Vassar, Wellesley, or Cornell, next year but [it] is a vain wish for no such future for me."[7]

Denied her dreams and despondent about her future, the young woman confided to her diary, "Life is surely not worth the living. Or at any rate where one is poor and has to sacrifice and struggle." What kept her going was her deep love for her mother and the voracious reading that substituted for the formal education she was denied. Outwardly, life appeared good. Talented, she earned spending money as a paid vocalist for churches, by selling hand-painted party cards, and by writing a society column for a local newspaper. A beautiful young woman, she had many eligible young bachelors taking her to dances, the theater, and other social events.[8]

Despite this male attention, Pattie's personal anxiety about marriage and relationships grew intense, influenced not only by her mother's situation but also by her sister Julia's divorce from an abusive husband. Agonized questions about marriage and passages from marital advice books fill the diary pages. In July 1896, pursued by many beaux, she wondered "whether to sink individuality and principle in a sea of conventionality"—the "conventionality" she feared marriage would bring.[9]

The increased urgency of her questioning resulted from "the certain knowledge that to me belongs the entire love of the one man whose heart I covet." Despite Pattie's misgivings about marriage, a new suitor, Solon Jacobs, had captured her heart. A native of Kansas, Jacobs had recently arrived in Birmingham as an employee of a railroad but soon began to build on business opportunities afforded by the young Magic City.[10]

Pattie delayed her decision about marriage by persuading her mother's brother to accept some paintings in exchange for enough funds to study music, art, and foreign languages in New York City for a year. Living frugally, she roomed with eight other girls and relished the excitement the city and her studies provided. She also rejoiced in the daily letters from Jacobs promising that he would wait for her. She returned to Birmingham in 1897, set aside her fears, and joined her future with Solon in February 1898. Ironically, the union brought her the stability, emotional support, and financial security that allowed her to "stretch her limbs" and eventually to pursue a public career.[11]

During the early years of their marriage, Solon left his position as the Birmingham general agent for the Central Railroad and Banking Company of Georgia and undertook various business endeavors related to the city's industries. Solon Jacobs and Company dealt in mine, mill, and furnace supplies, but his greatest success came when he and fellow businessman Henry Badham organized the Birmingham Slag Company in 1909. The men realized that slag, supposedly a waste by-product of the steel mills, had great economic potential as ballast for railroad tracks and later as an aggregate for road construction. In 1916 Solon sold the company to the Ireland family, and it became the core of what later became the Vulcan Materials Company, a global concern.[12]

As Solon's wife, Pattie Jacobs entered the social world of the city's industrial elite. With the financial resources to employ help to care for two daughters, born in 1901 and 1907, she expanded her experience through travel and cultural activities. In 1906 she joined a three-month tour of Europe, leaving Solon and daughter Madelein in the care of a nurse and cook. Although Pattie's letters begged for more news of "baby and her sayings," she was still having "the trip of my life, so full of educational benefit, besides the pleasure."[13]

In Birmingham, Pattie Jacobs became increasingly involved with a circle of women who promoted cultural and civic activities. Alabama women of the late nineteenth and early twentieth centuries who moved into public roles usually followed a path similar to women across the nation: participation in church work and missionary societies, the Woman's Christian Temperance Union, women's clubs, education reform efforts, and crusades such as the anti-child-labor campaign. Jacobs's life followed many of the same patterns. She served as president of the Birmingham Art League and vice president of the Music Club. She campaigned against Alabama's convict lease system and child labor even though some of the men in her social circle utilized children and convicts in their industries.[14]

For Ruffner, republican motherhood (the expectation that American women were responsible for nurturing their husbands, children, and communities) began to intersect with public politics (crusades for various reforms that would protect children and enhance their communities) when she appeared before the Birmingham City Commission to request funds to allow the Music Club to host performances in public parks. Years later, Jacobs recounted how the cavalier rejection of her request convinced her that had she represented four hundred registered voters instead of four hundred voteless women, the outcome would have been different. She also recalled the horrors of child labor and her belief that it would never be eradicated until women could vote.[15]

Recruiting sympathetic women from conventional venues (the Highland Book Club, Independent Presbyterian Church, and coalitions against child labor and convict lease), Jacobs channeled her frustrations over male resistance to reform into the Birmingham and Alabama Equal Suffrage Associations. Lillian Roden Bowron and Nellie Kimball Murdock attended church with Jacobs and had already begun to take active roles in reform movements. Bowron's father-in-law was one of the city's leading industrialists, and Murdock chaired the Alabama Child Labor Committee. Bossie O'Brien Hundley, the third of Ruffner's key lieutenants, was a devout Catholic, daughter of a former mayor, and wife of a prominent judge.

In 1911 Pattie Jacobs and Nellie Murdock formed the Equal Suffrage League of Birmingham, and within eighteen months it had grown from the original thirty charter members to five hundred. A year later, local clubs joined together to form the Alabama Equal Suffrage Association (AESA). Both the Birmingham and state groups elected Jacobs president. She rented the entire floor of a downtown office building to serve as headquarters for the combined organizations, attracting female store clerks by providing working women with a place to sit down, eat their lunches, and (perhaps most importantly) use the toilet, since some workplaces had no inside sanitary facilities. Although Jacobs belonged to a liberal Presbyterian church not known for aggressive evangelism, she spread the suffrage gospel among female clerks in a manner that even the apostle Paul would have appreciated.

As president of the Equal Suffrage League, Jacobs focused on a single theme each year (the status of women; the way local and state governments worked; the historical evolution of women's rights) before attempting to push a women's suffrage amendment through the 1915 Alabama legislature.[16]

Educating women gathered in union halls, churches, and study, garden, and book clubs required Jacobs to speak constantly, a task made possible by her husband's wealth and the endless supply of gardeners, nurses, cooks, and housekeepers who kept her two daughters safe and the Jacobs home functioning efficiently. Jacobs gradually became one of the suffrage movement's most articulate and confident speakers, a consummate diplomat when that role advanced her cause but a wickedly satirical debater when required. Aided by her own careful study of political structures and the sage advice of well-placed men (especially Judge Oscar Hundley, Bossie O'Brien Hundley's husband), Ruffner also became a tactically gifted legislative lobbyist. She quickly realized that few of her opponents, male or female, had read as extensively, researched as thoroughly, or thought as strategically as she had. Courteous or curt as the situation required, she was the intellectual match for all male antagonists and the master of most, sometimes directing savage and dismissive wit at the traditional pabulum they used against women's suffragists.

In 1912 her obvious skills attracted the attention of the National American Woman Suffrage Association (NAWSA), whose leaders were impressed by her strong support of a federal suffrage amendment over endless campaigns to enfranchise women state by state. But many of her AESA colleagues still paid homage to the tainted goddess of state's rights. Most southern state suffrage leaders also demanded that efforts to enfranchise women proceed through state legislative channels.

Although Jacobs never had confidence that Alabama legislators would enfranchise women, she also did not want to divide her legions along state's rights and federal lines. In 1914, therefore, she focused Alabama suffragists' undivided attention on the state legislature. She organized committees and began fundraising. Oscar Hundley drafted a simple women's suffrage amendment to the state constitution. Bossie Hundley chaired the AESA's Legislative Committee and served as chief state lobbyist. Jacobs hired out-of-state advisers, including both influential leaders of the Southern States Woman Suffrage Conference, who rejected federal action, as well as NAWSA leaders, who endorsed it. Both organizations pledged to make Alabama's 1915 legislative session the year's pivotal campaign.

Pattie Jacobs began the crusade with a statewide membership drive featuring public rallies and downtown speeches from atop soapboxes and soft drink crates. Bossie Hundley began a petition drive at local fairs, seeking ten thousand signatures calling on the legislature to submit a constitutional amendment to voters. Hundley also appointed a suffrage "godmother" in each of the state's sixty-seven counties tasked with contacting, polling, and convincing local legislators, who were also deluged with suffrage clippings and literature. A committee of four, including Pattie Jacobs and Bossie Hundley, prepared to lobby the legislature during its entire 1915 session in Montgomery, the state capital. They endorsed Representative Malcolm Smith Carmichael of Coffee County, an enthusiastic suffragist, as their candidate for House Speaker.

Jacobs also organized an auxiliary Men's League of the AESA. She recruited influential pro-suffrage males, especially prominent husbands of suffragists, asking AESA members to nominate five or six prominent males in each community.[17] Ominously, the effort was not a statewide success, although chapters were established in Cullman and Birmingham.

Bossie Hundley prepared a questionnaire for each member of the legislature, and Amelia Worthington, a schoolteacher from a prominent Birmingham family who had been suspended for a month while in teacher training for distributing suffrage literature, began work on the first issue of the *Alabama Suffrage Bulletin* in October 1915. A four-page tabloid, the newsletter celebrated the growth of the suffrage cause in Alabama from two leagues with a handful of members to sixty-nine chapters with three thousand members, making it one of the South's largest state suffrage associations.[18]

The third annual AESA convention, which had met in Tuscaloosa in early February 1915, was devoted almost entirely to the upcoming legislative campaign. It attracted forty-seven delegates, nearly twice as many as the year before. The convention began on a sour note when the pastor of Tuscaloosa's Presbyterian Church, who had been asked to open the gathering with a prayer, prefaced the prayer with a disquisition on why he opposed women's suffrage. Seething with rage, the AESA's secretary recorded in her notes, "After thus clearing his conscience and making peace with his Maker for the crime of praying in the presence of Suffragists, he proceeded to pray."[19] It was not a promising omen for the proceedings to come.

Perhaps reacting to the parson's lecture, AESA created a Standing Church Extension Committee to educate church members and ministers about suffrage. Delegates reelected Pattie Jacobs president and Bossie Hundley vice president and then turned their attention to legislative strategy. Some timid attendees suggested that AESA push for limited suffrage in presidential elections or local contests. Both Jacobs and Hundley argued forcefully against any compromise short of full political equality.[20]

Jacobs then turned to the looming legislative session, reporting that she had written to Alabama's congressmen concerning suffrage and reading aloud their replies. Only Representative Richmond Pearson Hobson of Greensboro was unreservedly supportive. Jacobs then urged delegates to send postcards, telegrams, and letters to Alabama legislators, who had just begun the new session. She reported that some positive legislation had already passed, including a bill that allowed women to serve on school boards.[21]

Jacobs's attempt to involve Alabama's members of Congress in the 1915 drive for a state suffrage amendment revealed her tactical shrewdness and their insincerity. She informed each congressman about the bill to submit the question of equal suffrage to Alabama voters. Because most of the delegation had declared that women's suffrage should be left for states to decide, she asked each congressman merely to assist the AESA in securing for the people the right to do so, not necessarily to endorse the cause. If congressmen were sincere in their state's rights philosophy, they could not object to allowing Alabama's white male voters to resolve the question by ballot. She therefore urged Alabama's U.S. representatives to contact state legislators on behalf of the bill. She particularly targeted U.S. senator Oscar Underwood, who had defeated Representative Richmond Hobson, a pro-suffrage progressive, in a bitter Democratic primary. Jacobs wrote to Underwood that suffragists had made no public attacks on him during the primary (though they had worked hard for Hobson behind the scenes) because they believed that the suffrage question was a state rather than federal issue. Her argument was disingenuous: Jacobs clearly did not believe that voting was a state matter, though many other AESA members did. Nevertheless, she told Underwood that Alabama suffragists "prefer obtaining the ballot at the hands of the men of our own State and we are now giving them for the first time the opportunity to act. We hope very much that we shall not be forced to seek suffrage by Federal action."[22] Hobson was the only member of Congress to swallow her bait.

Jacobs had no better luck with the state's chief executive. When she saw Governor Emmet O'Neal in a Montgomery restaurant during a break from legislative lobbying, she invited the governor to her table. He declined this invitation to indigestion.[23]

Events were not going the suffragists' way. In fact the timing of the legislative session could hardly have been worse. If Jacobs's strategy consisted of three parts—education, organization, and legislation—the educational phase had been entirely too brief. But faced with a system in which the legislature met only once every four years, she had no choice. If legislators failed to act during the 1915 session, Alabama suffragists would have to look to the federal government for relief.

Jacobs appealed to suffragists nationally for speakers and money through the pages of the *Woman's Journal*, the weekly publication of the Southern States Woman Suffrage Conference. The response was heartening. Money flowed in, and suffragists such as Kentucky's Madeline Breckinridge and Tennessee's Dr. Lilian Johnson volunteered to speak.[24] Although Jacobs's first choice, Jeannette Rankin, a Montana suffragist who in 1916 became the first woman elected to the U.S. House of Representatives, was not available, NAWSA sent Lavinia Engle, a 1912 graduate of Antioch College. Jacobs had originally intended to use Engle as a lobbyist, but in light of legislators' questions about whether Alabama women really desired the franchise, using Engle to lobby in Montgomery seemed counterproductive. Her presence in the capitol would open AESA to charges that northern outsiders were trying to dictate to the legislature. Engle consequently spent her time organizing new suffrage locals, a job she did with energy and success, and advising on political strategy. Her efforts and the enthusiasm generated by the legislative campaign resulted in the creation of nearly three dozen new chapters in 1915.[25]

In December 1914, Bossie Hundley wrote to each legislator asking his position on women's suffrage. Anyone who did not return the form received a personal visit from local suffragists, who completed the form themselves. Hundley then created a file on each legislator. The questionnaire also solicited the legislator's job and religion and whether he was married or a Confederate veteran. Suffragists often embellished the responses with editorial comments.

These files provide tremendous insight into Alabama legislators in the early years of the twentieth century. H. A. Bradshaw of Florence wrote frankly that he favored suffrage personally but would not vote for it because that would constitute an act of political suicide. B. F. Ellis wrote that he opposed suffrage, prompting the local suffragist who interviewed him to add, "Mr. Ellis is distinctly of the old school, quite an elderly man and violently and unreasonably prejudiced." John W. Lapsley, a Presbyterian attorney, opposed women's suffrage because he did not think it "in the Divine plan of salvation." John A. Darden of Goodwater opposed because African American women would be allowed to vote. Hundley had difficulty discerning clear patterns among the replies. Most respondents were noncommittal. Among those who gave opinions, four Methodist legislators opposed suffrage, while five favored it. Baptists split four to three against, Presbyterians were three to one in favor, and Episcopalians split evenly. The Black Belt, which had a large black population, was more united in opposition to suffrage than other regions.[26]

Judge Hundley advised the AESA's lobbying committee about how to frame the bill as well as the best strategy for dealing with racial concerns. The grandfather clause, he told them, would disfranchise black women just as it did black men, thus eliminating one powerful argument raised by opponents.[27]

Engle, though not officially a lobbyist, utilized her considerable skills from other battlegrounds. She studied the state's legislature and its procedures, then advised the AESA executive committee that she anticipated a split legislative session with a recess in the middle. She thought it wise to introduce the bill during the first part of the session, then concentrate lobbying efforts in the second half. This approach would enable members to focus on individual legislators based on early assessments about their positions.[28]

Kate Gordon, state's rights leader of Louisiana suffragists, added her endorsement by furnishing each legislator with copies of the *Woman's Journal*, which would presumably sanctify and sanitize the issue for legislators who opposed federal determination of a state's voting standards.[29]

AESA opened a Montgomery headquarters in the Grant Theater Building near the capitol on January 12, 1915. From this base, suffragists spread out across the city, leaving suffrage literature in hotel lobbies, plastering buildings with posters, and buttonholing legislators.[30] The quality of the legislature, its dominance by special interests, and the legislative process were working against the suffrage cause. Although Jacobs announced in September 1914 that five of the seven legislators from Jefferson County favored women's suffrage, a *Birmingham Age-Herald* poll of all legislators a month later predicted that women's suffrage would lose badly. However, a large number of legislators remained uncommitted and might be open to persuasion.[31]

The amendment proposed to the legislature stated the issue simply: "The right of citizens of this State to vote, shall not be denied or abridged on account of sex."[32] But the process of passage was more complicated. A proposed amendment to Alabama's constitution required a three-fifths majority of the 106 members of the House and 35 senators. If passed by the legislature, the amendment would be placed on the November 1916 general election ballot, a simple majority vote would either approve or defeat the measure. That referendum would require a second costly campaign by AESA.

Alabama's legislature was not renowned for either its disinterested public spirit nor its forward-looking progressivism. The Progressive Era had altered the body's reputation a bit as a modest reform program trickled through its halls. But beyond the emotional Prohibition issue, little substantively had changed. Senator Ed Norman, a legislative power, wrote to his friend Oscar Underwood early in the 1915 session that although a large majority favored banning alcohol, beyond that issue "the legislature appears to be evenly balanced and conservative. It appears . . . no freakish or drastic legislation is to be encouraged by the lawmakers." At around the same time, Forney Johnston, a Birmingham attorney and key Underwood lieutenant, complained that the Alabama Power Company had helped Prohibitionists organize the legislature because the corporation wanted to protect itself from unfavorable regulation. As a result, representatives from the Tennessee and Coosa River Valleys who desired electrical power had voted for Prohibition at the company's urging.[33]

When the legislature opened in January, the suffrage cause gained an unlikely champion in the House. Representative J. W. Green of Selma (Dallas County) presented the bill to his colleagues. Green was a locomotive engineer who had pulled the train carrying Birmingham delegates to the 1913 AESA convention in Selma. When the train stopped for lunch, suffragists had engaged him in conversation and had "converted" him to their cause. The following year he asked for the privilege of introducing the suffrage amendment, a request the AESA gladly granted. The story was a public relations coup and soon entered suffragist mythology, with press releases referring to Green as "the Sir Walter Raleigh of the legislature."[34] H. H. Holmes of Baldwin County, who had no such dramatic conversion experience to relate, introduced the bill in the Senate.

Suffragists presented their arguments to a joint session of the committees on privileges and elections on January 28. Bossie Hundley marshaled an impressive array of advocates, including Engle, Jacobs, and Julia Tutwiler, a prison reformer and teacher and one of the state's most respected women. Rabbi B. C. Ehrenreich of Montgomery and Representative Green also testified on behalf of the bill, addressing virtually every major issue: action by the legislature would forestall federal government intervention in the state's right to determine suffrage; women's suffrage was inevitable; national Democratic Party leaders had endorsed state action; Alabama had an opportunity to be the first southern state to enfranchise women; traditional measures designed to restrict voting by black men would also apply to black women; a vote for the bill did not reflect the personal preference of legislators on the merits of women's suffrage but merely extended to male voters the democratic right to decide the issue themselves. Green offered the most emotional testimony, arguing that opposition to the bill came mainly from whiskey interests.[35] But following these presentations, the House committee voted to postpone the bill indefinitely.

On February 5 Dr. Anna Howard Shaw, president of NAWSA, spoke for an hour to a joint session of the legislature on behalf of the bill; then, as Engle had predicted, the legislature adjourned until July without taking action. Suffragists were prepared to use the recess to their advantage. Bossie Hundley sent the Recess Joint Committee on the Judiciary a carefully reasoned argument in favor of action by the state as opposed to federal involvement and then began an intensive lobbying effort. The legislative battle furnished invaluable publicity and inspired suffragists to even greater efforts.[36]

Despite her doubts, Pattie Jacobs was indefatigable. While a nurse, a cook, and her husband cared for the Jacobs daughters, Pattie Jacobs devoted virtually all her time between March and August to the cause. In March she spoke in East Lake and Jasper as well as to the Young Men's Hebrew Association of Birmingham. In April she toured west-central Alabama. In May she spoke three times in Gadsden and Clanton, twice in Anniston and Talladega, and once each in Oxford, Columbiana, Calera, Childersburg, and Wilsonville. From just one of these trips she returned with 610 signatures on a petition in favor of a referendum. New suffrage associations sprang up in small communities and larger towns across the state: Jackson, Muscadine, Fruithurst, Edwardsville, Heflin, Beason's Mill, Wedowee, Demopolis, Anniston, Talladega, Goodwater, Alex City, Ozark, Citronelle, Sheffield, and Northport. Montgomery's Huntingdon College also formed a suffrage group. By November 1915, the AESA had nearly seventy chapters, each of which circulated petitions, contacted legislators, and lobbied for the appointment of women to city and county school boards.[37]

Pattie Jacobs and Bossie Hundley used an appearance before the Recess Committee on the Judiciary to increase petition activity. One committeeman told them he was willing to vote for suffrage if petitioned to do so by 25 percent of male voters. Jacobs urged AESA members, including isolated suffragists in small chapters, to help obtain those signatures by circulating petitions at church and club meetings, at social gatherings, and in stores and other public places. The Mobile Association placed a coupon in city newspapers reading, "I am in favor of submitting the question of equal suffrage to a vote of the people," with a line for a signature, and then placed a box at a central location in which people could deposit signed coupons. The Birmingham Men's League, which consisted primarily of males whose wives were active in the Equal Suffrage League of Birmingham, petitioned legislators separately for favorable action on the amendment.[38]

When the legislature reconvened in mid-July, Jacobs and Hundley had become more optimistic about their chances: they had a petition containing more than ten thousand signatures demanding action. On August 11 the bill came before the House for full discussion. The following day Hundley locked horns with acid-tongued congressman Tom Heflin at a barbecue in Wetumpka. After Hundley asked the crowd of some two thousand to support women's suffrage, Heflin urged women to stay home where they belonged and mold public opinion by their "own sweetness of character" and influence over their sons and husbands. He had not enjoyed Hundley's speech and declared that he did not believe that many Alabama women desired to vote. In fact, he was willing to allow Alabama women to decide the issue for themselves. If a majority of women wanted the vote, he would not object. Hundley, who knew Heflin's position well and who had tried to bait him into a debate for some time, was waiting to spring a trap. She interrupted Heflin and asked if he would yield to a question. Heflin, accustomed to such parliamentary maneuvers in congressional debates but never by a woman on the stump in Alabama, was caught by surprise and yielded. Hundley seized the advantage, chiding that Heflin surely knew very well that such a referendum by women was impossible because the Alabama Constitution had no provision for it and that suffragists therefore depended on chivalrous men to voluntarily extend the vote. Heflin ignored her argument, told a funny story, and dropped the subject of women's suffrage altogether, to the considerable delight of correspondents, who reported his retreat from the formidable Hundley.[39] This incident simply added to Hundley's and Jacobs's cautious optimism as the legislature moved toward final action.

But late in August, their optimism vanished, the casualty of two sudden developments that undid years of careful planning. Legislators received copies of an anonymous fifteen-page pamphlet, *A Protest against Woman's Suffrage in Alabama*, sponsored by "Alabama Democrats on Behalf and in Defense of the Large Unorganized Majority of the Women of Alabama." The publication claimed that women's suffrage was the "most dangerous blow aimed at the peace and happiness of the people of Alabama and white supremacy since the Civil War." Northern advocates of suffrage were trying to destroy both sexual and racial distinctions in the state. Forcing women to serve on juries violated southern traditions and would result in white women being locked up all night in a jury room with white and black men. Alabama suffragists consisted of "a few misguided enthusiasts" who were unhappy with their lives or desired personal political advancement. The suffrage enthusiasm of the times grew from feminism, which advocated the right of all women to be mothers, whether married or not. Reopening the suffrage question imperiled Alabama with the possibility of African American rule and federal intrusion, violated state's rights, and was inspired by the Republican and Bull Moose Parties.[40] Jacobs and other Alabama suffragists believed that Joseph B. Evans, clerk of the City Court of Selma, had written the pamphlet after suddenly realizing that the amendment had a real chance of passing.[41]

Jacobs and Hundley worked desperately to contain the damage, laboring all night to prepare a rebuttal pamphlet for distribution to legislators the following day. They argued that the bill before the legislature merely gave male voters the right to determine the issue. Women would not be forced to sit on juries but could choose to do so. Advocates of the bill were not foreign radicals but members of local suffrage associations and 10,600 Alabama men and women whose names appeared on petitions. Alabama women wanted down from any pedestal that they shared with aliens, idiots, and criminals. Their demand for action by their own legislators should itself refute the charge that they opposed state's rights. Suffragists were loyal southern Democrats who did not seek African American suffrage. They reassured legislators that the same restrictions that disfranchised black men would continue to disbar black women. Finally, they denied allegations that Shaw was a radical feminist and an advocate of free love. She was, in fact, a Christian minister who opposed both licentiousness and the liquor traffic.[42]

On August 24, the second blow fell. Representative J. W. Green, the suffragists' Sir Walter Raleigh, betrayed them, withdrawing support for his own bill. Whether influenced by the pamphlet written by his fellow Selma resident, Evans, or by more sinister motives—suffragists alleged that he had been bought by liquor money—Green attacked women's suffrage as a plot by NAWSA to re-enfranchise southern blacks. Pattie Jacobs privately acknowledged that Green's defection was devastating but publicly tried to put the best spin possible on the defection. In a statement laced with sarcasm, she argued that "few causes could so nobly stand the desertion of a man so faithful, so stable, so strong in his convictions, so unswerving in his devotion as Mr. Green has proved himself to be."[43]

Frantic efforts by Jacobs and Hundley postponed the vote by a day, but on August 25, the issue finally came up for resolution. Suffragists filled the semicircular balcony of the historic House chambers, the same room where Alabama had seceded from the Union and the Confederate government had been formed. A huge banner hung from the balcony, proclaiming "Alabama Women Ask the Ballot on the Same Terms as Alabama Men." Bedecked in yellow sashes, supporters of the vote watched their allies below, many of them wearing yellow flowers to demonstrate their allegiance. Representative Isadore Shapiro of Birmingham dealt first with the pamphlet and then with the turncoat Green. The anonymous antisuffrage pamphlet, Shapiro argued, was "a book of lies and its authors . . . curs and renegades." Warming to his subject, he reminded his colleagues that in January Green had said that the only opponents of suffrage were "whiskyites and crooked politicians." Looking straight at the Selma representative, Shapiro inquired angrily, "Which one are you?" Green, sputtering with rage, denied making the earlier statement and said he had changed his mind after talking with his wife. Should he listen to her, he asked rhetorically, or to Shaw? Shapiro landed the last punch: "If I had been in favor of a measure for twenty years and had been a fool, I'd rather remain a fool than be a traitor."[44] Bossie Hundley agreed. She wrote on the bottom of the legislative questionnaire where Green had proclaimed his longtime support for women's suffrage: "Introduced the Bill at his request. Betrayed the trust, speaking and voting against it."[45] When debate ended, the amendment carried by a vote of fifty-two to forty-two, twelve votes short of the required three-fifths supermajority. Laughter greeted Representative Green's negative vote.[46] Senators saw no reason to anger constituents on behalf of a cause already lost in the House, and when the bill came to a vote in the upper chamber, it went down to defeat by a vote of twenty to twelve.

Pattie Jacobs publicly promised to return every four years until women possessed the right to vote; privately, however, she knew that her best legislative effort had failed. Many legislators who personally opposed women's suffrage had been willing to allow voters to decide the issue, and convincing a majority of Alabama males to support the referendum would be a much harder task. After the Louisiana legislature passed a similar bill in 1918, the state's male voters rejected women's suffrage despite active support from the governor, the state Democratic Executive Committee, and most legislators and elected officials. Jacobs realized that her problem was not the legislature but Alabama's male voters and quickly steered the AESA in a new direction.

Pattie Jacobs had always had little confidence in state's rights or Alabama males. The 1915 campaign was tactical, preserved the unity of state suffragists, and proved her point. Henceforth, she turned her efforts toward passage of a federal law and never looked back on the legislative charade.

As the youngest state president of a suffrage association, Jacobs had shown poise and speaking skills in 1913 when invited to testify before the U.S. House Rules Committee. A satirical exchange with Alabama congressman Thomas Heflin left the suffragist gallery in stitches and Heflin in a sputtering rage. After the 1915 defeat, Jacobs became an uncompromising advocate of the Susan B. Anthony Amendment.[47]

Since Jacobs had already proven her mettle as a confident, spell-binding debater, NAWSA now dispatched her on national speaking tours until the Nineteenth Amendment went into effect in 1920. She won election as a national officer in NAWSA as well as its successor, the League of Women Voters. State Democratic leaders forgave her alleged radicalism by electing her their first National Democratic Committeewoman. She also was chosen by the Democratic National Committee and to its executive committee. She met and became friends with Eleanor Roosevelt, who entrusted her agenda to Jacobs for advocacy while struggling to keep Franklin Delano Roosevelt's political career alive during the 1920s. A grateful President Roosevelt later rewarded Jacobs's friendship and administrative skills by naming her to head the Women's Division of the National Recovery Administration's Consumer Advisory Board and to serve as a spokesperson for the Tennessee Valley Authority. In 1933, Alabama's Democrats tapped her to head the state effort to repeal Prohibition. These endeavors did not come without costs, taking her away from her family, but there is no evidence that she ever doubted or regretted the course she had plotted for her life. And few Alabama political leaders ever advanced so unpopular a cause so near legislative victory as she did in 1915.

Pattie Jacobs suffered a heart attack and died on December 22, 1935, by which time she had been casting ballots for a decade and a half. But Alabama had still not ratified the Nineteenth Amendment. In fact, it did not do so for another eighteen years.

NOTES

1. Pattie Ruffner Diary, "Heart Throbs," July 11, 1895, Jacobs Collection, Special Collections, Samford University Library.

2. For Ruffner family history, see Charles Hedrick, *History of the Ruffner Family* (Charleston, W.Va.: *Charleston Gazette*, 1884); sketches originally published in *Charleston Gazette*, 1884, Frank Barton Thompson Collection, MSS A T471 585, Filson Club; W. S. Laidley, *History of Charleston and Kanawha County, West Virginia, and Representative Citizens* (Chicago: Richmond-Arnold, 1911);

William Henry Ruffner, "The Ruffners," *West Virginia Historical Magazine Quarterly*, April 1901, 31–38; George W. Atkinson, *History of Kanawha County* (Charleston, W.Va.: *West Virginia Journal*, 1876); Mark Flasch and Pam Flasch, *Peter Ruffner and His Descendants* (Luray, Va.: Ruffner Family Association, 2007).

For descriptions of the salt industry and the Ruffners' involvement, see Anne Royall, "Description of Burning Spring and the Kanawha Valley Salt Industry," in *Sketches of History, Life, and Manners in the United States, 1826*, available at http://www.wvculture.org/history/royalsalt .html (accessed January 26, 2014); Ruth W. Dayton, *Pioneers and Their Homes on Upper Kanawha* (Charleston, W.Va.: West Virginia Publishing, 1947); John E. Stealey III, *The Antebellum Kanawha Salt Business and Western Markets* (Lexington: University Press of Kentucky, 1993); "Articles and Pledge of the Kanawha Salt Association," Rebecca Putney Beattie Collection, MS92-12, West Virginia State Archives.

3. Hedrick, *History*, 9–11; Atkinson, *History*, 303–5; Dayton, *Pioneers and Their Homes*, 157.

4. Hedrick, *History*, 6–8; Atkinson, *History*, 180–85; Laidley, *History*, 234, 256–57; Dayton, *Pioneers and Their Homes*, 197–99; *The National Cyclopedia of American Biography* (Clifton, N.J.: White, 1892), 217–19; Richard J. Altenbaugh, *Historical Dictionary of American Education* (Westport, Conn.: Greenwood, 1999), 317–19.

5. Stealey, *Antebellum Kanawha Salt Business*, 184–97.

6. Nashville City Directories, 1882–93; Tennessee Marriage Book 8, 143, 220, Metro Archives of Davidson County, Tennessee; Flasch and Flasch, *Peter Ruffner*, 101; "Announcement 1884–85 W. E. Ward's Seminary for Young Ladies," Tennessee State Library, Nashville; "Announcement, 1885–86, W. E. Ward's Seminary for Young Ladies," Williams Library, Belmont College.

7. Ward's Seminary, "Alumnae Card," "Catalog, 1892–93," Williams Library, Belmont College; Ruffner Diary, December 29, 1893; for summer in Birmingham, see entries beginning August 5, 1892; for move to Birmingham, see August 8, 1893; for Teacher Training School, see entries beginning September 24, 1893. The 1892 Nashville City Directory lists separate residences for her parents. Virginia Ruffner subsequently identified herself as a widow even though her husband was alive and they were not divorced.

8. Ruffner Diary, September 24, 1893. Numerous diary entries from 1893–95 give names of beaux and list social events to which young men took Pattie. The diary also includes a list of thirty-six books read in 1894–95. Scattered entries note a bidding war between two prestigious city churches for her vocal talents. Despite her active social life, bouts of "the blues" frequently appear in entries. She mentions writing for the *Birmingham Age-Herald* in the entries for March 7, 1895, and April 7, 1895.

9. Ruffner Diary, May 19, 1895; Circuit Court Records, Jefferson County Kentucky, #7727, Equity Action, 1895, Kentucky Department of Libraries and Archives; Ruffner Diary, July 25, 1896 (followed by passages she copied from a variety of books about relationships between men and women).

10. Ruffner Diary, March 10, 1896 (mentions of Solon Jacobs begin in March 1895); Albert Burton Moore, *History of Alabama and Her People* (Chicago: American Historical Society, 1927), 2:521; George M. Cruikshank, *A History of Birmingham and Its Environs* (Chicago: Lewis, 1920), 2:361–63.

11. Ruffner Diary, February 8, 1898; Flasch and Flasch, *Peter Ruffner*, 104. On December 10, 1896, Pattie began a new diary, "Bohemia," about her time in New York, but she was too busy to make many entries.

12. Moore, *History*, 521; Cruikshank, *History*, 362–63; Ed England and Irene Preston, "Part 1: The Birmingham Slag Company," *Profile: A Publication of Vulcan Materials* (n.p.); Birmingham City Directories, 1888–1909.

13. Pattie Jacobs to Solon Jacobs, August 30, 1906, from the Grand Hotel in Venice. Letters from Pattie Jacobs to Solon Jacobs, July–September 1908, while on a trip to Canada and Chicago, discuss household affairs concerning the cook, redecoration of the Birmingham home, Birmingham friends also vacationing in Canada, and the purchase of fall wardrobes for Pattie and the children. "Mammy" accompanied Pattie and the daughters. Collection of letters and postcards from Joel Hillhouse, Birmingham, Alabama, to be deposited in Jacobs Collection.

14. *Alabama Blue Book and Social Register, 1929* (Birmingham: Blue Book Publishing, 1920), 126; "Biographical Service, Alabama Women, Mrs. Solon Jacobs," Alabama League of Women Voters Correspondence, File 91A, Auburn University Archives.

15. Mrs. Solon Jacobs, Biographical Service—Alabama Women, National American Woman Suffrage Association, [1919?], Series H, Box 126, National League of Women Voters, Library of Congress. In another autobiographical sketch, Jacobs alluded to frustrations over her inability to end child labor while omitting the reference to musicals in the park as a source of her support for women's suffrage: "Mrs. Solon Jacobs (Pattie Ruffner), Birmingham, Alabama," Box 1261, Eleanor Roosevelt Papers, Franklin Delano Roosevelt Library.

16. Unidentified clipping, Jacobs Scrapbooks, vol. 2, Birmingham Public Library.

17. Alabama Equal Suffrage Association Minute Book, beginning October 9, 1912, Alabama State Archives.

18. *Alabama Suffrage Bulletin*, October 1915, Jacobs Papers.

19. AESA Minute Book.

20. Ibid.

21. Ibid.

22. Pattie Jacobs to Oscar W. Underwood, January 20, 1915, Oscar Underwood Papers, Alabama State Archives.

23. Unidentified clipping, Jacobs Scrapbooks, vol. 2.

24. *Woman's Journal*, December 12, 1914.

25. AESA Minute Book.

26. James H. Pride to Bossie O'Brien Hundley, December 12, 1914, "A Record of the Unsuccessful Campaign Waged by the Alabama Equal Suffrage Association to Get the 1915 Legislature to Submit an Equal Suffrage Amendment to the Vote of the People: A Scrapbook Kept by Mrs. Bossie O'Brien Hundley, State Legislative Chairman, Alabama Equal Suffrage Association, Birmingham, Alabama, 1914–1915," Archives, Birmingham Public Library (hereafter Hundley Scrapbook).

27. AESA Minute Book.

28. Ibid.

29. Lee N. Allen, "The Woman Suffrage Movement in Alabama" (master's thesis, Auburn University, 1949), 74.

30. Ibid., 74–75.

31. Unidentified clipping, Jacobs Scrapbooks, vol. 2; *Birmingham Age-Herald*, October 4, 1914.

32. For a copy of the bill and the enabling legislation, see Hundley Scrapbook.

33. Ed Norman to Senator Oscar W. Underwood, January 27, 1915, Forney Johnston to Underwood, January 12, 1915, both in Underwood Papers.

34. Unidentified clipping, February 2, 1913, Jacobs Scrapbooks, vol. 2.

35. Allen, "Woman Suffrage Movement," 74–77.

36. Ibid., 78–80.

37. AESA Minute Book; "Report of the Organization Committee, 9 February 1916," Alabama Woman Suffrage Organization Papers, Correspondence, 1914–1919, Alabama State Archives.

38. AESA Minute Book; H. H. Snell to Hon. ——, July 12, 1915, "Correspondence, 1914–1919," Alabama Woman Suffrage Organization Papers.

39. *Montgomery Daily Times*, n.d., Hundley Scrapbook.

40. *A Protest against Woman's Suffrage in Alabama*, Alabama Woman Suffrage Organization Papers.

41. Nellie N. Somerville to Laura Clay, November 18, 1915, Laura Clay Papers, University of Kentucky Archives.

42. *Reply to the Anonymous "Protest against Woman's Suffrage in Alabama,"* Alabama Woman Suffrage Organization Papers.

43. *Birmingham Age-Herald*, August 25, 1915, Hundley Scrapbook.

44. Ibid.; Allen, "Woman Suffrage Movement," 84.

45. J. W. Green Questionnaire, Hundley Scrapbook.

46. Ibid.

47. *Birmingham News*, December 6, 1913, Jacobs Scrapbooks.

Ida E. Brandon Mathis

The One-Crop System and the Limits of Progressive Economic Reform

REBECCA S. MONTGOMERY

The emergence of Ida Mathis as a central figure in the early twentieth-century movement for crop diversification signaled how much had changed in the status of southern women since the Civil War. A married woman with a master's degree and penchant for scientific agriculture, she launched a career advising men on how to make farming pay. She held her own with bankers and businessmen, managed unruly tenants, and canvassed the state and nation multiple times spreading her message of economic cooperation and social uplift. Her approach to reform defies easy categorization, as it combined aspects of male and female political culture and promoted cooperation while accepting the basic tenets of white supremacy. A bundle of contradictions, Mathis also illustrates how much white southerners resisted change. Her crusade against the one-crop system provided hope to poor farmers in a time of uncertainty and left the state well positioned for economic mobilization during World War I, but it did little to challenge a racial order that perpetuated rural poverty. In this she epitomized the limits of southern progressivism, the blind spot that plagued otherwise forward-thinking men and women.

Ida Elizabeth Brandon was born in 1856 in Lauderdale County, on the Tennessee River in the northwest corner of Alabama. She spent her early years in Florence, the county seat, and graduated from the Florence Synodical Female College in 1874. Even though some newspaper accounts would later claim she had no background in agriculture because she lived all of her life in town, her father owned farmland in the area and took her with him on visits to the property. They had a close relationship, in part because Brandon's mother died when she was fourteen years old, and she credited her father with teaching her the "practical side of farm life." She taught natural science at Oxford College in

IDA E. BRANDON MATHIS, 1917, SPEAKING TO FARMERS

From *America Magazine*.

Oxford, Alabama, before marrying cotton merchant Giles Huffman Mathis in November 1882. She then moved with her husband to the rural community of Gadsden in the northeastern part of the state and for the next two decades spent most of her time absorbed in raising a son and two daughters. When she decided to begin investing in farm properties around 1903, she tackled farming as an intellectual challenge, determined "to learn it scientifically, and then go and apply it practically." Her first experiment with farm management was such a success that she established a career rehabilitating worn-out lands and reselling them for profit.[1]

Ida Mathis chose to take on a difficult set of problems that dated back to the 1860s–70s, when the economic impact of the Civil War reduced farmers' self-sufficiency. Financial hardship during the last few years of the war stripped many farmers of their livestock and crops, and the postwar shortage of cash and credit made economic recovery difficult. Most farmers lacked the resources to expand production or grow crops more intensively, and they were poor risks in the unlikely event that they had access to formal credit. Informal credit, such as that extended by landlords and merchants, was frequently exploitative. Those who had no choice but to purchase supplies on credit paid higher prices than customers paying cash and were charged exorbitant interest rates on what they owed. One result was a cycle of indebtedness that steadily increased the ranks of tenancy: by 1910 more than 60 percent of Alabama farmers were tenants. A related problem was farmers' overreliance on cotton: its relatively high value per acre influenced them to focus all of their resources on cotton cultivation in hopes that good prices would finally free them from debt. Moreover, landlords dictated the terms of leases and merchants who extended credit frequently required farmers to grow mostly cotton. As farmers abandoned their traditional "safety-first" practice of prioritizing household needs, they had few alternate sources of income when cotton did poorly. These aspects of the one-crop system helped to create a population of poor farmers who were at the mercy of fluctuating cotton prices and had little opportunity for upward mobility.[2]

Against the advice of family and friends, Mathis deliberately purchased properties that had lost their value and set about rehabilitating both land and tenants. Her larger goal was to prove that diversified farming using sustainable methods could be profitable even when practiced on a small scale. She divided her first purchase of 1,060 acres into 50-acre plots and required the tenants on each farm to plant 22 acres in cotton and 16 acres in corn, with the remaining acreage divided among food and feed crops. She specified exactly how fields would be prepared for planting and the number of hogs and cattle her tenants had to raise for food purposes. Mathis initiated farming operations with winter

cover crops that were plowed under to enrich the soil, a practice tenants repeated every year. The remedies she implemented had been advocated by agricultural experts in the U.S. Department of Agriculture and state colleges of agriculture since at least the 1870s, but few southerners implemented them in such
a regimented and systematic manner. Mathis used detailed tenant contracts,
provided chore lists for every week of the year, and offered incentive prizes to
obtain her tenants' cooperation. She bought her first property for eight dollars
an acre and sold it six years later for forty dollars an acre.[3]

Although the degree of control Mathis asserted over her tenants' lives was
intrusive, to say the least, she was genuinely committed to promoting their
economic independence. Instead of treating them simply as a source of cheap
labor, she treated them as partners—albeit unequal ones—and encouraged
them to be more ambitious. She took them to her banker and cosigned loans
so they could pay off past debts, certain that her farming plans for the next year
would enable them to repay the loans with cash to spare. The tenants' greater
self-sufficiency—resulting from her insistence on safety-first farming—would
keep them debt-free and allow them eventually to purchase their own homes.
Mathis's scheme sought not only to generate profit for her but also to release
poor farmers from indebtedness and transform them from transient tenants to
responsible property owners. Improvements would accrue to the larger community as well. Financially secure parents would send their children to school
rather than keeping them in the fields, property values would rise, and local
businesses would thrive from the increased customer base.[4]

Mathis tried to convince townspeople and businessmen that her cooperative
model of rural reform would benefit everyone. A favorite story used to drive
home this message involved her efforts to help a home demonstration agent
with a girls' tomato canning club. When the local agent complained about lacking the resources necessary to reach the neediest girls, Mathis loaned the agent
a horse and buggy so that she could deliver tomato seed in the hills of Etowah
County. The agent returned five weeks later to say that the girls were eagerly
growing tomatoes but did not have the money for cans. Mathis's first attempt
to solicit donations met with defeat when the chamber of commerce turned her
down. She then pressured members of a local women's club into taking out a
loan for the supplies and secured their help in selling the tens of thousands of
cans of tomatoes the club produced. This effort required briefly boycotting local
merchants, who insisted they sold only Maryland and Virginia tomatoes, until
the stores agreed to place the local tomatoes on shelves. Mathis triumphantly
concluded that the four-hundred-dollar loan produced six thousand dollars
worth of business for the town, as the girls used the proceeds from tomato sales

to purchase clothing, household goods, and farm supplies. The obvious moral of the tale was that the prosperity of town and country was linked: everyone in the community benefited from helping its poorest members.[5]

Despite her remarkable success as a progressive farmer and rural reformer, Ida Mathis probably would have remained only locally known if not for the outbreak of war in Europe in 1914. The beginning of the First World War created a crisis for cotton farmers, who had increased production in response to favorable prices and were set to harvest a record sixteen million bales when foreign trade was interrupted by the onset of war. Between July and November, cotton prices fell from twelve cents per pound in 1913 to seven cents per pound, a 40 percent drop. In his report for the fiscal year that ended in September, Alabama commissioner of agriculture and industries R. F. Colb declared, "If cotton is still king, for the present at least he is a monarch without a crown." Still reeling from the suddenness of the disaster, he and his department were "at a complete loss to know what to do or what to recommend" to farmers. Southern bankers who had extended credit based on the projected value of the cotton crop were equally alarmed. In November the Alabama Bankers' Association (ABA) held an emergency meeting and developed a two-pronged response to the crisis. First, the bankers resolved to organize businessmen and farmers into county committees to promote diversification and encourage the substitution of food crops for cotton. Second, they resolved to extend credit only to producers who agreed to reduce acreage in cotton to no more than half the amount planted in 1914.[6] Encouraged by U.S. treasury secretary William McAdoo's statement that the war would increase demand for food crops, Alabama bankers decided to use their control of credit to shape the state's agricultural policies.

Mathis quickly emerged as a central figure in Alabama's response to the financial crisis. In early 1915 she represented the Anniston Chamber of Commerce at a statewide meeting of business and professional leaders that convened in Birmingham to discuss the problems facing the agricultural economy. Impressed by her knowledge and speaking abilities, the group employed Mathis to address farmers on crop diversification and safety-first practices in a series of meetings held across the state during February and March. At the conclusion of the tour, businessmen, bankers, and farmers gathered at the Tutwiler Hotel in Birmingham to discuss how to maintain the momentum. Attendees formed the Alabama Diversified Farming Association and chose Mathis to serve as temporary president at the state level, with three men representing branches in the northern, central, and southern parts of the state. On behalf of the organization, Mathis returned to the Tutwiler Hotel in mid-May to address the bankers gathered there for the ABA annual conference. After hearing her success story, the banking association's agricultural committee promptly hired her to work as its field agent and arranged to share her salary and travel expenses with the state commissioner of agriculture. Several months later she agreed to participate in a separate diversification crusade that canvassed eighty-three counties in four states surrounding the city of Memphis, Tennessee.[7]

The campaigns launched in Alabama and Tennessee set a precedent for Mathis's career as a public figure by casting her in a leadership role typically held by men. The ABA had no female members, and Mathis was the only woman temporarily accorded a position on one of its committees. Other leaders in the bankers' crusade were male professionals in the Alabama Department of Agriculture, state extension services, and local business organizations. The Tennessee movement was sponsored by the Memphis Business Men's Club, which had created a Farm Development Bureau to determine how to respond to the agricultural crisis. Club members worked to form a broad base of support that included local businessmen, social clubs, railroad and telephone companies, agricultural schools and colleges, and newspapers. Although seven of the ten office workers who orchestrated the fieldwork were women, Mathis was one of only two women employed as speakers. They distributed literature and gave talks in three counties per day for twenty-three days in November and December, addressing topics that ranged from diversified farming and eradication of the cattle tick to canning and home sanitation.[8]

Although it was not at all unusual for women to be active in rural reform, Ida Mathis was unique in her focus on business and financial concerns. Southern conservatism on the issue of gender equality had historically constrained women's public activism, and female reformers typically provided leadership in areas that could be construed as a natural extension of their domestic roles. The field of domestic science established women's expertise in public health matters that directly affected home and family, such as household sanitation and nutrition, and their interests as mothers justified leadership in child labor and educational reform. Women often worked productively with men in campaigns aimed at shaping public policies on such issues. For example, the Alabama School Improvement Association and members of the educational and school improvement committees of the Alabama Federation of Women's Clubs worked closely with officials in the Alabama Department of Education to build public support for a slate of legislative reforms.[9] Conversely, leadership in fields still defined as masculine remained solidly male. Mathis transcended this barrier in scientific agriculture and finance because her practical knowledge and impressive business acumen quickly gained the respect of male professionals. Equally important, male professionals who needed to gain public support for agricultural reforms valued her ability to draw a crowd and keep it enthralled while she outlined solutions to farm problems.

Bankers and businessmen believed that a long-term commitment to diversification was necessary for economic growth and stability and hoped that Mathis could influence farmers to stay the course. Declines in cotton production had already occurred following the boll weevil's arrival in Alabama in 1913, prompting the quick response to the drop in prices the following year. Worried that farmers would abandon food and feed crops as soon as the international market crisis passed, the Birmingham Chamber of Commerce brought Federal Reserve Board member William P. G. Harding to town in March 1916 to reinforce the diversification message. An Alabamian and former ABA president, Harding declared that cotton prices had risen slightly in 1915 only because of reduced production. He cautioned farmers against assuming that the European war would soon end and that pent-up demand for cotton would send prices soaring. Harding also praised Mathis's work as ABA field agent, calling her "perhaps the most useful citizen of Alabama."[10]

Mathis was even more valuable than bankers realized, as she brought national attention to their diversification campaign and the possibilities for economic investment in the state. Her May 1915 address before ABA members was the beginning of a whirlwind schedule of appearances. Her speeches to bankers in Chicago and St. Louis that fall made such an impression that excerpts from her talks were widely printed in business journals and newspapers. The Farm Mortgage Bankers Association of America, sponsor of the St. Louis conference, was so awed by Mathis that its officers sent a copy of her speech to President Woodrow Wilson. The related publicity led to invitations for Mathis to speak the following year in Georgia, Kansas, Michigan, North Carolina, South Carolina, Ohio, and Virginia. Although the ABA initially had a difficult time getting the local press to cover the diversification campaign, the situation changed dramatically as a result of Mathis's popularity. In the spring of 1916 Frank Willis Barrett, associate editor of the *Birmingham Age-Herald*, assigned a reporter to accompany Mathis on her journeys across the state and began publishing detailed accounts of every appearance. When the newspaper held a reception in her honor at the Tutwiler Hotel, Barrett introduced Mathis as the "Joan of Arc" of agriculture, "the person who would lead the people of Alabama out of the wilderness."[11]

One reason for Mathis's popularity was that her speeches were a carefully crafted combination of folksy language and humor, shrewd analysis, and practical solutions. She began talks by addressing her audiences in a manner designed to disarm them. She opened her speech at the Banker-Farmer Conference in Chicago with the salutation, "Well, neighbors!" and she often began talks to farmers by saying matter-of-factly, "I am just a farmer, like you are." She also had a knack for getting people to laugh at themselves while acknowledging that she spoke the truth. One saying often repeated in the press was her observation that Alabama farmers were "killing the grass to raise the cotton to buy the grass." Growing cotton required farmers to suppress the grasses that grew so well in the state's temperate climate, but keeping the grasses down required purchasing imported hay at more than double the cost of growing it. Farmers could only laugh ruefully at their foolishness when it was described in such persuasive, commonsense terms. In this and many other instances, Mathis used everyday language to put audiences at ease, presenting, as one admirer put it, "the 'hog and hominy' view as it was never presented before." This approach helped her gain acceptance from farmers who would have viewed with skepticism the message of an agricultural expert in a business suit.[12]

Mathis's ability to present herself as an ordinary woman who truly cared about the plight of farmers helped to narrow the cultural distance that separated an educated wealthy woman from the rural poor. As ABA field agent she toured the state delivering speeches as many as five times per day to the thousands of men and women from town and countryside who flocked to hear her. A large woman with a kindly face who looked like someone's aunt, she delivered a message of hope and a plan of action. Mathis commonly stated that her main concern was the producer, the person suffering most from the collapse of cotton prices. Referring to unfavorable terms of credit, she complained that "everybody wants to get interest FROM the farmer, while very few take interest in the farmer." She spoke of the hardships endured by tenant farmers and promised that they could escape debt if they grew their own food and made cotton a surplus cash crop. Audiences were heartened by the thought that following a simple plan of diversification would enable families to establish bank accounts, own their homes, and educate their children.[13]

However, Mathis's early speeches and articles for professional audiences often portrayed poor farmers in a less flattering light than the message she delivered in the field. Her talks at bankers' and investment conferences on the financial opportunities offered by Alabama's moderate climate and cheap land often employed humorous stories that played to negative stereotypes of poor whites. She described the mountain whites of northeastern Alabama as an ignorant and shiftless bunch and was fond of explaining how she convinced them to knuckle down and work by having them jailed for drunkenness and fighting. In other instances Mathis appeared to blame tenants for their poverty, complaining that they would not grow gardens and that the average farmer was poor because "he likes to be poor and don't want to be anything else." She frequently claimed that tenants were renters by choice, describing them in one article as "a good-natured happy hearted set of people who prefer to have a jolly good time rather than to own a home." Her depiction of tenants as naughty but amiable children who needed to be taught self-discipline drew laughter and applause from businessmen North and South.[14]

Such comments were less damning than they appear at first glance because Mathis usually tempered them with environmental explanations of the origins of irresponsible white tenancy. She described how the one-crop system had produced indolence among a formerly self-sufficient, self-respecting yeomanry by creating long periods of idleness. Farmers who grew only cotton were accustomed to having four months of rest between October and March, and the fields did not require their daily attention during the rest of the year. Mathis maintained that cotton really only required about 160 days of labor scattered throughout the growing season, meaning that farmers were idle for 200 days per year. This life had been their lot for so long that they had no impetus to change and no knowledge of how to improve their situation; however, they could be lifted up and restored to their former state with kindness, encouragement, and guidance. Naturally, they would resist, as the tasks associated with year-round diversified farming would infringe on the time they normally spent fishing, hunting, or loafing.[15]

Mathis's description of her black tenants' shortcomings was equally patronizing but lacked the optimistic message about the potential for uplift. When addressing southern professionals she was blunt, speaking to them in the racial terms with which they were familiar. She told South Carolina bankers that she had hesitated to accept their invitation to speak because she was "so busy with the poor white folks and 'niggers'" that she had no time to spare. For northern audiences she explained how blacks had degenerated under the conditions of freedom. She recounted how mountain whites gradually replaced former slaves in the fields of northern Alabama after the Civil War because the generation of blacks born after emancipation "felt that they really were not called upon to do anything." She discussed her racial employment practices at some length with agricultural experts in Kansas, insisting that whites and blacks could be hired to work the same property as long as certain rules were enforced. She had her tenants sign contracts stipulating that "the negroes shall stay to their side of the farm and the whites to theirs." To make her position perfectly clear, she added, "We do not have any social equality between the whites and the blacks. [The Negro] must stay in his place; if he does not he is put there. Upon that fact depends the peace and prosperity of the country."[16]

The destructive impact of such attitudes on the plight of rural African Americans can be seen in Mathis's response to the torrential rains of 1916. A severe tropical storm hammered the state during the month of July, causing widespread flooding and crop damage. The state agricultural commissioner estimated that the storm reduced overall crop yields by as much as 50 percent. The flooding was especially devastating for black farmers, leaving thousands without food, clothing, and shelter; however, only after they sent flyers to northern cities with desperate pleas for help did Mathis take an interest in the matter. Her public comments about the need for quick action display genuine concern, suggesting that she might not have realized the extent of the suffering until northern friends brought it to her attention. She was not completely insensitive to the needs of black tenants. She extended to them the same terms and benefits offered to white tenants, including encouragement to become property owners. But her assumptions regarding white racial superiority influenced her to believe that African American farmers would always have a low standard of living. She claimed that black tenants who purchased land by following her instructions and work schedule returned to their shiftless ways as soon as they were freed from her supervision. In her eyes, their suffering appeared to be a natural result of inherent flaws rather than a problem that could be remedied through rural uplift.[17]

Even though Mathis sometimes blamed poor farmers of both races for their own impoverishment, she had to address the root causes of their condition in the business practices that crippled the rural economy. She knew that most tenants did not have gardens or diversify production because of restrictive leases, and she acknowledged that "the landlords had forced the tenants to this condition" because of cotton's greater profitability relative to other crops. She also knew that landlords often benefited from keeping tenants in debt, because when crop prices were low, landowners made more money from providing goods on credit than from the sale of cotton. Supply merchants who advanced credit on the two-price system were culpable, as were rural bankers whose refusal to provide loans on reasonable terms left tenants with no alternatives. Local bankers were especially wary of extending credit for crops other than cotton, and Mathis found that those who had been supply merchants before entering banking were particularly resistant to financing diversification. Just because the ABA leadership acknowledged the need for reform did not mean the average small-town banker was convinced that it was feasible, and change could not happen without the support of bankers across the state.[18]

These sources of opposition required the ABA to take a grassroots approach to reform, and Mathis sought to convince all members of the community that diversification would work to their collective advantage. The campaign in each county began by engaging the support of local bankers. As Mathis later put it, because the "crop subject was so largely a credit subject, the solution had to come along the line of credit in addition to advice." ABA president James Keith Jr. asked rural banks to donate money to fund Mathis's work, and she asked bankers in communities where she was scheduled to appear to write personal letters of invitation to nearby farmers. Securing the support of business leaders was a crucial step, since reformers needed their help in providing credit and finding markets for new crops. Mathis promoted the ABA strategy of giving loans only to farmers who diversified operations, but rural bankers with limited capital would endorse the plan only if they were convinced that it would succeed. Reformers were counting on Mathis's considerable oratorical skills to persuade businessmen as well as farmers that her achievements could be easily replicated.[19]

Mathis took pains to present diversification as a benefit to urban consumers, whose support also was necessary for the creation of markets. When addressing townspeople, she frequently appealed to community loyalty, promoting the purchase of locally grown produce as a way to strengthen the local economy. She noted that businessmen passed along to the consumer the costs of importing products from other regions, while farmers lost a portion of their profit to middlemen when transporting crops to external markets. Consumption of local products would solve both of these problems by lowering food prices for urban families and increasing farmers' income. Mathis drew on her experience with the tomato canning club, meeting with women's groups and urging them to demand that merchants carry local products. In addition, she promoted urban business schemes, such as a plan to open a large cannery in Birmingham, as a way to provide farmers with guaranteed markets for their food crops. Such measures were crucial for the long-term success of reform, since farmers would return to growing cotton if they had to scramble to find markets for food crops and were forced to sell at low prices to avoid a complete loss.[20]

Although Mathis's role in the diversification movement was stereotypically male in its focus on the nuts and bolts of farming and finance, her message was decidedly female in taking the family as its model for reform. She combined the traits of progressive men and women, joining the male emphasis on rational organization and efficiency with the female focus on human needs and the greater social good. Her approach to farming reflected this melding of male and female political culture. She was very businesslike in her employment of methods carefully chosen to maximize yields, but her goal was not merely the accumulation of personal wealth. She believed that the landlord-tenant (or employer-employee) relation could be mutually beneficial and even facilitate the cooperative uplift of community. In speech after speech, Mathis urged bankers, merchants, and farmers to recognize their common interests and act as a family. As she explained to the ABA, the ideal model for reform was citizens acting as "one great household—one great family—thinking and acting for each other that all may receive good." Her association with this vision of cooperative change was so great that she was mentioned by name in the chapter on "Cooperation" in a 1921 college textbook on agricultural economics.[21]

In urging Alabama citizens to act as a family, Mathis used a metaphor that looked both backward and forward in time. In equating community with family and asking landowners to promote tenants' upward mobility in the interest of the greater good, she hearkened back to the slaveholder's ideal of paternalism, in which the master's responsibility for his dependents' well-being supposedly limited his exploitation of their labor. Moreover, her promotion of an approach to farming that prioritized family needs was contrary to national trends toward specialization and the subordination of the household to the market. At the same time, Mathis was forward-looking in her appeal to the progressive ideal of collective social responsibility, a core value underlying female reformers' concept of municipal housekeeping. Just as urban women argued that cities were simply a collection of interdependent households in which the welfare of one affected the welfare of all, Mathis argued that a unity of interests existed between town and country, banker and farmer, and producer and consumer.

Mathis's message was especially well suited for mobilization of the economy after the United States entered the First World War in April 1917, as food production and conservation required extensive cooperation within and across communities. In early May, McAdoo called her to Washington for a conference. When Governor Charles Henderson created the Alabama Council of Defense about a week later, he appointed Mathis to serve on the Food Production and Conservation Committee and as field secretary for the central office. In the month before the council's first meeting in June, she traveled to twenty-three counties to speak on the importance of food production for the war effort. As field worker for the state council, she was charged with organizing community councils of defense and helping to coordinate their work with county councils. The effort she already had put into organizing bankers, merchants, and farmers paid off both in terms of laying the foundation for local councils and in establishing a blueprint for further organization. In some cases, local bankers continued to cover Mathis's travel expenses, at least partially compensating for a scarcity of state funding.[22]

Mathis's reputation as a persuasive speaker put her in great demand, resulting in numerous appeals for her help throughout the two years of U.S. involve-

ment in the war. She corresponded with Carl Vrooman, assistant secretary of
the U.S. Department of Agriculture, and acted as a conduit for the department's
propaganda intended to spur farmers to greater food production. Shortly after
the creation of the U.S. Food Administration in August 1917, the agency's head,
Herbert Hoover, hired her to serve as a lecturer. She was one of several speakers chosen to spearhead Alabama's second campaign to enroll women in the
pledge card program for food and fuel saving. And the Birmingham Food Preparedness Committee hired her to expand her work in urban areas to all of
northern Alabama, facilitating the cooperative marketing of crops and meeting
with women and girls to promote liberty gardens, canning, and consumption
of locally grown food: farmers had responded so enthusiastically to President
Wilson's call for increased food production that they struggled to find markets
for their 1917 crops.[23]

Even though some of Mathis's war work addressed women's domestic roles,
her contributions to the Alabama Council of Defense and other wartime agencies defied gender stereotypes, much as her work for the ABA had done. She
was not a member of the Women's Committee, which in addition to the food
conservation campaigns focused on child welfare, Liberty Loans, and services
for soldiers and female workers. The only other woman on the state council was
Nellie Hooper, who served as chair of the Women's Committee and president
of the Alabama State Federation of Women's Clubs. Hooper acted as organized
women's representative on the state council's executive committee and the Co-
ordination of Societies Committee. Mathis was the sole woman hired by the
Birmingham Food Preparedness Committee, which comprised local businessmen who compiled and disseminated information on the marketing, storage,
and transportation of agricultural products. For the most part, she continued
the same work she had done for bankers, though it now had a patriotic purpose.
The diversification message was intended to ensure that southern farmers produced food for Americans and American allies rather than diverging from the
path of reform to pursue higher cotton prices.[24]

Mathis was aware of the uniqueness of her position as spokesperson for male
bureaucrats and businessmen but chose to let her abilities speak for themselves
rather than highlighting the cause of gender equality. However, she also did not
run from the issue. A Birmingham reporter who met with Mathis in March
1917 was correct in saying that she did not make derogatory comments about
men and was not an "ardent suffragist," but the interviewer was wrong in saying she did not "speak of woman's opportunities." Mathis had long promoted
agriculture as a career for women, especially widows, claiming in one speech
that they owned half the farmland in Alabama. She argued that farm property

was the best investment a woman could make and encouraged female property owners to assert direct control of its management rather than entrusting its operation to hired hands or tenants. She also made more general claims regarding women's financial abilities, contending that even those not actively involved in business could competently handle their own investments. She predicted that women's demonstration of business abilities would soon persuade men to give them the vote.[25]

Although Mathis was overly optimistic in thinking that female competency would persuade southern men to support women's suffrage, the war did advance the cause of equality by requiring women to fill roles normally held by men. The Women's Committee was kept busy by the large numbers of women seeking employment in virtually all sectors of the economy. They became elevator operators, drove delivery wagons, and worked in lumberyards. Banks, post offices, department stores, and laundries hired women to fill positions vacated by men. In most cases both black and white women were hired for these jobs, although one Birmingham scrap iron business advertised openings specifically for African Americans. The Committee on Women in Industry placed women in positions, provided information and training as needed, inspected places of employment to ensure sanitary conditions, and tried to protect workers from exploitative practices—a difficult task, as Alabama had no protective legislation for female workers.[26]

As women's contributions to the war effort proved the artificiality of gender distinctions, Mathis was emboldened to more openly support equality. Georgia suffragists cheered her prominent role in the diversification campaign, and the national secretary of the National American Woman Suffrage Association contacted her to ask advice on the organization's plan to establish agricultural training programs for women. Mathis reciprocated by lending her oratorical skills to suffragists' events. She provided the keynote address at a luncheon staged by Alabama suffragists for Margaret Wilson, the president's daughter. She also shared the podium with the suffrage association's honorary president, Anna Howard Shaw, at a public meeting in support of the war effort. After the ratification of the Nineteenth Amendment in 1920, Mathis added stump speeches for women voters to her busy schedule of appearances. That year, she gave thirteen addresses in six days on issues related to political campaigns.[27]

Mathis's later support for women's suffrage suggests that her previous reticence on the issue had been a strategy to avoid controversy that might interfere with her goals of diversification, social uplift, and economic improvement. She was acutely aware of the fact that many southern whites opposed female public activism of any type, a characteristic she described in one interview as a

"failing" of the region. She faced the additional hurdle of being a woman advising men on a profession defined as male. In many ways farming has been
the profession most rigidly defined as masculine, because property ownership
historically served as the basis of male citizenship and provided the economic
independence that separated men from women and children. Mathis chose to
showcase her common sense and practical savvy, to win respect from men on
her merits rather than make a demand for respect and equality her starting
point. As southern blacks knew all too well, that approach had distinct limitations. When asked by a reporter if her public activities had received criticism,
she said she had heard of none but thoughtfully added, "I don't know how it
would be, though, if I were running for office."[28]

While Mathis's wartime activities reveal her progressivism on gender issues,
the same was not true of her attitudes toward class and race. Government propaganda designed to mobilize public sentiment behind the war effort depicted
critics of public policies as agents of Germany, encouraging citizens to view
dissent as un-American and traitorous. Mathis, whose emotions were no doubt
heightened by her son's tour of duty in France, became convinced that Alabama
was teeming with German spies. She was particularly concerned that they were
the source of dissatisfaction among black steelworkers and miners. When she
spoke to miners in Empire, she stridently maintained that "America is honey-
combed with German spies," and she urged her audience to hunt them down
and hang them "just as fast as you find them." She later told Labor Department
officials that she had seen evidence that German spies were using the miners'
union to spread discontent among black workers and encourage aggressive
behavior toward whites. Her open endorsement of lynching must have been
chilling for black Alabamians already under attack from discriminatory work-
or-fight laws and a sharp increase in vigilante violence. Newspapers offered
no further information regarding the one hundred that Mathis said departed
Birmingham on the night train after her Empire speech was published.[29]

While it would be unfair to gauge Mathis's legacy by the hysteria of 1918,
the culmination of her diversification crusade in the economic mobilization
for war did reveal important truths. She had succeeded in the part of her work
based on the business efficiency model. Her fieldwork was a crucial aspect of
Alabama's organizational plan for mobilization, which the National Defense
Council used as a model for other states. The larger goal of diversification remained elusive, however, and white racial attitudes played an important part in
landowners' failure to embrace her cooperative model of the family as basis for
community. White landlords who assumed black inferiority had no reason to

put forth the effort required to promote their tenants' economic independence, and most returned to the one-crop system as soon as cotton prices recovered. Reformers' failure to give rural blacks equal consideration came back to haunt reform efforts during the war, as those who migrated after the flooding of 1916 left the communities around Selma without the agricultural labor needed to increase food production.

Mathis's willingness to embrace a cooperative approach to community uplift shows how progressive intentions could create a space for reform in spite of the biases of reformers. She was willing to promote the economic independence of groups she considered her social inferiors because she knew that the health of the family was only as good as the health of its members. She had the audacity to launch a serious challenge to the exploitative labor practices that underpinned the one-crop system, a quite remarkable development in itself. Ida Mathis proved that her methods worked, and the fact that her story did not convince other landlords to follow suit spoke more to their shortcomings than to hers. It was not unusual for the male model of reform based on individualist private enterprise to triumph, especially as the conservative politics of the postwar Red Scare began to cast doubt on the legitimacy of women's model of collective responsibility.[30] Remaking the state's system of agricultural production was a massive undertaking that required every landlord to invest time and resources in tenants who might or might not respond effectively. In the end, perhaps that was something only a mother would do.

NOTES

1. Thomas McAdory Owen, *History of Alabama and Dictionary of Alabama Biography* (Chicago: Clark, 1921), 4:1175; Benjamin Franklin Riley, *Alabama as It Is; or, The Immigrant's and Capitalist's Guide Book to Alabama*, 3rd ed. (Montgomery, Ala.: Brown, 1893), 12–14; "'Feed Yourselves,' Says Mrs. Mathis," *Country Gentleman*, October 28, 1916, 1895; "'Mrs. Mathis Might Easily Make Many Who Belong to the Masculine Persuasion Sorry They Were Born—Men,' Says Dolly," *Birmingham Age-Herald*, March 7, 1917.

2. Pete Daniel, *Breaking the Land: The Transformation of Cotton, Tobacco, and Rice Cultures since 1880* (Urbana: University of Illinois Press, 1985), 160–62; Gilbert C. Fite, *Cotton Fields No More: Southern Agriculture, 1865–1980* (Lexington: University Press of Kentucky, 1984), 24–27; Wayne Flynt, *Poor but Proud: Alabama's Poor Whites* (Tuscaloosa: University of Alabama Press, 1989), 59–62.

3. Mrs. G. H. Mathis, *Tenant and Landlord*, Redpath Chautauqua Collection, Special Collections, University of Iowa Libraries; "How the Success of a Woman Farmer Is Inspiring the South," *Banker-Farmer* 3 (January 1916): 11; Fite, *Cotton Fields No More*, 62–65.

4. "Woman Expert Uses Circus to Revive Farms," *Chicago Daily Tribune*, July 8, 1915, 9; Mrs.

G. H. Mathis, "The Big Problems of the South—The Renter and Cotton," *Banker-Farmer* 2 (August 1915): 13; Mrs. G. H. Mathis, "From Hired Man to Landowner in the South," *Banker-Farmer* 3 (December 1915): 12.

5. "What One Southern Woman Has Done," *The Outlook*, December 8, 1915, 870–71; Mrs. G. H. Mathis, "A Message from the South," *Report of the Kansas State Board of Agriculture for the Quarter Ending March, 1916* (Topeka: Kansas State Printing, 1916), 72–73.

6. Fite, *Cotton Fields No More*, 91–92; *Annual Report of the [Alabama] Commissioner of Agriculture and Industries for the Fiscal Year Ending September 30, 1914* (Montgomery, Ala.: Brown, 1914), 12; *Resolutions Adopted by Bankers Convention, November 17, 1914, at Montgomery, Alabama*, Alabama Associations Collection, Box 500, Folder 1, Alabama Department of Archives and History.

7. "Feed Yourselves," 1896; "Follow Up Work Is Greater Than Campaign Itself" (clipping), program, 1915 meeting of the ABA, both in Ida Elizabeth Brandon Mathis Scrapbook, Alabama Women's Hall of Fame, Judson College.

8. C. M. Carroll, *Every Farm Is a Factory: The Opportunity of the Town Lies in the Country* (Chicago: International Harvester, 1916), 5–8; "We Must Feed Ourselves," *Manual Training and Vocational Education* 17 (March 1916): 563–65; "A Profitable Farming Campaign," *American City* 14 (March 1916): 272–73; "Building Up the Run-Down Farm," *Country Life in America* 29 (April 1916): 16-j; "A City with a Vision," *Town Development* 17 (April 1916): 45; Emmet A. Jones to Ida Mathis, October 17, 1916, "State Chamber of Commerce Planning Great Things for Inauguration of Activities" (clipping), both in Mathis Scrapbook.

9. Judith N. McArthur, *Creating the New Woman: The Rise of Southern Women's Progressive Culture in Texas, 1893–1918* (Urbana: University of Illinois Press, 1998); Mary Martha Thomas, *The New Woman in Alabama: Social Reforms and Suffrage, 1890–1920* (Tuscaloosa: University of Alabama Press, 1992); "Summary of Work of the School Improvement Committee," *Alabama Federation of Women's Clubs Yearbook, 1907–1908* (n.p.), Alabama Associations Collection, Box 441, Folder 27; Department of Education of Alabama Circular No. 1, *To the People of Alabama* (Montgomery: Brown, n.d.), Circular No. 2, *Local Organizations* (Montgomery: Brown, n.d.), both in School Improvement Association Records, Alabama Associations Collection, Box 465, Folder 12.

10. "Harding Sounds Note of Warning Urging Farmers to Limit Acreage," *Birmingham Age-Herald*, March 11, 1916; J. Allen Tower, "Cotton Change in Alabama, 1879–1946," *Economic Geography* 26 (January 1950): 7–8.

11. "Bankers Pleased with Week's Work for the Farmers" (clipping), "Several Hundred Representative People Greet Noted Woman at Reception Tendered Her Yesterday by *Age-Herald*" (clipping), H. M. Hanson to Ida Mathis, November 4, 1915, all in Mathis Scrapbook.

12. "High Lights of the Conference," *Banker-Farmer* 2 (August 1915): 2; "Profit 3,000 Percent Building Up Farms" (clipping), "Mrs. Mathis Has Busy Week among Farmers in Lower End of State" (clipping), "Captain White Praises Work of Mrs. Mathis" (clipping), "Tells Why Farm Lands Are Cheap All over Alabama" (clipping), all in Mathis Scrapbook.

13. "Fine Address by Mrs. G. H. Mathis" (clipping), "Mrs. Mathis Receives Royal Welcome" (clipping), "Famous Woman Farmer Speaks at Greenville" (clipping), all in Mathis Scrapbook; "The 'Feed Ourselves' Gospel and the Woman Who Proved It," *Outlook*, February 28, 1917, 356–57.

14. Mathis, "Big Problems of the South"; Mrs. G. H. Mathis, "Agricultural Common Sense for the Cotton States," *Commerce and Finance*, November 3, 1915, 846; Mathis, "Message from the South," 65; Mrs. G. H. Mathis, "Opportunities of the Moneyless Man in the South," *Commerce and Finance*, January 5, 1916, 26; Mrs. G. H. Mathis, "Agriculture in the South," *Thirtieth Annual Convention of the Michigan Bankers' Association* (Detroit: Bland, n.d.), 84; Mrs. G. H. Mathis, "Diversification

in Farming," *Proceedings of the Fifth Annual Convention of the Investment Bankers Association of America* (Chicago: Lakeside, 1916), 131.

15. Mrs. G. H. Mathis, "How to Help the Unambitious Tenant" (clipping), Mathis Scrapbook; Mathis, "Message from the South," 64; Mrs. G. H. Mathis, "Reasons for Poor Credit in the South," in Harold G. Moulton, ed., *Principles of Money and Banking: A Series of Selected Materials, with Explanatory Introductions* (Chicago: University of Chicago, 1916), 371.

16. Mrs. G. H. Mathis, "More Money on the Farm, and How to Make It," *Report of Proceedings of the Sixteenth Annual Convention of the South Carolina Bankers' Association* (Florence, S.C.: South Carolina Bankers' Association, 1916), 200; Mathis, "Agricultural Common Sense," 846; Mathis, "Message from the South," 65.

17. "Mrs. Mathis Says Negroes Have Made Appeal for Help," November 9, 1916 (clipping), Mathis Scrapbook; *Annual Report of the [Alabama] Commissioner of Agriculture and Industries for Fiscal Year Ending September 30, 1916* (Montgomery: Brown, 1917), 6; "One Way to Help Tenants," *Progressive Farmer*, July 31, 1915; Mrs. G. H. Mathis, "The Problem of Tenant and Landlord in the Cotton States," in *Agricultural Extension: Something of Its Meaning, the Forces Engaged in the Work, and of the Results Obtained* (Chicago: National Implement and Vehicle Association, 1916), 118.

18. "For Better Live Stock" (clipping), Mathis Scrapbook; Mathis, "Message from the South," 68; "Feed Yourselves," 1896.

19. "Mrs. Mathis Points to Next Great Duty of Alabama Farmer" (clipping), "President Keith Asks Bankers to Aid in Big Work" (clipping), both in Mathis Scrapbook; Mathis, "More Money on the Farm"; Mathis, "Diversification in Farming," 129; Mathis, "Agriculture in the South," 88; "Feed Yourselves," 1895–96.

20. "Mrs. Mathis Delivers Splendid Address" (clipping), "Mrs. Mathis Tells How to Reduce Cost of Living" (clipping), "Mrs. Mathis Tells Housewives How to Cut Down Expenses" (clipping), all in Mathis Scrapbook; "Greatest Woman Farmer of the South," *New Orleans Times-Picayune*, May 12, 1918.

21. *Proceedings of the Twenty-Fifth Annual Convention of the Alabama Bankers' Association, Held at Mobile, Alabama, May 10–12, 1917* (Atlanta: Press of the *Southern Banker*, n.d.), 68; James E. Boyle, *Agricultural Economics* (Philadelphia: Lippincott, 1921), 158–9; Maureen Flanagan, *Seeing with Their Hearts: Chicago Women and the Vision of the Good City, 1871–1933* (Princeton,: Princeton University Press, 2002).

22. Hastings H. Hart, *Social Problems of Alabama: A Study of the Social Institutions and Agencies of the State of Alabama as Related to Its War Activities Made at the Request of Governor Charles Henderson* (New York: Sage, 1918), 17; *Proceedings of the Alabama State Council of Defense, Senate Chamber of Alabama, June 1, 1917* (Montgomery: Brown, 1917), 3, 9–11; *Report of the Alabama Council of Defense, Covering Its Activities from May 17, 1917, to December 31, 1918* (Montgomery: Brown, 1919), 5–6, 12–13; "Alabama Woman to Lecture on Food," *Christian Science Monitor*, September 12, 1917; Ida Mathis to L. M. Hooper, September 16, 1918, Box 5, Folder 8, Alabama State Council of Defense Administrative Files, Alabama Department of Archives and History; "Mrs. Mathis Is Called to Confer With McAdoo" (clipping), "Mrs. Mathis Called to Washington" (clipping), Mathis Scrapbook.

23. "Mrs. Mathis Busy on Speaking Tour" (clipping), "Fourth of Fund for Food Work Is Already in Hand" (clipping), both in Mathis Scrapbook; "Some Bad Mistakes Emanating from the United States Department of Agriculture," *Manufacturers Record*, June 14, 1917, 43; *Food Conservation* (Council of National Defense Bulletin), September 8, 1917, Alabama State Council of Defense Administrative Files, Box 2, Folder 33; *Proceedings of the Twenty-Sixth Annual Convention of the Alabama Bankers' Association, Held at Birmingham, Alabama, May 9–11, 1918* (Atlanta: Press of the

Southern Banker, n.d.), 82; Robert H. Zieger, *America's Great War: World War I and the American Experience* (Lanham, Md.: Rowman and Littlefield, 2000), 72–73.

24. *Report of the Alabama Counsel of Defense*, 40–41, 51–56; "In Every Crisis There's a Woman" (clipping), "Mrs. Mathis Points Next Great Duty" (clipping), both in Mathis Scrapbook; *Report of the Birmingham Food Preparedness Committee, Merchantable Farm Products*, Alabama Associations Collection, Box 540, Folder 22; Carl R. Woodward, "Woodrow Wilson's Agricultural Policy," *Agricultural History* 14 (October 1940): 138–39.

25. "Farming Best Investment for Women, Says Woman, Who Addresses Bankers" (clipping), "Business Ability to Win Women the Ballot" (clipping), both in Mathis Scrapbook; "'Mrs. Mathis Might Easily Make Many Who Belong to the Masculine Persuasion Sorry They Were Born—Men,' Says Dolly," *Birmingham Age-Herald*, March 7, 1917.

26. *Report of the Alabama Council of Defense*, 58–60; "Alabama Women Taking Men's Places," *Christian Science Monitor*, May 21, 1918.

27. "Mrs. Mathis' Work Noted" (clipping), "Miss Wilson Guest of Honor at Lunch at Club Thursday" (clipping), "Meeting for Women," Emma Rogers to Ida Mathis, March 8, 1917, all in Mathis Scrapbook.

28. "Southern Woman Planter Tells How She Helps Ne'er-Do-Well Renters to Become Land Owners," *St. Louis Post-Dispatch*, October 10, 1915; Sally Shortall, *Women and Farming: Property and Power* (New York: St. Martin's, 1999).

29. "Mrs. Mathis Says America Getting Enough of Spies" (clipping), "Spies of Germany Should Be Crushed without Mercy, Says Mrs. Mathis" (clipping), "Says the Spies Are Being Driven Out" (clipping), all in Mathis Scrapbook; H. S. Murphy to Monroe N. Work, October 3, 1918, Lloyd Hooper to Robert R. Moton, October 10, 1918, Alabama State Council of Defense Administrative Files, Box 5, Folder 8; Brian Kelly, *Race, Class, and Power in the Alabama Coalfields, 1908–1921* (Urbana: University of Illinois Press, 2001), 155–56.

30. Robyn Muncy, *Creating a Female Dominion in American Reform, 1890–1935* (New York: Oxford University Press, 1991), 128–30, 135–50; Molly Ladd-Taylor, *Mother-Work: Women, Child Welfare, and the State, 1890–1930* (Urbana: University of Illinois Press, 1994), 170–74.

Zelda Sayre Fitzgerald and Sara Martin Mayfield

"Alabama Modern"

REBECCA CAWOOD MCINTYRE

❀ ❀ ❀

On a sunny fall day in 1910, Zelda Sayre strapped on her roller skates. She stood at the summit of Sayre Street and looked down the hill. Then she crouched down and pushed off. Picking up speed, she careened past her elementary school and whizzed by the playground where her classmates were gathered. And then, right as she was about to go headlong into the red brick building at the bottom of the hill, she feinted to the left and came to a graceful stop. Her classmates were awestruck. The ten-year-old Zelda bowed and then climbed back up the hill to do it again. Little Sara Mayfield was on that playground. Five-year-old Sara had just gotten her first pair of skates. She immediately decided that she was going to do exactly what Zelda did and amaze her schoolmates with her daring and skill. The nursemaid who always took "Miss Sara" to school told her not to follow that wild Sayre girl. Sara ignored her. She was a kindergartener and certainly old enough to skate down a sissy hill in mostly flat Montgomery, Alabama. Sara stood at the top of the street, took a deep breath, and pushed off. Going faster than she ever thought possible, Sara zoomed past the school and the playground and kept on going. Then suddenly, she lost control. About to hit that brick wall, she braced herself for the crash. Watching, Zelda quickly assessed the situation and headed down the hill at breakneck speed. With just inches to spare, she pushed Sara to the left, away from the building. As Sara stood, visibly shaken, Zelda fussed and scolded the little girl for risking a broken neck by skating like that. And then Zelda smiled and told Sara not to worry: next time, Sara could hold on to Zelda's waist, and she would teach the younger girl how to swerve away from the wall. From that day forward, Sara wrote years later, she

ZELDA SAYRE FITZGERALD, C. 1935

William Stanley Hoole Special Collections Library, University of Alabama, Tuscaloosa.

SARA MARTIN MAYFIELD, C. 1927

William Stanley Hoole Special Collections Library, University of Alabama, Tuscaloosa.

was spellbound: Zelda "had a dash, a style, and a daring that left me wide-eyed and open-mouthed with admiration."[1]

The story could have ended there, a precious vignette from a precocious girl who adored wild Zelda Sayre, the pied piper of childhood excitement in sleepy Montgomery. Yet that hill was the beginning of a bond that lasted almost forty years. As adults, the two women chose different paths—Zelda, a famous flapper; Sara, a well-known novelist—yet their lives were inextricably intertwined. And while each woman was significant in her own right, examining their adult years in tandem provides a novel interpretation not just of these two figures but of the ideal of modern womanhood beginning to emerge in the decades after World War I. These Alabama natives would challenge the norms of their conventional and conservative southern upbringing and become the forerunners in defining the modern woman of the twentieth century.

When discussing modernity and women, particularly in the 1920s, the Deep South often is overlooked. The southern ideal of a woman appears too far away from the modern woman of New York and Chicago in the Jazz Age. Not that Zelda is ignored. Most of her story is well known. The dazzling gypsy queen and her equally beautiful husband, F. Scott Fitzgerald, are standard fare in any history of the 1920s. In the typical scenario, Scott represents the great American novelist and Zelda becomes the epitome of the American flapper. *American* is the key. While the best biographers look at her southern roots, many writers see her southern upbringing as a quaint sidebar rather than a key to understanding her psyche. Talented but more sedate intellectuals such as Sara Mayfield are ignored. Yet both women used modern sensibilities and their southern skills to erode the conservative traditions in which they had grown up. Both turned away from the orderly restraints of Victorian womanhood and entered into a chaotic and exciting world that began offering new independence for women. For Mayfield, that meant attending college, becoming a journalist, and building a professional career in what was still a man's world. For Fitzgerald, modern meant drinking, smoking, going to big parties, wearing short skirts and even shorter hair, having a lack of inhibition and a new freedom from conservative cultural mores that enabled a woman to openly express her sexuality.[2]

These outside personas, though, masked much deeper insecurities. For Mayfield and Fitzgerald, truly daughters of the South, being modern created insurmountable problems, as neither could fully divest herself of the ingrained culture of her upbringing. According to the accepted norms, well-bred girls of marriageable age could coyly play the coquettish belle, and flirting was acceptable and indeed encouraged, but only as long as the goal was a respectable marriage. Once married, good southern wives removed themselves from the public sphere to become the doyennes of domesticity, raising and training up their children, catering to their husbands' needs, and managing their households. In reality, some leeway existed. Outside of the private sphere, society encouraged elite women to join social clubs focused on charity and social uplift. But mainly, southern society expected respectable ladies to be demure, undemanding, and content at home. As the saying went, a southern woman should be mentioned in the papers three times in her life: when she was born, when she married, and when she died.[3]

Both Mayfield and Fitzgerald ran roughshod over those dictums. While both women married, and Fitzgerald had a child, their ideal of a lady was neither private nor demure. Both wanted to be in the limelight, not pushed behind the scenes. Both craved equality and personal autonomy. And both wanted independent identities attached to meaningful work—Fitzgerald as a dancer and artist and Mayfield as an inventor and novelist. Yet independence eluded them: neither could totally break free from her southern roots.

Mayfield and Fitzgerald are worthy of study simply because of their accomplishments, but their lives also have a larger significance. Their experiences offer a more nuanced look at the making of modern womanhood, demonstrating that the "New Woman" of the early twentieth century could spring even from the rocky soil of the South. Yet Mayfield and Fitzgerald also demonstrate the limitations of a southern upbringing. Both became victims of their quests for self, fighting the odds but in the end paying dearly for their dreams of independence. They were "Alabama Modern," women striving toward an autonomous future but unable to separate themselves from the comfort and the security of the traditional South.

The Sayres and the Mayfields were typical southern elites of their time. Sara Mayfield was born in Tuscaloosa on September 10, 1905. Her father, James Jefferson Mayfield Jr., was a respected lawyer, while her mother, Susie Fitts Martin, came from a distinguished Memphis family. In 1908, James Mayfield was appointed an associate justice on the Alabama Supreme Court, and the family, which also included Sara's younger brother, James Jefferson Mayfield III, moved to Montgomery. Theirs was a comfortable life. A combination of James's salary and family money meant that the Mayfields lived in the best section of Montgomery and gave their children the finest education. Sara, a bright girl, was enrolled at the prestigious Margaret Booth School, the best private girls school in the city.[4]

Zelda Sayre came from a similar background, though her family often skirted the edge of elite society. She was born on July 24, 1900, in Montgomery, the youngest of six children. Her father, Anthony Dickinson Sayre, had studied law, and he, too, served as an associate justice on the Alabama Supreme Court. Zelda's mother, Minnie Buckner, grew up on a tobacco plantation in Kentucky and married A. D. Sayre after meeting him while visiting relatives in Montgomery. Theirs was an attraction of opposites. "Mama Sayre" was artistic and loving, while A. D. was dour and intellectual. Both doted on Zelda, however. The Sayres lived in a nice house with a cook, a nanny, and a gardener but constantly worried about the lack of money because they had no family money to serve as a cushion. Judge Sayre so feared debt that he never bought a home and always rented at the edge of Montgomery's good neighborhoods. He did not send his children to private academies, so Zelda, like her brother and sisters before her, attended Sidney Lanier School, the city's public high school.[5]

Monetary worries aside, the Sayres carved out a good living in turn-of-the-century Montgomery. The southern city was large for the region, boasting more than forty thousand residents in 1920. It was the state capital and the center of Alabama's political life. The city's money, however, came not from politics but from cotton, which was still king. Montgomery thrived because it was an excellent transportation hub, set in the fertile Black Belt, along the Alabama River, which ran to New Orleans, and with a railroad system that connected it to the region and beyond. The city had warehouses, industrial cotton gins, and a large textile factory. Boosters proclaimed Montgomery the New South, with big banks, modern hotels, and the first electric streetcar in America. During the First World War, Montgomery gained an even more modern image with the construction of two military camps tasked with training pilots for service in Europe.[6]

Yet despite the city's pride at being modern, Montgomery was rooted in a mythical romanticized past. It was the Cradle of the Confederacy, where Jefferson Davis had stood on the balcony of the state capitol and been sworn in as president of the Confederate States of America. An embedded star marked the spot where Davis gave his inauguration speech. Across the street from the capitol stood the Davis residence, the First White House of the Confederacy. In 1920, these echoes of the Lost Cause were the pride of white Montgomery and tourists alike. The contradiction between the ideals of the New South and the Old South seemed to provoke little concern.[7]

Sara Mayfield loved the romance of her childhood city. It was a place, she wrote, filled with ghosts of the Confederacy that still haunted the city's "somnolent oak-lined streets." It was a city of tradition, she boasted, where citizens held their heads high not because it was the capital of Alabama but rather because the first flag of the Confederacy had been raised there. Zelda Fitzgerald also remembered the drowsy air of her hometown, "where lazy gossiping [went on] in the warm sun . . . in a climate too hot for anything but sporadic effort." It was a place, she wrote, where one could "lie long and sleepily under the Spanish moss." She regularly indulged her romantic yearnings by lying among the graves of the soldiers at the Oakwood Cemetery, where, she wrote in 1919, "all the broken columns and clasped hands and doves and angels mean romances."[8]

While dead Confederates conferred a southern identity on Montgomery, it was truly southern because of its strict code of racial segregation, dictated by both custom and law. White Montgomery residents believed that giving blacks the vote would destroy all white privilege. Giving them social equality was unthinkable. A. D. Sayre played a critical role in disfranchising blacks. The 1893 Election Law, dubbed the Sayre Law, allowed registration of voters only in May, arranged candidates alphabetically and without party identification under the office they sought, and required voters to present both registration certificates and identification. The system was designed to disfranchise both African Americans and poor whites. Whether de facto or de jure, maintaining the color line was paramount to the city leaders, and any African American who crossed it faced deadly consequences. Lynching was not commonplace but did occur.[9]

Segregation gained stronger legal footing with the 1901 Alabama Constitution, which restricted voting to people who could pass literacy tests and satisfy property requirements. The constitution also included provisions mandating separate schools for African American and white children and outlawing interracial marriage. Judge Mayfield supported the constitution, and both the Sayre and Mayfield families accepted their Jim Crow world without comment. They understood the landscape of Montgomery segregation. This city of forty-seven square miles had sections for wealthy whites, blue-collar whites, poor whites, and blacks. The Sayres lived right on the edge of one of the older elite neighborhoods, in the southeastern portion of the city. The Mayfields lived in the heart of the old-line Alabamians. Middle-income whites lived in the city's northeastern quadrant, while the poorest whites occupied western Montgomery and black people lived mainly in the northern sector. Most residents stayed within their zones except in their workplaces, where the classes mixed, although the obvious divisions between domestic, blue-collar, and white-collar workers persisted.[10]

African Americans in 1920s Montgomery endured inequality and limited job opportunities, but members of the white and privileged class had access to a good life. Mayfield and Fitzgerald remembered it as idyllic. Sara tended to be the good girl who listened to her elders, while Zelda was a rebel whose goal was to shock. As a young girl, Zelda combined her wild stunts with a recklessness unheard of for proper southern girls. The examples are legion. One day, when young Zelda was bored, she called the fire department and reported that a house was on fire and that a girl was trapped on the roof. Then she climbed a ladder to the roof, pushed the ladder away, and waited to be rescued. The firemen were annoyed yet amused; Zelda was overjoyed by the commotion she had caused. Her mother forgave such caprices, and even her father ignored all but the worst. What Mayfield later described as Zelda's "special combination of nerve and defiance" was not modern: it was just boredom and a need for excitement.[11]

When Montgomery's girls reached a suitable age for dating (typically their senior year of high school), they attended chaperoned dances or shared ice cream sodas with boys (typically college students home for weekends) at the downtown drugstore. Ideal beaux for well-bred white girls appeared educated, possessed the proper social graces, and hailed from an old, distinguished and hopefully wealthy family—in short, they constituted suitable marriage material.[12]

Impatient Zelda, however, could not wait until her senior year to get on the social circuit. At fifteen, with her mother's permission, she started attending subscription dances sponsored by college men at the local country club. One of the men would post a sheet of paper on the door of the downtown drugstore. Down the left side would be names of local girls; a boy would write his name next to that of the girl he wanted to escort. Zelda's name was always on the list, and she had no shortage of escorts. On one occasion, the local paper ran her picture with a caption reading that "the classically beautiful fifteen year old" who danced at the country club every Saturday night would "be even more striking at sweet sixteen."[13]

By the time she reached the more eligible age of seventeen, Zelda had mastered the techniques of the elusive southern belle. She would pit her admirers against each other, giving one a goodnight kiss and accepting a pledge pin from another. She made the rounds of college football games, traveling to Tuscaloosa, Auburn, and Atlanta. She even went to Boodler's Bend, a Montgomery hideaway where she could drink corn whiskey with the boys. She danced the Shimmy, the Charleston, and the Black Bottom while most young women still waltzed as they had learned at cotillion. But Zelda had little concern for what other girls did. She could "do anything and get away with it." Gossip always followed Zelda. A contemporary wrote that she "was attractive, vivacious, daring, and a dashing type." Mayfield recalled that she was simply a young girl who was unusually attractive and wanted to have a good time—a southern flirt who could tempt young men to a point just shy of "going the limit."[14]

Zelda's audaciousness resulted in part from the rise of the automobile, which permitted young couples to court away from the eyes of anxious parents and chaperones. In addition, Zelda came of age during the final year of the First

World War. Soldiers came to Montgomery to train at Camp Taylor and Camp Sheridan before receiving orders to fight in France. Officers from the camps met local girls at Montgomery Country Club dances. Morals loosened with the sense of urgency that war often brings. Mayfield described "the New Freedom" as "rich Yankees stood cheek to jowl with Montgomery bluebloods." Almost nostalgically, she added that the New Freedom burned with a zeal that "dimmed the phosphorescence from the decaying ethos of the late Confederacy." At this heady time, Montgomery's young women were rebels born in an "ultraconservative place in which revolt was long overdue."[15]

Zelda Sayre fell hard for one of those officers whom she thought was a rich Yankee. Francis Scott Fitzgerald saw Sayre dancing at the country club in the summer of 1918 and told his army buddy that he had to have that girl. She seemed equally smitten with the boy who glowed as brightly as she did. A Minnesotan who had attended Princeton University, Fitzgerald was not wealthy but came from a respectable family, and he seemed exotic compared to southern college boys. He boasted that he was a novelist and was going to write a bestselling book that would make him rich. After the war, he moved to New York, and he and Sayre became engaged in March 1919. She wrote to him from Montgomery with all the syrupy sentimentality expected from a young girl in love but also had trouble being attached to just one man. Still the belle and despite their engagement, she wrote to Fitzgerald in June 1919 that she loved him so and then added that she needed to go to the Georgia Tech football game so she could try her "hand in new fields" and that he could visit her in Alabama but "she would be mighty tired" because the boys always wanted to dance until breakfast. Soon thereafter, she was pinned by the star quarterback at Auburn University. She soon changed her mind and wrote him a sentimental letter returning his pin but accidentally sent the letter to Fitzgerald. Furious, he traveled to Alabama and tried to persuade her to marry him immediately. When she refused, he broke off their engagement for several months.[16]

Sayre could have married Fitzgerald at any time. She had graduated from Sidney Lanier and had no intention of pursuing further education or finding a job. And she was not expected to do either of those things. She lived with her parents and enjoyed her leisure time and her various flirtations. However, she also knew that she must eventually marry, and she appears to have wanted the security of a husband as much as her independence—a dichotomy, she later wrote, that forced her "to be two simple people at once, one who wants to have a law to itself and the other who wants to keep all the nice old things and be loved and safe and protected." Though she wanted to marry Fitzgerald, she would not do so until he could prove that he could provide for her, a condition that mattered to her as much as to her father. In the early spring of 1920, Fitzgerald's first novel, *This Side of Paradise*, was published, receiving wide acclaim and quickly going through three editions. Two weeks after its release, Sayre boarded a train to New York City, where they married on April 3, 1920.[17]

When Sayre left for New York, Sara Mayfield was just fifteen. She was studying at the Margaret Booth School and doing well in the rigorous academic atmosphere. In 1922, she entered Goucher College in Baltimore under the guidance of Sara Haardt, a close friend from Montgomery and a graduate of the Margaret Booth School. Haardt, also a friend of Zelda Sayre, was incredibly intelligent though relatively poor. Her father was a second-generation German American, while her mother, Venetia Hall Haardt, was from Montgomery. Haardt had received a scholarship to attend Goucher, where she majored in English literature, graduating Phi Beta Kappa in 1920. She was involved in politics and in the women's rights movement and spent much of her time writing collections of short stories. Hired to teach English at Goucher, Haardt became Mayfield's mentor when she enrolled there in the fall of 1922. Where Sayre had shown Mayfield a rebellious path to the new, Haardt offered modernity as education and self-independence.[18]

Mayfield enjoyed Goucher but left school after two years and returned to Montgomery to marry the charming and wealthy John Allen Sellers, whose father owned a prosperous cotton brokerage. Mayfield later wrote that Sellers was "like all southern gentleman," a master at "putting their girls on pedestals, glorifying them, and abasing themselves." At nineteen, Mayfield began her life in Montgomery as the respectable Mrs. Sellers, but their marriage lasted less than three years.[19]

The reasons for the couple's divorce are unclear. In a 1926 letter to Zelda Fitzgerald, Mayfield wrote that she had married Sellers "in the time of my innocence . . . and divorced him when I came of age." She also said that there were "too many parties, too many hangovers, and too much money." Fitzgerald exclaimed that there could never be too much money, but admitted that marriage and drinking did not mix. In her later years, Mayfield softened and remembered her former husband as "tall, blonde, immaculate, and distinguished."[20]

Mayfield may simply have been bored. Intelligent and with a thirst for knowledge, Mayfield began studying at the University of Paris a year before her divorce was final. The next year she enrolled at the University of Chicago, and the following year she received a bachelor's degree from Goucher. She then did graduate work at the University of London and in 1938 earned a master of arts degree from the University of Alabama. Such a path was unheard of for a young lady from Montgomery: even Sara Haardt did not have a graduate degree.[21]

Divorce provided Sara Mayfield's entrance into a new professional life. In contrast, marriage launched Zelda Fitzgerald into a new modern lifestyle. Her trip to New York to get married was the first time that she had ever traveled outside of the South. Her parents did not attend the wedding, and her three sisters were her only witnesses. Scott Fitzgerald rushed the ceremony and did not even take a picture of Zelda in her midnight-blue suit. The bacchanal of the honeymoon, however, starkly contrasted the tiny wedding. Mr. and Mrs. Fitzgerald went first to the city's elegant Biltmore Hotel, but management asked them to leave a few days later because they were disturbing the other guests. The management of the Commodore Hotel proved more willing to put up with the Fitzgeralds' rowdy and outlandish behavior, resulting in a wild three weeks that created Scott and Zelda's reputation and cemented them in the public's eye. They spun endlessly around the Commodore's revolving front door, drank heavily and danced wildly in the bars and the clubs and the streets of Manhattan, and rode on top of taxis. They frolicked in public fountains and went to parties with the smart set. The golden couple of the moment splashed onto the New York scene, young and beautiful with cash to burn.[22]

Zelda Fitzgerald's new modern life was that of a party girl, independent from any cultural restraints. Zelda claimed that she was "good for nothing but useless pleasure-giving pursuits" that all she had ever wanted was to be young and "very irresponsible." In an age sobered by the trauma of the war, Scott and Zelda offered gaiety and a new joie de vivre. Conspicuous consumption was their credo. The Fitzgeralds began a great, gaudy, wonderful spree of unending excess. Scott would light up hundred dollar bills for the hell of it. They dressed themselves up for a studio portrait that demonstrates their indulgence and need for notoriety. They stare into the camera, Scott wearing a tailored overcoat with velvet lapels, Zelda bundled in a massive fur coat, her bobbed hair just barely visible under a lovely art deco hat. She was a flapper—a richer, wilder form of the southern belle, still a tease and a flirt but on a much greater scale. Zelda had been born to play this role, which provided her with a freedom that she could never have found as a married woman in Montgomery.[23]

After their Manhattan honeymoon, the Fitzgeralds rented a gray-shingled house in Westport, Connecticut, a quiet location away from the city intended to encourage Scott in writing his second novel. Instead, it became a six-month house party. Their New York friends would come out on Friday night and stay until Sunday. Though Scott had never graduated from Princeton, he had a coterie of good college friends, some of whom, such as literary critic Edmund "Bunny" Wilson and drama critic and editor George Jean Nathan, would become famous in their own right. The Fitzgeralds' house on Compo Road represented the beginning of a pattern that continued for the rest of their married life—short-term rentals and outrageous parties.[24]

While New York treated the couple as the new celebrities of a new age, Montgomery society thought differently. In July 1920, after three months of marriage, Zelda became homesick, and she and her husband drove to Alabama in a ramshackle car. Scott Fitzgerald satirized their trip in "The Cruise of the Rolling Junk" published in *Motor* magazine in 1924. Southerners were most shocked by the Fitzgeralds' outfits—matching white knickerbockers. After hotel operators in Virginia did not want to give Scott and Zelda a room because of her mannish clothes, she slipped a dress over the pants when entering a southern hotel or restaurant. According to Mayfield, the outfits were designed for coolness in the heat of the city, but they did startle the "Confederates." Quipped another childhood friend, Zelda "left here in long dresses and came back in short pants."[25]

In early 1921, Zelda discovered that she was pregnant. To celebrate, the couple boarded an ocean liner and took a grand tour of Europe, visiting London, Paris, and Rome before returning to Montgomery when she was six and a half months pregnant. After deciding that Alabama was too hot, she and Scott went north to Minnesota to be near Scott's friends and family. Born on October 26, 1921, their daughter, Frances Scott Fitzgerald, nicknamed Scottie, was a happy and healthy baby. Zelda loved her daughter but seemed disconnected from her maternal role, preferring parties with friends and occasional visits with Scottie to the constant demands of serving as primary caregiver to the child. Instead, a long line of nannies assumed that role.[26]

Zelda also was dealing with Scott's drinking and mood swings. For his part, Scott saw Zelda as his baby. Scott privately sought to claim much of the credit for Zelda's rise as a flapper and public figure. Zelda initially seemed pleased to serve as Scott's muse. He freely acknowledged that he borrowed heavily from their life and that Zelda was his inspiration and greatest critic. He wrote to his publisher, for example, that a work he had submitted could be edited, but Zelda really did not think it was necessary. Scott also told Bunny Wilson that Zelda was "the most enormous influence" on the author's life. Most academics agree that Zelda had an important role; others contend that Zelda had a primary role. Sara Mayfield, for example, declared that Scott was a good writer "as long as Zelda supplied the copy."[27]

Zelda did push for a voice of her own. In the first years of her marriage, she wrote several articles for publication. "Eulogy of a Flapper," published by *Metropolitan* magazine in June 1922, was a light, slightly snobby, and rather illogical puff piece. Zelda proclaimed the flapper dead because the novelty had worn off once "shop-girls and co-eds" began mimicking the look. Zelda articulated what the modern girl should be as a flapper: risqué, audacious, and flirtatious. She ended by connecting flappers to the modern businessman: flappers capitalized on their natural resources to get their money's worth. Zelda's wittiest piece was a review of Scott's second novel, *The Beautiful and the Damned*, in which she playfully noted that she "recognized a portion of an old diary" that had mysteriously disappeared when she married. Her husband, she quipped, "believes plagiarism begins at home."[28]

In the summer of 1924, the Fitzgeralds moved to France. Money lay at the heart of their decision to be émigrés. *The Beautiful and the Damned* had not sold as well as *This Side of Paradise*, and Scott was chronically short of money. Zelda and Scott never lived within any sort of budget, and when they had extra money, they spent it. France made sense because the dollar was strong compared to the franc. Like many other American expats, they did not integrate themselves into the French society but instead became part of several tight-knit groups of artists and consorted with the likes of Gertrude Stein and Ernest Hemingway, living in Europe intermittently for seven years.[29]

Zelda tried to live by a creed of her own, an independence that would affirm her outward appearance as the modern woman, but she was inextricably bound up with Scott—more of an appendage, she complained, than a person. As Zelda chafed at her dependence, Sara Mayfield began enjoying professional successes. In 1927, she was living in New York City and working as a theater casting director. The next year she went back to the Deep South and tried her hand at ethnomusicology, traveling to small towns and backwaters in Mississippi and Alabama to collect and record African American songs, years before the famous folklorist Alan Lomax made the trip. Mayfield then turned more seriously to journalism. Between 1928 and 1929, she went to Paris as a special correspondent for the *Baltimore Sun* while pursing her graduate education in languages as well as in science. By 1938, she was an established freelance reporter working the majority of the time for Transradio Press.[30]

By the mid-1920s, Zelda was showing signs of mental strain and was floundering as a mother, a wife, and a woman. The Fitzgeralds had been moving between winters in Paris and summers in the south of France, where Scott would work on his third novel and Zelda had very little to do. The Riviera was affordable and comfortable at the time, and Scott rented an inexpensive villa a bit away from the beach. On his good days, Scott wrote during the afternoon and then went drinking with friends like Sara and Gerald Murphy, wealthy American expats. But when Scott was writing, Zelda was bored. She would go to the beach with

Scottie and her nanny, swimming and reading. At night, she joined Scott in his drinking, causing scenes that topped any of their earlier escapades. More often than not, they went home and passed out.[31]

Friends now found the Fitzgeralds' nighttime antics less amusing and complained about their conduct. Zelda often engaged in self-destructive behavior—for example, diving off of high cliffs into the Mediterranean despite the large rocks below. One evening, she threatened to drive off a cliff; on another night she flopped in front of their car and dared Scott to drive over her. Visiting that summer, Sara Mayfield worried about Zelda, though not because she doubted her longtime friend's sanity. Rather, Mayfield thought that Scott was "committing suicide on the installment plan" by drinking himself to death, usually with gin. Adding to Mayfield's fears was the fact that when Scott drank, he often turned mean, breaking objects and verbally tearing apart his friends. At other times, he wallowed in self-pity, complaining that Zelda was going "southern on him" with her flirtations. He also claimed she had been having an affair with Eduard Jozan, a French aviator who lived along the beach. Both Zelda and Jozan denied the affair, and Zelda responded by taking an overdose of sleeping pills. At that point, the Fitzgeralds left the coast and returned to Paris for the winter.[32]

Yet despite the earlier problems, the next summer Scott and Zelda headed back to the Riviera. Scott decided that he was going to flirt and embarrass his wife. When famous dancer Isadora Duncan, who had long been Zelda's idol, walked into a restaurant where the Fitzgeralds and the Murphys were having a boozy dinner, Scott prostrated himself at Duncan's feet, while the dancer stroked his hair and called him "my centurion." Zelda responded by throwing herself down a stone staircase at the rear of the room, somehow suffering only minor injuries.[33]

The Fitzgerald family finally moved back to the States in January 1927, when they rented Ellerslie, a massive thirty-room Georgian home located just outside of Wilmington, Delaware. It appeared to be the perfect place where Scott could write and Zelda could spend more time with Scottie, but both Scott's and Zelda's self-destructive behaviors escalated. Now in her late twenties, Zelda no longer served as Scott's muse and was searching for her own identity. She flitted from writing and painting to dancing, displaying talent in all three arenas, but as Scottie later wrote, "It was my mother's misfortune to be born with the ability to write, to dance, and to paint . . . and then never to have acquired the discipline to make her talent work, for, rather than against her."[34]

Indeed, Zelda was a talented though untutored writer. Her prose was amusing and metaphorically lyrical, and though her earliest pieces are fluff, they are delightful fluff. In 1925, the *Chicago Sunday Tribune* ran "Our Own Movie Queen," a short story based on the adventures of Zelda's friend and fellow Alabamian, Tallulah Bankhead. Though not particularly clear, the story explores the rise of an ordinary girl to movie stardom, and the newspaper paid a thousand dollars for it. But it was published solely under Scott's name—Zelda was not even credited as a coauthor. The Fitzgeralds used this arrangement repeatedly in the late 1920s and early 1930s because they were heavily in debt, and newspapers and magazines would pay ten times as much for a story by F. Scott Fitzgerald as for one by Zelda Fitzgerald. *College Humor* printed six stories credited to Scott and Zelda together, although Zelda wrote them alone, and the joint byline earned them four times what Zelda's name alone would have brought. Zelda claimed that she wanted to use the money for dancing lessons, but the situation hurt her ego, which by now had become very fragile.[35]

At Ellerslie, Zelda also began painting again, mostly for Scottie. She painted whimsical scenes on her daughter's bedroom walls and five series of exquisite watercolor paper dolls: Goldilocks, the Court of Louis XIV, King Arthur's Roundtable, Joan of Arc, and Little Red Riding Hood. A sixth set depicted the members of the Fitzgerald family, with Scott's various costumes including one with wings. Zelda also started to paint more seriously on canvas.[36]

Dancing, however, became Zelda's obsession. While at Ellerslie, twenty-seven-year-old Zelda decided that she was going to become a prima ballerina. Dancing had long been one of Zelda's passions, and she had begun ballet lessons at age nine. As a teenager, Zelda was renowned for her grace and elegance as a dancer, performing regularly at women's clubs, charity events, and local dances. She played the lead role, Folly, in *The War and Peace Pageant*, written by her mother and staged by her sister, Rosalind. According to the local paper, Zelda was attractive in her harlequin outfit and beautifully executed her jester's performance. When Scott first saw Zelda at the Montgomery Country Club, she was performing a ballet, *Dance of the Hours*, and during their courtship she sent him several photographs of herself in dancing costumes, including one of her sitting in her mother's rose garden.[37]

In Alabama, dance allowed Zelda a public forum and added to her popularity. The *Montgomery Advertiser* declared that Zelda Sayre might someday "dance like Pavlova if her nimble feet were not busy keeping up with the pace [of] a string of young but ardent admirers." But marriage put an abrupt end to Zelda's dancing, and she made no attempt to return until 1927, when she began taking professional ballet classes under the tutelage of Catherine Littlefield, director of the Philadelphia Opera Ballet Corps.[38]

Scott's behavior likely provided the catalyst for Zelda's return to dancing. Between leaving France and settling in Delaware, the Fitzgeralds had spent two months in Hollywood, where United Artists had hired Scott to write an original screenplay for the princely sum of sixteen thousand dollars. The film was intended as a vehicle to allow Constance Talmadge to show off her talents as a flapper. United Artists gave Scott a thirty-five-hundred-dollar advance, a much-needed cash infusion for the extravagant Fitzgeralds. While Scottie stayed with Scott's parents and a nanny, Scott and Zelda boarded the train for sunny southern California and booked a room at the tony Ambassador Hotel. At first, Scott worked diligently to get the script done, writing during the day before he and Zelda went out in the evening. However, his productivity diminished after his new friend, writer and photographer Carl van Vechten, introduced him to Lois Moran. Barely eighteen years old and a rising film star, Moran was pretty, petite, and quite intelligent. Scott was smitten, an infatuation that was obvious to everyone who knew him, including Zelda. Lois did not worship Scott in the same way he idolized her, but she did become attached to the thirty-year-old novelist, who escorted her to parties while her widowed mother acted as their chaperone. Most observers noted that Moran looked very much like a younger Zelda. Zelda maintained her outward composure, appearing pleasant and even polite when meeting Moran, but privately fumed. After one humiliating episode, Zelda threw all her clothes into her bathtub and set them on fire.[39]

After just a few months in Hollywood, the Fitzgeralds left. Scott had an argument with Talmadge, and United Artists rejected the screenplay. They departed without the additional $12,500 for the completed script but with even more bills. They boarded a train for Delaware, but even that turned into a disaster when Zelda learned that her husband had invited Moran to visit them at Ellerslie. After a tremendous public row, Zelda slid open the train window and flung her diamond-and-platinum watch—an expensive gift from Scott during their courtship—out of the car.[40]

The bitter fighting continued after they arrived at Ellerslie. During one argument, Scott remarked that at least Moran had made something of herself—something that required not just talent but real effort. He could have uttered no crueler words. Zelda's renewed interest in ballet might have constituted her attempt to prove him wrong.[41]

Zelda took the train to Philadelphia three times a week for lessons. At Ellerslie, she had a ballet bar installed in the living room and practiced every other day and often into the night. Sara Haardt came to visit, found Zelda seemingly happy in her dancing, and remarked that dancing had given her friend both self-confidence and self-esteem. Haardt knew that becoming a prima ballerina at Zelda's age was impossible but nevertheless told her that she was as charming as she had been at eighteen "with all the deep sense of tragedy and beauty of the aristocratic South to which she was born."[42]

But Haardt was mistaken: ballet did not make Zelda happy. Scott resented her lessons and made no secret of his feelings. He could neither share nor take credit for this hobby. He drank even more heavily, using alcohol not as a spur to his creativity, as had previously been the case, but as a diversion from his craft. Zelda suffered several frightening emotional episodes. She was exhausted from dancing and became resentful herself when Moran and her mother came to visit. On several occasions, Scott called a doctor to the house to inject Zelda with morphine to calm her down. She also developed a horrible case of eczema, a painful skin rash that had plagued her throughout the marriage, flaring up when her mental state was at its most unstable. And her marriage and mental health were as fragile as they had ever been.[43]

The Fitzgeralds' Delaware sojourn ended in April 1928, after a fire at Ellerslie destroyed all of their new and very expensive furniture. They, Scottie, and her nanny headed back to Paris for the summer, where they rented an apartment on the Left Bank and Scott began his usual routine of writing in the afternoon and boozing at night. Instead of joining him in carousing around the capital, Zelda went to the studio of Madame Lubov Egorova, a Russian émigré who had been a prima ballerina with the famed Ballet Russe and who had trained Littlefield. Littlefield's recommendation won Zelda admittance to Egorova's prestigious Paris dance school, although Egorova certainly knew that Zelda was too old for a dancing career. Zelda, too, may have known it: even her close friend, Gerald Murphy said, "There are limits to what a woman of Zelda's age can do and it was obvious she had taken ballet up too late." Egorova was distant and professional, a strict and rigorous taskmaster, but Zelda, searching for an anchor, became hopelessly attached.[44]

Zelda bought her new idol flowers nearly every day, gave her whimsical gifts, and took her out to expensive dinners. Zelda attributed her teacher's poverty to her total dedication to her students. For Zelda, Egorova became a parental figure, much like her stern father, and she was willing to do nearly anything to please Egorova. Zelda's semiautobiographical 1932 novel, *Save Me the Waltz*, offers some insight into the relationship: the narrative stresses the rigor of dancing and the toll it takes on the mature body of Alabama Beggs, Zelda's alter ego, as well as the tremendous feeling of reward she experiences when Madame gives her a single compliment.[45]

From 1929 to 1930, ballet utterly consumed Zelda's life. But when Madame Egorova procured for Zelda the title role in a production of *Aida* put on by the

San Carlo Ballet Opera Company in Naples, Zelda for some reason turned it down, even though the company was a good one and living in Italy was inexpensive. She was desperately unhappy and Scott looked haggard. Possibly in hopes of saving their marriage, the couple booked a vacation to Algeria, but it did not help. Zelda took on a wraithlike appearance, with her shoulders hunched and circles under her eyes. She was angry that she was missing her ballet lessons, and she and Scott continued to fight. They returned to Paris, and Zelda resumed her lessons.[46]

On April 23, 1930, friends of the Fitzgeralds from Minnesota, Oscar and Xandra Kalman, were visiting Paris. Xandra was Zelda's only close friend from Scott's hometown. The two couples were eating lunch, and drinking heavily. In the middle of the meal, Zelda became agitated and began to shake, terrified that she would miss her lesson with Madame Egorova. She declared that she needed to go to the studio immediately. Since Scott made no move to get up, Oscar decided to escort Zelda. As they rode in a taxi toward the studio, Zelda struggled into her ballet costume and tied her pink slippers. When the taxi became snarled in a traffic jam, Zelda bounded from the car and began running to the studio. When Kalman caught up with her, she was nearly incoherent. Kalman called Scott, who seemed not to care but urged Zelda to go to a hospital. That night she checked herself into Sanitarium Malmaison, a clinic recommended by Madame Egorova. The admittance report declared that Zelda was "in a state of acute anxiety," repeating that she needed to go back to Madame and work.[47]

Located about five miles from Paris, Malmaison was a large luxurious house set in a picturesque park. Despite its beautiful grounds, Zelda hated the place and checked herself out after less than two weeks and went directly to Egorova's studio, claiming that she needed to work or she would die. Over the next three weeks, Zelda's mental state continued to decline, and she became suicidal and hallucinatory. Scott then had her committed against her will to one of the finest clinics in Europe, Les Rives de Prangins, outside of Geneva, Switzerland.[48]

Like Malmaison, Prangins was beautiful and exclusive. The property, an old chateau set on the banks of Lake Geneva, had belonged to Joseph Bonaparte and boasted music rooms, billiard rooms, a large stable, and tennis courts. Zelda had a spacious and comfortable room with a double bed and a sitting area. Zelda's doctor, Oscar Forel, eventually diagnosed her as a schizophrenic and prescribed therapies that are harsh by modern standards: powerful sedatives, electric shock treatments, and induced comas. The stress caused Zelda's eczema to return, this time all over her body, making her skin feel as if it were on fire. Zelda tried to escape and was sent to a small cottage on the grounds where the most intransigent patients were locked in for treatment.[49]

Miserable, Zelda begged Scott to allow her to return to Egorova since part of her was dying with the "bitter and incessant beating I am taking." After Zelda demanded that Scott write to Madame Egorova to ask about Zelda's future in dance, Egorova answered kindly but directly that Zelda danced well but would never achieve starring roles because she had started too late in life. Her dancing days were over.[50]

Zelda gradually accommodated herself to her new routine at the sanitarium. She could walk, play tennis, and even dance, and her life had a stability that eased her mind considerably. Her doctors urged her to write. Sara Mayfield came to visit and declared her view that Zelda was not a schizophrenic and did not belong in Prangins. According to Mayfield, of course Zelda had a split personality—she was the well-bred, witty, and charming daughter of a conservative Montgomery family as well as "cold, aloof, [and] fey, trapped in the maelstrom of literary cocktail parties and café society . . . where she frequently appeared to be bored." Mayfield believed that Zelda "had brilliant gifts, an unconquerable urge to express herself and a very sensible desire to earn a living for herself." Mayfield diagnosed Zelda's problem as an inability to express herself as an independent woman.[51]

Released from Prangins in September 1931, Zelda and Scottie returned to live in Montgomery, where A. D. Sayre was dying. Scott accompanied them for a few weeks but found life dull and went to Hollywood to try again to write screenplays. In his absence, Zelda began a period of intense writing, composing eight short stories and sending them to Harold Ober, Scott's agent. One, "A Couple of Nuts," appeared in the August 1932 issue of *Scribner's* magazine. Zelda appeared happy—at least until Scott visited. Then her eczema came back with a vengeance, and he thought she seemed irrational. He had her admitted to the Phipps Psychiatric Clinic at the Johns Hopkins University Hospital.[52]

Scott told Zelda's doctor at Phipps, Adolph Meyers, that Zelda had been a wild child in Montgomery, totally indulged by her mother. Meyers listened, evaluated Zelda, and concluded that both Fitzgeralds needed help. Meyers told Scott that he needed to stop drinking and might even benefit from a therapeutic stay at Phipps. Scott refused on the grounds that he was a writer and must feel his subject, not analyze it.[53]

Another doctor, Mildred Squires, encouraged Zelda to write as therapy. In Montgomery, Zelda had started *Save Me the Waltz*, a very thinly fictionalized version of her life. She finished the 250-page novel in just six weeks at Phipps and immediately sent it to Ober. Though rambling and filled with showy metaphors and cryptic allusions, *Save Me the Waltz* reveals much about Zelda and the conflicts between her southern upbringing and her adult life. The story centers on Alabama Beggs from Jeffersonville, Alabama, the youngest child of Judge Austin Beggs and Millie Beggs. Alabama admires her strict but loving father, who chides her for hanging out with the Yankee officers preparing for the First World War. One soldier, aspiring artist David Knight, sweeps her off her feet, and she marries him in New York City after the war. The marriage begins in a frenzy of parties, David becomes famous, and they move to the Riviera. They have a little girl, Bonnie, and Alabama becomes a ballet dancer in her late twenties. The ballet sections offer a fascinating glimpse of what it must have been like for Zelda to try to achieve any status in that competitive field. The plot then diverges from Zelda's real-life experiences: instead of turning down the opportunity to dance in Naples, Alabama leaves her husband and daughter to play a lead role in *Faust*. The reviews are good, and although Alabama misses her little girl, she is happy. But then Alabama injures her foot, develops blood poisoning, and spends weeks in a Naples hospital. When her husband comes with Bonnie, the doctors tell Alabama that she is well but will never dance again. The Knights return to Jeffersonville, where Alabama's father is on his deathbed. Despite the sadness of his death, the book ends on a happy note, with Alabama and David together.

The book received mediocre reviews, leaving Zelda depressed even though she had finally become a published author under her own name. She continued to write privately but turned her public energies to painting. Through the 1930s, Zelda was a prolific painter. Some of the best work was her children's illustrations, particularly a later series on Alice in Wonderland with brilliant shades of red and blue. She also did still-lifes, primarily of flowers, that show a strong influence by Georgia O'Keeffe. In the 1940s, Zelda painted cityscapes of places she had been, including New York and Paris. Her most prized works show androgynous ballet and circus characters with massive musculature. The figures focus on the legs, with the bodies diminishing toward the heads, which are tilted and fairly small. Her final paintings feature biblical scenes, with characters writhing through the landscape in unnatural light.[54]

In the mid-1930s, Scott organized public exhibitions of her work in New York and Baltimore. The exhibitions sparked more marital discord, creating a public rivalry between Scott and Zelda. *The New Yorker* touted the show as featuring "paintings by the almost mythical Zelda Sayre Fitzgerald with whatever emotional overtones or associations may remain from the so-called Jazz Age." *Time* magazine declared her works to be the product of a "brilliant introvert" and found her dancers with their muscular legs reminiscent of Picasso. Reviewing Scott's latest novel, *Tender Is the Night*, a few days later, *Time* offered only middling praise.[55]

Scott refrained from public comment about his wife but privately sniped. He wrote to Scottie that he was trying to write his next big novel, "but when your mother started to catch up with Pavlova at 28 it was fantastic and impossible." In 1938, writing from Hollywood, where he was living with gossip columnist Sheilah Graham, he told his daughter that his mistake in life had been marrying her mother: she was spoiled and soft, without the strength to make it in the public eye, and she had only wanted Scott to work for her gain and had failed to realize that work conferred dignity. By the time Zelda herself tried working, "it was too late and she was broken forever." He repeatedly cautioned Scottie to avoid following Zelda's example and to limit her time with her mother. In December 1940 Scott died of a heart attack brought on by acute alcoholism. Zelda mourned his death but could not attend the funeral and soon slipped out of the public eye.[56]

Zelda appeared much happier after Scott's death. She split her time between her mother's house in Montgomery and Highland Mental Hospital in Asheville, North Carolina, voluntarily checking herself in whenever she had had enough of a visit with her mother and sisters. She enjoyed the peace and the routine of the hospital and was content exercising, painting, and writing, particularly a novel she called *Caesar's Things*, though she never finished it. She also experienced a new spirituality and often carried a Bible and quoted Scripture.[57]

Sara Mayfield's journalistic career peaked in 1945, when she covered the Inter-American Conference on Problems of War and Peace held in Mexico City in March. The conference sought to foster pan-Americanism and resulted in the Act of Chapultepec, in which twenty Western Hemisphere nations agreed to work jointly to repel any aggression in the Americas. The conference was a series of complex diplomatic negotiations on complicated issues, and Mayfield reported events superbly. A few months later, she went to San Francisco to cover the United Nations Conference on International Organization, which brought together representatives from fifty nations to sign the United Nations charter. Covering it represented a journalistic coup for Mayfield.[58]

Mayfield also spent large amounts of time on her inventions. After studying chemistry in college and graduate school, she invented at least twelve new products, the most successful of which was Plasticast, a liquid plastic used for molding and particularly for setting jewelry that she patented in 1939.[59]

After World War II, Mayfield's freelance career came to an end. She returned to Alabama in 1948 and took up residence in the basement of her mother's home in Tuscaloosa, sleeping most of the day and writing and drinking through the night. Her brother, James, became concerned. Eight years earlier, he had claimed that she was having a mental breakdown and had her remanded to

Baltimore's Sheppard-Pratt Hospital and subsequently committed to Tusca-loosa's Bryce Hospital. However, she accused him of sending her to the hospital because he had seen the Plasticast patent applications and wanted some of the royalties. While hospitalized, she reported him to the U.S. Justice Department for illegally transporting her across state lines from Maryland to Alabama. The Justice Department did not respond, and she spent most of 1940 in the asylum. After her release, she returned to work for Transradio. It is not clear whether James Mayfield's worries about his sister's mental health were genuine. In 1948, however, he had her recommitted to Bryce, and she spent most of the next two decades there. At age forty-three, her quest for independence appeared to have ended.[60]

Shortly after Sara Mayfield returned to the hospital, Zelda Fitzgerald died when a fire broke out on a lower floor of Highland Hospital, trapping Zelda and several other patients on the top floor. At her funeral, she was no longer the famous Zelda; she was simply the widow of a once-famous novelist.[61]

Institutionalized at Bryce, Sara Mayfield mourned Zelda's death. Unlike the luxurious private hospitals where Fitzgerald had received treatment, Bryce was a state institution notorious for its horrid conditions, and Mayfield's descriptions are more reminiscent of a prison than a hospital. She lived in a dormitory with eighty-four other women, sharing three toilets and one laundry tub. The food was inedible, with rat pellets in the rice. According to Mayfield, she had been at her mother's house when four local deputies broke in and took her to the hospital without a warrant, a trial, or even a hearing. Mayfield did not understand why she had been committed, although some of that confusion may have resulted from the treatment she received—heavy sedatives and a course of electric shock therapy, the same treatments that Zelda Fitzgerald had received at Prangins. She wrote letters claiming that her brother, James, and his wife, Betty, had wanted her out of the way during their messy divorce and custody case. Then she blamed the hospital's director, W. D. Partlow Jr., whom she claimed was in league with First National Bank and the superintendent of the Alabama State Hospital System, Dr. J. Tarwater. She also implicated University of Alabama football coach Paul "Bear" Bryant in her incarceration and compiled a three-page list of people who had testified to keep her at Bryce, including staff and what she labeled "so-called" patients. Mayfield tried to make her stay more palatable, starting a social club and editing the hospital's newsletter, but her time at Bryce was awful.[62]

Mayfield gained her freedom in 1965, eleven years after her mother's death and nine years after her brother's suicide. No documentation survives to explain her release. Mayfield returned to her mother's house and immediately resumed writing—unlike Fitzgerald, Mayfield's productive periods occurred outside the hospital walls. She lived on a small inheritance from her mother and the money she had received from selling the patent for Plasticast. In 1968, she published *The Constant Circle: H. L. Mencken and His Friends*. Mayfield had met the Baltimore newspaperman when she was a student at Goucher and he had come to the school to award her the prize for best freshman essay. He had invited Mayfield and Sara Haardt out to dinner and been entranced by Haardt. After a long courtship, the acerbic Mencken and the sedate Haardt had married in 1930, living together happily until Haardt's death in 1935. Mayfield was close to the two and very much admired their work. Mayfield wrote the biography of Mencken and his colleagues using a variety of archival sources and her own reminiscences. The result is a sympathetic and nuanced portrait that does not ignore Mencken's barbed wit, especially toward the South.[63]

Royalties from *The Constant Circle* enabled Mayfield to write her most popular book, *Exiles from Paradise*, a dual biography of Scott and Zelda Fitzgerald. Perhaps not surprisingly, Mayfield sympathizes with her lifelong friend and is hard on Scott. The book depicts Zelda as burning brightly and Scott as a gentleman at times but more often a cad whose drinking turned his wife into a wreck. Mayfield's final book, *Mona Lisa: The Woman in the Portrait*, offers a fictionalized account of the relationship between Leonardo da Vinci and his most famous subject.[64] Mayfield died in 1979.

No one could have predicted that the two girls who met that fall day on a Montgomery street would grow up to have lives that not only remained intertwined but also had notable parallels. Both Zelda Sayre Fitzgerald and Sara Mayfield struggled to find their own identities as women navigating the tricky terrain of modernity. And for both women, the consequences of that struggle included hospitalization for psychiatric issues. While it is certainly possible and perhaps even likely that both women suffered from genuine medical maladies, it is also true that in the first half of the twentieth century, women in Alabama who sought to break out of the traditional mold of southern women ran the risk of being labeled hysterical, a term that had originated a century earlier to describe uncontrolled and extreme emotion resulting from disturbances of the uterus. Both women ultimately found paths to peace and fulfillment, but doing so ultimately proved much harder than either would ever have imagined.

NOTES

1. Sara Mayfield, *Exiles from Paradise: Zelda and Scott Fitzgerald* (New York: Delacorte, 1971), 13–18.

2. Lynn Dumenil, *The Modern Temper: American Culture and Society in the 1920s* (New York: Hill and Wang, 1995), 56–98.

3. Sara Mayfield, *The Constant Circle: H. L. Mencken and His Friends* (New York: Delacorte, 1968), 25; Anne Firor Scott, *The Southern Lady: From Pedestal to Politics, 1830–1930* (Charlottesville: University Press of Virginia, 1995).

4. Henry Holman Mize, "The Life of James Jefferson Mayfield" (master's thesis, University of Alabama, 1935); James Benson Sellers, *History of the University of Alabama* (Tuscaloosa: University of Alabama Press, 1953), 484.

5. Helen Friedman Blackshear, "Mama Sayre, Scott Fitzgerald's Mother-in-Law," *Georgia Review* 19 (1965): 465–70; Nancy Milford, *Zelda: A Biography* (New York: Harper and Row, 1970), 4–13.

6. *Polk's Montgomery City Directory,* 1928; Wesley Phillips Newton, *Montgomery in the Good War: Portrait of a Southern City, 1939–1946* (Tuscaloosa: University of Alabama Press, 2000), 20; Wayne Flynt, *Alabama in the Twentieth Century* (Tuscaloosa: University of Alabama Press, 2004).

7. Paul M. Gaston, *The New South Creed: A Study in Southern Mythmaking* (New York: Knopf, 1970); Don Harrison Doyle, *New Men, New Cities, New South: Atlanta, Nashville, Charleston, Mobile, 1860–1910* (Chapel Hill: University of North Carolina Press, 1990).

8. Mayfield, *Constant Circle,* 23–25; F. Scott Fitzgerald and Zelda Fitzgerald, *Dear Scott, Dearest Zelda: The Love Letters of F. Scott and Zelda Fitzgerald,* ed. Jackson R. Bryer and Cathy W. Barks (New York: St. Martin's, 2002), 386.

9. Wayne Flynt, "Alabama's Shame: The Historical Origins of the 1901 Constitution," *Alabama Law Review* 53 (2001): 69.

10. Ibid., 67–76; R. Volney Riser, *Defying Disfranchisement: Black Voting Rights Activism in the Jim Crow South, 1890–1908* (Baton Rouge: Louisiana State University Press, 2010).

11. Mayfield, *Constant Circle,* 24; Milford, *Zelda,* 11.

12. Emily Holt, *Encyclopaedia of Etiquette: What to Write, What to Do, What to Wear, What to Say: A Book of Manners for Everyday Use* (Oyster Bay, N.Y.: Doubleday, Page, 1921), 188–89.

13. Milford, *Zelda,* 15; Sally Cline, *Zelda Fitzgerald: Her Voice in Paradise* (New York: Arcade, 2003), 9.

14. Mayfield, *Exiles from Paradise,* 22–26.

15. Nathan Miller, *New World Coming: The 1920s and the Making of Modern America* (New York: Scribner, 2003), 261; Mayfield, *Exiles from Paradise,* 25.

16. F. Scott Fitzgerald and Fitzgerald, *Dear Scott, Dearest Zelda,* 4, 5, 36, 37.

17. Zelda Fitzgerald, *Save Me the Waltz* (1932; Carbondale: Southern Illinois University Press, 1967), 56.

18. H. L. Mencken and Sara Haardt, *Mencken and Sara: A Life in Letters: The Private Correspondence of H. L. Mencken and Sara Haardt,* ed. Marion Elizabeth Rodgers (New York: McGraw-Hill, 1987), 17.

19. Mayfield, *Exiles from Paradise,* 42–43.

20. John Allen Sellers to Sara Mayfield Sellers, n.d., Sara Mayfield Papers, Division of Special Collections, University Libraries, University of Alabama; Mayfield, *Exiles from Paradise,* 43, 126–27.

21. Finding Aids, Mayfield Papers.

22. F. Scott Fitzgerald and Fitzgerald, *Dear Scott, Dearest Zelda,* 46–47; Milford, *Zelda,* 65–69.

23. Zelda Fitzgerald and Eleanor Anne Lanahan, *Zelda, an Illustrated Life: The Private World of Zelda Fitzgerald* (New York: Abrams, 1996), 22; Joshua Zeitz, *Flapper: The Notorious Life and*

Scandalous Times of the First Thoroughly Modern Woman (New York: Crown, 2006), Milford, *Zelda*, 16–17.

24. F. Scott Fitzgerald and Fitzgerald, *Dear Scott, Dearest Zelda*, 50; Mary Jo Tate, *Critical Companion to F. Scott Fitzgerald: A Literary Reference to His Life and Work* (New York: Facts on File, 2007), 392–93.

25. Kirk Curnutt, "The Cruise of the Rolling Junk by F. Scott Fitzgerald," *F. Scott Fitzgerald Review* 10 (2012): 154–63; Mayfield, *Constant Circle*, 41; Milford, *Zelda*, 73.

26. F. Scott Fitzgerald and Fitzgerald, *Dear Scott, Dearest Zelda*, 68; Geraldine Youcha, *Minding the Children: Child Care in America from Colonial Times to the Present* (New York: Scribner, 1995), 252.

27. Lewis M. Dabney, *Edmund Wilson: A Life in Literature* (New York: Farrar, Straus, and Giroux, 2005), 93; Mayfield, *Constant Circle*, 6.

28. Zelda Fitzgerald, *The Collected Writings of Zelda Fitzgerald*, ed. Matthew J. Bruccoli (Tuscaloosa: University of Alabama Press, 1997), 387–94.

29. Karen Lane Rood, *American Writers in Paris, 1920–1939* (Detroit: Gale Research, 1980), 162–64.

30. African American Songs, Recorded by Sara Mayfield, 1929–30 (phonograph records), Mayfield Papers, Box 1219, Folder 124a–b; journalistic writings, Mayfield Papers, Box 1219, Folders 129–74.

31. Amanda Vaill, *Everybody Was So Young: Gerald and Sara Murphy: A Lost Generation Love Story* (Boston: Houghton Mifflin, 1998), 146–47.

32. Mayfield, *Exiles from Paradise*, 116–17; Kirk Curnutt, *A Historical Guide to F. Scott Fitzgerald* (New York: Oxford University Press, 2004), 33–36.

33. Milford, *Zelda*, 129–31; Harold Bloom, *F. Scott Fitzgerald* (New York: Chelsea House, 1985), 31–32.

34. Zelda Fitzgerald and Lanahan, *Zelda*, 29; F. Scott Fitzgerald and Fitzgerald, *Dear Scott, Dearest Zelda*, 59–60.

35. Zelda Fitzgerald, *Collected Writings*, 273–97, 108–10; Ashley Lawson, "The Muse and the Maker: Gender, Collaboration, and Appropriation in the Life and Work of F. Scott and Zelda Fitzgerald," *F. Scott Fitzgerald Review* 13 (2015): 76–109; Linda Wagner-Martin, *Zelda Sayre Fitzgerald: An American Woman's Life* (New York: Palgrave Macmillan, 2004), 109–11.

36. Matthew J. Bruccoli and Scottie Fitzgerald Smith, *Some Sort of Epic Grandeur: The Life of F. Scott Fitzgerald* (New York: Harcourt Brace Jovanovich, 1981), 258–61.

37. Milford, *Zelda*, 17–18; Scrapbook, c. 1917–26, Zelda Fitzgerald Papers, Box 6, Folder 15, and Box 7, Department of Rare Books and Special Collections, Princeton University Library.

38. Mayfield, *Exiles from Paradise*, 126; Sharon E. Friedler and Susan Glazer, *Dancing Female: Lives and Issues of Women in Contemporary Dance* (Amsterdam: Harwood Academic, 1997) 23–44.

39. Bruccoli and Smith, *Some Sort of Epic Grandeur*, 255–56; Mitford, *Zelda*, 127–130.

40. Milford, *Zelda*, 131; Bruccoli and Smith, *Some Sort of Epic Grandeur*, 256.

41. Tate, *Critical Companion*, 303.

42. Cline, *Zelda Fitzgerald*.

43. Koula Svokos Hartnett, *Zelda Fitzgerald and the Failure of the American Dream for Women* (New York: Lang, 1990), 175; F. Scott Fitzgerald and Fitzgerald, *Dear Scott, Dearest Zelda*, 63.

44. Milford, *Zelda*, 140.

45. Zelda Fitzgerald, *Save Me the Waltz*.

46. Milford, *Zelda*, 156–57; Kirk Curnutt, "Once Again to Zelda," *Southern Review* 49 (2013): 203–13; Bruccoli and Smith, *Some Sort of Epic Grandeur*, 288–89.

47. Mayfield, *Exiles from Paradise*, 148–49; Bruccoli and Smith, *Some Sort of Epic Grandeur*, 288–89.

48. Wagner-Martin, *Zelda Sayre Fitzgerald*, 128–29.

49. Ibid., 130–31; P. K. Gilbert and Mary Elene Wood, "The Writing on the Wall: Women's Autobiography and the Asylum," *Contemporary Psychology* 41 (1996): 390.

50. F. Scott Fitzgerald and Fitzgerald, *Dear Scott, Dearest Zelda*, 80–102; Wagner-Martin, *Zelda Sayre Fitzgerald*, 134.

51. Mayfield, *Exiles from Paradise*, 151–52.

52. Wagner-Martin, *Zelda Sayre Fitzgerald*, 143–44; Mayfield, *Exiles from Paradise*, 171–72.

53. Mayfield, *Exiles from Paradise*, 182–84.

54. Zelda Fitzgerald and Lanahan, *Zelda*, 77–83.

55. F. Scott Fitzgerald, *The Letters of F. Scott Fitzgerald*, ed. Andrew Turnbull (New York: Scribner, 1963), 95.

56. Mayfield, *Constant Circle*, 206; F. Scott Fitzgerald, *Letters*, 32, 64, 88–89.

57. Milford, *Zelda*, 377–82.

58. Inter-American Conference, Mexico City, 1945, Mayfield Papers, Box 1219, Folders 142–48.

59. Patents and Research Notes, 1939–61, in ibid., Box 1218, Folders 99–118, Box 1219, Folders 129–74; U.N. Conference on International Organization (UNICO), San Francisco, 1945, box 1219, folders 160–74, Mayfield Papers.

60. Outgoing Correspondence, Mayfield Papers, Box 1220, Folders 202–14.

61. Milford, *Zelda*, 382–83.

62. Descriptions of Bryce are scattered through the Mayfield Papers.

63. Mayfield, *Constant Circle*, 131–213.

64. Sara Mayfield, *Mona Lisa, the Woman in the Portrait: A Fictional Biography* (New York: Grosset and Dunlap, 1974).

Ruby Pickens Tartt

Composing a New Score

TINA JONES

❀ ❀ ❀

In 1936, while on a trip to Birmingham to evaluate folk material from Alabama for the Federal Writers' Project (FWP) as the national adviser for folklore and folkways for the Works Progress Administration (WPA), ethnomusicologist John A. Lomax asked Alabama FWP director Myrtle Miles where a stack of spirituals originated. Miles replied that a "Mrs. Tartt collected them." Acknowledging that he had not heard half of the songs recorded by Ruby Pickens Tartt, Lomax said, "There are twenty-five spirituals here. One woman couldn't have done that, not in one place. Just not possible."[1]

Lomax's incredulousness at Tartt's accomplishment probably stemmed from his memory of his first October 1934 recording efforts in Alabama, when he found whites "indifferent" and blacks "unusually stupid and unfolksongy." Some people in Huntsville were even hostile to his recording efforts.[2]

Tartt (1880–1974), however, proved to Lomax that the people of Alabama, particularly Sumter County, were plenty "folksongy," and she was willing to do the recording and serve as his avenue into the black community from which the spirituals came. In 1937, Lomax and his wife, Ruby Terrill Lomax, traveled to Livingston to meet Tartt and witness firsthand the folk material she collected in her notebooks.

Over Tartt's ninety-four years, the relationships between blacks and whites and between men and women underwent many changes. At her birth in 1880, Jim Crow laws kept African Americans separated from whites and restricted the voting rights of black men. Women could not vote at all. At midlife, Tartt found herself able not only to cast a ballot but also to help others exercise their voting rights through her role as county registrar. And despite continued second-class citizenship, African Americans gained distinction with contributions in art, literature, music, and academia. Tartt saw the civil rights and women's rights

RUBY PICKENS TARTT, 1974

From *Sumter County Record-Journal.*

movements capture headlines and legal segregation of the races end. Each of these changes redefined relationships, and the lines of acceptable and unacceptable behavior blurred. With her early interest in folk singing and later in her work with the WPA, Tartt navigated uncharted territory in the changing relationships.

As a fifth-generation native of Sumter County, Alabama, Tartt found herself part of a prominent cotton family surrounded by not only devoted parents, Fannie West Short and William King Pickens, but an artistic grandmother, Mary Champ, and a supportive older brother, Champ. Educated at Livingston Female Academy and Alabama Normal College under the tutelage of Julia Strudwick Tutwiler, a progressive educator intent on broadening women's horizons, Tartt learned to investigate the world around her. Catering to every desire, Tartt's father provided her with one of the state's first automobiles and her own gas tank in the front yard. He paid for her to study art and English at Sophie Newcomb College in New Orleans in 1899, and she returned to Alabama Normal College as the head of the art department in 1900. In the summer of 1901, she studied painting with American impressionist William Merritt Chase at the New York School of Art. She returned to Livingston to teach and married her childhood sweetheart, Pratt Tartt, in 1904. Tartt gave birth to her only daughter, Fannie Pickens Tartt, in 1906. Her life seemed to lack nothing.

According to Tartt's biographers, Tartt's parents and in-laws "had illusions that Ruby might settle down and conform to a conventional life for a young Livingston matron" after her marriage. Reflecting the attitudes of the Victorian era, conventional life in the Black Belt would have meant Tartt staying at home, her husband handling public affairs, and the black and white races remaining segregated.[3] However, Tartt's delight in storytelling, disregard for domestic duties, and frequent visits to the black community soon proved she had no intention of being a "proper" southern lady.

Folklorist Harold Courlander captured Tartt's habit of collecting folk songs and folktales in his book *The Big Old World of Richard Creeks*. The novel features Sumter County folksinger Rich Amerson, aka Richard Creeks. Tartt appears as Miss Judy. Creeks explains, "I heard from some old men that Miss Judy has been doing that ever since she was a little girl. Instead of going to church on Sunday, her daddy would take her in his buggy and go off somewhere to hear the Negro people sing, and I guess she aint never stopped that kind of thing, it got to be a sort of habit."[4] Near the end of her life, Tartt found a kindred spirit in Alabama folklorist Kathryn Tucker Windham. The two met while Windham was compiling *Alabama: One Big Front Porch*, a collection of tales about people and places from Alabama's folk history. Tartt told Windham, "Come to think of it, I was nearly always alone in the enjoyment of my interest. Therefore I was 'nuts' according to [white] public opinion—and to think I'm still at 90 running true to form."[5]

Historian Anne Firor Scott writes that the image of the southern lady lived on despite some people's belief of its passing following women's suffrage and the dawn of the "modern" era of the 1920s and 1930s.

> [The image] lived on, not as a prescription for a woman's life but as a style which as often as not was a façade to ward off criticism of unladylike independence or to please men. It gave an illusory uniformity to the southern female personality. In fact, many varieties of women were visible in the new southern culture which had once allowed only domestic talents to blossom. Economic independence, education, and professional opportunity gave the chance for many kinds of development. Even so, the outward forms of ladylike behavior were carefully maintained.[6]

To the white citizens of Sumter County, Tartt was an "artist." While their use of the term carried with it an air of disapproval, it also allowed them to attribute Tartt's more "disturbing" activities, such as attending black churches on Sunday and lobbying for fire protection in black neighborhoods, to her "artistic" disposition.

As a result, when the depression hit and Tartt found herself forced to work for the first time in her life, the WPA and the FWP offered her a means of resisting social mores and preserving the southern black culture she valued. Tartt recalled, "I found overnight in 1936, we not only had no jobs and no money, but we were in debt. At once I fired the cook, had the phone taken out and sold the car. I went all over town and asked if anyone knew of jobs for the most inefficient person on earth. Finally someone suggested I inquire at the Welfare Department, perhaps there was a WPA job I could get."[7]

In addition to providing money, her job at the WPA legitimized Tartt's interest in the black community despite the white community's lack of enthusiasm for her lifelong interest in folk songs and spirituals.[8] Known as a woman willing to push the envelope of what was socially acceptable, Tartt nevertheless understood that a woman had a certain place to maintain.[9] During the 1920s and 1930s, writers spent countless reams of paper describing the changed social status of women following the passage of suffrage legislation, but contemporary historical studies reveal that women's roles were not as different as the media maintained.[10] Therefore, the economic circumstances of the depression afforded possibilities for public service and access to positions of power for which few precedents existed. The basic designs of social culture did not change, but the depression created opportunities for those designs to alter or shift slightly. For Tartt, unlike Lomax, the WPA represented a chance to do what she had always wanted with little public scrutiny. As a result, she went into the homes of both blacks and whites, and they entered her home with little difficulty despite segregation.

The way Tartt described her hometown when she was eighty-one reveals her insight regarding the careful balance that held the peace. Livingston was "a small old town with many odd and provincial people; a town where the best somehow seems impossible, but the worst never happens; a town where silly simple episodes can get much bigger than they deserve to be, and often even State and Church regard it as a threat to the established order of society. This can be both amusing and touching as comedy invariably is."[11] The order of society was not to be changed; otherwise, the troublemaker could be held accountable not to family but to the higher authorities of church and government. In other words, family business was town business.

Author Carl Carmer, a friend of Tartt's, wrote of the struggles of an artist living in the South. His 1934 book, *Stars Fell on Alabama*, received negative reviews from Alabamians, leading him to decide not to return to the state. In a letter to Tartt, he wrote, "One thing the people of the South pretty generally are incapable of even conceiving, . . . is artistic integrity—a creative worker's compulsion to write or paint the thing as he sees it. I don't need to tell you this though—for you have had to combat them on this point more often than I."[12] To live and work in her own town, Tartt had to find a middle ground that allowed her to express herself as well as to avoid completely ostracizing herself and her family from the community. Painting and collecting folklore, both songs and tales, provided such a middle ground.

According to Carmer, Tartt's choice of cemetery plot reflected her negotiation of the space between the two worlds. In the 1950s, Carmer and Tartt listened to singer Earthy Anne Coleman's rendition of "Wake Up Noah," and Tartt exclaimed, "When I die I want all the old-time singers to sing at my funeral in the cemetery." After Coleman said, "We'd do it, but they won't let us sing in a white-folks cemetery," Tartt replied, "That's why I got a corner lot right by the fence and you can all walk down that singing and be right beside me." Indeed, her grave lies at the edge of the Myrtlewood Cemetery.[13]

This episode raises a number of important complications about "crossing" and failing to really cross boundaries. Carmer, Tartt, and Coleman inhabit a common position as artists, but other identities intrude into this common position. The meeting brings together the pinnacle of political and social power (the white man) with the most politically and socially disadvantaged member of American society of the era (the black woman). Between these two individuals is a white woman, connected on the one hand to the white man by race and on the other hand to the black woman by gender. Metaphorically speaking, Tartt for this moment becomes the fence that both connects and separates the two halves of the town's cemetery. Tartt does not question the fence, while Carmer does not question either the fence or the connection between the two women. The fence, like color and gender lines, is a boundary around but not necessarily through which they work.

Music provides the means by which the women work around the fence. The two women continue to discuss what song would be appropriate for the service and agree on the spiritual "Free at Last." Today, the song is inextricably connected to Martin Luther King Jr. and the civil rights movement, but the words have long symbolized triumph in the face of a struggle. A common language connects individuals, enabling them to articulate shared experiences and order them so that meaning continues to be shaped by those who speak and listen.

Although Coleman died before Tartt did, "Free at Last" was not sung at Tartt's funeral, and legalized segregation was a thing of the past by the time she died on November 29, 1974, the episode demonstrates Tartt's understanding of her place between two cultures. For feminist critic Nelly Furman, the lives of women who write, such as Tartt, are texts, just like pieces of literature that beckon us to read them. Furman defines a text as a space of transition that either leads us to a new path or becomes a site where change occurs. When Carmer, Tartt, and Coleman met, American society was teetering on the brink of change, with the 1954 *Brown v. Board of Education* decision in the process of bringing about the desegregation of public schools. Nonetheless, many other fences continued to separate and connect individuals, and even in death, Tartt served as a liaison between the white community in which she lived and the black community in which she found much beauty. On the day of her funeral, both communities gathered to mourn their loss. Without introduction, Dock Reed, one of Sumter County's most noted African American folksingers, stepped forward to offer what he had shared with Tartt so many times before—his voice.

To the outsider reading the newspaper account of Tartt's funeral, Reed's act speaks on many levels. Much could be made of the obvious differences between these two individuals—a poor black man who struggled to support a wife and two children in rural West Alabama at the height of racial segregation and a white female from a prominent family who fell on hard economic times, wrestled with the idea of proper southern womanhood, and found an alternative model for herself. Any effort to analyze complex negotiations among race, sex, and class neglects one aspect of existence—humanity. This moment stands as an expression of one human being's grief at the loss of another human being.

To express his emotion, Reed chose the language in which he and Tartt had communicated for more than fifty years—music. For them, as with Coleman, the language articulated itself in the form of a spiritual. With the words of "Steal Away Home," Reed voiced his own understanding of death.

Taken from Psalm 77:18, the spiritual begins with a familiar refrain:

> Steal away, steal away,
> steal away to Jesus.
> Steal away, steal away home,
> I ain't got long to stay here.

For the uninitiated listener, the song sounds of a time long gone and signifies simply the praise of one's God. However, for the initiated—a group that included Reed and Tartt—the meaning was quite different. This spiritual and many others formed part of the code of the Underground Railroad that helped escaped slaves find freedom.[14] Since singing about freedom was considered a criminal act, lyrics that entertained this subject had to be couched in ambiguous phrases that would be clear to slaves yet not arouse suspicion among whites. Harriet Tubman used "Steal Away Home" to inform Underground Railroad passengers that she had arrived and would not stay long. In addition, slaves used the song to announce to their family and friends that they intended to escape. In his classic study, *American Folklore*, Richard M. Dorson noted that spirituals "summoned the bondsmen for African-type secret meetings, encouraged them to flee via the underground railroad. . . . All the time they employed the white man's phrases for their own meanings. 'Freedom' which to the Christian signified freedom from sin, to the slave meant physical freedom; the white man's 'Canaan' was for [the slave] the North."[15]

The words *steal away home* therefore stand as a verbal mask signifying the spiritual meaning of traveling to heaven while subversively referring to the struggle for freedom. The second verse also holds double meaning:

> My Lord, He calls me,
> He calls me by the thunder;
> The trumpet sounds within my soul,
> I ain't got long to stay here.

The verse reveals the secretive nature of the song. The singer has been singled out by "the trumpet sounds within my soul." Since only the singer can hear the sounds, only the singer understands the words' true meaning. One might argue that although Reed understood the significance of the words he sang, Tartt, as a white woman, never truly did. However, this argument overlooks Tartt's long association with Reed and her lifelong participation in the black community's funerals, church services, and singings.

The song, chosen by Reed, is traditionally executed as a call and response, with the choir performing the refrain or chorus and a soloist singing the verses. Reed thus spoke directly to Tartt, while she announced her desire for heaven (freedom), a place located outside of society's restrictions.[16] Reed indicated that he understood her desire and that he, too, would seek heaven as a freedom from society's restrictions.

The spirituals sung by Reed and recorded by Tartt crossed the color line and conveyed solace between two people whose very relationship in both the black and white communities had often been construed as dangerous and taboo. On at least two other occasions, Reed and Tartt came together and used the spiritual tradition to communicate. Tartt sought out Reed when her father died in 1923. The loss was a tremendous blow to Tartt, since her father had financially and emotionally supported what she called her "pilgrimages" and had understood his daughter's restlessness in Sumter County.[17] In addition, William Pickens had shared his daughter's love of spirituals and in fact had introduced her to Reed's singing. After her father's death, Tartt told Reed that William Pickens had felt that no one could sing the way Reed did. At Pickens's funeral, Reed had sung "Oh, The Sun Will Never Go Down, Go Down," a song of hope with words that promise the listener that whatever else happens, the sun will continue to shine and flowers will continue to bloom. Although another line acknowledges the emptiness caused by the loss of a loved one (in the song's case, a mother), the words provide reassurance that life will continue. Tartt reached for consolation from Reed by traveling to his home, and he supplied that solace through his singing. When he finished, Reed asked Tartt where her notebook was since "Yo' pa always have you take down what I sung." Tartt answered, "Next time, Dock."[18] Tartt undoubtedly received expressions of sympathy from the white community over the loss of her father, and the local newspaper printed a lengthy obituary reminding Sumter County citizens that Pickens had served as clerk of the circuit court since 1904 and as secretary-treasurer of Alabama Normal College and was a respected member of the Methodist church. Tartt's need to seek Reed's companionship during a time of grief, however, suggests that he offered a different kind of consolation. The words of the white world acknowledged Pickens's place in society and undeniably evoked a sense of pride; Reed's words reassured a child that mourning the loss of a parent was natural and normal.

Tartt and Reed also came together at the January 1948 death of John Lomax, who had offered both Tartt and Reed artistic encouragement and monetary support.[19] In a letter to Ruby Lomax, Tartt said she and Reed stood in the middle of the road and wept over Lomax's death. A few days later, Reed (who was illiterate) asked Tartt to request that Ruby Lomax send him a picture of her late husband because "I've got to get pacified somehow."[20] Tartt then remembered that Reed had received a tribute in Lomax's autobiography, *The Adventures of a Ballad Hunter*, which closed with a spiritual sung by Reed to Lomax. Tartt traveled to Reed's farm and told him that she had a message for him from Lomax. She then read the words of the spiritual aloud from the autobiography:

> Angel flew from the bottom of the pit,
> Gathered the sun all in her fist,
> Gathered the moon all 'round her waist,
> Gathered the stars all under her feet,
> Gathered the wind all 'round her waist,
> Cryin, "Holy Lord,"
> Cryin, "Holy Lord,"
> Cryin, "Holy my Lord,"
> Cryin, "Holy!"

> Weep like a willow, moan like a dove,
> You can't get to Heaven 'thout you go by love.

As Tartt read, Reed hummed and then sang. Finally, Reed said, "I's pacified, Miss Ruby. Glory, glory. Thanky, thanky."[21] The song offered a reminder that possessions do not open heaven's door, love does. Reed had previously lamented not having done more for Lomax, especially since Lomax had given Reed so much materially. By reading the spiritual, Tartt assured Reed that he had given just as much to Lomax. In grief, the song bridged the cultural gap separating Tartt and Reed, providing them with a language in which to communicate. Such a language was particularly important when the ruling members of society enforced strict standards that rendered the relationship between a black man and a white woman unequal and even in some instances dangerous.

Tartt's whiteness allowed her privilege regardless of her fallen financial status. Despite losing the family home and seeking government relief, she remained a part of the aristocracy of a small southern town. Accordingly, her presence in the black community demanded deference, even though many of the singers from whom she collected songs owned the land on which they lived, while Ruby and Pratt Tartt moved from rental house to rental house. Perhaps Tartt's understanding of herself as aristocrat also explains her constant gifts of money, clothing, and even furniture to neighbors both black and white, no matter her financial situation. Tartt's activities caused much comment in Livingston, particularly among members of Tartt's family.[22]

Mahnaz Kousha suggests that the dynamic between black domestics and their white employers in the South was structured by the codification of African American subordination through Jim Crow legislation. This codification removed southern white women's need to maintain social distance to assert authority and to establish superiority.[23] Though Tartt apparently did not employ either Coleman or Reed, Kousha's argument offers insight into the complex layering of the relationships between Tartt and the black community of Sumter County. Before the boll weevil devastated cotton crops in 1915, William King Pickens had employed many black families, including Reed's. Even after the Tartts' financial position declined, Ruby Tartt remained the "boss's daughter," evoking the codification of behavior Kousha discusses. This identity allowed Tartt certain liberties. She could attend funerals and call on sick people within the black community with little scrutiny because she was upholding the duty of her class and race in caring for those less fortunate than she. Her status ensured that African Americans would allow her to enter their homes and churches to avoid displeasing the boss. Though genuine affection may have existed between these two groups, codes of behavior incorporated tension into the relationships.

Tartt's understanding and valuing of the folk songs and the people who sang them seem to contradict her need to maintain her appearance as a wealthy white woman who bestowed money, food, and clothing on the less fortunate. According to historian Terry Cooney's examination of the 1930s as a clash between traditional values and modern solutions, "mixed meanings may offer important messages, and the presence of contradictions is seldom a simple matter of hypocrisy."[24] Economics often codified the relationships between black and white. The depression displaced many from their normal economic status.

For Reed and Tartt, music held a special place beyond cultural barriers and societal restrictions. Music crossed the color line. Reed was both a folksinger, representing the black voice, and an artist who sought another language in which to express himself. The double-voiced text of the folk song permitted expression of the unspeakable and explanation of the unrecognized.

In Tartt's later years, people repeatedly asked why she collected folk material, particularly folk songs. She answered that "folksongs are more than music, they are in the deepest sense a part of the life of a people. Not an adopted past that could be disbursed with but a very basic and organic part of common life."[25] Tartt understood the black community as having a past that could not be "disbursed with" despite white society's adoption of another past for the African

American community. Blacks' music represented a link to their true past. Elsewhere, Tartt wrote that folk songs "tell us more about the heart of a nation than a hundred history books."[26] Tartt's words indicate a perception of the gaps in published history books. Despite its claims of universality, the dominant white voice alone cannot tell the whole story of society.

The music Tartt heard uncovered voices of different generations, races, and genders. Tart saw the genre as representing the life of a people but retaining room for individuals to leave their marks on each song:

> After these songs have been passed on to school children, many changes have been made in the order and music until they are sung in many different ways by both young and old. . . . Some of these have as many different tunes as words. All of these however are traceable to the parent stem, so that the individual has his share in the song, and the race has its share . . . which has led someone to call folk music an individual flowering on a common stem and that definition of folk music I should like to call my own.[27]

Tartt's discussion of folk songs as a symbolic understanding of herself and the people whose music and lives she recorded begins an articulation of how communities of people, no matter their differences, connect. The "stem" named by Tartt signifies the passage of time as well as the connective possibilities that music holds. She acknowledges that the "songs" or voices have as many different tunes as words. No matter the tune we sing, we all have a place on a common stem.

Tartt answered questions regarding folk songs by writing on the backs of index cards, adding notations in the margins of letters, or by directly corresponding with those who inquired. Her answers repeatedly returned to the issue of language: "I've been particularly interested not only in what [the black man] said but the way he said it—*His own words* for I believe we can better *understand* a person if we know the very *language* in which he expresses his *thoughts* and *feelings*. If I have succeeded in that I'm satisfied."[28] These words indicate that she was not attempting racial masquerade or even linguistic imitation at this point unless the act of transcription is imitation. However, transcription typically means an accurate rendering of the words, song, or recording of an event. Tartt's efforts at transcribing language received notice in Washington: FWP staff member Harry Bennett wrote to his boss, B. A. Botkin, that Tartt "shows much intelligence and discernment. Her renderings of dialect are fair, though they are sometimes spoilt by exaggerated pseudo-phonetic transcription."[29] Tartt sought to capture individual nuances of voice—that is, each word represented a unique aspect of the individual being recorded. As a result, different spellings of the same word are not uncommon in Tartt's work. In *Dim Roads and Dark Nights: The Collected Folklore of Ruby Pickens Tartt*, editor Alan Brown explains that he "elected to publish her works exactly as she recorded them so that the reader can have the experience of 'hearing' pure folklore, coming from the mouths of the storytellers."[30]

Although Tartt's expression in folklore itself would not emerge until she began recording life histories for the WPA, her father had her emulate the voices of Sumter County folksingers to learn the art of folk song. William Pickens had "John Campbell, a Negro with a good voice, . . . come out and get me straight on some of the words."[31] Campbell served as Tartt's teacher. While Tartt's father may have seen his daughter's antics as merely the act of a precocious child seeking adult attention, his act of asking Campbell to "get" Tartt "straight on some of the words" established a precedent in Tartt's life and her work with the folk songs and folklore of the black community. Tartt was not to mock or appropriate the dialect strictly for her own use; she was to learn it and understand it.

NOTES

1. Lomax's quote appeared as the opening to Virginia Pounds Brown and Laurella Owens's original unpublished manuscript for *Toting the Lead Row: Ruby Pickens Tartt, Alabama Folklorist*, Ruby Pickens Tartt Collection, FF-5, 25, #70, Alabama Room, Julia Tutwiler Library, University of West Alabama.

2. Nolan Porterfield, *The Last Cavalier: The Life and Times of John A. Lomax* (Urbana: University of Illinois Press, 1996), 77, 334–35. Porterfield admits that Lomax could be a bundle of contradictions. While he spent his life recording the music of cowboys, blues singers, country laborers, and black and white folk artists alike, his attitude toward people could be patronizing, paternalistic, and racist.

3. Virginia Pounds Brown and Laurella Owens, *Toting the Lead Row: Ruby Pickens Tartt, Alabama Folklorist* (Tuscaloosa: University of Alabama Press, 1981), 10; Glenn N. Sisk, "Social Life in the Alabama Black Belt, 1875–1917," *Alabama Review* 8 (1955): 83–103.

4. Harold Courlander, *The Big Old World of Richard Creeks* (Philadelphia: Chilton, 1962), 104.

5. Kathryn Tucker Windham, *Alabama: One Big Front Porch* (Tuscaloosa: University of Alabama Press, 1975), 56.

6. Anne Firor Scott, *The Southern Lady: From Pedestal to Politics, 1830–1930* (Chicago: University of Chicago Press, 1970), 225.

7. Miscellaneous Papers, Tartt Collection, Box 2, Folder F-1.

8. Brown and Owens, *Toting the Lead Row*, 10–12. Brown and Owens document the white community's lack of enthusiasm for Tartt's work. I also interviewed Tartt's relatives and Sumter County citizens to gauge the town's reaction to Tartt's interest in folklore and folk songs from the black community.

9. Jean Ennis, interview by author, October 4, 1997. When Ennis moved from Washington State to the town of Livingston as a new bride, she quickly learned that her actions were to be dictated

by the family into which she had married. The Ennis and Scruggs families, like the Tartts, were among the first families to settle Sumter County following the 1830 Treaty of Dancing Rabbit Creek.

10. Terry A. Cooney, *Balancing Acts: American Thought and Culture in the 1930s* (New York: Twayne, 1995); Lynn Dumenil, *The Modern Temper: American Culture and Society in the 1920s* (New York: Hill and Wang, 1995).

11. Ruby Pickens Tartt to W. H. Sadler, May 4, 1961, private collection of Billy Stuart, Livingston, Alabama.

12. Tartt Collection, Folder FF-1.

13. Carl Carmer, *My Most Unforgettable Character* (Livingston, Ala.: Livingston University Press, 1975).

14. PBS, "American Roots Music," http://www.pbs.org/americanrootsmusic/pbs_arm_es_religious .html (accessed July 30, 2016).

15. Richard M. Dorson, *American Folklore*, rev. ed. (Chicago: University of Chicago Press, 1977), 180.

16. Tartt lived her last days in the Sumter County nursing home and left behind manuscripts in which she articulated her feelings about old age. Material provided by Tartt biographer Virginia Pounds Brown.

17. Virginia Pounds Brown (interview by author, January 15, 2001).

18. The incident appears in chapter 3, "Pilgrimages," of the manuscript version of Brown and Owens, *Toting the Lead Row*.

19. Brown and Owens, *Toting the Lead Row*, 52; Porterfield, *Last Cavalier*; John A. Lomax and Alan Lomax, *Adventures of a Ballad Hunter* (New York: Macmillan, 1947).

20. Ruby Pickens Tartt to Ruby Terrill Lomax, February 28, 1948, Tartt Collection, FF-3, 24, #58.

21. Ibid., February 12, 1948.

22. Annie Bestor Mitchell, great-niece of Ruby Pickens Tartt, interview by Virginia Pounds Brown, February 1, 1978. Mitchell discussed the strained relationship between Ruby Pickens Tartt and the Tartt family, particularly her mother-in-law, Ba-ma Tartt.

23. Mahnaz Kousha, "Race, Class, and Intimacy in Southern Households: Relationships between Black Domestic Workers and White Employers," in Barbara Ellen Smith, ed., *Neither Separate nor Equal: Women, Race, and Class in the South* (Philadelphia: Temple University Press, 1999), 77–89.

24. Cooney, *Balancing Acts*, 61.

25. Tartt Collection, Box 25, Folder 1-3.

26. Ibid.

27. Ibid.

28. Ibid., Box 3, Folder 1-1.

29. Kathie Farnell, "Narratives of Former Alabama Slaves," *Alabama Heritage* 51 (1999): 40.

30. Ruby Pickens Tartt, *Dim Roads and Dark Nights: The Collected Folklore of Ruby Pickens Tartt*, ed. Alan Brown (Livingston, Ala.: University of Livingston Press, 1993), ii.

31. Tartt Collection, Box 2, Folder G.

Bess Bolden Walcott

A Legacy of Women's Leadership at Tuskegee Institute

CAROLINE GEBHARD

❀ ❀ ❀

Bess Bolden Walcott (1886–1988) lived almost all of her 101 years in rural Alabama. Her remarkable life included combating the pandemic flu of 1918, overseeing emergency relief during the Great Depression, serving her country and community in both world wars, and helping children recover from polio, a disease that killed and crippled thousands. Over her long, remarkable life, she volunteered her gifts as a leader, speaker, and writer, and when action was needed, she knew how to get things done. Others looked to B. B., as her friends called her, in times of crisis, and she never gave up in the face of overwhelming tasks or the grossly unequal treatment she and other African Americans faced. In 1918, she helped found the all-black American Red Cross chapter at Tuskegee Institute, and it went on to serve with distinction during both peace and war.

For almost all of the thirty-three years she served as the chapter's executive secretary, she also held down a full-time position at Tuskegee Institute (now Tuskegee University). However, she faced one of her greatest challenges during the Second World War, when she became the first African American, male or female, to serve as a Red Cross field director for the new cadets who arrived at Tuskegee Army Air Field to begin their pilot training in 1941.

Bess Adeline Bolden was born on November 4, 1886, in Xenia, Ohio, and graduated from Oberlin College in 1908, placing her among the tiny minority of African American women who earned college degrees. Then as now, Oberlin was an elite college with a long history of enrolling talented African Americans, but blacks made up only a small percentage of the student body at the turn of the twentieth century. She was one of only six African Americans, including three women, enrolled at the time.[1]

Not much is known about her parents, William Pinkney Bolden and Fannie Bizzell Bolden, or how they managed to send her to college, but in a 1983 talk,

BESS BOLDEN WALCOTT

Known as "The Red Cross Lady," B. B. Walcott was photographed
in her Red Cross uniform for the cover of the March 1944
issue of *Service*, a Tuskegee Institute publication.
Used by permission of the Tuskegee University Archives.

Walcott suggested that they cared about her education and helped spark what she called her "insatiable curiosity." She recalled "leaning against" her father when she was nine years old and he took her to hear Booker T. Washington speak. The educator, she remembered, told his Cleveland audience that students at Tuskegee did not write compositions beginning, "Beyond the Alps lies Italy" but instead wrote about what they knew and experienced every day: the turnips they were growing in the garden and the hogs they fed. Even at that early age she was fascinated by writing and especially by the message of writing what you know, though she recollected that she personally had never grown any turnips. Still, she said, Washington's approach to writing "has influenced me all through the years."[2]

In 1908, during her senior year, Washington hired Bolden to come to Tuskegee. The yearbook shows a serious young woman with hair fashionably swept up. Her classmates credited her with solving the question, "Has an isolated cat self-consciousness?," though they did not record her answer.[3] For an ambitious female college graduate, the chance to work at the school founded by her childhood hero—though far from the lofty heights of Oberlin—proved irresistible.

When Bolden arrived at Tuskegee in 1908, the school had only recently celebrated its twenty-fifth anniversary. Tuskegee Normal School had been founded on July 4, 1881, for the primary purpose of preparing black teachers to educate the children of former slaves. Washington himself had been born a slave, as had renowned scientist George Washington Carver, who had come to Tuskegee a dozen years before Bolden and who ultimately became her lifelong friend. Although Tuskegee had added *Industrial Institute* to its name in 1891, when the school's mission expanded to include "industrial" education, it continued to devote considerable resources to preparing teachers.

Later in her life, Walcott remembered Tuskegee's campus as unlike the rural South that surrounded it although the campus's roads were also made of "soft, mushy, bountiful red clay." Because Washington hired the best and brightest from Harvard, Yale, Cornell, Brown, Oberlin, and elsewhere, Walcott recalled, the campus atmosphere was "cosmopolitan." The result was a vibrant social life, with debates, plays, and even dancing—though only off campus and for teachers. According to Walcott, "Every teacher had her little bag and in the bag were her dancing shoes," which she would put on after walking along muddy roads to get to the off-campus dances. Tuskegee did not pay a lot: Bolden's starting salary was twenty-five dollars a year, plus room and board. Yet she and other talented young African Americans flocked to Tuskegee to participate in the advancement of the race and help perpetuate its record of success. Walcott remembered the stirring sight of students marching to chapel led by a brass band, the young men in blue uniforms with brass buttons shining, the young women in dark blue calico dresses (light blue for nursing students). The sight moved some observers to tears: "Nothing but the band and the sound of their feet: all of these young people marching together, going somewhere, going in order—you felt it; it was in the air. You couldn't help but feel it. . . . The whole place was interlaced with romance and interesting things."[4]

One of those dashing young figures was another young Tuskegee instructor, Jamaican-born William Holbrook Walcott, whom Bess Bolden married in 1911. They lived on campus and went on to have three daughters and a son, who were reared on the school's grounds.[5]

Like other female faculty, Bess Walcott became an active member of the Tuskegee Woman's Club, founded by Washington's third wife, Margaret Murray Washington. The club not only held literary and social evenings but also undertook projects to improve African Americans' living standards locally as well as regionally. Walcott recalled Margaret Washington as a dynamic leader who saw to it that Tuskegee's female faculty volunteered to serve the rural poor, including participating in Mothers' Meetings she had started. The organizations Washington created led to the formation of other important Tuskegee civic groups, including the Tuskegee Institute Red Cross Chapter and the Tuskegee Civic Association.[6]

Booker T. Washington initially recruited Bess Bolden to come to Tuskegee to do research for Dr. Robert E. Park, a sociologist whose work at Tuskegee laid the foundation for his later career at the University of Chicago. She was also assigned to catalog Washington's private library, an extensive collection of significant work by and about people of African descent, and to instruct students in library science.[7] She soon found that Washington's "byword was correlation—meet the need, do the thing that needs to be done, but adjust it to the need."[8] That meant finding ways to make what students were learning in the classroom connect to what they were doing outside the classroom, and it meant being willing to adapt to the needs of the students and the school. Walcott was so thoroughly imbued with Tuskegee's mission of connecting learning with the practical needs of people that decades later she continued to preach correlation.[9]

Walcott also ran Tuskegee's rural circulating library, and she eventually taught English composition and American literature. In addition, she directed student performances and founded the *Tuskegee Messenger*, one of many publications in which she played an instrumental role. She proved a dedicated teacher, embracing Washington's revolutionary educational philosophy, which called for reaching students by showing them the practical applications of academic subjects such as English and mathematics. Walcott recalled that the goal was "to unite what [the students] were learning in the academic [curriculum] with what they did in the shops," so students studying architecture, agriculture, and masonry had to write compositions about their future occupations. Not content merely to correct their English, Walcott decided that she "had to know what they were doing in the shop. So I went every day [to] talk with them about their work. . . . And, then I would incorporate it in to my teaching." She recalled she "had all the boys' sections" because discipline was never a problem for her. When football later became popular at Tuskegee, she taught the players in the same way, speaking their language and using what they knew—sports—to teach them English grammar and composition.[10]

One particular experience drove home to Walcott the importance of never giving up on any student. One young man was doing poorly in Walcott's American literature class: despite his efforts, he simply could not understand the meaning of William Cullen Bryant's poem, "To a Waterfowl." He ultimately dropped out of school and went home to tend to his ailing mother. When she died, according to Walcott, "it was the end of everything. And he had just walked out in the yard by himself and said he happened to look up . . . and there was a bird flying across the sky. And then he said it was just like a light had broken and he said that's the thing we have been reading in class. That's what Mrs. Walcott's been telling me." In that instant, he told Walcott, he completely understood Bryant's poem about a lone bird being guided through the "boundless sky." Moreover, he believed that his mother was telling him to return to school. "From then on," Walcott said, "there was no student I found impossible," and his experience "encouraged me, [to] just teach my head off."[11]

But Walcott's talents were in demand beyond the classroom, and over the many years she worked at Tuskegee, she served four school presidents and took on many roles, using her considerable organizing and administrative skills to do whatever Mother Tuskegee required. For example, she headed the committee arranging Frederick D. Patterson's inauguration as Tuskegee's third president, arranged the celebration honoring Carver's forty years at the school, and took charge of fund-raising efforts to commission a bust of Carver.[12]

Walcott worked closely with Robert Russa Moton, who succeeded Washington as Tuskegee's president after his death in 1915. Serving as his editorial assistant and in other capacities, Walcott helped as he oversaw the school's transformation into a two- and then a four-year college. In 1923, he spearheaded the establishment of a Tuskegee veterans' hospital staffed by black doctors and nurses, with the school donating the land and the plan succeeding despite the opposition of many white Alabamians, including the governor and members of the Ku Klux Klan.[13]

In 1918, Margaret Washington, Bess Walcott, and other Tuskegee women founded the institute's all-black Red Cross chapter. Created in 1881, the same year as Tuskegee, the Red Cross had initially ignored racial lines in its efforts to provide relief services "free from all shadows of sex or race." However, the organization also granted local chapters a great deal of leeway to follow local customs, particularly in the South, leading to gross violations of African Americans' rights.[14] White citizens of Macon County had been granted a Red Cross charter in 1917, but the Tuskegee women sought to form a chapter outside the control of local whites. Doubtless, they also saw it as an opportunity to show their mettle.

Moton initially had hesitated to agree to a Red Cross chapter on campus but changed his mind at the urging of the members of the Tuskegee Woman's Club. The school applied to form an independent chapter that would report directly to the Gulf Division in New Orleans. It would be the first black-led Red Cross chapter, an idea that encountered stiff opposition both locally and across the South. The chair of the Atlanta Red Cross chapter objected because "of the problems connected with colored people making bandages"—that is, "the amount of tuberculosis and disease that the negro may spread." For this reason, the Atlantans allowed "only certain kind of work to be done by our colored branch." Tuskegee succeeded only after enormous effort and with the backing of the head of the Southeastern Division, Harry Hopkins, and former president William Howard Taft. In Walcott's words, the charter was granted only after "months of correspondence and a series of qualifyings," including a visit by Hopkins. On July 29, 1918, the chapter, chaired by Moton, gathered at his home to choose its officers: members selected Walcott to serve as executive secretary, a position she held until 1951. When the executive committee met again on September 13, 1918, members focused first on locating "suitable headquarters," finding hosts for visiting soldiers' families, and organizing a membership drive.[15]

The men and women of Tuskegee Institute responded enthusiastically to the creation of the Red Cross chapter and to the message of patriotism and democratic ideals promoted by its founders. By October 8, the chapter had three hundred members. Later in the month, organizers held a program to encourage students to join, with one speaker proclaiming, "This country is your country, it is my country, that flag is your flag and my flag, . . . it is because of these high ideals of honor, and peace, and of freedom, and of brotherhood, and of devotion and of an equal chance, that black men and white men all over our country have gone across the sea." Campus leaders told the crowd of students assembled in the school's chapel that "the Negro is on trial, he must prove to the world, not only that he is patriotic, not only efficient, but that he can serve and serve effectively." Tuskegee Institute's fledgling Red Cross chapter had to demonstrate that it could become a self-supporting, highly effective unit.[16]

The new chapter soon found itself responding to its first disasters. The school's main trades building burned on October 14, 1918, and a few days later, students began to come down with the flu, Tuskegee's first victims of the deadly 1918–19 worldwide epidemic that ultimately killed more people than the First World War did. At the height of the epidemic, 250 Tuskegee students were hospitalized, and the institute's hospital treated a total of 449 cases, with 33 people developing pneumonia.[17]

Tuskegee's response to the epidemic included an aggressive quarantine ordered by the school's medical director, Dr. John A. Kenney; a high level of care from the school's hospital; and extraordinary efforts by seven hundred Red Cross volunteers. The *Tuskegee Student* reported proudly, "Not one death resulted from the dreaded 'Spanish' influenza" and praised the "beautiful spirit" shown by the Red Cross chapter. Volunteers not only stepped in to relieve the overburdened nursing staff but also "worked like Trojans" to produce the hospital supplies needed, with the women sewing "1,000 napkins for sputum, 100 masks, 135 bags for beds, 59 bed protectors, 11 pairs of slippers and 14 kimonas" and "a force of boys" making thirty beds. Treasurer Warren Logan, who had been at the school almost since it opened, publicly thanked Kenney, the nurses, and the Red Cross workers, declaring that "many would have perished but for the deeds of love of these faithful men and women cooperating for the common good."[18]

Moreover, despite its massive workload at home, the Tuskegee Institute Red Cross sent a shipment of sewn and knitted goods to the Gulf Division headquarters on November 25, 1918. On December 21, the *Tuskegee Student* declared, "One cannot help but admire the women of the Red Cross chapter at Tuskegee Institute. Faithful, persistent, patient, industrious; they have accomplished in a short interval a vast amount of work under great odds." Most of the volunteers, it noted, had school duties from Monday through Saturday, and some also taught at Tuskegee's night school. The Red Cross workers had been sewing and knitting at night, during lunch, and in any other spare moment they could find.[19] Tuskegee's Red Cross earned the respect of those on campus as well as those beyond it.

Tuskegee Institute's Red Cross Chapter continued this extraordinary esprit de corps, with Walcott emerging as the central figure, though the institute's president always served as the organization's formal chair. Under Walcott's leadership, the chapter took a broad view of its mandate to extend aid and support to those in need. In the 1920s, while the white Macon County chapter fell dormant, the Tuskegee chapter fought tuberculosis and pellagra, a lethal disease caused by a severe niacin (vitamin B-3) deficiency brought on by a poor diet. Poverty and new grain-processing methods had led to an explosion in pellagra cases in the American South, but after scientists discovered that niacin-rich dry brewer's yeast could help prevent the disease, "hundreds of pounds of Red Cross yeast were distributed throughout Macon County," Walcott reported.[20] The chapter also furnished portable units to screen rural patients for tuberculosis and in 1924 constructed and equipped Alabama's second health center and staffed it with a public health nurse.[21] With the construction of a new Veterans Administration Hospital in Tuskegee, the chapter helped provide stationery and other support for servicemen's families.

African American hopes that wartime service abroad would bring change to segregation at home did not reach fruition; instead, succeeding decades brought the terrible flood of 1927, drought, boll weevils, crop failures, and economic ruin throughout the South, including Macon County. Tuskegee Institute remained a beacon of hope in this bleak landscape, and the institute's Red Cross chapter played a significant role in responding to the needs of rural black communities. During the depths of the Great Depression, the chapter secured a four-thousand-dollar grant to provide food and supplies for black farm families in need and distributed "flour by the carloads, hundreds of bolts of cotton, blankets, stockings, socks, and underwear." When a 1939 tornado ravaged dozens of black homes in Macon County, Walcott's unit played a key role in distributing relief. In addition, the chapter responded to the national Red Cross's annual and special appeals for funds for disaster relief worldwide.[22]

Although Tuskegee Institute's chapter had originally been chartered to serve only the campus and the surrounding black neighborhood, the national Red Cross recognized the expansion of its jurisdiction during the depression to include the entire black population of Macon County (twenty-two thousand of the county's twenty-seven thousand residents) as well as the Veterans Administration Hospital. When the white Macon County chapter renewed its charter in 1932, it agreed to this new arrangement. However, when the authorities at Red Cross headquarters in Washington attempted to start a separate chapter specifically to serve the Veterans Administration Hospital, the Tuskegee chapter balked, retaining responsibility for the hospital.[23] Walcott and the other leaders of Tuskegee's chapter resisted the creation of a separate hospital chapter because doing so would severely deplete the Tuskegee Red Cross's numbers and resources. Very few of the area's black women could afford to volunteer, and those women were already fully committed. In addition, the Red Cross had provided Walcott with a part-time salary that enabled her to add relief responsibilities to her duties at the Institute. And regional and national Red Cross officials recognized Walcott's value to the organization, declaring that she "wields a strong influence and is largely responsible for the various services rendered."[24]

Walcott's most unusual Red Cross activity occurred in 1941, when she pulled together a work party to salvage the cotton crop set to be destroyed to make way for the construction of a new U.S. Army air field. She obtained special permission to have the cotton picked, ginned, and sold on the market, earning more than two thousand dollars for the Tuskegee Red Cross.[25] By the Second World War, Walcott had become widely known as the Red Cross Lady, and she and the chapter's station wagon had become the organization's local symbols.[26] Edward L. Pryce, Walcott's friend and colleague at Tuskegee and chair of the chapter's Disaster Committee, later remembered using the old wood-panel station wagon to distribute household goods "in rural areas where fires, floods, tornadoes, and other disasters had left residents in dire need."[27]

Walcott and the Tuskegee Red Cross took on even greater responsibilities during the Second World War, when Walcott became the first African American to serve as a Red Cross field director. With Germany's 1939 invasion of Poland, the American Red Cross had begun helping refugees as well as Americans in Europe eager to return home. The national organization issued a pamphlet, *War Relief Abroad*, explaining that providing warm clothing to civilians in war-torn regions not only addressed a practical need but also carried symbolic meaning: "The value of these supplies . . . must also be measured by the strength and courage which comes to the war sufferers with the realization that the help received comes from the working hands of American volunteers."[28]

And the Tuskegee Red Cross had many working hands. Early in 1941, Walcott wrote to almost two dozen local women's and girls' organizations, "This is an SOS . . . Do you knit? Do you crochet? Do you sew? Can you follow instructions in putting together garments already cut out? Can you sew on tapes, buttons, bindings? Can you pull basting threads? Press seams? The Red Cross needs your help in all these ways to complete the spring quota of production." As the chapter returned to garment production for the first time since the Great War, Walcott urged, "We need your help to duplicate the fine showing we made at that time."[29] Over the next five years, Tuskegee volunteers turned out hundreds of men's, women's, and children's sweaters, operating gowns, layettes, and other items sorely needed by victims of the Nazis' bombing raids on Britain and other civilians suffering from the ravages of war. In addition, the chapter raised funds to support the Red Cross's efforts, with Walcott announcing proudly in February 1942, "The Tuskegee Institute Chapter has never failed."[30]

In the fall of 1939, the U.S. government selected Tuskegee to host a Civilian Pilot Training Program. On July 19, 1941, the U.S. Army and Tuskegee Institute commissioned the nation's first black U.S. Army Air Corps cadets—the first African American fighter pilots. Even before the Tuskegee Airmen arrived, Walcott and Tuskegee's president Frederick D. Patterson worked to bring Red Cross services to the new air field.[31]

For the first year after the base opened, Walcott served as Red Cross field director and helped train her successor, Roger Gordon, who was to receive official credit as the first African American to serve as a Red Cross field director.[32] In addition, she oversaw the Tuskegee chapter's fund-raising efforts and various other programs, which included operating a motor corps; providing instruction in first aid, nutrition, and home nursing; and offering training programs for nurse's aides and other volunteers at the Veterans Administration Hospital.[33] By February 1942, she reported, "Chapter activities have been stepped up one hundred per cent with defense activities, services to Negro families of Macon County who have boys in the army or navy, and service to the several hundred enlisted men and flying cadets at the 99th Pursuit Squadron Air Base."[34]

The "services to Negro families of Macon County who have boys in the army or navy" fell under the Red Cross's category of "home service." Red Cross workers assisted soldiers, veterans, and their families with obtaining information, counseling, filing claims, and obtaining benefits—that is, generally serving as social workers. This aspect of Walcott's Red Cross duties took up increasing amounts of her time, and on more than one occasion, regional Red Cross officials visited Tuskegee Institute only to find her out on a call. Reported one field director, "In as much as there are not many colored social workers, and Mrs. Walcott is forced to do most of her own investigations, the writer can well understand her irregular schedule."[35] The same field director also described her as "very charming and very capable."[36]

In March 1942, Gordon replaced Walcott as field director at the air base, relieving her of some of her workload. However, she was also tasked with finding him a temporary place to live since the post still lacked officers' quarters. The military had decreed that although most of the base personnel, including the officers being trained, would be African Americans, the officer in charge had to be white. But the U.S. government's proposal to house white and black officers together provoked outrage not only among white southerners but also from such high-ranking officials as the assistant chief in charge of the Air Corps,

General George H. Brett, who said, "I happen to be from Cleveland and I'm sure I don't want to live with a nigger."[37] Many white officers at Tuskegee refused to go to the officers' club because black officers were admitted. Other white officers, however, took a different view. Noel F. Parrish, a southerner who served at Tuskegee first as a flight instructor and later as commander of the air base, relaxed racial policies in accordance with both his own beliefs and army regulations.[38]

The issue of recreational opportunities for the men stationed at the Tuskegee Army Air Field also posed a problem early on. Higher-ups expressed concern that "the Post is without a recreation building and . . . as time goes on it will continue to offer a greater problem."[39] The base was located seven miles outside the town of Tuskegee, and no public transportation from the base to the town was offered; moreover, the small, white-dominated town offered nothing in the way of recreation for black soldiers except the institute's campus. According to Major James A. Ellison, the base's first commander, "The facilities at the Institute are taxed to the utmost . . . and although Mrs. Walcott and Doctor Patterson have tried to work out programs for the soldiers, it has been entirely inadequate." He continued, "Mrs. Walcott reports that a great many negro soldiers from Fort Benning come to Tuskegee over the week-end and the matter of recreation for soldiers not only on the Post but in the town is now presenting itself as a problem." Ellison therefore recommended that a recreation building be constructed at the Tuskegee Air Field despite the relatively small number of men assigned there.[40]

Walcott, too, recognized that "providing wholesome recreation" for soldiers was a must for Red Cross chapters near army bases, and she was instrumental in getting the campus, the community, and the Veterans Administration Hospital to plan "receptions, tours, teas, dances, 'home' evenings and Sunday dinner invitations for the boys in uniform."[41] A recreation hall was built, and by September 1942, the base newsletter, *Hawk's Cry* (whose creation resulted from Walcott's efforts), announced that a new hall was nearing completion. The previous facility, which had served as a post chapel, lecture hall, theater, and classroom, would now become a lounge for soldiers and their guests, with furniture provided by the local Red Cross chapter "through the remarkable work of Mrs. B. B. Walcott," whose help had been "inestimable."[42]

The war years transformed the entire community of Tuskegee, especially for its black citizens. The air base brought a "whole new outlook on life," increasing the community's size and raising "the general standard of living." The Red Cross chapter turned Dorothy Hall on campus into an unofficial guesthouse, and the community's women, especially students, enthusiastically sought to keep soldiers' morale high. Many of the young soldiers who trained at Tuskegee wrote to Walcott after shipping out: one referred to her as his "other Mother," while another addressed her as "Dear Mrs. Red Cross" before explaining, "When I got on the bus I felt that I had not thanked you [enough]. I am beginning to realize that I miss something more than I miss the girls back home. I miss the warm affection of an interested and interesting adult."[43]

At the same time that the United States was fighting the Axis powers abroad, the country was also engaged in another battle at home: the fight against polio, a disease that disproportionately affected African Americans. Black Americans in the South who became ill or injured had few treatment options, since white hospitals and clinics banished black patients to "colored waiting rooms" and hospital basements, where they often waited hours until every white patient had been seen. In 1938, President Franklin Roosevelt, who had been paralyzed by polio, founded the National Foundation for Infantile Paralysis (now the March of Dimes) to combat the disease. The following March, Tuskegee Institute appealed directly to the president for his support for the establishment of one of the nation's first polio treatment centers for black children and adults. Beginning in 1940, Walcott served as executive secretary of the foundation's Tuskegee Institute chapter, and on January 15, 1941, the institute dedicated its new Infantile Paralysis Center, a state-of-the-art facility modeled on the Warm Springs, Georgia, center where Roosevelt himself was treated. It became one of the few places in the South where black polio patients could receive the best professional treatment, which in the days before the development of a vaccine included round-the-clock care, expert massage, and physical therapy.[44]

According to Walcott, by 1942 "the crippled children's ward and the Infantile Paralysis Center keep their beds filled and have a long waiting list, despite the dozens of children that have been sent home able to run and play for the first time." Nevertheless, Walcott conceded, "There is one gloomy side to the picture. Hundreds who look to Tuskegee for hospital care are unable to get it. They have no money—and Tuskegee has no budget to provide for indigent cases."[45] Through the 1940s and into the early 1950s, Walcott led the Tuskegee chapter of the National Foundation for Infantile Paralysis in its efforts to raise funds for patient care and to provide comfort to black children suffering from polio. In addition, when members of the Tuskegee community organized to combat mental illness, they, too, turned to Walcott, who served as executive secretary of the Mental Hygiene Society from 1940 to 1951. In 1951, the group's work led to the establishment of Tuskegee's first mental health clinic.[46]

When the war ended in 1945, Walcott's Red Cross chapter found that it was needed more than ever. The institute's classes swelled with hundreds of return-

ing veterans taking advantage of the G.I. Bill. Still others hospitalized at the
Veterans Administration Hospital needed aid, as did Macon County families
experiencing hardships or natural disasters. Walcott again served as acting Red
Cross field director at the air base in 1946–47.[47] That year, some fifteen hundred
veterans enrolled at the institute, the hospital had a total of twenty-three hundred beds, and her normal home service caseload averaged "397.5 over a four
months' period."[48]

Like the Tuskegee Airmen with whom she had worked, Walcott broke down
barriers. She was part of a generation whose work and sacrifices paved the way
for the postwar changes in the American racial order that would finally end de
jure segregation. Moreover, she was also part of a generation that often overlooked the contributions of women. Indeed, one letter from national Red Cross
Headquarters written by the national vice chair in charge of domestic operations mistakenly congratulated "Mr. B. B. Walcott" on the "fine program you
have developed." While the Second World War had brought new opportunities
for women, it also caused losses that forever changed many lives. The aftermath
of the conflict brought personal changes to Bess Walcott's life as well: William
Walcott accepted a job elsewhere, she chose to stay in Tuskegee, and the couple
divorced in 1947.[49]

The Tuskegee Red Cross chapter led by Walcott continued to provide a range
of services. In 1948, the chapter provided help for nearly a thousand people—
cash assistance to veterans and tornado victims, clothing and household goods
to eleven families who lost their homes to fire, and similar assistance to forty
needy families. The chapter also issued 247 certificates in training courses in
such areas as accident prevention, first aid, nutrition, and water safety. And the
chapter sponsored movies, talks, and exhibits and made referrals to the Department of Public Welfare, the John A. Andrew Hospital, and other agencies.
Moreover, as it had since the First World War, the Tuskegee Red Cross recruited
Macon County schoolchildren to join the Junior Red Cross, where they participated in projects such as filling gift boxes to be sent overseas. In the spring
of 1949, Walcott became a full-time Red Cross worker, though she remained
executive secretary of the institute chapter. With the Cold War, her focus shifted
to civilian defense and overseeing hundreds of Red Cross volunteers.[50]

In 1951, at the age of sixty-five, Walcott stepped down from all of her leadership posts in volunteer organizations. In June of that year, the Red Cross chapter
held a celebration in her honor in the institute's chapel, where nearly thirty-five
years earlier she had first helped to inspire students and faculty to join the Red
Cross. She continued to work at Tuskegee Institute until 1962 and remained active even after her retirement, playing a key role in the school's designation as a

National Historic Site in 1965. She also became involved in the Women's International League for Peace and Freedom and spent 1964–65 in Liberia, helping to establish the Tubman Center for African Culture.[51]

By the 1980s, she was the last living link to Tuskegee's founders, and she never tired of sharing her knowledge of the institute's rich history. She admitted that her time there had included "a lot of disappointments" but emphasized that it had also featured "a lot of opportunities."[52] Like many other educated black Americans born at a time when slavery remained a living memory, Walcott embraced the mission of service to her people. In Tuskegee Institute, she found like-minded men and women eager to change America for the better, and many of the students educated there became part of the black southern middle class, which in turn helped to spark the civil rights movement.[53] But Walcott stands out even among the middle-class African American men and women of her time: few others made as much of the opportunities presented to them or gave of themselves so generously. When she died on April 18, 1988, her community, state, and nation lost a precious tie to its storied past. In March 2003, Walcott was inducted into the Alabama Women's Hall of Fame, honoring a life lived to the fullest in the service of humanity.

NOTES

I thank William Penn White for his invaluable assistance in my research at the National Archives, College Park, Maryland, and Tuskegee University archivist Dana Chandler and his staff for their help with my notes.

1. B. B. Walcott, "B. B. Walcott/H. E. Hanna: History of Tuskegee Institute—Early History, Culture as Well as Trades," September 22, 1981, Bess Bolden Walcott Papers, Box 23, Tuskegee University Archives; "Summary of Negro Graduates of Oberlin College," 1844–1972, *Oberlin College Archives*, http://www.oberlin.edu/archive/holdings/finding/RG5/SG4/S3/summary.html (accessed July 30, 2016).

2. B. B. Walcott, Interdisciplinary Forum Talk, April 27, 1983, Tuskegee University Archives.

3. Oberlin Yearbook (copy), 1908, Tuskegee University Archives. I thank B. B. Walcott's granddaughter, Marian Garmon, for allowing me to make a digital copy of the yearbook.

4. Walcott, Interdisciplinary Forum Talk.

5. "Walcott, Bess Bolden," in *Who's Who of American Women, 1974–75*, 8th ed. (St. Louis: Van Hoffman, 1973), 999.

6. Walcott, Interdisciplinary Forum Talk. The Tuskegee Civic Association, which counted Walcott as one of its members, was dedicated to civic education, desegregating public schools, and securing voting rights. It brought several landmark lawsuits, including *Gomillion v. Lightfoot*, the 1960 U.S. Supreme Court case that barred electoral districts from being drawn to disenfranchise African Americans.

7. B. B. Walcott, "Library," Walcott Papers, Box 20.

8. Walcott, "B. B. Walcott/H. E. Hanna."

9. Walcott, Interdisciplinary Forum Talk.

10. Walcott, "B. B. Walcott/H. E. Hanna."

11. Ibid.

12. Walcott Papers, Boxes 6, 8, 22.

13. John A. Kenney Papers, Boxes 3–4, Tuskegee University Archives.

14. Marian Moser Jones, *The American Red Cross from Clara Barton to the New Deal* (Baltimore: Johns Hopkins University Press, 2013), 32, 20n, 199–200.

15. "Red Cross Entertainment Committee Presents Interesting Program," *Tuskegee Student*, October 19, 1918; Walter T. Colquitt to Dr. Guy E. Snavely, June 29, 1917, Records of the American National Red Cross, 1947–64, Record Group 200, Box 1391, File 711, National Archives; "Red Cross Chapter Organized at Tuskegee Institute," *Tuskegee Student*, August 17, 1918; C. H. Whelden Jr. to Leslie C. Bell, October 9, 1958, Red Cross Records, Box 1391, File 711 Tuskegee Institute Chapter; *Tuskegee's Service in National Recovery* (Tuskegee, Ala.: Tuskegee Institute Press, 1935), 5; Handwritten Minutes, September 13, 1918, Walcott Papers, Box 8. Walcott later singled out Jennie Moton, Lena Cheeks Shehee, Ernestine Suarez, and Emma J. Scott for their unstinting work in getting the chapter established (B. B. Walcott, "Red Cross Girds for Victory, Then and Now," *Service* [February 1942]: 9). The Tuskegee chapter's original charter has been lost. Records at the national Red Cross headquarters in Washington indicate that the chapter was officially chartered on December 18, 1918 (Red Cross Records, Box 1391, File 711 Tuskegee–Macon County).

16. Handwritten Minutes, October 8, 1918, Walcott Papers, Box 8; "Red Cross Entertainment Committee Presents Interesting Program," *Tuskegee Student*, October 19, 1918.

17. U.S. Department of Health and Human Services, "The Great Pandemic: The United States in 1918–1919," http://www.flu.gov/pandemic/history/1918/the_pandemic/index.html (accessed July 30, 2016); "Quarantine Removed: Influenza Controlled at Tuskegee by Hospital Staff and Red Cross Volunteers," *Tuskegee Student*, November 16, 1918 *Thirty-Eighth Annual Report of the Principal and Treasurer, Tuskegee Normal and Industrial Institute for the Year Ending May 31, 1919*, 10, Tuskegee University Archives; "Service of a Negro Hospital," *Southern Workman* (April 1921), 167.

18. "Quarantine Removed," *Tuskegee Student*, November 16, 1918. Kenney later reported one death ("Service of a Negro Hospital," *Southern Workman* [April 1921], 167).

19. "The Red Cross Chapter Finishes Its Allotment and Ships It November 25," *Tuskegee Student*, December 21, 1918.

20. Margaret Humphreys, "How Four Once Common Diseases Were Eliminated from the American South," *Health Affairs* 28 (2009): 1734–44; Kumaravel Rajakumar, "Pellagra in the United States: A Historical Perspective," *South Medical Journal* 93 (2000): 272–76; Walcott, "Red Cross Girds for Victory," 10.

21. "The Tuskegee Institute Chapter of the American Red Cross Honors Bess Bolden Walcott for Thirty-Three Years of Service as Executive Secretary, 1918–1951," February 27, 1952, Walcott Papers, Box 23.

22. Ibid.; Walcott, "Red Cross Girds for Victory," 10; "American Red Cross Gray Lady Training Course, Oct. 16, 1950," attached to Mary Ellen Gardner, report, September–October 1950, Red Cross Records, Box 2035, File 1000, Alabama, Tuskegee Veterans Administration Hospital.

23. U.S. Census, 1930; Porter Tull to [W. W.] Jefferson, January 23, 1950, Red Cross Records, Box 1391, File 711 Tuskegee Institute. Mary F. Swiggart reported that her efforts to set up a separate Red Cross volunteer group at the hospital was a "complete failure" (Swiggart to Eleanor C. Vincent, February 24, 1935, Red Cross Records, Box 1707, File 1000 Alabama, Tuskegee Veterans Administration Hospital). It seems that there was also some friction between the Veterans Administration Hospital and Tuskegee Institute (Ruth Wadman memorandum to files, May 5, 1931, Red Cross Records,

Box 1707, File 1000 Alabama, Tuskegee Veterans Administration Hospital). Relations between the Tuskegee chapter and the county chapter were always complicated, though the white chapter was happy to cede the county's black population to the institute (Hazel Hart, memorandum, January 20, 1932, C. H. Whelden Jr., memorandum, July 19, 1956, both in Red Cross Records, Box 1391, File 711 Tuskegee Institute Chapter). With the end of legalized segregation, two chapters merged to form the Tuskegee–Macon County chapter.

24. B. B. Walcott to Earnest J. Swift, December 21, 1931, attached to C. H. Whelden to Leslie C. Bell, October 9, 1958, Walter C. Derrick Jr. to W. W. Jefferson, October 28, 1947, W. W. Jefferson to [?] Eaton, March 31, 1949, all in Red Cross Records, Box 1391, File 711 Tuskegee Institute Chapter.

25. "Tuskegee Institute Chapter of the American Red Cross Honors Bess Bolden Walcott." Walcott's daughter Carolyn W. Ford also relayed this story during a March 10, 2003, celebration at Tuskegee of Walcott's induction into the Alabama Women's Hall of Fame.

26. "The Cover," *Service*, March 1944, 7.

27. Edward L. Pryce, letter in support of Walcott's nomination to the Alabama Women's Hall of Fame, July 19, 2002, copy in the author's possession.

28. *War Relief Abroad: A Review of Foreign War Relief Operations, Sept. 1, 1939 to June 30, 1941* (Washington, D.C.: American National Red Cross, 1941), 11.

29. B. B. Walcott, copy of form letter addressed to Miss Smitherman of the Alphas, February 8, 1941, Walcott Papers, Box 5.

30. Walcott, "Red Cross Girds for Victory," 10.

31. B. B. Walcott, "First Negro Officers Commissioned in the U.S. Air Corps," press release, March 8, 1942, Walcott Papers, Box 22.

32. James L. Meacham to Frank H. Grayson, April 2, 1942, Red Cross Records, Box 1707, File 1000 Tuskegee Army Flying School.

33. Walcott, interview by Robert Durr, WSGN July 8, 1942, Walcott Papers, Box 23.

34. Walcott, "Red Cross Girds for Victory," 11.

35. Joseph W. Hildebrand to Roy J. Spearman, March 31, 1944, Red Cross Records, Box 1707, File 1000 Tuskegee Veterans Administration.

36. Joseph W. Hildebrand to Rexford Shaffer, October 7, 1943, in ibid.

37. William H. Hastie to Lieutenant General H. H. Arnold, July 13, 1942, General George H. Brett and unnamed secretary to Senator Lister Hill (Alabama), transcript of telephone conversation, April 28, 1941, both in Records of the Army Air Force, Record Group 18, Project Files: Air Fields 1939–42, Tuskegee, Alabama, 331.1 Inspections to 400 Miscellaneous, Folder 350, Miscellaneous, National Archives.

38. Daniel L. Haulman, "Tuskegee Airfields during World War II," February 4, 2015, *Air Force Historical Research Agency*, http://www.afhra.af.mil/shared/media/document/AFD-141118-041.pdf.

39. Asbury Cecil to Frank Grayson, March 31, 1942, Red Cross Records, Box 1707, File 1000 Tuskegee Army Flying School.

40. Ellison quoted in Roy E. Johnson to Don Smith, December 8, [1941?], in ibid.

41. Walcott, "Red Cross Girds for Victory," 11.

42. *Hawk's Cry*, September 16, 1942, 8, copy enclosed in John T. Bryant to Carolyn Ford, June 8, 2007; "Tuskegee Institute Chapter of the American Red Cross Honors Bess Bolden Walcott."

43. Jessie L. Guzman, *Contributions of Tuskegee Institute, 1927–1952: Address Delivered by J. Guzman, May 4, 1952* (Tuskegee, Ala.: Tuskegee Institute, 1952), Walcott Papers, Box 20; Lieutenant R. L. Weaver to B. B. Walcott, August 25, 1943, Private Went Miller to Mrs. Red Cross [B. B. Walcott] care of Miss Florence May, November 1, 1943, both in Walcott Papers, Box 23.

44. Edith Powell and John F. Hume, *A Black Oasis: Tuskegee Institute's Fight against Infantile Paralysis, 1941–1975* (Tuskegee Institute, Ala.: n.p., 2008), 29, 36, 72, 125–31, 66–70; B. B. Walcott, "The Tuskegee Institute Infantile Paralysis Center, Tuskegee Institute 1941," Edith Powell Papers, Box 7, Tuskegee University Archives.

45. Walcott, interview by Durr.

46. Walcott, "The Tuskegee Institute Infantile Paralysis Center," Powell Papers, Box 7; "Walcott, Bess Bolden," *Who's Who*, 999; C. P. Prudhomme, "A Mental Hygiene Society Organized at Tuskegee," *Journal of the National Medical Association* 33 (1941): 34–35; Correspondence of Mental Hygiene Society at Tuskegee Institute, Charles Goode Gomillion Papers, Box 4, Tuskegee University Archives; Dr. Eugene H. Dibble, Jr., "Activities of the John A. Andrew Memorial Hospital for the Fiscal Year Beginning June 1, 1950 and Ending May 31, 1951," October 22, 1951, Eugene H. Dibble Papers, Box 31, Tuskegee University Archives.

47. "Tuskegee Institute Chapter of the American Red Cross Honors Bess Bolden Walcott." The Tuskegee Army Air Field closed permanently on June 12, 1947, Daniel L. Haulman, "Tuskegee Airmen Chronology," October 29, 2015, *Air Force Historical Research Agency*, www.afhra.af.mil/shared /media/document/AFD-100413-023.pdf (accessed July 30, 2016).

48. Walter C. Derrick Jr. to W. W. Jefferson, October 28, 1947, Red Cross Records, Box 1391, File 711 Tuskegee Institute Chapter.

49. James L. Fieser to Mr. [*sic*] B. B. Walcott, February 6, 1941, Walcott Papers, Box 5; "Walcott, Bess Bolden," in *Who's Who*, 999; information provided by Marian Garmon.

50. *Founder's Day Activities, April 9–19, 1949*, Walcott Papers, Box 23.

51. Edward L. Pryce, letter in support of Walcott's nomination to the Alabama Women's Hall of Fame, July 19, 2002, copy in the author's possession; "Walcott, Bess Bolden," in *Who's Who*.

52. Walcott, Interdisciplinary Forum Talk.

53. See, for example, J. William Harris, *Deep Souths: Delta, Piedmont, and Sea Island Society in the Age of Segregation* (Baltimore: Johns Hopkins University Press, 2001), 331. Civil rights leaders educated at Tuskegee included Amelia Boynton Robinson, who stood on the front lines in Selma, Alabama, on Bloody Sunday, March 7, 1965.

Lebanese, Italian, and Slavic Immigrant Women in Metropolitan Birmingham

"Just Mud Roads"

STACI GLOVER

In the post–Civil War era, southern leaders found themselves faced with the problem of how to compete effectively with the North on an increasingly industrializing national stage. In the antebellum period, southern industry had been small at best, confined mostly to textile mills, small mining operations, and small ironworks, while heavy industry was practically nonexistent. James M. McPherson and others have shown that the South's lack of capital investment in industry outside agriculture resulted not from insufficient financial resources but rather from a conscious decision on the part of the wealthy to invest their money in the economy of agriculture and slaves and the consequent lack of incentive to invest in much else.[1] To compete effectively with the North, southern investors needed not only to capitalize business and infrastructure but also to obtain ample sources of labor. While emancipation might have proved the logical answer, racial attitudes inherent in the South's slave society lead to postwar labor problems. Many southerners believed that African Americans' ethic and industrial output were vastly inferior to those of whites.[2] In 1894 Charles H. Otken elucidated the position of white southerners of the period when he wrote, "The men do much less work than [those born into slavery], and the women do next to nothing."[3] With these racial attitudes coloring the region's hiring practices, investors began looking to the North and to Europe to find workers who would better fit the ideal of an industrial worker. As a result, thousands of European immigrants found their way south, with many settling in the Birmingham industrial district.

ANNE SCHUMANN SOKIRA

With new husband John Sokira in Brookside in the early 1900s.

Courtesy of Barbara Sokira.

The original immigrants left behind few primary sources. However, over the past forty years, historians have become interested in the contributions made by these immigrants and have consequently conducted interviews with surviving immigrants and their children and collected documents regarding family and community life. These oral histories have vastly enriched historians' understanding of immigrants' lives and their roles in their neighborhoods, city, and state. Nevertheless, the lives of immigrant men have frequently overshadowed the lives of women. This essay sheds new light on the experiences and contributions of immigrant women from three groups in the Birmingham industrial district in the first two decades of the twentieth century. Though they resided in different parts of the metropolitan area and had different economic backgrounds, Lebanese, Italian, and Slavic immigrant women had parallel life experiences. For some immigrant women, the trauma of entering the United States represented the first hint of the other challenges they would face, including prejudices against their language, dress, religion, and skin tone. Moreover, they also confronted changing attitudes regarding women's roles. Some immigrant women felt few effects, remaining secluded in their comfortable ethnic neighborhoods, while others responded to these external challenges both subtly and dramatically. Yet the ways in which these women adapted to their changing environments are as individual as the women themselves and cannot easily be quantified. Regardless of ethnicity, these women made significant contributions to the development of the Birmingham metropolitan area and surrounding industrial district, and their stories help increase our understanding of immigrant life in Birmingham and in Alabama.

Realizing the industrial potential of the combination of iron ore and coal deposits in the Jones Valley area and the meeting of two railroad lines there, Jefferson County land speculators founded the Elyton Land Company in 1871 and created the New South city of Birmingham at the foot of Red Mountain. Within two years, waves of financial depression and cholera threatened to draw the new city into a downward spiral of destruction and devastation before it had even really begun to establish itself. Nevertheless, Jefferson County became both an economic hub and a center for ethnic diversity, with Birmingham developing into an industrial center during the 1880s. Iron ore, steel, and coal became the Birmingham district's primary industries, attracting workers from all over the world and growing into the region's industrial behemoth. Birmingham's iron and steel industry depended heavily on the development of a surrounding mineral district and the presence of both skilled and unskilled labor.

After 1870, most U.S. states and cities, including those in the South, employed recruitment agents to attract European workers.[4] Industrial boosters blanketed both the United States and Europe with newspaper articles and broadsides extolling the job opportunities available in the sprawling industrial hub of Birmingham. Slavs, Italians, Greeks, Scots, and, later, Lebanese snapped up the bait, making their way to the area, and by 1890, immigrants comprised 17 percent of the coal miners in the Birmingham industrial district. By 1910, the area had 5,730 immigrants, most of them aged between twenty-five and thirty-five. The 1930 U.S. Census found that Birmingham's population included 1,418 Italians, 735 English, 531 Russians, 462 Greeks, 436 Scots, 315 Syrians and Palestinians, and 400 Germans, with others residing in the surrounding industrial/ metropolitan district. Brookside, just northwest of Birmingham within the metropolitan district, exemplified the area's rural settlement patterns. Rich in coal, such towns provided the fuel for Birmingham's blast furnaces. By 1900, Slavs comprised approximately 30 percent of the coal miners living and working in Brookside.[5]

Those who settled in Birmingham proper in these years found a growing city struggling to offer certain public amenities readily available in more mature cities. According to Nellie Lusco Saia (1899–1988), whose family emigrated from Italy just after the turn of the century, her mother lamented, "I left my beautiful Sicily, with cobblestone and paved roads everywhere, and everything was beautiful, and here are just mud roads where you can't walk anywhere without getting your shoes nasty."[6] Others who settled in Brookside or other towns in the outlying mineral district found their surroundings more amenable. Many of Brookside's immigrants hailed from the rural areas of Spiš, Sariska (Sáros), and Zemplín near the Galician region of the Austro-Hungarian empire and found that the Alabama countryside resembled their homeland. Elizabeth Duchock Beck (b. 1944) remembered that her immigrant grandparents found "the conditions similar to the village they left in that it was a rolling hill terrain. . . . The ground was fertile, so they can grow crops and make a living in the coal mines. In Slovinky, Slovakia, their ancestral home, there were copper mines, so they were used to mining and that was what they knew. . . . Life here was just a continuation of life in the old country."[7]

These immigrants encountered not only the growing pains of an adolescent city and metropolitan area but also both new challenges and old prejudices. Despite appearing superficially homogenous, the South always swirled with undercurrents of political, racial, and ethnic diversity, a phenomenon well represented in the sprawling Birmingham industrial district. Each ethnic group resided in a different area, and they experienced varying degrees of occupational and economic mobility.

The Lebanese who settled Birmingham originally lived along Avenue C. As they became more prosperous, they relocated to the city's Southside, along Eighth Avenue South from Twelfth to Twentieth Streets. According to Mary Bohorfoush Pharo (1904–91), the neighborhood was racially mixed, with whites living along one side of Eighteenth Street South and African Americans on the other. Before Lebanese dry goods stores and groceries peppered Twentieth Street, Pharo recalled, many people in her community looked forward to the arrival of peddlers because they had no other means of getting their goods from merchants in town. Most Lebanese were small business owners who sold goods to members of a variety of other groups, including African Americans and Italians.[8] Lebanese women helped run the small groceries and dry goods stores, giving those women access to different people and their cultures. Lebanese business owners became increasingly upwardly mobile, particularly after the maturation of members of the second generation, a process that in many ways eased their assimilation to American language and practice.

Lyda Faires Deep (1899–1990), the daughter of Abelah and Nazira Faires, was born in Lebanon and immigrated with her mother to the United States in 1900. The family settled in Birmingham in 1904.[9] Abelah Faires began peddling soon after his arrival and later opened a grocery with his uncle, Norman Faires, and Abdallah Joseph on the corner of First Avenue between Nineteenth and Twentieth Streets. The family store afforded Lyda an education that schools could not offer, though she received no pay for her work. Lyda encountered all manner of people and learned to appreciate cultures other than her own. Lyda married Louis Deep in 1920, and they owned and operated the Southside Rag Company until his death in 1954. Similarly, although she was born in Birmingham in 1904, Mary Bohorfoush Pharo, the daughter of grocer George Bohorfoush and Susan Joseph Bohorfoush, worked at her husband's grocery store, near Avondale Mills. The store opened for business between four and five in the morning and closed as late as ten at night. Second-generation members of Birmingham's Lebanese community used such hard work and perseverance to make their mark in the city.[10]

Born in Birmingham in 1918, Elizabeth Boohaker (1918–2004) was the only girl among Abdalla and Nezha Boohaker's eight children. Though a farmer in his native Lebanon, Abdalla Boohaker worked for seven years as a peddler in Birmingham before opening a store at Avenue C and Thirteenth Street. Prior to her father's unexpected death, Elizabeth attended business school while working in the administrative office at Miller Foundry, where she earned fifteen dollars a week. However, Abdalla's absence meant that Nezha and her children had to take over the family business. Elizabeth never married because she had "to take care of" her brothers, and remained employed outside the home until late in her life. In addition, she decried intermarriage and other changes that forever altered her community.[11]

Birmingham's Italian community was the most geographically widespread and the most fractured occupationally. Many Italians lived on Birmingham's west side, in Ensley, between Twelfth and Seventeenth Streets and in Tuxedo Junction, or in Thomas; however, other Italians lived in Southside. While the Southside Lebanese community looked forward to the arrival of Lebanese peddlers, Italians attached some stigma to the occupation. Interviewed decades later, Rose Maenza (1901–83) stressed that her family had not been peddlers but instead owned a grocery.[12] According to historian Dino Cinel, by 1900 about twenty-five Italian agents controlled Birmingham's truck farms and employed three hundred people.[13] Indicators of success among Italian immigrants included working for oneself rather than working for someone else, white-collar rather than blue-collar employment, and homeownership.

Nellie Lusco Saia was born in Birmingham in 1899 to a family that owned a forty-five-acre farm near the L&N depot. The Luscos grew fruits and vegetables and sold them to area hospitals, hotels, and the Britling cafeteria chain. The business was so successful that Nellie's father purchased an automobile for four thousand dollars in cash. Nellie often filled the role of second mother to a brood of siblings, serving "as chief cook and baby tender. I didn't work the farm but I helped fill orders."[14]

Rose Maenza's family arrived in New Orleans in the 1880s before moving to Ensley, where her father, Louis, found employment as a water boy at the Tennessee Coal and Iron Company. Louis Maenza bounced between Birmingham and New Orleans, where Rose was born around the turn of the twentieth century, before settling in Ensley around 1906 and opening a grocery with his brother, Joseph. The business was situated between the Italian section of Ensley and Birmingham, providing Rose an opportunity to interact with a smorgasbord of people.[15]

Argentine Morganti (1921–95) was the daughter of a Tuscan immigrant, Richard Morganti, who settled in Birmingham between 1923 and 1924. Though Richard Morganti had a high school education, he had difficulty finding employment, and unlike earlier arrivals who opened groceries, he worked as a coal miner in Pratt City for U.S. Steel.[16]

Unlike the Lebanese and Italians who settled in the Birmingham urban area and mingled with each other, other immigrant families found the rural areas just north of the city appealing and remained in ethnic enclaves. The Slavs of Brookside, approximately twelve miles northwest of Birmingham's city center, remained rather isolated until a 1920 mining strike forced many of the community's men to seek employment elsewhere.

Nestled in a picturesque valley, surrounded by Five Mile Creek, and accessible only via bridges from Mount Olive, Cardiff, and Republic, Brookside harbored a large community of Slavic immigrants beginning in the 1890s and 1900s. Most men from the community worked in the area's coal mines, though others engaged in small businesses selling items such as feed and grain. By 1900, Slavs occupied the town's residential core and accounted for almost one-third of Brookside's coal miners. Most native whites employed by Sloss-Sheffield Iron and Steel Company lived in the company-owned houses in the mining camp on the town's east side. Therefore, Brookside's Slavs, while working and occasionally associating with native-born whites, were geographically separated from them. Slavs dominated several streets in Brookside's downtown area, insulating the community from outside influences at least through 1917.[17]

Most of the immigrant women of Brookside's Slavic community followed a traditional life as homemakers. Many immigrated to the United States between 1890 and 1910 or were born in Brookside during that period, and their lives were difficult, with assimilation posing a daunting challenge. Annie Letanosky Patchen (1913–2006) was the daughter of Dolphina Lesko Letanosky and her second husband, Josef Letanosky, both of whom came from the Spiš region of Austria-Hungary in the 1890s, but they traveled separately and settled independently in Brookside, where both already had relatives. Joe Letanosky, who was twenty years older than Dolphina, worked as a coal miner until a mine collapse took his life in 1937. Annie married Alabama-born Joseph Patchen and spent her entire life in the town where she was born.[18]

Annie Schumann Sokira (1894–1990), a coal miner's wife, experienced the most traditional life of an immigrant woman, moving away from home during her twenties, working as an office clerk, leaving the Russian Orthodox Church of her parents, and marrying a native-born American man. For her part, Alice Slovensky Harmon (1905–1994) was a traditional second-generation immigrant woman, proud of her heritage but engaged with the larger community.

Different ethnic groups followed different immigration patterns. Italians migrating into the Birmingham district tended to migrate as intact families: fathers, mothers, and children.[19] Among the Lebanese and Slavs, however, men often immigrated first, leaving behind their sweethearts, wives, and families while searching for jobs in America. Weeks, months, or even years might pass before women and children joined their loved ones in the United States, and in some cases, the separations became permanent. Abelah Faires left Lebanon just before 1900 with promises from friends to help him establish a peddling business in the United States. When he earned enough money to send for his wife, Nazira, and their two daughters, however, Nazira's father told her, "You can't take both of my girls," and took the older daughter "off the boat." Nazira sailed alone with baby Lyda, who grew up hearing the story of how "that child cried and my mama cried. And she never saw her daughter any more." Not until 1956, seventeen years after their mother's death, did Lyda and her sister see each other again.[20]

Transatlantic immigration had other intrinsic problems, including weather hazards, language differences, and fear of separation from traveling companions. Sixteen-year-old Dolphina Lesko (1881–1958) left Slovakia with a group of neighbors, arriving in New York Harbor in August 1897. The seventy-dollar ticket for her passage had been purchased by Michael Ziach, her fiancé, who was already living in Brookside, as were her sister and brother-in-law. Passport problems kept Dolphina in New York for about three weeks, and when she finally arrived in Alabama, no one had come to meet her at the train depot. After a policeman gave Dolphina a ride to town, she made her way to her sister's home, where she lived until she married Ziach in 1900. Just a year later, both Ziach and the couple's infant son died in a typhoid epidemic.[21]

As they built new lives in the Birmingham industrial district, immigrants created social and community organizations that replicated those that had structured their lives in the Old Country. Churches in particular played an incalculable role in the well-being and survival of the immigrant community and particularly in the transmission of culture. The church provided not only spiritual nourishment but also social and educational opportunities that reinforced the cohesion of the ethnic enclave. Most ethnic neighborhoods in the district were anchored by the church and the schools and fraternal organizations it hosted.[22] Slavic immigrants to Brookside purchased homes, founded the Saints Cyril and Methodius Catholic Church and Saint Nicholas Russian Orthodox Church, and created social and fraternal organizations.[23]

Moreover, religious celebrations such as weddings, funerals, and baptisms brought together not only members of the community but also those who had moved away. According to Mary Bohorfoush Pharo, "The church has kept us together. The Lebanese stick together—especially for funerals. You'll see people you haven't seen in a long time. And holidays—they'll flock to the church."[24] Wedding celebrations could last as long as three days, bringing together members of both the Roman Catholic and Orthodox Churches. These gatherings attracted so many of the town's coal miners that operators had to close the mine.[25]

However, Catholics also seemed to experience bigotry and prejudice. Between the 1920s and the 1950s, several incidents of anti-Catholic terrorism occurred in the Birmingham area, among them a 1949 Ku Klux Klan night raid against Catholic café owners in Brookside. Recalled Rose Maenza, "If you were a Catholic you had a black mark against you."[26]

Although Alabama had always had Catholic residents, many native-born whites were unfamiliar with the religion, and anti-Catholic sentiment could reflect ignorance rather than outright hostility. Lyda Faires Deep recalled an incident in which a native-born white woman came into Abelah Faires's store and asked, "'Where do you send your children to school?' She was going to send hers up there to Glen Iris. So I told her I sent them to Our Lady of Sorrows. . . . And she said 'Oh no, I won't send them to a Catholic school.' I said, 'Well, I'm not asking you to.'" The woman later returned to the store, and Deep encouraged her to familiarize herself with the principles of Catholicism. The woman did so and a year later enrolled her children in Catholic school; she and her children subsequently converted, and Deep became a godmother to one of the children. Deep, too, expanded her religious and cultural horizons by attending a neighbor's baptism at Southside Baptist Church. When chastised by her priest for attending the service without his permission, Deep asked how attending a religious service could possibly constitute a sin. The American-born child of Lebanese immigrants, Deep exemplifies the role of members of the second generation in connecting ethnic communities to native whites and as active agents of change. In addition, she demonstrates how immigrant families were not simply subject to one-way pressure to assimilate into the native white culture; rather, the acculturation process worked in both directions, producing a hybrid that reflected both immigrant and native influences. In Deep's words, "We are all Americans . . . Irish, Scotch, or something." Deep did not distinguish between an "American" way of life and a "southern" way of life and believed that Americanness included people of all ethnicities. Alice Slovensky Harmon echoed this view, declaring, "I feel like an American. I mingle with them. Being a Slavic never crosses my mind." Harmon always remained proud of her heritage but felt that she had integrated into the greater community.[27]

John Shelton Reed and other historians have posited that the South possesses indomitable and distinct characteristics that set it apart from the rest of the United States, but these women never felt such distinctions.[28] Their sense of belonging may have resulted in part from the fact that many of them spent time in larger, more cosmopolitan areas of the United States such as New York and New Orleans before migrating to the Birmingham district. Rose Maenza recalled that her parents' time in New Orleans strongly influenced her mother's cooking, which was "more French than . . . Italian." According to Mary Pharo, her mother and the other Lebanese women of their neighborhood prepared not only Lebanese foods such as kibbe and cabbage but "American" foods as well. In addition to Lebanese foods, Elizabeth Boohaker's mother cooked spaghetti, hotdogs, and turnip greens. For these immigrant women and others, food became a means of bridging the gap between foreign and native-born. Although Annie Letanosky Patchen's mother spoke little English, native-born whites "would smell the bread" she baked and "really come on our side."[29] These American-born second-generation women bore traces of an Alabama hill-country accent but no other easily discernable "southern" characteristics.

While immigrants distinguished others based on ethnicity but viewed everyone as American, many native-born whites lumped all immigrants, whatever their origins, into one ethnic category, Italian. The predominance of Italians in Birmingham may have led native whites to assume that all of the area's immigrants hailed from that country, and this perception may have been heightened by the darker skin tones that generally prevailed among Slavs, Italians, and Lebanese. Moreover, white Alabamians failed to perceive the American-born children of immigrants as American. Said Maenza, "All my friends were American, and even though I was born here and was American, they couldn't see it that way. As long as you had Italian parents, they still claimed that you were a foreigner." In addition, according to Maenza, "All foreigners were called dagoes."[30] Southern racist attitudes also could come into play: Argentine Morganti remembered an executive at U.S. Steel questioning the whiteness of an Italian man's son, declaring the boy "a little on the dark side." The father responded that if Italians had known of the reception that they would receive in the United States, "Christopher Columbus would have turned around and gone home."[31]

Helen Slovensky (1927–97), a Slav who grew up in Brookside, did not take kindly to a sixth-grade classmate who thought Slovensky was Italian:

> She just didn't like me for some reason, and she called me a dago. And I told her I was not a dago. [And she said,] "Oh, you speak another language, and all that food" and this and that and everything. And I said, "Well, I am not a dago. I am a Slavic," and I tried to explain it to her. And one evening school was out, and we were waiting for the school bus, and she come up and said, "Oh, there's that little dago again." And I had the eraser—I was cleaning the board, and I took that eraser and I went right in her face with it. We got into a fight. And the teacher asked Betty why she called me a dago, [and the teacher] said, "Why, Betty, you should be honored to be Helen's friend. Just look—at her age, she can speak two languages. Betty, can you do that?"[32]

As children of immigrants became increasingly Americanized, they also encountered changing attitudes toward women's public and private roles. Upper-

and middle-class women during the Progressive Era formed organizations that addressed issues of poverty, industrialization, health care, and temperance.[33] Immigrant women in the lower and lower-middle classes also found themselves with new choices. Having learned English in school and no longer bound to traditional ethnic customs, they began to change their manner of dress and marry outside their ethnic groups. Though most of these women did not work outside the home, others, among them Harmon and Boohaker, took advantage of new opportunities to work in offices.

As Owlen Hufton has shown, life for peasant women changed little before 1920. Peasant women not only bore responsibility for duties inside the home such as cooking, making and repairing clothes, and taking care of children but also tended farm animals, fetched water, and maintained vegetable gardens.[34] The Industrial Revolution brought only minimal changes to this routine, and Alabama's working-class immigrant women typically spent their days caring for their homes and children. European-born Annie Schumann Sokira, for example, moved to the United States with her parents and settled in Brookside in 1900, when she was five. At the age of fifteen, she married John Sokira Jr., a coal miner, and gave birth to the first of her eleven children in October 1911. Annie Sokira awoke before daybreak, packed her husband a lunch, and then saw him off to work before waking her children and getting the older ones ready for school. She then spent the rest of the day attending to her younger children and performing household chores. She made and mended her children's clothes, bathed and fed them, and put them to bed before their father returned home from work late at night. According to Sokira, "He never saw his kids. . . . Half of them didn't see their daddy for a whole week."[35]

Lebanese and Italian immigrant women also frequently contributed to family businesses. Lyda Deep and others worked in stores owned by their fathers or husbands; all of the women in Rose Maenza's family grew the vegetables that their husbands sold.[36]

Like native-born women, immigrant women increasingly began to find wage employment outside the home, generally before marriage but in some cases continuing to work even after they wed. Kathryn Evancho Sokira (1921–2010), a Slav living in Brookside, worked part-time as a grocery store clerk after marrying. Katie Duchock (1910–2002) found employment as a waitress at a bakery in Fairfield but left the job soon after her marriage.[37] Women who worked outside the home, whether in family businesses or for wages, needed to learn and speak proper English to interact with customers and coworkers. Mary Pharo, Lyda Deep, and Nellie Saia, all of whom came from families that operated small businesses, reported that their immigrant mothers spoke English; Deep's father did not.[38] Feiza Mickwee (1895–1988), a native of Lebanon who immigrated to the United States with her parents when she was a small child, had an aunt who owned a business that sold linens and lace. The aunt also served as an agent for those unable to speak English, helping them purchase foodstuffs and medicines, and thus realized the importance of linguistic skills for women's lives. Mickwee remembered,

> She was an aunt, a mother, a grandmother wrapped up in one. She had so much sense of humor—she was a trouper. Mama said she wished she could be like Sultana. . . . If it weren't for her we would have had no education. She saw to it that we went to Catholic school. . . . She gave me the courage to live on my own after my mother died. . . . My mother was quiet. She kept everything to herself, but Sultana would tell us everything.[39]

In contrast, Mary Pharo's grandmother and Dolphina Lesko never worked outside their homes and did not learn English. They did not need to do so, since they could buy goods at immigrant-owned stores or from peddlers who spoke the same language.[40]

Leslie Woodcock Tentler has argued that the workplace played a greater role than any other factor in assimilating immigrant women, offering a wide array of possibilities, including suitors, new ideas, and new understandings of women's place in the world.[41] The experiences of Birmingham's immigrant women support this argument. However, the issue of language was more than a simple matter of necessity. Some immigrants sought to learn English as quickly as possible to avoid discrimination: according to Nellie Lusco Saia, her parents spoke "beautiful English . . . because people were prejudiced."[42] Nellie Saia's parents avoided using Italian in public. Rose Maenza's parents spoke fluent English and rarely conversed in Italian; Maenza learned Italian from her grandmother, who never learned English.[43]

In other cases, however, immigrants sought to stave off assimilation by continuing to use their native tongues and by enrolling children in parochial schools that offered non-English instruction. A U.S. Slavic newspaper, *Jednota*, published seventeen articles concerning education between 1902 and 1911, with eleven of them lauding parochial schools for maintaining children's knowledge of ethnic language and customs.[44] Brookside's Alice Slovensky Harmon recalled that when she began attending public schools, "I wasn't mingling with Slavs, I was mingling with American people."[45] At age fifteen, influenced by her American-born piano teacher, she left her family's congregation, Saint Nicholas Russian Orthodox Church, and began attending Methodist church services.

Unlike her older siblings, who had left school to work to support the family, Alice not only graduated from high school but attended business college until family resentments forced her to drop out. And when Alice married Frank Harmon, she felt even more alienated from the members of her community who decried her marriage to an "outsider"—an Alabamian who was not a member of the Slavic community.[46]

Marriage outside of the ethnic group provoked condemnation among Italian and Lebanese immigrants as well, as many parents sought to keep the "breed pure" and "recommended" suitable spouses for their children and grandchildren. Elizabeth Boohaker's mother was so upset when her grandchildren married non-Lebanese women that she did not want to see those grandchildren again. Fifteen-year-old Mary Bohorfoush married George Pharo in February 1920 after her parents "told her to get married" to a man from the Lebanese community.[47]

As historian Anne Firor Scott has explained, after the First World War, women "felt freer to express their ideas about sexuality, divorce, and paid work outside the home." Though many women continued to work solely inside the home, others no longer experienced "the desperate need to find a husband. A woman could wait for a man who suited her or she could choose not to marry at all."[48] Immigrant women, like their American counterparts, experienced these changes. Alice Slovensky Harmon, for example, had a different worldview from her mother. Whereas Mary Slovensky saw marriage as a normal process of life, Alice saw it as a gamble: "You don't know if you want to stay married or not. You're taking a chance."[49] Harmon and other second-generation immigrant women resembled their nonimmigrant counterparts much more closely than earlier immigrant women did."[50]

Nina Miglionico (1913–2009) perhaps best represents the new avenues available to the American-born daughters and granddaughters of the women who immigrated to the Birmingham area at the end of the nineteenth century. The daughter of Italian immigrants Joseph and Mary Miglionico, Nina graduated at sixteen from Woodlawn High School and later attended Howard University (now Samford University). At age twenty-two, she earned a law degree from the University of Alabama. When she had difficulty finding a job with an established firm, Miglionico opened her own law practice, becoming one of the first women in the state to do so. She continued to practice for seventy-three years, championing the rights of women and minorities. In 1963, she became the first female member of the new Birmingham City Council, and she remained on the council for twenty-two years, serving as its president from 1978 to 1981. Her progressive racial views made her a target: in 1965, she found an undetonated bomb on her front porch, and in 1974 someone burned a cross in her front yard. In 1974, she became the first Alabama woman nominated by a major party for a seat in the U.S. House of Representatives, though she lost the race. On March 1, 2012, Nina Miglionico was inducted into the Alabama Women's Hall of Fame.[51]

The influence of the Lebanese, Italian, and Slavic women who settled in the Birmingham industrial district between 1890 and 1910 can still be felt in the area. Those women and their daughters and granddaughters paved the way for the women involved in the city's political, business, and community affairs in the early twenty-first century. In addition, since the last quarter of the twentieth century, metropolitan Birmingham's ethnic communities have experienced a resurgence. The churches founded by immigrants nearly a century earlier continue to preserve the religious and cultural rituals of their ancestors, while women from the Greek, Lebanese, and Slavic communities host food festivals that highlight traditional cuisine and culture. And countless other women have followed in Nina Miglionico's footsteps, making their mark among the ranks of Birmingham's professionals.

NOTES

1. James M. McPherson, "Antebellum Southern Exceptionalism: A New Look at an Old Question," *Civil War History* 29 (1983): 233.

2. Katherine M. Pruett and John D. Fair, "Promoting a New South: Immigration, Racism, and 'Alabama on Wheels,'" *Agricultural History* 66 (1992): 20–21.

3. Charles H. Otken, *The Ills of the South; or, Related Causes Hostile to the General Prosperity of the Southern People* (New York: Ayers, 1894), 237.

4. Dino Cinel, "Italians in the South: The Alabama Case," *Italian Americana* 9 (1990): 11.

5. Staci S. Simon, "A Study of the Slovak Community at Brookside, Alabama" (master's thesis, University of Alabama, 1997), 87.

6. Frances Saia and Nellie Lusco Saia, interview, May 8, 1981, Birmingfind Oral History Collection, Birmingham Public Library Archives, Linn-Henley Research Library.

7. Elizabeth Duchock Beck, interview by Junius Jackson, November 20, 2009, transcript in possession of the author.

8. Mary Bohorfoush Pharo, interview, September 19, 1980, Birmingfind Oral History Collection.

9. Lyda Faires Deep, interview, October 29, 1980, Birmingfind Oral History Collection.

10. Pharo, interview.

11. Elizabeth Boohaker, interview, October 2, 1980, Birmingfind Oral History Collection.

12. Rose Maenza, interview by Karen Rolen, March 25, 1981, Birmingfind Oral History Collection.

13. Cinel, "Italians in the South," 17.

14. Saia and Saia, interview.

15. Maenza, interview.

16. Argentine Morganti, interview, April 2, 1981, Birmingfind Oral History Collection.

17. Simon, "Study," 20.

18. Annie Letanosky Patchen, interview by Peggy Hamrick, January 3, 1982, Birmingfind Oral History Collection.

19. Cinel, "Italians in the South," 17–18.

20. Deep, interview.

21. Patchen, interview; Simon, "Study," 10–11.

22. John Bodnar, *Immigration and Industrialization: Ethnicity in an American Mill Town, 1870–1940* (Pittsburgh: University of Pittsburgh Press, 1977), 102, 127.

23. Simon, "Study," 1.

24. Pharo, interview.

25. Simon, "Study," 37.

26. Ibid., 27–28; Maenza, interview.

27. Deep, interview; Alice Slovensky Harmon, interview by Peggy Hamrick, February 21, 1983, Birmingfind Oral History Collection.

28. John Shelton Reed, *My Tears Spoiled My Aim and Other Reflections on Southern Culture* (Columbia: University of Missouri Press, 1993). In general, Reed's work analyzes the South from a sociological perspective and concludes that the region is very similar in character to an ethnic group in terms of shared religion, culture, and norms. Moreover, pockets of this southern ethnic grouping can be found throughout the United States, not unlike other traditionally recognized ethnic groups.

29. Pharo, interview; Boohaker, interview; Patchen, interview; Maenza, interview.

30. Maenza, interview.

31. Morganti, interview.

32. Helen Slovensky, interview by author, February 2, 1997.

33. Mary Martha Thomas, "White and Black Alabama Women of the Progressive Era, 1890–1900," in Mary Martha Thomas, ed., *Stepping Out of the Shadows: Alabama Women 1819–1990* (Tuscaloosa: University of Alabama Press, 1995), 77.

34. Owlen Hufton, *The Prospect before Her: A History of Women in Western Europe, 1500–1800* (New York: Knopf, 1995), 175–76. Hufton focuses on Western Europe, but her argument also holds true for women from Lebanon, Italy, and the Slavic countries.

35. Annie Sokira, interview by Selena Casson, July 24, 1975, Special Collections, Samford University Library.

36. Deep, interview; Maenza, interview.

37. Michele Sokira, interview by author, February 1997; Elizabeth Duchock Beck, interview by author, June 11, 1997.

38. Pharo, interview; Deep, interview; Saia, interview.

39. Feiza Mickwee, interview, November 13, 1980, Birmingfind Oral History Collection.

40. Pharo, interview; Patchen, interview.

41. Leslie Woodcock Tentler, *Wage-Earning Women: Industrial Work and Family Life in The United States, 1900–1930* (Oxford: Oxford University Press, 1979), 60–69.

42. Saia, interview.

43. Ibid.; Maenza, interview.

44. M. Mark Stolarik, *Immigration and Urbanization: The Slovak Experience, 1870–1918* (New York: AMS Press, 1977), 161. According to historian Alan M. Kraut, Italian and Greek parents who did not enroll their children in parochial school often organized private after-school language lessons for those children (*The Huddled Masses: The Immigrant in American Society* [Arlington Heights, Ill.: Harlan Davidson, 1982], 135–36).

45. Harmon, interview.

46. Ibid.

47. Pharo, interview.

48. Anne Firor Scott, *The Southern Lady: From Pedestal to Politics, 1830–1930* (Charlottesville: University Press of Virginia, 1995), 214, 215, 216.

49. Harmon, interview.

50. Simon, "Study," 64–65.

51. Samuel Rumore Jr., "Nina Miglionico," December 7, 2011, *Encyclopedia of Alabama*, http://www.encyclopediaofalabama.org/face/Article.jsp?id=h-3184 (accessed July 30, 2016); "Nina Miglionico," n.d., *Alabama State Bar 2011 Lawyers' Hall of Fame*, https://www.alabar.org/membership/alabama-lawyers-hall-of-fame/2011-lawyers-hall-of-fame/ (accessed July 30, 2016); Michael J. Brooks, "Former Birmingham Council Member Miglionico Inducted into Women's Hall of Fame," *Judson College News*, March 27, 2012, http://judsoncollege.infomedia.net/news.asp?record_no =23374 (accessed August 20, 2014).

Margaret Charles Smith

Lessons from Midwifery

JENNY M. LUKE

In May 1985, the Eutaw, Alabama, city council gave the key to the city to its first African American recipient, seventy-nine-year-old lay midwife Margaret Charles Smith, and declared Margaret Charles Smith Day in honor of her commitment and dedication to improving maternity care for women in the community. Until the late 1970s, when Alabama and other southern states outlawed midwifery, thousands of lay midwives provided maternity care to women who would otherwise have received no care. Much has been written about the demise of southern black midwives. However, by focusing mainly on the midwives' elevated role in society and the process by which they were eradicated, these studies have neglected to explore the midwives' work. Midwives satisfied the community-centered, culturally appropriate aspects of care that are today considered an essential part of good, accessible health care.

During Margaret Charles Smith's life (1906–2004), childbirth in Alabama transitioned from a traditional, community-centered affair to a medicalized, hospital-based event. As a young woman, Smith's experience of childbirth resembled that of countless other poor women in Alabama: her children were delivered by a midwife whose elevated position in the community was validated by a supernatural calling to serve and whose skill set and knowledge base were entirely traditional. The political, economic, and social conditions of the Jim Crow South created a unique space in which African American lay midwives developed their model of maternity care and associated childbirth culture. In the face of overwhelming poverty and almost total isolation from the medical establishment, the enduring institution of midwifery filled a crucial void. Revered as models of wisdom, spirituality, and strength, midwives represented authority and prestige in the community and were central to the formation of social networks and relationships.

MARGARET CHARLES SMITH, 1990
Alabama Department of Archives and History, Montgomery.

As a licensed midwife in the 1950s, 1960s, and 1970s, Smith became integrated into a larger, more modern maternity system that slowly emerged out of the increasing state and federal presence in health care. In 1992, she declared, "I want a book about me," giving voice to the thoughts of numerous African American women entrenched in the isolation and intractable poverty of rural Alabama who are largely silent in the historical record. Smith's life and work expose the choices made by poor African American women in their search for safer childbirth. These women ultimately sacrificed the familiarity and comfort of tradition for modern medical care, even if they had to tolerate disrespectful professionals to access that care. Moreover, Smith helps illuminate the complex dilemma that black lay midwives faced as they not only navigated the increasingly formalized health care options developing in Alabama and across the South but also accommodated the shifting cultural demands of the women they served. It was a double-edged sword: Smith was instrumental in helping women gain access to modern maternity care, but she also insisted that her midwifery skills were invaluable and that her trusting, respectful relationships with her patients were critical.

By 1981, Smith had reportedly delivered more than three thousand babies. Nevertheless, her license to practice was terminated after the Alabama legislature redefined the role of the midwife to include only registered nurses specifically certified in midwifery. The legislation also required births to take place in hospitals under doctors' supervision. Thirty-five years later, Alabama is again struggling to meet the maternity needs of its population, and the professional care model is incorporating a greater cultural awareness.[1] Once deemed backward and discarded as obsolete, the grassroots-level skills demonstrated by Smith and her fellow lay midwives are now being rehabilitated in an attempt to reach communities currently neglected by the health care system. The new approach demands a cultural and linguistic competence from its professionals and recognizes the relationships among culture, spirituality, and treatment.[2] Perhaps lessons can be learned from the past.

Margaret Charles was born in Eutaw, a rural community in Greene County, in western Alabama. Her mother, Beulah Sanders, died shortly thereafter, and Margaret was brought up by her grandmother as the youngest of eleven children. Her early experiences share two significant features with the handful of black lay midwives on whom documentation exists: a strong matriarchal role model, and a family of good reputation. Smith understood how cultural stability gelled and strengthened her community and recognized the value in the traditions passed down from one generation of women to the next. Margaret had a profound relationship with her grandmother, who had been born a slave, and delayed her marriage as a consequence of her reverence for "Mama." This deep sense of commitment to a woman who had many years earlier been "put on a stage and sold for three dollars" and had given birth to only one child but raised ten others connected Smith to the past and guided her future. She always lived by the example set by her grandmother.[3]

All of the documented midwives came from families that were less economically vulnerable than most members of their communities. Smith's grandparents were not sharecroppers: they owned the land on which they lived and worked, and with daily tasks distributed between eleven children they were reasonably self-sufficient. Though Smith's life certainly included strenuous physical work and hardship, she remained acutely aware that she was better off than poorer members of her community trapped in a desperate cycle of poverty and deprivation.[4] Her elevated position as a midwife granted her an unusual degree of influence in her community, and she and other midwives used that position to foster positive change and improve the maternal and child health in their communities.

Concern about maternity care in the South arose in the wake of a disturbing Children's Bureau study published in 1917 that found that the United States had a much higher maternal mortality rate than other industrialized nations. Moreover, black women in Alabama had a maternal mortality rate 70 percent higher than the rate for the state's white women. The study concluded that the disparity between the races showed "without a doubt a very great difference in standards of care at childbirth in these two groups."[5] With unquestionable faith in the value of medical science and professionalism, the government blamed this disparity squarely on the shoulders of lay midwives—more specifically, the African American lay midwives who served the South's black population. The medical establishment determined that these providers' gender, race, and lack of professionalism made them grossly inadequate and sought to eradicate them.

In response to this study, Congress passed the Sheppard-Towner Maternity and Infancy Act of 1921. The act provided federal funding to cover the cost of state programs for mothers and babies, and in 1922 and 1923 Alabama received more than thirty-five thousand dollars for the "provision of instruction in the hygiene of maternity and infancy through public health nursing, consultation centers, and other suitable methods."[6] The lack of medical facilities and doctors willing to care for African Americans forced the state to accept lay midwives as a temporary necessary evil; to minimize the "danger to the public," the midwives were brought under the auspices of county health departments; given rudimentary training in asepsis, personal hygiene, and standardized care; and were required to be licensed annually.[7] Margaret Charles herself bore children in 1922 and 1926, as this process was taking place, though her recollections of her experiences do not include any oversight by the Greene County Health Department. Just sixteen when she had her first child, Smith later described herself as "a mess" during the pregnancy and delivery. She resisted using some traditional but ineffective methods of accelerating labor and criticized the harsh techniques employed by her midwife. When she had her second child, therefore, she decided, "I'd rather be by myself . . . just me and the good Lord." She delivered the baby alone, just managing to finish work and get home before he was born.[8] These experiences influenced her approach to midwifery, which featured firm kindness, patience, and trust.

Although the Sheppard-Towner Act expired in 1927, it ushered in an era of supervision, collaboration, and improved standards of care, allowing lay midwives to enhance their skills with elements of modern scientific care. In 1942, after her grandmother's death, Margaret Charles married a childhood friend, Randolph Smith, and she gave birth to another child in 1943. By then, increased funding for public health nurses and diligent supervision of midwives by the county health departments had lowered Alabama's maternal mortality rate from 13.1 deaths per 1,000 live births in 1935 to 4.3 in 1941.[9] During this pregnancy, Smith received instruction from one of Alabama's seventeen hundred lay midwives on how to prepare to give birth, and by the time she went into labor, she "had all the confidence" in the midwife. Instead of attempting to force Smith to consume herbal emetics, as the first midwife had, this midwife rubbed Smith's back and stomach, providing comfort and reassurance.[10]

The Smiths were a sharecropping family, meaning that they were completely dependent on a white landowner for their livelihood. After he took most of their possessions to repay a debt he claimed they owed, Margaret Smith told her husband, "I'm going to look for a job. If I get a start again, no Mr. White Man is going to come up here to tell me he wants my things."[11] She had previously offered informal assistance to friends or neighbors in labor but hesitated to become a licensed midwife. The economic rewards were minimal, and she knew that midwives had to "stay away from home all night and no coffee the next morning. Nowhere to wash your face, and you look like you've come out of a sewer."[12] But the biggest problem she foresaw was her lack of transportation to women in labor, a legitimate concern in a county with few cars and paved roads.[13]

Despite her concerns, Smith began a three-month midwifery course at the Greene County Health Department.[14] Whereas midwives traditionally had learned via apprenticeship, the Department of Health required candidates to receive recommendations from two reputable physicians and to be in good health, literate, and capable of carrying out instructions.[15] Smith possessed those qualifications as well as the requisite "good moral character and reputation." She subsequently attended a two-week residential course at the Tuskegee Institute where she learned basic principles of asepsis, appropriate management of delivery, and compliance with health department procedures.[16]

Midwives necessarily enhanced this science-based training with their innate resourcefulness—what one Alabama lay midwife, Onnie Lee Logan, described as an ability to "use whatcha got."[17] They combined new ideas with their knowledge of prevailing culture to create a better environment for themselves and the women they served. In the past, for example, most women had delivered on quilts, which the midwives later had to wash and sterilize. After some basic instruction, midwives refined techniques to make disposable pads, sanitary towels, and basins from newspaper, focusing on preparation to create a clean environment at delivery.[18] According to Smith, when she arrived at a delivery, she would immediately check to see if disposable pads had been made; if not, she made them, taking twenty sheets of newspaper and "twirl[ing] that newspaper together and tack it so it won't slip and slide." She also used newspaper to make a receptacle to hold waste.[19]

For the black community, Tuskegee's John A. Andrew Memorial Hospital represented a beacon of hope in a landscape largely devoid of medical access.[20] For Margaret Charles Smith, training there was a "real big thing," since it introduced her and three hundred other midwives from surrounding counties to sophisticated, scientific health care, and she sprinkled her memoir with references to skills she "learned at Tuskegee." However, Smith also enormously valued her on-the-job training with midwife Ella Anderson: "Everything, everything I learned, I learned from Miss Anderson."[21] Smith and other midwives faced the challenge of finding the optimum blend of both aspects of care, negotiating between compliance with policy set by a racially prejudiced medical establishment unfamiliar with the realities of African American lives and satisfying the important cultural requirements of the women they served.

State regulations required each licensed lay midwife to carry her instructional manual at all times: any deviation from the prescribed scope of practice could jeopardize her license. In addition, the regulations not only decreed that all midwives carry special bags containing eleven specific items but also prescribed where in the bag each item had to be placed. A significant portion of the manual explained how to prepare for a safe delivery, including three home visits during the pregnancy.[22] But providing maternity services in the homes of the desperately poor usually involved improvising within the boundaries of state standards. Smith excelled in this area, able to "make a way out of no way" and mindful of the fact that "can't nobody prepare what they don't have."[23] This familiarity with the families they served and the collective philosophy of self-help allowed midwives to better meet each mother's individual needs.

Community social networks provided lay midwives with information on new pregnancies. Midwives, in turn, needed to encourage pregnant women to obtain medical care, since state law dictated that a woman obtain a medical release before having a midwife delivery and a midwife could lose her license if she delivered a woman who lacked such clearance. Wrote Smith, "I'd been trained all along not to fool with somebody unless the doctor ok'd the paper stating that the patient is ok for a midwife. [Patients] knew that upfront."[24] In the days before the hospital-construction boom of the late 1940s and 1950s, that medical clearance came from clinics, which lacked the full facilities available at hospitals but nevertheless offered a more modern, scientific approach to childbirth.[25] As early as 1941, more than thirteen thousand Alabama women, most of them black, attended a clinic.[26] Thus, the lay midwife program opened up some level of medical care to a population that previously had none.[27] Adequate prenatal care had long been identified as the single-most-important factor in lowering maternal mortality rates, and indeed, the creation of the lay midwife program led to a drop in mortality rates.

Many poor black women distrusted white physicians and local government, but the midwives' presence at the prenatal clinics provided much-needed reassurance. Smith worked at local prenatal clinics for twenty-eight years: Eutaw on Tuesdays, Tishibe on Thursdays, and Boligee on Fridays. Her presence eased women's transition into the unfamiliar world of modern medicine, and they often requested that she deliver their babies, thus creating a continuity of care that is ideal but difficult to achieve in practice.[28] Lay midwives taught women how to improve their diet despite their limited resources, explained the importance of abstaining from alcohol and tobacco, and encouraged as much rest as possible to promote healthy pregnancies.[29] Patients preferred midwife deliveries to a physician's intervention and knew that such deliveries were possible only in the absence of complications, providing a powerful incentive for women to maintain their good health. The accepted cultural authority of the midwives and the consistency of their presence in the community, neither of which was associated with physician-led care, made them extremely influential in the prenatal education of women.

The lay midwives' acceptance of their pivotal role in the community and eagerness to expand their knowledge base suggests that they were well aware of their potential to effect positive change. Midwife training classes and prenatal clinics became the nexus for traditional and scientific components of care. Prenatal clinics provided a link to medical expertise, a dimension of health care not previously available to poor women, and the training classes spread information about elements of scientific care.

The culturally specific aspects of the care provided by lay midwives are now accepted as crucial elements in providing effective health care but were overlooked in medically driven obstetric care in the Jim Crow South. The childbirth customs of poor rural African American women were not rooted in the Western scientific tradition as practiced by white doctors and nurses but rather reflected the collective culture of black people in America, blending West African traditions with Native American and local customs and adapting herbal remedies and treatments with local flora. Although some treatments clearly conflicted with conventional medical wisdom, some folk practices employed by midwives were compatible with scientific theory, such as using preparations containing natural coagulants such as spiderwebs, soot, and cherry tree bark to treat hemorrhage.[30] Rather than the physiology-based medicine typically used by professionally trained and usually white doctors, philosophies of healing emphasized psychological, social, and spiritual components, and these motifs were evident in the care given by lay midwives.[31]

These practices reached back to folk traditions used in the eighteenth and nineteenth centuries under slavery. Enslaved women who gave birth increased their owners' wealth, and every year from 1750 until emancipation one of every five black women between the ages of fifteen and forty-four gave birth.[32] Smith's grandmother had to marry a "breeding man" who had presumably been approved by her owner based on his perceived virility.[33] But pregnancy offered no benefits to slave women: they either received little or no reprieve from the daily burden of physical labor (except perhaps from the most arduous tasks) and punishment or were subjected to experimental interventions and humiliating examinations by plantation physicians.[34] In this light, it is not surprising that later generations of African American women did not immediately accept childbirth as a disease requiring treatment, continued to work when they became pregnant, and retained a fundamental distrust of white doctors that led to a reluctance to submit to medical examinations during pregnancy. As Logan wrote, "Childbirth is not a sickness. . . . I declare a woman gonna have a baby if she out there in the middle of the street. She gonna have it. All she need is somebody to wrap it up and put some clothes on it. Fact of business, she can get up and do that herself."[35] The white medical establishment, however, not only rejected this laissez-faire attitude toward childbirth but used it to confirm the racist assessment that African American mothers were essentially like animals and required little in the way of comfort and pain relief during labor. Furthermore, white public health nurses interpreted a reluctance to engage a doctor as an indifferent negligence and emotional detachment from the unborn child.[36] Whereas, in Smith's words, "most of the doctors weren't too lovely with the colored folk," midwives possessed a cultural empathy that helped to persuade women of the need to undergo medical examinations during pregnancy.[37]

The lay midwife's claim to authority was rooted in a deep spirituality and a belief in her God-given skills; similarly, a woman's confidence in the midwife lay in the acceptance that the midwife's actions were guided by a higher power. When managing long, difficult labors, Smith asked God to have mercy, believing that if her patients called "Him pure and sincere from [the] heart," he would hear them. For their part, her patients believed that "couldn't no doctor in town or anywhere else could of made me feel any better than Mrs. Smith in assuring me that everything was going to be all right, and it was."[38]

Some midwives kept up other aspects of traditional practice. Herbal teas to augment labor, placing a knife under the bed to "cut" pain, and perineal and abdominal massage persisted despite health department bans. Laboring women's insistence on such practices, which brought a sense of comfort and familiarity to an anxiety-provoking experience, created a conflict for midwives. Smith had to stop using teas, which caused women to ask her, "Miss Margaret, how come you are not using some of that stuff you used on Emma or Lucille? She was telling me about what good stuff you had. Why don't you give me some? Fix me some so I can get through with this baby." But Smith had seen two midwives stripped of their licenses for failing to comply with regulations and was unwilling to take that risk: her patients were "just going to have those babies with what the [midwifery] guide says, 'cause [public health nurses] told us not to" break the rules.[39] These restrictions gradually reinforced the idea that midwifery was an inadequate service that should be usurped by scientific obstetrics and that ultimate knowledge lay in the realm of the physician.

But in the event of an emergency, lay midwives had only limited access to medical support and hospital facilities. Midwives consistently decried the lack of support from the larger medical establishment. Though some of that absence of support was philosophical, much resulted from the reality that doctors were scarce and hospitals were inaccessible. In a handful of cases, Smith experienced emergencies that required transporting women the 170 miles to Tuskegee to receive care. Though other hospitals were closer, she knew that they might well turn away African American patients. And any white hospital that would accept Smith's patient would not accept Smith, leaving the woman at the mercy of the white medical establishment. Smith believed that in such cases, the long journey to Tuskegee was in the best interest of her patients.[40]

Despite the medical establishment's overall lack of support for midwives, individual midwives and doctors frequently developed supportive working relationships based on mutual respect. Dr. Rucker Staggers had a high regard for Smith's abilities and knew that if she requested his help, the situation was serious. He did not hesitate to act. In fact, after 1976, when Alabama legislated that hospital doctors must supervise all deliveries, Smith and Staggers worked around the restrictions as long as possible so that she could continue to provide her vital services. When midwifery was finally phased out in 1981, Staggers had tears in his eyes as he told Smith that he could no longer provide her with medical support and declared, "I'd put you up against anybody delivering a baby."[41]

The shift from home to hospital childbirth accelerated with the increase in the number of hospital beds across the South in the wake of the 1946 Hill-Burton Hospital Construction Act, which bore the name of Alabama senator Lister Hill. Hill-Burton permitted "separate but equal" hospital facilities, meaning that African Americans continued to face racially discriminatory practices, but the increase in access to hospital care began to alter attitudes toward childbirth and heightened expectations regarding levels of care.[42]

Birmingham's Slossfield Hospital and other black institutions initially incorporated traditional, lay-provider elements into their vision of community-based maternity care. Slossfield saw the family as a unit and consequently offered child care for older children when a mother was in labor and allowed midwifery to coexist alongside modern medicine. However, Hill-Burton required hospitals to meet certain standards to receive funding, and Slossfield needed an obstetric department to train black physicians, forcing the hospital to shift to a more mainstream, professionalized care model. Like their white counterparts, pregnant black women sought professional maternity care when presented with the option. In 1935, midwives attended 74.8 percent of Alabama's pregnant African American women; by 1953, that figure had dropped to 44.5 percent.[43]

The shift toward hospital delivery began much earlier in Birmingham and other urban areas, but options remained limited in rural, more isolated locales such as Eutaw. In 1941, the Tuskegee School of Nurse-Midwifery had opened with the goals of enhancing the education and supervision of lay midwives and studying the specific problems of providing maternity services in rural areas with few medical facilities. The program attracted high-caliber African American graduate nurses with backgrounds in public health. The thirty-one nurse-midwives who completed the program melded modern nursing skills learned in their formal training with a cultural competency that was plainly lacking in other professionals, resulting in a significant decline in Macon County's maternal mortality rate.[44] However, African American nurse-midwives experienced much more racism than lay midwives, whose embeddedness in their communities lent them some protection. The Tuskegee graduates, for example, found that their salaries were determined by their race and had to accept segregation-related restrictions on housing and social activities. Many black nurse-midwives found these discriminatory practices intolerable, and the program faced overwhelming difficulties with recruitment and retention.[45] Moreover, the school's success was undermined by a lack of support from the Tuskegee Institute and John A. Andrew Memorial Hospital. To the black medical establishment, the promotion of midwifery, even at a professional level, perpetuated a "racial dualism" in maternal health—the continued exclusion of African Americans from mainstream health care and society at large.[46] Branded as substandard, midwifery came to be accepted as a vestige of the past. In the context of the Jim Crow South, going to a hospital became a marker of status for some African American women: a midwife delivery was seen as an indication of exclusion, poverty, and backwardness, while a hospital delivery signified inclusion within a larger, modern, and scientific society.[47]

Smith reluctantly acknowledged the new preference for hospital delivery and the desire for a medically managed, pain-free labor, though she thought the choice misguided. She insisted that black women did not receive the same level of hospital care as did white women, and she was right. White doctors and nursing staff gave African American women little attention, even after the Civil Rights Act of 1964 required virtually all hospitals to abandon discriminatory practices. In 1966, for example, Eutaw's recently opened Greene County Hospital avoided desegregating by remodeling the semiprivate rooms into private rooms, and the hospital's administrator admitted that he had no intention of making nonracial room assignments.[48] Black maternity patients were often admitted to general nursing floors, exposing mothers and newborns to women suffering from a variety of diseases. In addition, African American women often remained on the general floor throughout the first stage of labor, without constant observation by nurses, meaning that laboring women could not receive any pain relief. At least some white nurses continued to believe that "more primitive" black women lacked white women's capacity to feel pain. When delivery was imminent, nurses whisked patients up to the delivery room, but many did not make it, delivering their babies in the elevator with at best limited medical supervision and a complete absence of privacy or dignity.[49] Declared Smith, "But these mothers, they still rather be in hospital where they can whoop and holler, thinking the doctor is going to give them something to ease them pains, but the doctors won't be there. . . . You need somebody back there with you. Now a midwife, she's got to be right there, sitting aside the bed or sitting over you, holding you, rocking you, rubbing you."[50]

Nevertheless, access to scientific hospital care offered blacks an entrée into American society at large and brought with it hope for positive change. African American women accepted that despite its drawbacks, hospitalized childbirth represented an improvement.[51] Such an attitude altered long-held customs surrounding pregnancy and birth and in turn undermined the prestige of midwifery. Anthropologists have suggested that the preference for hospital birth required changes in belief structures. The community as a whole came to accept that younger bodies had altered in such a way that they no longer responded to traditional methods and remedies, making medically managed births more suitable.[52] Smith reflected this changing belief when she wrote, "I just think the younger race having babies now don't be what the elder people, the old heads, used to be."[53]

As demand for her services dwindled, Smith supplemented her income with private nursing duties, which lacked the prestige of midwifery. In addition, she claimed, "I've saved more babies, but they're losing a whole lot of babies now." Moreover, she continued to advocate a place for midwifery: "So many people can't afford a hospital. And if you get in labor and don't know what to do, you could have a midwife standing by."[54]

Ironically, Smith began to receive accolades for her service only after midwifery was fully eradicated from Alabama's health care system and home birth was deemed illegal. The West Alabama Health Services chapter of the National Black Women's Health Project honored her in 1985, and in 2003, she received national recognition from the Congressional Black Caucus in Washington, D.C., and the International Center for Traditional Childbearing.[55] She would not wish to be defined by these recognitions, though, nor did she need to be validated by them. She believed that she "had to do my part. . . . [T]he Lord had something to do with it. . . . [I]f you can help somebody, help them." That service made her feel as though she was "worth millions."[56]

The development of a professionalized, hospital-based health care system unquestionably brought essential benefits to Alabama's desperately underserved African American population. However, the pendulum has to some extent swung back in the other direction over the past twenty-five years, with the medical establishment and others recognizing that some aspects of the care provided by Smith and other midwives were invaluable. The Office of Minority Health at the Alabama Department of Public Health worked to reduce continuing disparities in care by rehabilitating such strategies as disseminating knowledge through culturally appropriate lenses, utilizing community leaders to encourage people to access care, creating faith-based programs, and promoting linguistic competency.[57] As one obstetrician argued recently, "What works isn't flashy, not expensive, but it's human intensive."[58]

The life and work of Margaret Charles Smith illuminate the ways in which Alabama's African American midwives accommodated and adjusted to the transforming maternity care system. Moreover, they expose how the cultural needs and expectations surrounding childbirth influenced the choices made by black women in the Jim Crow South. As the debate about maternity continues, Alabamians would do well to "listen good" to Smith's experiences and wisdom.

NOTES

1. Alabama Department of Public Health, Center for Health Statistics, Division of Statistical Analysis, *Selected Maternal and Child Health Statistics: Alabama 2013*, December 2014, 17, http://www.adph.org/healthstats/assets/MCH%20book_Final%2013.pdf (accessed July 30, 2016); Alabama Department of Public Health, *Alabama Department of Public Health 2013 Annual Report*, 51, http://www.adph.org/publications/assets/2013annrpt.pdf (accessed January 22, 2016).

2. Alabama Department of Public Health, *Alabama Department of Public Health 2011 Annual Report*, 61, http://www.adph.org/publications/assets/2011annrpt.pdf (accessed January 22, 2016); Emilie Townes, *Breaking the Fine Rain of Death: African American Health Issues and a Womanist Ethic of Care* (New York: Continuum, 1998), 152. For more on the association between culture and health, see Collins O. Airhihenbuwa and Leandris Liburd, "Eliminating Health Disparities in the African American Population: The Interface of Culture, Gender, and Power," *Health Education and Behavior* 33 (2006): 488–501.

3. Margaret Charles Smith and Linda Janet Holmes, *Listen to Me Good: The Life Story of an Alabama Midwife* (Columbus: Ohio State University Press, 1996), 23–30; *Miss Margaret: The Story of an Alabama Granny Midwife*, DVD, directed by Diana Paul (Tiburon, Calif.: Sage Femme, 2010).

4. Smith and Holmes, *Listen to Me Good*, 73.

5. Grace L. Meigs, *Maternal Mortality from All Conditions Connected with Childbirth in the United States and Certain Other Countries* (Washington, D.C.: U.S. Government Printing Office, 1917), in Judy Barrett Litoff, ed., *The American Midwife Debate: A Sourcebook on its Modern Origins* (New York: Greenwood, 1986), 61; Carey V. Stabler, "The History of the Alabama Public Health System" (PhD diss., Duke University, 1944), 193. In 1913 the United States experienced 15.2 maternal deaths per 100,000 whites and 26.1 deaths per 100,000 blacks. The United States ranked fourteenth among the sixteen industrialized countries in the study.

6. Grace Abbott, "Federal Aid for the Protection of Maternity and Infancy," *American Journal of Public Health* 12 (1922): 737–42.

7. E. R. Hardin, "The Midwife Problem," *Southern Medical Journal* 18 (1925): 347–50, in Litoff, ed., *American Midwife Debate*, 146.

8. Smith and Holmes, *Listen to Me Good*, 44, 47, 49.

9. Stabler, "Alabama Public Health System," 263.

10. Smith and Holmes, *Listen to Me Good*, 55; Paul H. Jacobson, "Hospital Care and the Vanishing Midwife," *Millbank Memorial Fund Quarterly* 34 (1956): 257.

11. Smith and Holmes, *Listen to Me Good*, 59.

12. Ibid., 71.

13. *Miss Margaret*.

14. Paul H. Jacobson, "Hospital Care and the Vanishing Midwife," *Millbank Memorial Fund Quarterly* 34 (1956): 257.

15. Stabler, "Alabama Public Health System," 264.

16. Smith and Holmes, *Listen to Me Good*, xvii, 67, 68–72; Alabama Department of Public Health, *The Alabama Midwife: Her Book* (Montgomery: Alabama Department of Public Health, 1956), 1.

17. Onnie Lee Logan, as told to Katherine Clark, *Motherwit: An Alabama Midwife's Story* (New York: Dutton, 1989), 68.

18. Alabama Department of Health, Bureau of Maternal and Child Health, "Oral Quiz for Midwives," [1950s], Alabama Department of Health, Bureau of Maternal and Child Health, "Demonstration of Preparation for Delivery," [1950s], both in Datcher Family Collection, Box 2, Folder 8, Alabama Department of Archives and History; Alabama Department of Public Health, *Alabama Midwife*, 9–20.

19. Smith and Holmes, *Listen to Me Good*, 88; Alabama Department of Public Health, *Alabama Midwife*, 14–15.

20. Eugene H. Dribble Jr., Louis A. Rabb, and Ruth B. Ballard, "John A. Andrew Memorial Hospital," *Journal of the National Medical Association* 53 (1961): 103–18.

21. Smith and Holmes, *Listen to Me Good*, 72, 88, 96, 75.

22. Alabama Department of Public Health, *Alabama Midwife*, 5–7, 9–20.

23. Smith and Holmes, *Listen to Me Good*, 88, 75; Logan, *Motherwit*, 93–96.

24. Smith and Holmes, *Listen to Me Good*, 78.

25. Edward Beardsley, *A History of Neglect: Health Care for Blacks and Mill Workers in the Twentieth-Century South* (Knoxville: University of Tennessee Press, 1987), 277; Karen Kruse Thomas, *Deluxe Jim Crow: Civil Rights and American Health Policy, 1935–1954* (Athens: University of Georgia Press, 2011), 60, 86.

26. Stabler, "Alabama Public Health System," 262.

27. Alabama State Department of Health, Bureau of Maternal and Child Health, "Prenatal Instructions for Cases Attended by Midwives," 1955, Datcher Family Collection, Box 2, Folder 8; James H. Ferguson, "Mississippi Midwives," *Journal of the History of Medicine* 5 (1950): 89; Alabama Department of Public Health, *Alabama Midwife*, 1.

28. Smith and Holmes, *Listen to Me Good*, 77.

29. "A General Daily Guide during Normal Pregnancy," 1958, Datcher Family Collection, Box 2, Folder 8; Alabama Department of Public Health, *Alabama Midwife*, 10–11.

30. Thomas, *Deluxe Jim Crow*, 83.

31. Harriet A. Washington, *Medical Apartheid: The Dark History of Medical Experimentation on Black Americans from Colonial Times to the Present* (New York: Anchor, 2006), 48.

32. Ibid., 44.

33. Smith and Holmes, *Listen to Me Good*, 24.

34. Marie Jenkins Schwartz, *Birthing a Slave: Motherhood and Medicine in the Antebellum South* (Cambridge: Harvard University Press, 2009), 127, 136, 312.

35. Logan, *Motherwit*, 130.

36. Stabler, "Alabama Public Health System," 262; Gertrude Jacinta Fraser, *African American Midwifery in the South: Dialogues of Birth, Race, and Memory* (Cambridge: Harvard University Press, 1998), ch. 6, 133.

37. Smith and Holmes, *Listen to Me Good*, 104; Logan, *Motherwit*, 102.

38. Smith and Holmes, *Listen to Me Good*, 91, 83.

39. Ibid., 101, 99.

40. Ibid., 104.

41. Ibid., 88, 147.

42. Beardsley, *History of Neglect*, 90–100; Karen Kruse Thomas, "The Hill-Burton Act and Civil Rights: Expanding Hospital Care for Black Southerners, 1939–1960," *Journal of Southern History* 72 (2006): 823–70; Thomas, *Deluxe Jim Crow*, 116.

43. Jennifer Nelson, "Healthcare Reconsidered: Forging Community Wellness among African Americans in the South," *Bulletin of the History of Medicine* 81 (2007): 594–624; Jacobson, "Hospital Care," 257; Stabler, "Alabama Public Health System," 260. Among Alabama's white women, 12.6 percent had midwife deliveries in 1935, while just 1.6 percent did so in 1953.

44. *Twenty Years of Nurse-Midwifery, 1933–1953* (New York: Maternity Center Association, 1955), 58–59, 61.

45. Lucinda Canty, "The Graduates of the Tuskegee School of Nurse-Midwifery," (master's thesis, Yale University, 1994), 34; *Twenty Years of Nurse-Midwifery*, 61.

46. Bruce Bellingham and Mary Pugh Mathis, "Race, Citizenship, and the Bio-Ethics of the Maternalist Welfare State: 'Traditional' Midwifery in the American South under the Sheppard-Towner Act, 1921–1929," *Social Politics* 1 (1994): 158–59.

47. Fraser, *African American Midwifery*, 103.

48. U.S. Commission on Civil Rights, *Title VI . . . One Year After: A Survey of Desegregation of Health and Welfare Services in the South* (Washington, D.C.: U.S. Government Printing Office, 1966), 11–12.

49. Penfield Chester, *Sisters on a Journey: Portraits of American Midwives* (New Brunswick, N.J.: Rutgers University Press, 1997), 139; Thomas, "Hill-Burton Act," 826.

50. Smith and Holmes, *Listen to Me Good*, 148.

51. Fraser, *African American Midwifery*, 136.

52. Ibid., 166.

53. Smith and Holmes, *Listen to Me Good*, 155.

54. Ibid., 149; Rhonda Pines, "Margaret Charles Smith: She Knows Motherhood by Heart," *Tuscaloosa News*, May 12, 1985.

55. Rhonda Pines, "Margaret Charles Smith: She Knows Motherhood by Heart," *Tuscaloosa News*, May 12, 1985; *Miss Margaret*; International Center for Traditional Childbearing, *About ICTC*, http://ictcmidwives.org/about-ictc/ictc-history/ (accessed January 22, 2016).

56. Smith and Holmes, *Listen to Me Good*, 150, 156.

57. Alabama Department of Public Health, *Alabama Department of Public Health 2011 Annual Report*, 60–61.

58. Dr. Heidi Rinehart quoted in *Deadly Delivery: The Maternity Health Care Crisis in the USA* (London: Amnesty International Secretariat, 2010), 92.

Virginia Foster Durr

"The Liberation of Pure White Southern Womanhood"

PATRICIA SULLIVAN

When she was in her sixties, Virginia Foster Durr attempted to write her memoir, intending to call it *The Liberation of Pure White Southern Womanhood*. Durr's life, which spanned the twentieth century, is a story of a woman who defied the expectations that structured the lives of white southern women of her generation. Personal characteristics and experiences along with historical timing combined to create Durr's opportunities. Born to privilege in the shadow of the Civil War, she had a keen mind, a restless curiosity, and a sharp moral compass. Her social awareness and political sensibilities were informed in large part by her experience of the Great Depression and the culture and politics of New Deal Washington. Her activism was given full rein in the movement to end the South's racial caste system and democratize its politics.

Virginia Foster was born in 1903 in Birmingham, Alabama, the industrial hub of the New South, just as segregation and disfranchisement laws were tightening their hold on the state and the region. Her father, Sterling Foster, minister of the prestigious South Highland Presbyterian Church, had grown up on his family's plantation in Union Springs "in an atmosphere of wealth and abundance and servants." Virginia's mother, Anne Patterson Foster, was the daughter of Josiah Patterson, who earned the rank of colonel in the Fifth Alabama Cavalry regiment of the Confederate Army. "The Confederacy was still sacred when I was young," she later recalled. As a young girl, she volunteered as a page at the annual state Confederate reunion held in her hometown.[1]

Summers spent on the Foster plantation in Union Springs were among Durr's most vivid childhood memories. Her grandmother, Virginia Heard Foster, for whom Durr was named, presided over a household run by formerly enslaved African Americans and their immediate descendants. Through Virginia's

VIRGINIA FOSTER DURR, C. 1947
C. B. Baldwin Papers, Special Collections and University
Archives, University of Iowa, Iowa City.

youthful eyes, it seemed Granny Foster "never had to do anything in life but be charming." Easter, a woman born into slavery, was in charge of the household. Durr remembered her as "dignified and aristocratic" and "probably one of the smartest women I ever knew." That was one reason, Durr recalled, that it was difficult for her "to swallow the prevailing theory that blacks were inferior."[2] When Virginia was ten, the well-being of her immediate family took a drastic turn when her father lost his parsonage. The Princeton-educated minister, who had also studied theology at the Presbyterian seminary in Edinburgh, had refused to accept a literal interpretation of the Bible and been tried and found guilty of heresy. After losing his church, Sterling Foster supported his family by selling insurance and relying on income from the Union Springs plantation. From then on, Durr recalled, there was "always a sense of insecurity, of not knowing what was going to come next," as the Fosters strived to maintain their social standing in the community.[3] Virginia attended Birmingham's public schools, with a year at Miss Finch's Finishing School in New York and one at the Cathedral School for Girls in Washington, D.C. She was an avid reader and had an inquisitive nature, causing her father to worry that his "bookish" daughter might never marry. Hugo Black, then a young labor lawyer courting Virginia's older sister, Josephine, encouraged Virginia's interests and, she recalled, "he treated me like an equal."[4] In 1921, Hugo and Josephine married, and Virginia enrolled at Wellesley College, a prestigious women's school outside of Boston.

Wellesley broadened Virginia's horizons. Her studies of economics, religion, and history taught her how "to use my mind and get pleasure out of it." Beyond the intellectual stimulation of her classes, her female professors challenged her ideas about women. She recalled an old professor "with white hair" who taught Shakespeare "and was one of the happiest creatures I had ever seen. She never had a husband." She realized that women "could use their minds," accomplish things, and find happiness and fulfillment. "For the first time, I realized women could be something." That, she recalled, "was the real liberation that I got at Wellesley."[5]

Virginia faced the first challenge to her racial beliefs and practices while at Wellesley. A policy of assigned seating in the dining halls placed her at a table with one of the college's few black students. When an indignant Virginia insisted that she "could not possibly eat at the table with a Negro girl," the dining hall supervisor replied that if she was unable to abide by the rules, she could withdraw from the college. Virginia could not bear the thought of leaving Wellesley. After talking late into the night with her roommates, she realized that what worried her most was what her father would say. She decided not to tell him. She subsequently wrote, "That was the first time I became aware that my attitude was considered foolish by some people and Wellesley College wasn't going to stand for it. That experience had a tremendous effect on me." While it did not constitute an epiphany in terms of her racial attitudes, "it planted a doubt."[6]

Virginia's time at Wellesley was cut short when, as she put it, "the boll weevil ate up my education." The pest's infestation of the South during the early 1920s sent cotton prices and land values plummeting, eroding the Foster family's primary income source. Her English professor thought she could help secure a scholarship to cover Virginia's tuition and suggested that she consider the "Self Help House," where students did their own cooking and cleaning up and minimized the cost of room and board. Sterling Foster believed that such an arrangement was beneath his family's social status and would further mark his financial failure. Consequently, at the end of her sophomore year, Virginia withdrew from Wellesley.[7]

In the immediate years following her return to Birmingham, the trappings of status lingered and the pressures to find a husband became more pronounced. In 1923, Virginia made her debut with a whirl of parties. She also took a job as librarian for the county bar association to help support the family, a source of humiliation for her parents. Durr later explained that marriage was viewed as "the only safe economic route" for a young white woman of her status in Alabama. Looking back, she recalled that so much was happening around her that would later occupy the center of her attention—"anti-lynching fights and child labor fights and the suffrage movement. [But it] was only after I was safely married that I could really be interested in anything else."[8]

Virginia Foster's marriage to Clifford Durr in April 1926 marked a union that would transform both their lives. Clifford Durr, from Montgomery, was a graduate of the University of Alabama and had been a Rhodes Scholar. He was a partner in one of Birmingham's leading corporate law firms when he met Virginia. The marriage enabled Virginia to move in circles that expanded her intellectual and political range and gave full rein to desires and questions that simmered just beneath the surface.

The assumptions and certitudes that defined the lives of the privileged unraveled in the face the Great Depression. Virginia was pained by the hardships endured by her mother and father, a situation compounded by her exposure to the raw face of poverty. As a Junior League volunteer, Virginia accompanied Red Cross workers to the steel mill villages on the edge of Birmingham to investigate families of unemployed steel workers and determine their eligibility for relief. She recalled, "All of a sudden Birmingham broke on me and I just couldn't believe it." The Tennessee Coal and Iron Company evicted families from company housing; those who remained had no electricity or water. According to

Durr, "They were cold, they were sick and many children had rickets . . . simply because they didn't have any milk." The desperate conditions and callous indifference of the steel companies, she later recalled, was her "first ineradicable lesson on the injustice and inequalities . . . of society."[9]

The Durrs read and studied in an effort to understand the causes of the depression, deepening their sense of social responsibility. In a February 1933 letter to a college friend, Corliss Lamont, Virginia expressed interest in his views on socialism and said that she was going to hear Socialist Party leader Norman Thomas the following week. She continued, "The depression has shown that no one group is omnipotent and that when the powers and the money get concentrated in a few hands that all of the rest of the people are bound to suffer. I believe we are bound to see in the next few years some startling changes."[10]

Early in 1933, Cliff opposed the firing of several clerical staff and junior members of his law firm just as relief funds were drying up in Birmingham. He proposed that the firm's senior partners take a cut in pay to avoid further dismissals. His colleagues rejected the idea, leading to Durr's departure from the firm. Hugo Black, who had become a U.S. senator, helped Durr obtain a temporary position in Washington, D.C., with the Reconstruction Finance Corporation shortly after Franklin Roosevelt's inauguration. The job quickly became permanent.[11]

Arriving in Washington in the spring of 1933, Virginia later recalled, "was like light after darkness." Until then, she said, "I didn't have a framework for the way I felt. . . . I was almost completely apolitical." That changed dramatically in the excitement and tumult of New Deal Washington.[12]

Virginia, Cliff, and their six-year-old daughter, Ann, settled into an old farmhouse on Seminary Hill in Alexandria, six miles outside of Washington. Over the next seven years, Virginia gave birth to Clifford Jr. (1935), Lucy (1937), and Virginia "Tilla" (1939). A fifth child, Lulah, was born in 1947. Able to afford help with household work and with the children, Virginia became part of the wider world of Washington politics. After meeting Eleanor Roosevelt at a party, she volunteered with the Women's Division of the Democratic National Committee a couple of days each week.[13]

The Women's Division had conducted a study on the South and identified the poll tax as the major barrier that kept many poor people, especially women, from voting. This issue resonated with Virginia. After they married, Cliff had paid her fifteen-dollar accumulated poll tax so that she could vote. For a family of lesser means, such a cost was prohibitive. The study found that many families paid the tax solely for the male head of the household. Such conditions stoked Virginia's resentment of the constraints on the lives and opportunities of southern white women. After the Women's Division initiated a campaign to eliminate the poll tax, Virginia began going to the headquarters every day.[14]

Washington's various groups and organizations, including the Women's Division of the Democratic Party, reflected the fact that the city was segregated. No black women worked in the Women's Division. But a chance meeting with Mary McLeod Bethune, a noted black educator and close friend of Eleanor Roosevelt, had a significant impact on Virginia. Bethune attended a meeting of the Women's Division as Roosevelt's guest. Bethune advised the women that if they planned to do something about voting rights in the South, they should become acquainted with the work of black lawyers such as Charles Houston and William Hastie, who were leading an effort to challenge voting barriers in the region. Virginia Durr followed through on Bethune's advice and met with Hastie in the restaurant of the YWCA, one of the city's few nonsegregated eating places. Her connections with Hastie and Houston, two of the leading constitutional lawyers in the country, further bored away at racial ideas and attitudes with which she had grown up and proved important as she became more deeply involved in the issue of voting rights in the South.[15]

New Deal Washington was a crossroads for young people who, like the Durrs, were attracted to the possibilities that blossomed as government sought to meet the crisis of the depression and remedy the deep economic inequities that it exposed. Eleanor Roosevelt helped to broaden the visibility and roles of women in government affairs, as did Secretary of Labor Frances Perkins, the first woman to serve in a presidential cabinet. Their actions informed Virginia Durr's sense of opportunities for women.

Fellow southerners who shared the Durrs' backgrounds and concerns for the region formed the core of Cliff and Virginia's social and political lives. Virginia renewed her acquaintance with Clark Foreman of Atlanta, whom she had known when she was at Wellesley and Foreman was at Harvard. Foreman served as special adviser on the economic status of the Negro under Secretary of the Interior Harold Ickes, a novel attempt to ensure the inclusion of blacks in New Deal programs as well as within the administration. Initially shocked by Foreman's advanced racial views, Virginia found him to be a major influence as her own ideas and associations began to change. Aubrey Williams, fellow Alabamian and director of the National Youth Administration, became one of the Durrs' closest friends. Other southerners who were part of the Durrs' social network included Arthur "Tex" Goldschmidt, a key architect of the Works Progress Administration program; Florida Congressman Claude Pepper; Lyndon and Lady Bird Johnson; and Alan Lomax, who was creating the Archive of American Folk Song at the Library of Congress.

In 1937, Virginia had begun attending hearings chaired by Senator Robert La Follette on antilabor violence in violation of the National Labor Relations Act when the committee turned its attention to the practices of the Tennessee Coal and Iron Company in Birmingham and Bessemer. She was riveted by accounts of the massive show of force that met efforts to organize workers in the mill villages she had visited just a few years earlier. And she was startled to learn that leading citizens of Birmingham—the fathers of children with whom she had grown up—were accused of actively supporting the violent repression of labor activity. Testimony regarding Joseph Gelders struck a deep chord. Gelders, a University of Alabama professor turned labor activist, had been beaten by Tennessee Coal and Iron police and left for dead. Gelders had attended the University of Alabama with Cliff, and Virginia was acquainted with his younger brother. She arranged to meet him during her next visit to Birmingham.[16]

Meeting Joe Gelders, Virginia later recalled, was probably "one event that really changed my life." His journey from apolitical physics professor to a labor and human rights activist resonated with her own experience. After witnessing abject poverty and human suffering during the depression, Gelders sought to understand the causes and found the most satisfactory explanation in Karl Marx's critique of capitalism. Gelders became affiliated with the Communist Party and was involved in investigating and exposing the violent repression and often illegal arrests of labor organizers. Despite the beating he received, he continued his work in the South. Gelders's integrity and raw courage inspired Virginia. He was, she recalled, "prepared to give his life. . . . [H]e was struggling to get something accomplished."[17]

In the spring of 1938, tragedy struck the Durr family when two-and-a-half-year-old Clifford Jr. died after the family pediatrician failed to diagnose appendicitis. The boy's parents were "absolutely devastated," Ann later recalled. In the months that followed, Virginia began attending the La Follette Committee hearings on a regular basis and became more deeply involved in politics because "staying at home was too painful for me." The hearings helped "to take my mind off my boy's death, at least during the day."[18]

The La Follette Committee hearings were "where I got my education," Durr later explained. The hearings offered stark evidence of the ways in which powerful interests used the cloak of "law and order" and charges of communism to justify wholesale assaults on union organizers and their supporters. For Durr, the hearings revealed the economic and political relationships at the core of the struggle around the New Deal. They also introduced her to a radical group of New Dealers and labor activists. Throughout the summer of 1938 she frequently lunched with members of the committee's staff: Charles Kramer,

Robert Lamb, John Abt, Luke Wilson, and others. Some were members of the Communist Party and some were not, but all were staunch defenders of the labor movement.[19]

That year was pivotal for the New Deal and Franklin Roosevelt's presidency. In the aftermath of his landslide reelection in 1936, Roosevelt's failed effort to expand the number of justices sitting on the U.S. Supreme Court had triggered the open rebellion of southern Democrats anxious to contain the reformist policies of the New Deal and the progressive movements and labor activism that had grown up in its wake. In response, Roosevelt, on the advice of Clark Foreman, commissioned Foreman, Clifford Durr, and a group of other southern New Dealers to write a "report on the economic conditions of the South." The report emphasized the importance of federal aid in cultivating the rich resources of a region that Roosevelt described as "the nation's number one economic problem." In conjunction with the report, Roosevelt supported challenges to several powerful anti–New Deal southern representatives in the Democratic primaries. The effort failed in part because the strongest supporters of the New Deal in the South were disfranchised by a variety of voting restrictions.[20]

During this period, Gelders and Lucy Randolph Mason, the Virginia-born publicist for the Congress of Industrial Organizations, sought Virginia Durr's assistance in organizing a major conference in the South, an idea that Franklin and Eleanor Roosevelt supported. The conference would be dedicated to rallying support for workers' right to organize and to promoting the expansion of voting rights and political democracy in the region. With Durr's assistance, this labor-oriented group joined with Foreman and other contributors to the report to organize a three-day meeting in Birmingham over Thanksgiving weekend in 1938. Attendees then founded the Southern Conference for Human Welfare (SCHW).

Durr attended the meeting as a representative of the Women's Division of the Democratic National Committee. The conference sought to provide a broad forum for addressing the issues raised by the report. Organizers drew from the networks that had grown up around the New Deal, convening an eclectic group of southerners that included business executives, state and federal officials, labor organizers, sharecroppers, newspaper editors, and college students from across the political spectrum. Participants included Eleanor Roosevelt; Mary McLeod Bethune; Hugo Black, whom President Roosevelt had appointed to the U.S. Supreme Court in 1937; poet Sterling Brown; and University of North Carolina president Frank Porter Graham. About 20 percent of the twelve hundred people in attendance were African American. Sociologist Arthur Raper described the gathering as "one of the most exaggerated expressions of change in the South. . . . [H]ere was a revival, a bush-shaking, something that just jumped up."[21]

The group met on a nonsegregated basis, but organizers did not intend to directly confront the issue of race. During the second day of the meeting, however, Birmingham police, led by Eugene "Bull" Connor, ordered the group to segregate in accordance with a municipal ordinance. With limited options available, organizers decided to comply so that the meeting might continue. When Eleanor Roosevelt returned to the newly segregated hall, she sat on the side with the black participants. A policeman promptly informed the First Lady that she would have to move. Roosevelt took her chair and placed it in the middle of the aisle dividing the two sections, a powerful gesture that further elevated the segregation issue. SCHW members pledged never again to meet at a venue where segregation could be enforced.[22]

Durr described the meeting as "a wonderful sort of love feast because it was the first time all of these various elements from the South had gotten together."[23] Her mood, however, was tempered by the response of her closest friends in Birmingham, who bitterly opposed Franklin Roosevelt. The disturbance over segregation at the meeting confirmed their fears that racial equality was a part of the president's agenda, and they rebuffed her efforts to explain her support for the New Deal. People she had known since childhood labeled her "an outright traitor, an outlaw. It was very painful for me to see my friends against me, but I never had a moment's doubt of where I stood."[24]

The SCHW catalyzed Durr's development as a political activist and strategist and civil rights advocate. She served as chair of the SCHW's Committee on Civil Rights, with Gelders as the committee's executive secretary. Together, they helped lead the organization's first major campaign to abolish the poll tax. Durr and Gelders worked with California congressman Lee Geyer, who introduced a bill to ban the poll tax in federal elections. "All hell broke loose," Durr recalled. Southern Democrats strongly opposed any federal regulation of voting requirements, and the chair of the Democratic National Committee ordered the Women's Division to stop all work on the issue. Durr resigned from the Women's Division, and began working full time out of Geyer's office.[25]

The anti-poll-tax movement became the opening salvo in the struggle for federal protection of voting rights, and Virginia Durr was one of its most effective organizers. Working through a growing network of contacts in the labor movement along with the National Association for the Advancement of Colored People (NAACP) and other civil rights groups, she helped build a broad coalition of support for legislation. Durr persuaded Eleanor Roosevelt to help secure Florida senator Claude Pepper as cosponsor of the bill in 1941, when it passed the House, only to be blocked by a southern-led filibuster in the Senate. That year the National Committee to Abolish the Poll Tax was created to serve as a clearinghouse and center for anti-poll-tax activity, and Durr served as the director. An unpaid volunteer, Durr built a small army of other volunteers to aid in the effort. Congressional staffers worked in the National Committee's cramped office in the evenings, and college students showed up to stuff envelopes and run the mimeograph machine. After enlisting young historian C. Vann Woodward to aid in a publicity campaign, she wrote confidently, "I have an invincible belief that if the right people ever get together something is bound to happen."[26]

Durr proved herself a talented strategist and organizer, displaying a deep faith in the democratic process and an insatiable interest in people. A close friend, British writer Jessica Mitford, described Durr as "a spellbinder whose peculiar charm lay in her enormous curiosity about people, her driving passion to find things out, to know about the details and the motives." The Durrs' home on Seminary Hill became a favorite Sunday-afternoon gathering place for a broad cross-section of friends and political allies. According to Mitford, a "kaleidoscopic mix of people" turned up each week, among them "judicial dignitaries, Southern legislators—who Virginia was forever trying to proselytize for the anti–poll tax cause—New Deal functionaries, earnest young radicals." Mitford particularly recalled Lyndon and Lady Bird Johnson and Virginia and Clifford Durr relaxing barefoot on the lawn, "chinning away" in a "near incomprehensible patois about the ins and outs of Southern politics."[27]

During the 1940s, the pull of politics and the urgency of the voting rights fight competed with the demands of children and domestic life. The Durrs' younger daughters remember their mother as an active if not constant presence in their lives. She was a firm believer in public education and served as head of the Parent-Teacher Association for the Lee-Jackson School, which they attended. She often read to her daughters, sharing her love of Louisa May Alcott, Charles Dickens, and other writers. The Durr children were not sent away during parties or other social gatherings but instead "roamed freely," as Lucy recalled. The vast variety of people coming and going made Tilla "feel included in the whole world."[28]

In many ways, Virginia and Clifford Durr presented a study in contrasts. He was conservative by nature, slow and deliberate; she was, as Mitford put it, "one of nature's rebels."[29] But their political beliefs and values developed in tandem. Cliff, like Virginia, was greatly influenced by his experiences in Washington. His opportunities within the Roosevelt administration and his participation in the city's broader social life nurtured his transition from corporate lawyer to an active proponent of the public interest and stalwart defender of civil liber-ties. Cliff left the Reconstruction Finance Corporation in 1941, when President Roosevelt appointed the Alabamian to serve on the Federal Communications Commission, where he played a leading role in securing frequencies for public programming.[30]

Politics in the service of changing the South became Virginia Durr's passion. During the Second World War, while the anti-poll-tax bill and other liberal legislative efforts stalled, her activities extended beyond Capitol Hill. As chair of the SCHW's Washington committee, she participated in efforts to desegregate public facilities in the nation's capital. Starting in 1944, the SCHW expanded its program to include local and state affiliates around the South. She joined the Arlington branch of the NAACP and served as cochair of SCHW's Committee for Virginia with Luther Porter Jackson, a professor at Virginia State College, a historically black school in Petersburg. In a state where less than 12 percent of eligible voters were registered, the Virginia Committee worked with labor unions, NAACP chapters, and other civic groups to promote voter registration and organize coalitions of black and white southerners around a program of progressive political action. The NAACP's 1944 Supreme Court victory overturn-ing the all-white Democratic primary removed the most effective barrier to black voter participation in the South. At the same time, returning black war veterans determined to exercise the full rights of citizenship energized efforts by civil rights and labor groups to broaden the base of voters and political engage-ment in the South.[31]

Durr's political activism in Virginia and Washington was part of a region-wide biracial movement that mounted a robust challenge to conservative Democrats' "solid South" in the immediate postwar years, and the effort gained considerable ground during the 1946 electoral season. At the same time, the Cold War poli-cies of the Truman administration, with its rampant anticommunism, fractured the Democratic Party and undermined the confident democratic spirit of the New Deal era. The SCHW was among the organizations that refused to bar or purge Communist Party members, a policy Durr endorsed. "My position on the Communists is as it has always been," she explained. "They represent the extreme left of the political circuit and I often disagree with their programs and methods. But I see so clearly that when one group of people is made untouch-able the liberties of all suffer and our Democracy is on the way to ruin. I see and feel so clearly how it has crippled the lives and hopes of both white and Negro people in the South."[32]

Former vice president Henry Wallace emerged as a vocal critic of President Harry S. Truman's Cold War policies and stood out among national political figures as an active supporter of political, economic, and racial democracy in the South. During 1947, Durr, Foreman, and several other SCHW leaders joined with other progressives to sponsor Wallace on several national tours, providing a forum for his views on foreign and domestic policies. In the South, Wallace refused to appear before segregated audiences. After Wallace declared his candidacy for the presidency on the Progressive Party ticket late in 1947, Durr and other leading SCHW figures joined with southern labor and civil rights activists to organize support for Wallace. The Progressive Party campaign built on the postwar work to expand voter participation, support New Deal policies, and challenge the color line. Wallace's supporters included noted black activist W. E. B. Du Bois; Charles Houston; Daisy Bates, an NAACP leader from Little Rock, Arkansas; and Coretta Scott, future wife of Martin Luther King Jr. Blacks and whites ran for local and state office on the Progressive Party ticket across the region.[33]

Durr chaired the Progressive Party in Virginia and ran as the party's U.S. Senate candidate, challenging Democratic incumbent Harry F. Byrd. She also served as president of the Northern Virginia Parent-Teacher Association, focusing on the abysmal state of Virginia's public school system. She spoke mostly at small community forums and in black churches. Clifford Durr, who did not publicly support Wallace, wrote to the Durrs' daughter, Ann, "I suspect you realize that your mother is a rather exceptional person with a first class mind and more than one person's share of guts. And she has faith!" She received nearly six thousand votes, twice as many as Wallace garnered in Virginia.[34]

In the aftermath of the 1948 presidential campaign, a Cold War consensus infused the political climate in Washington, ultimately leading to the Durrs' departure. President Truman offered Clifford Durr a second term on the Federal Communications Commission, but Durr declined because of his opposition to the administration's loyalty program, which he described as fraught with the "potentialities of injustice, oppression, and cruelty." In 1949, Virginia and Cliff joined a group of noted scientists, lawyers, and media figures that traveled to Europe under the sponsorship of the One World Committee. The trip confirmed both Durrs' skepticism about the direction of American foreign policy. Clifford Durr's opposition to Cold War orthodoxies made it difficult for him to make a living for his family in Washington. After a temporary move to Denver, Colorado, and with no other options, the family settled temporarily in the Montgomery home of Cliff's mother.[35]

Virginia Durr had never imagined that she would return to live in the Deep South. At nearly fifty years of age, after two decades in Washington, she returned to a place where social and racial relations remained much as they had

been when she had left. Their dependence on Cliff's family, all staunch segregationists, compounded a feeling of loss and isolation. Virginia Durr described
life in the Cradle of the Confederacy as like "living in a closed room, simply
struggling for air."[36]

Durr fought loneliness and despair by writing an outpouring of letters to
friends from New Deal days. The correspondence connected her to a world
beyond the confines of Montgomery and enabled her to sustain friendships,
political engagement, and the constant dialogue that had been at the center of
her life in Washington. She described the painful adjustments to life in Alabama as she struggled to understand her native state and searched for signs of
change. In the process, she created a remarkable chronicle of life in the South
from the days of entrenched segregation through the peak years of the civil
rights movement.

Cliff established a law practice and Virginia worked as his secretary, focusing
on making a living and trying mightily to avoid attention and notoriety. Her
cover was blown in the spring of 1954, on the eve of the U.S. Supreme Court's
Brown v. Board of Education ruling, when she was subpoenaed to appear before
a Senate committee that was holding hearings in New Orleans to investigate
subversive activity in the South, including the SCHW. Her appearance before
the committee made headlines—with a photo capturing Virginia powdering
her nose after refusing to respond to Mississippi senator James O. Eastland's
interrogation. During the hearing, Clifford Durr suffered a minor heart attack.
The Durrs returned to Alabama, publicly exposed as "subversives" and anti-
segregationists.[37]

Shortly after returning to Montgomery, Virginia struck up a friendship with
Rosa Parks, an activist who served alternately as the youth leader and the secretary of the NAACP branch in the Alabama capital. As a seamstress, she occasionally did some sewing and alterations for the Durr women. In the summer of
1955, Virginia arranged for Parks to attend Highlander Folk School in Tennessee
for an interracial workshop on the implementation of school desegregation. For
Parks, meeting and living with white people on an equal basis was transforma-
tive. For the first time, she had found "that this could be a unified society."[38] On
December 1, Parks was arrested when she refused to give up her seat to a white
man on a city bus. Cliff and Virginia accompanied Montgomery NAACP activist
E. D. Nixon to the jail to post bond for Parks. The resulting one-day boycott of
the buses led to a yearlong protest, the emergence of Rev. Martin Luther King Jr.
as its leader, and ultimately a Supreme Court decision striking down segregation on municipal buses.

Virginia Durr immediately sensed that the boycott represented a historic shift. In her letters she strained to find the words to convey the new spirit reflected in a protest that united fifty thousand black people in opposition to segregation. "It has a quality of hope and joy that I wish I could give you," she wrote to Mitford. "I feel like I am in touch with all the rising forces in the world and the end of fear and slavery is in sight. I know this is just a moment but . . . it only takes a moment for a new world to be conceived."[39] The boycott lifted Durr's spirits and placed her at the center of a movement that would ultimately transform the South and the nation. In the aftermath of the boycott, she joined with black and white women in a prayer group of the Fellowship of the Concerned, one of the few interracial groups functioning in Montgomery.

As the civil rights movement gained momentum over the next decade, Durr worked to elevate awareness and organize support from around the country and in Washington, D.C. Her letters capture the drama, escalating violence, and halting nature of the struggle along with the failure of the nation at large to effectively respond until the early 1960s. Mass protests, fueled by student sit-ins and Freedom Rides in the spring of 1961 seized national attention and finally compelled the federal government to act. After receiving a letter and press clippings from Durr, Burke Marshall, assistant attorney general for civil rights, urged her to send more.[40] The Durrs' home became a safe house for young people traveling south, often compared to a station on the Underground Railroad. A student on his way to Mississippi to register voters described their home as "an oasis of normalcy, wisdom, and amazing good humor."[41] The dedication, commitment, and courage of young people working to topple Jim Crow and open up the South's political system filled Virginia Durr with gratification and hope.

To Durr, the passage of the 1964 Civil Rights Act, orchestrated by her old friend, Lyndon Johnson, seemed a "political miracle." The comprehensive bill dismantled segregation, broadened federal protection of citizenship rights, and specifically barred employment discrimination based on race and gender. A year later, following the triumphant march from Selma to Montgomery, Johnson signed the Voting Rights Act, the fruition of the long struggle for federal action to prevent voting discrimination that Virginia Durr and others had begun during the New Deal era.

But new challenges moved to the forefront. She observed with dismay as Johnson escalated the war in Vietnam during 1965, and despite the end of legal racial segregation, the more intractable problems of economic inequality and racial polarization persisted, and they, along with the war, tore at the nation's social fabric. George Wallace's hold on Alabama and his rising appeal beyond the state gave voice to a national politics of white backlash.[42]

Nevertheless, the achievements of the long struggle for civil rights renewed Durr's faith in the power of people to stand up to injustice and work together toward meaningful change. With the fall of the racial caste system, opportunities for her political activism broadened. She worked with federal antipoverty programs during the latter half of the 1960s and in 1966 was elected to serve on the Child Development Agency, the local sponsor of Head Start programs. In 1967, Durr joined in founding the National Democratic Party of Alabama, an interracial group that worked for a decade to broaden political participation at all levels and helped elect black candidates to office. Durr served as a delegate to the Democratic National Conventions of 1968 and 1972, and in 1974 she was elected to the state Democratic Party Committee.

The persistence of racial discrimination remained a focus of Durr's attention. It was abundantly evident in the flawed process of school desegregation, the lack of economic opportunity for large segments of the black community, and the glaring injustices of the criminal justice system and its devastating consequences for young black men as demonstrated by rising incarceration rates and the disproportionate number of African Americans on death row. In 1978 she and a group of local activists organized a committee against the death penalty. All the while, she continued to struggle with the nature of racial prejudice and its complex history. "It may be that these feelings do derive originally from economics . . . but I think a lot of it is just plain old original sin, greed, the desire to live a life of ease while someone else does the dirty work," she wrote to historian C. Vann Woodward.[43]

Clifford Durr's death in May 1975, a year shy of the Durrs' fiftieth wedding anniversary, devastated Virginia. The two had a rare partnership that grew stronger over the years and helped both of them endure and even thrive during the difficult years after their return to Alabama. Nevertheless, her family, her broad and always growing circle of friends, and her deep engagement with the concerns that had long captured her attention kept her fully engaged in life. As the country moved increasingly rightward and Alabama became a Republican Party stronghold, Durr continued to look for openings and seek out people working for change. She was a tremendous source of support to the Southern Poverty Law Center, the Equal Justice Initiative, and the other progressive organizations that took root in Montgomery in the wake of the civil rights movement. "You couldn't not know about her," an early Southern Poverty Law Center staffer commented. "She was at every [public] meeting of consequence and had a vast network of contacts." Observed her friend and neighbor, federal judge Myron Thompson, "She just never gave up."[44]

Durr never finished writing her autobiography but sat for oral history interviews that she and Hollinger Barnard used to craft a first-person narrative about her life and times. The University of Alabama Press published *Outside the Magic Circle: The Autobiography of Virginia Foster Durr* in 1985 to wide attention and acclaim. She appeared on *The Today Show*, the most widely viewed morning television program at the time, and told a *New York Times* reporter that she had initially thought that "hawking a book was rather cheap and beneath me" but was now having a wonderful time. "I am not used to fame that comes pleasantly," she laughed. But she also took the opportunity to speak out about the problems that loomed during the Reagan administration—the massive military buildup, the business community's tightening hold on government, and the growing gap between the rich and the poor. She wanted to know what people intended to do about these problems and welcomed the many invitations to speak on college campuses.[45]

When Virginia Durr died on February 24, 1999, at the age of ninety-five, the flag over the state capitol in Montgomery was lowered to half-staff, a gesture that would hardly have been imaginable several decades earlier and a measure of the change that she had helped to bring about.

NOTES

1. Virginia Foster Durr, *Outside the Magic Circle: The Autobiography of Virginia Foster Durr*, ed. Hollinger F. Barnard (Tuscaloosa: University of Alabama Press, 1986), 1–11; Virginia Durr, "The Emancipation of Pure White Southern Womanhood," *New South* 26 (1971): 51.

2. Durr, *Outside the Magic Circle*, 5.

3. Ibid., 25; Virginia Durr, interview by author, June 9, 1992.

4. Durr, *Outside the Magic Circle*, 41.

5. Ibid., 59–60.

6. Ibid., 57–58, 59.

7. Ibid., 63.

8. Ibid., 66.

9. Ibid., 78–79; Virginia Durr, interview by author, May 3, 1978.

10. Virginia Durr to Corliss Lamont, February 16, 1933, Virginia Foster Durr Papers, Schlesinger Library, Radcliffe Institute for Advanced Study, Harvard University.

11. Durr, *Outside the Magic Circle*, 84–85.

12. Virginia Durr, interview by author, June 9, 1992.

13. Ibid.

14. Durr, *Outside the Magic Circle*, 102–3.

15. Patricia Sullivan, *Days of Hope: Race and Democracy in the New Deal Era* (Chapel Hill: University of North Carolina Press, 1996), 113.

16. Virginia Durr, interview by author, June 9, 1992; Durr, *Outside the Magic Circle*, 108–11.

17. Sullivan, *Days of Hope*, 112–13; Virginia Durr, interview by author, June 9, 1992.

18. Ann Durr Lyon, interview by author, May 12, 2001; Durr, *Outside the Magic Circle*, 108.

19. Durr, *Outside the Magic Circle*, 108–11.

20. Sullivan, *Days of Hope*, 63–67.

21. Ibid., 97–99.

22. Ibid., 100.

23. Virginia Durr, interview by author, January 25, 1980.

24. Ibid., June 9, 1992.

25. Sullivan, *Days of Hope*, 113–15.

26. Virginia Durr to C. Vann Woodward, January 26, 1940, C. Vann Woodward Papers, Box 1, Manuscript and Archives, Yale University Library.

27. Jessica Mitford, *Daughters and Rebels: The Autobiography of Jessica Mitford* (Boston: Houghton Mifflin, 1960), 254–55, 257; Jessica Mitford, *A Fine Old Conflict* (New York: Knopf, 1977), 24.

28. Virginia Foster Durr, *Freedom Writer: Virginia Foster Durr: Letters from the Civil Rights Years*, ed. Patricia Sullivan (New York: Routledge, 2003), 15.

29. Mitford, *Fine Old Conflict*, 24.

30. John A. Salmond, *The Conscience of a Lawyer: Clifford J. Durr and American Civil Liberties, 1899–1975* (Tuscaloosa: University of Alabama Press, 1990), 57–58.

31. Sullivan, *Days of Hope*, 204–5.

32. Ibid., 240–43.

33. Ibid., 243–47, 249–51; David Levering Lewis, *W. E. B. Du Bois: The Fight for Equality and the American Century, 1919–1963* (New York: Holt, 2000), 536–37; Glenn Eskew, "Coretta Scott King: Legacy to Civil Rights," in Kathleen Ann Clark and Ann Short Chirhart, eds., *Georgia Women: Their Lives and Times* (Athens: University of Georgia Press, 2014), 347.

34. Durr, *Outside the Magic Circle*, 196–99.

35. Durr, *Freedom Writer*, 18–23.

36. Ibid., 23

37. Durr, *Freedom Writer*, 30–31, 65–68.

38. Jeanne Theoharis, *The Rebellious Life of Mrs. Rosa Parks* (Boston: Beacon, 2013), 35–39.

39. Virginia Durr to Jessica Mitford, February 1956, Jessica Mitford Papers, Ohio State University Libraries.

40. Burke Marshall to Virginia Durr, May 4, 1941, Durr Papers.

41. Jonathan Steele, "Stopping off at the Durrs," tribute written for Virginia Durr's ninetieth birthday, in possession of author.

42. Durr, *Freedom Writer*, 234–36.

43. Ibid., 414, 420.

44. Ibid.

45. Ibid., 421–22.

Rosa Parks

"I Don't Know Whether I Could Have Been More Effective . . . in the South Than I Am Here in Detroit"

JEANNE THEOHARIS

Rosa Parks may well be one of the most famous Alabamians in history. Born in Tuskegee and raised in Pine Level, Parks spent nearly twenty-five years of her adult life in Montgomery, tilling the ground for a broader movement for racial justice to flower. After joining a small cadre of activists in transforming Montgomery's chapter of the National Association for the Advancement of Colored People (NAACP), she served as secretary of the branch for most of the next twelve years and in the late 1940s was elected secretary of the group's Alabama State Conference. Through the organization, she pressed for voter registration, documented white brutality and sexual violence, pushed for desegregation, and fought criminal injustice in the decade after World War II.

On December 1, 1955, as she was on her way home from work, driver James Blake asked her to give up her seat on a segregated Montgomery bus. "Pushed as far as she could stand to be pushed," she refused and was arrested.[1] That act of courage galvanized a yearlong community boycott of Montgomery's segregated buses, catapulting a young Martin Luther King Jr. to national attention and leading to the U.S. Supreme Court's decision barring segregated seating in public transportation. Parks's actions and the bus boycott they produced are often seen as the opening act of the modern civil rights movement, which over the next decade rippled across the South and culminated in the passage of the Civil and Voting Rights Acts. Often called the Mother of the Civil Rights Movement, she became one of the most well-known figures of that movement and one of the most feted Americans of the twentieth century. She received the Presidential Medal of Freedom and the Congressional Gold Medal, and at her death in 2005, she became the first civilian, the first woman, and the second African American to lie in honor in the U.S. Capitol. In February 2013, a statue

ROSA PARKS, 1972

Photo by LeRoy Henderson.

in her honor was installed in the U.S. Capitol's Statuary Hall, the first full statue of a black person put there.[2]

But the fullness of Parks's life and politics are surprisingly less known. In 1957, eight months after the boycott's successful end, the Parks family was forced to leave Alabama. She spent the second half of her life in Detroit, protesting northern segregation and racial inequality. Like many of her comrades in both Montgomery and Detroit, her activism continued long after the passage of the Civil and Voting Rights Acts. Parks's political life thus provides a window onto the varied strands of black protest that crisscrossed the twentieth century, South *and* North.

Yet Parks is so associated with that one day on the bus in Montgomery that her broader history and political commitments in Alabama and Michigan receive short shrift. Her ideas on what it meant to grow up on the "tightrope" of Jim Crow, on the nature of white supremacy and on the movement she and others built in Montgomery, are unfamiliar. So intertwined in the public memory with the racism of the Deep South, the fact that she spent more than half of her political life in the North hardly penetrates public understandings of her.

The Jim Crow South is often treated as a racial world unto itself, an approach that obscures Parks's Detroit life and fails to treat it in tandem with her Montgomery work. Northerners at the time encouraged this focus on the South, preferring to advocate change there rather than in their own backyards. Many southerners found this tendency hypocritical. Stemming from Cold War interests that sought to frame the race problem as southern, the focus on race relations below the Mason-Dixon Line fit with larger national interests in seeing the race problem as a regional malady rather than a national plague. Many scholars, political figures, journalists, and citizens have continued to reproduce the tendency to treat Alabama, the Deep South, and the movement that grew there as the real story. And so what tends to be known about Rosa Parks is largely confined to a limited view of the Montgomery Bus Boycott.

Grappling with a larger landscape of segregation and struggle — with the fullness of Parks's political life — brings into sharp relief the migration histories and cross-fertilizations of the northern and southern movements and the national character of American apartheid. Understanding Parks requires foregoing the tendency to treat Montgomery as so very separate from Detroit and consequently to focus primarily on the first half of Parks's life. As Parks pointed out, Montgomery and Detroit "do have the same problems," and so she spent her entire life challenging racial inequality in the South *and* in the North. Alabama was emblematic of an entrenched if multivalent racial system across the entire country, as one of the century's most well-known Alabamians took pains to demonstrate and challenge.

When Rosa Louise McCauley was growing up in Alabama, "whites would accuse you of causing trouble when all you were doing was acting like a normal human being instead of cringing."[3] Born in Tuskegee on February 4, 1913, Rosa was raised by her mother and grandparents to act respectably, which for them meant not just the image put out into the world but also the respect expected and demanded from the surrounding society. Young Rosa imbibed the value of self-defense from her grandfather, a supporter of black nationalist and pan-Africanist Marcus Garvey. When white violence rose after World War I, he would sit out on the porch at night with his shotgun to protect the family house. Sometimes she would sit vigil with him.[4] While the Garvey movement is often seen as a northern urban phenomenon, historian Mary Rolinson has documented the ample history of Garveyism in the South.[5]

Rosa McCauley had difficulty growing up in this system, which forced her to walk "on a tightrope from birth" and perform a "major mental acrobatic feat" to survive. There was "no solution for us who could not easily conform to this oppressive way of life."[6] Recalling W. E. B. Du Bois's famous invocation of "the problem of the color line," Parks echoed, "There is always a line of some kind— color line hanging rope tightrope. To me it seems that we are puppets on the string in the white man's hand. They say we must be segregated from them by the color line, yet they pull the strings and we perform to their satisfaction or suffer the consequence if we get out of line."[7] She continued, "Little children are so conditioned early to learn their places in the segregated pattern as they take their first toddling steps."[8]

McCauley resolved to change the situation. Her grandmother worried about young Rosa's feistiness, cautioning her that she would not "live to be grown if you don't learn not to talk biggety to white folks."[9] McCauley told her grandmother, "I would rather be lynched than live to be mistreated, than not be allowed to say 'I don't like it.'"[10] This "determination never to accept it, even if it must be endured," led McCauley to "search for a way of working for freedom and first class citizenship." Her teenage and young adult years were filled with "frustration" and she later recalled how she felt "anger, bitterness, hopeless."[11]

Because school for black children ended in sixth grade, Rosa McCauley moved to the state capital, where she lived with an aunt and enrolled in Miss White's Montgomery Industrial School for Girls. Modeled on Booker T. Washington's philosophy of industrial education and run by white women, Miss

White's School nonetheless instilled a message of pride, self-respect, and re-solve in its black female students. Like McCauley, many others who attended the school—among them Johnnie Carr and Mary Fair Burks—went on to play decisive roles in Montgomery's freedom movement.[12]

Parks had a "life history of being rebellious" that started decades before the boycott and continued for many decades afterward.[13] Her adult political work began when she fell in love with and married "the first real activist I ever met," Raymond Parks.[14] When she met him, Raymond was working on the Scottsboro case: nine African American men between the ages of twelve and nineteen who had been falsely accused of raping two young white women on a train. The young men were quickly tried and convicted, and all but the youngest were sentenced to death. Raymond Parks became part of a grassroots movement to prevent the execution of the "Scottsboro Boys." The work was dangerous and often took place late at night or early in the morning at a table "covered with guns," and Rosa joined the effort after marrying Raymond in December 1932. She feared for Raymond's life.[15] In the early years of their marriage, Ray-mond was the more public activist, while Rosa worked more behind the scenes, though this dynamic shifted decisively over the years. Nevertheless, this shared vision of justice always remained a key component of their marriage.

By the 1940s, Rosa Parks was looking to register to vote and take more con-certed action regarding racial issues. When she saw her old schoolmate Johnnie Carr in a photo of the local NAACP chapter that appeared in a black newspaper, Parks realized that women could join the branch and decided to attend a meet-ing. The only woman present and "too timid to say no," she was promptly elected secretary.[16] She made it known that she wanted to register to vote, and E. D. Nixon, one of Montgomery's most stalwart activists and a leader in the Brother-hood of Sleeping Car Porters, came by her home to bring her materials, begin-ning a partnership that ultimately changed the face of American history. Over the next decade, she worked with Nixon to transform Montgomery's NAACP chapter into a more activist working-class chapter. Nixon was elected branch president in 1945, and Parks was reelected secretary. Their focus on "politicking" brought opposition from more middle-class members of the branch, but Nixon and Parks won reelection the following year.[17]

In 1943 and 1944, Rosa Parks made two unsuccessful attempts to register to vote. The registration test was administered differently for white and black people, so on her second try, she took the unusual approach of bringing two white women with her. Registrars commonly did not allow black and white people in the office at the same time to prevent African Americans from seeing the differential treatment accorded to whites. The registrar indicated that the white women should wait until Parks had departed, implying that they would then receive help.[18]

Parks tried again in 1945. Confident that she had passed, she decided to write down all the questions and her answers so that she could file suit if she were not permitted to register. The registrar noticed what she was doing, and she later learned she had passed. Her success not only was an anomaly but also indicated her determination: Raymond Parks and many other Montgomery blacks never got past the registrar barrier during this period. But one more hurdle remained: registered voters could not cast ballots until they paid poll taxes not only for the current year but also for every year since they had first become eligible to vote. The accumulated sums could pose a substantial and in some cases insurmountable burden for working-class families, but the Parkses scraped together the money to pay the twelve years' worth of poll taxes she owed. In 1946, Rosa Parks cast her first ballot, backing Jim Folsom in his successful run for the Alabama governor's office.[19]

Another key issue on which Nixon and Parks collaborated was criminal justice, both defending young black men in "legal lynching" cases and attempting to obtain justice for black people, particularly women, subjected to white brutality.[20] Parks traveled throughout Alabama, taking testimony from victims and witnesses and trying to persuade people to file affidavits and pursue cases with the U.S. Department of Justice.[21] But most of her efforts went nowhere, leaving Parks increasingly demoralized: "People blamed [the] NAACP for not winning cases" she explained, but did not support the organization "and give strength enough." Though she understood the pressures African Americans faced and their understandable fears, she was frustrated that in the decade before the boycott, "the masses seemed not to put forth too much effort to struggle against the status quo" and labeled those who challenged the racial order "radicals, sore heads, agitators, trouble makers." Despite her struggles with the perils of being a rebel and the "wounds cut deeply by oppression," Parks determined to fight on, undergirded by her faith in God.[22]

The arbitrary nature of Jim Crow in Montgomery touched the Parks family in many ways. The Parkses (including Rosa's mother, Leona) lived in the Cleveland Courts, a black public housing project that had opened in 1937. Cleveland Courts offered decent if cramped housing for poor and working-class African Americans, with modern cooking facilities and indoor plumbing. The government maintained the property and initially proved more reliable than many white landlords. Segregated Montgomery offered very little in the way of adequate housing for African Americans, and the construction of Cleveland

Courts had destroyed some black residences. Even wealthier blacks had difficulty finding homes to rent or buy, and most properties within the range of
working-class blacks lacked proper sanitary facilities.[23] More than 80 percent
of African Americans lacked hot water in their homes, while nearly 70 percent
used chamber pots and outhouses (compared to 6 percent of whites).[24] By the
mid-1950s, blacks faced a housing crisis as urban renewal efforts targeted and
further undermined black neighborhoods.[25]

Raymond Parks worked as a barber at Maxwell Air Force Base, which was
desegregated by President Harry S. Truman's 1948 order integrating the U.S.
military. The base's desegregated cafeteria, bachelor hall, swimming pool, and
public transportation to and from Montgomery existed cheek by jowl with the
city's segregated bus system, meaning that African Americans would ride desegregated buses on the base but switch to segregated buses as soon as they left
it. For Rosa Parks, "Maxwell opened my eyes up. It was an alternative reality to
the ugly reality of Jim Crow."[26] In 1954, she became the first woman hired as an
assistant tailor in the men's shop at a downtown department store, Montgomery
Fair, where the employee lunch room and elevators were segregated.

On Thursday, December 1, 1955, she left work. She passed up the first bus that
came because it was too crowded and went to buy a few things at a drugstore.
Around 5:30, she boarded a bus just off Montgomery's Court Square. Deco-
rated with Christmas lights, the square had a festive atmosphere that obscured
its troubled racial history: slaves had been auctioned there, and the Exchange
Hotel had been the first headquarters of the Confederacy.[27]

Parks sat in the middle section of the bus, which was not reserved for whites.
Black customers could sit in that section, though the driver could tell them to
move. When the bus filled up, one white man was left standing. By the terms
of Alabama segregation, all four black people seated in the row would have
to get up so that the man could sit down. Bus driver James Blake told all four
to move, but they did not budge. Blake then said, "Y'all better make it light
on yourselves," and the other three black passengers "reluctantly" got up. But
Parks refused: "I felt that if I did stand up, it meant that I approved of the way I
was being treated, and I did not approve." And she certainly did not think that
segregation "was making it light on us as a people."[28]

Parks was not the first black Montgomerian to resist segregation on the city's
buses—a steady trickle of such instances had occurred in the decade since World
War II. Earlier in 1955, fifteen-year-old Claudette Colvin had refused to give up
her seat and been arrested, an event that had a searing effect on Montgomery's
black community but did not result in a full-fledged movement. Many of Montgomery's civil rights leaders saw Colvin as not the right kind of plaintiff—too

young, emotional, feisty, and poor.[29] Parks, however, had tried to encourage Colvin's political spirit, bringing her into the activities of the youth branch of Montgomery's NAACP, which Parks had started in 1954. In October 1955, another young woman, Mary Louise Smith, had been arrested for refusing to give up her seat, but Nixon and other community leaders deemed her, too, an unsuitable plaintiff.[30] December was also not Parks's first act of bus resistance. She refused to comply when bus drivers sought to make black passengers pay at the front and then exit the bus and reboard through the back door, an "uppity" stance that had resulted in her eviction by a number of Montgomery's bus drivers, including Blake.[31]

The reaction to Parks's arrest cannot be understood outside the broader history of bus resistance, which had primed the ground for the movement. Numerous community efforts to press the bus company and city commissioner, Parks noted, were "always brushed off and given the run around," leaving the stage "well set for . . . action."[32] Her refusal to move was undergirded in large part by the decades of political work and courageous stands that she and others had already taken. She had no reason to think she would obtain better results this time, but she refused to move anyway. "People always say that I didn't give up my seat because I was tired but that isn't true. I was not tired physically, or no more tired than I usually was at the end of a working day. . . . No the only tired I was, was tired of giving in."[33] Parks knew that the Montgomery police had a history of violence against black resisters—one of her neighbors, Hilliard Brooks, a veteran, had been killed for his bus resistance in 1950—and she "didn't know if she would get off the bus alive."[34] Parks later said in an interview that she thought the police did not want to arrest her but just evict her from the bus. The driver, however, insisted, saying that he would come to police headquarters after he finished work to sign the arrest warrant.[35]

Montgomery's network of activists sprang into action. Nixon and Virginia and Clifford Durr, who numbered among the city's few progressive whites, posted bond for Parks and accompanied her back to her apartment to decide what to do next. Nixon wanted Rosa Parks to be a test case for bus segregation, but Raymond initially disagreed, not only worried about their safety but also fearing that the community would not continue to support them.[36] Ultimately, with support from both her husband and her mother, Rosa decided to pursue the case. Late that night, she asked Fred Gray, a young black lawyer whom she knew from the NAACP, to represent her. Gray, in turn, called Jo Ann Robinson, a professor at Alabama State College and the head of the Women's Political Council (WPC), a black women's group that had previously challenged bus segregation.[37]

Very late that evening, the WPC called a one-day bus boycott for the following Monday, when Parks would be arraigned in court.[38] Robinson and two students snuck into the college and ran off thirty-five thousand flyers. Around 3:00 a.m., Robinson called Nixon (but not Parks) to inform him of the plan. On Friday morning, the WPC began blanketing the black community with the leaflets announcing the boycott, while Nixon began calling the city's more political ministers, including King and Ralph Abernathy, to arrange a community meeting for that night. Rosa Parks did not find out about the boycott until she went to Gray's office for lunch.[39] The community meeting took place at King's Dexter Avenue Baptist Church: after Parks told her story, the ministers decided to back the boycott, and many preached about it on Sunday.[40]

Rosa Parks continued to worry about whether the community would stick together, so she found the sight of the empty buses on Monday morning "gratifying" and "unbelievable." "The only thing that bothered me was that we waited so long to make this protest," she later observed.[41] Emboldened by the boycott's success, community members met again that night at the Holt Street Baptist Church, giving Parks a long standing ovation. Participants agreed to continue the boycott, forming the Montgomery Improvement Association to convey their demands to city leaders. Those demands initially were very modest: respectful service; first-come, first-serve seating, with black people sitting from the back and white people from the front; and the hiring of black bus drivers. The twenty-six-year-old King, who had come to Montgomery the previous year to pastor his first church, emerged as the leader. As months passed and the city resisted even these modest demands, the community came to insist on full desegregation of the buses.[42]

Parks's action became a movement as a consequence of the efforts of Montgomery's seasoned activists and a community that united in struggle. Parks was one of those seasoned activists, playing a key role not just in sparking the protest but in maintaining and sustaining it over the next year. The Montgomery Improvement Association created an elaborate carpool system that required tremendous numbers of people and substantial resources. Despite her family's precarious finances—both Rosa and Raymond Parks lost their jobs, leaving them to subsist on whatever they could earn through informal sewing and barbering jobs and on donations that Virginia Durr helped to secure—Rosa Parks spent much of the year traveling the country to raise money for the movement at home. According to Clifford Durr, Parks was a "tremendous hit" and became one of the Montgomery Improvement Association's best fund-raisers.[43] Back at Cleveland Courts, the Parkses' phone rang incessantly with hate calls and death threats.

The city employed many tactics to try to break the boycott. Police gave out hundreds of tickets to carpool drivers. At the end of February 1956, eighty-nine leaders were indicted under an old antiboycott statute. Rather than waiting to be arrested, Rosa Parks and Nixon were among the first to present themselves to the sheriff.[44]

To avoid having the case become mired in the state court system, Gray filed suit proactively in federal court in February 1956. The case, *Browder v. Gayle*, included Colvin and Smith but not Parks as plaintiffs.[45] Gray worried that because Parks's case was already in state court, the federal suit could be thrown out on a technicality if it included her. In addition, Parks's long history with the NAACP could prove a liability given the mounting red-baiting of the organization. In June 1956, the same month that Alabama outlawed the NAACP, a three-judge panel of the U.S. District Court for the Middle District of Alabama declared bus segregation unconstitutional. Six months later, the U.S. Supreme Court upheld that decision, and on December 20, 1956, Montgomery's buses were desegregated.

Yet victory did not mean an end to the Parks family's difficulties. In August 1957, still unable to find work and still facing persistent death threats, Rosa Parks, her husband, and her mother moved to Detroit, where her brother, Sylvester, had settled after serving in the U.S. Army during the Second World War. He and thousands of other blacks fled the race-based oppression of the South for the relative freedom and jobs available in northern cities in what became known as the Great Migration.[46]

When Rosa Parks moved north, she found that the public signs of segregation and some of the daily humiliations were gone but otherwise "didn't find too much difference" between Detroit's unequal housing, schooling, jobs, and policing and the conditions in Montgomery.[47] Northern whites promoted structures that maintained segregation but then justified the inequities not through overt racism but rather through a slippery language of color blindness, cultural deprivation, law and order, and other cultural frames that blamed black people for the conditions they faced in the city.

As she had in Alabama, Rosa Parks challenged racism in her new hometown, following in the footsteps of other southern migrants. Over the next forty years, she maintained her political commitments to self-defense, criminal justice, economic rights, black political power, and school equality.

In the spring of 1956, Parks had visited Detroit as part of her fund-raising effort on behalf of the bus boycott. Local 600, a militant United Auto Workers local, had invited her to speak over the objections of union head Walter Reuther, with local members raising the money to bring her and putting her up at the black Garfield Hotel because downtown hotels did not accept African American guests. Warmly welcomed by Local 600 and the National Negro Labor Council, Parks explicitly linked northern and southern struggles against racial injustice.[48] Some of the labor activists she met became her lifelong friends and comrades.

The Parkses had difficulty finding both jobs and decent affordable housing in Detroit. They lived with family for a time and then became caretakers at the Progressive Civic League building (where they were squashed into a two-room apartment).[49] In 1961, the family rented the ground floor of a brick flat in the Virginia Park neighborhood. Parks described the almost completely black neighborhood as "the heart of the ghetto," and to her it seemed much like Montgomery: "I don't feel a great deal of difference here, personally. Housing segregation is just as bad, and it seems more noticeable in the large cities."[50] Previously a neighborhood with beautiful homes, trees, and high rates of homeownership, Virginia Park had grown increasingly crowded as urban renewal and highway construction in the Hastings area decimated the black business district and pushed residents into Virginia Park.

Parks played an active role in the open housing movement, which sought to highlight Detroit's entrenched segregation, as well as in various union struggles. In June 1963, nearly two hundred thousand people, virtually all of them African Americans, participated in the Great March for Freedom down Woodward Avenue. In addition to giving the crowd a preview of the "I Have a Dream" speech he would deliver from the Lincoln Memorial two months later, Martin Luther King Jr. urged listeners to challenge racial inequality in Detroit: "To help us in Alabama and Mississippi and over the South, do all that you can to get rid of the problem here."[51] Parks was at the front of the march, but no one interviewed her. In August, Parks journeyed to Washington, D.C., where she sat on the dais during the March on Washington and stood and was recognized. But neither she nor any other woman spoke.

In 1964, when Parks was sewing aprons at the Stockton Sewing Company for ten hours a day and getting paid per piece, she volunteered on the upstart congressional campaign of a young African American civil rights lawyer, John Conyers. A long shot running against seven other candidates and promising "jobs, peace, and justice," Conyers won the newly created seat in the First Congressional District. Parks helped persuade King to come to Detroit and support Conyers, earning the new representative's gratitude—and her first paid political position, working in his Detroit office. He considered her the most important civil rights activist in the state.[52]

Some people reacted to Conyers's hiring of Parks by sending rotten watermelons, voodoo dolls, and hate mail to her at his office. Spewed one writer,

"Why didn't you stay down South? The North sure doesn't want you up here. You are the biggest woman troublemaker ever."[53] The office also received "quite threatening" phone calls; Parks would listen to the callers' abuse and then say, "Have a nice day."[54] The hate calls she had encountered in Montgomery were thus replicated in Detroit. Fifteen years after her bus stand, many northern whites regarded Parks as a troublemaker and traitor and wanted to tell her so.

For the first decade that she worked for Conyers, Parks took care of constituent needs, particularly regarding welfare benefits, education, job discrimination, affordable and public housing, and Social Security. Traveling throughout Detroit and sometimes further afield, she often served as Conyers's surrogate at community events, listening to the inequities and injustices that black people continued to face.

She also took part in Detroit's growing black militancy. The Parkses were frequent visitors to Edward Vaughn's bookstore, the only black bookstore in Detroit, to browse, learn, and discuss. Rosa periodically joined discussion groups there that provided the foundation for the city's black arts movement.[55] A member of St. Matthew African Methodist Episcopal Church, Parks became deaconess, the highest rank a woman could attain. She also often attended events at the Central Congregational Church (later the Central United Church of Christ and then the Shrine of the Black Madonna), headed by Rev. Albert Cleage, one of the leading voices that blended Christianity, social criticism, and black nationalism. Parks thus aligned herself with Detroit's more radical elements, whose approach intersected with her long-standing commitments to self-defense, black political power, economic justice, global solidarity, and criminal justice. She also attended numerous lectures all over the city, soaking up as much black history as she could find. An admirer of Malcolm X, whom she later described as her "personal hero," she heard him speak and met him three times before his assassination in February 1965.[56]

By the mid-1960s, she was helping to run Detroit's Friends of the Student Nonviolent Coordinating Committee (SNCC) with Dorothy Dewberry. Many of Detroit's African Americans had come from Alabama and still had friends and family there, so the Friends took particular interest in supporting the independent black political movement and new black political party that developed in Lowndes County in 1965 and 1966.[57] The Friends collected money and goods, and in 1966, Parks and Dewberry journeyed to Lowndes to deliver the donations and lend support. While there, Parks spoke at a rally. As activist Stokely Carmichael (later Kwame Ture), a notoriously fast driver, drove them through the county, a terrified Dewberry thought, "We're going to kill the Mother of the Civil Rights Movement." But Parks remained completely calm. In October 1966,

Carmichael traveled to Detroit and spoke before a packed house at the Central Congregational Church. With Parks in the audience, he opened his Black Power address by singling her out as his "hero."[58]

In July 1967, rioting broke out in Detroit about a mile from where the Parkses lived. The five-day uprising was initially sparked by a police raid on an after-hours bar, but Parks saw it as rooted in white "resistance to change that was needed long beforehand." In her view, "The establishment of white people . . . will antagonize and provoke violence. When the young people want to present themselves as human beings and come into their own as men, there is always something to cut them down."[59] Parks was dispirited by the violence and looting of small businesses, including her husband's barbershop, but her activism nonetheless continued.

She served as a juror at the People's Tribunal, a SNCC-led effort to investigate the police killings of three young black men at the Algiers Motel during the riot. Police claimed that the men had been shot in a gun battle, but no weapons were found, and witnesses told a different story. In the absence of any official or media investigation, SNCC leader H. Rap Brown came to Detroit and convened the People's Tribunal at Rev. Cleage's church on August 30, 1967. Parks and the other jurors found the police officers guilty of murder, and journalists from around the world covered the event.[60]

Parks also became one of the founders of the Virginia Park District Council, a community economic initiative to help rebuild and encourage economic development in the area. The council's efforts led to the construction of one of the country's first black-owned, nonprofit shopping centers in 1981. Decades before food justice movements would capture the nation, Parks and her Detroit comrades realized the need for access to quality, affordable produce. When fellow SNCC activists founded the People's Food Co-Op in the late 1960s, Parks immediately joined.[61] She helped tend Sylvester McCauley's huge garden, taught others how to can and preserve all that they grew, and in her later years became a vegetarian.

Rosa Parks's final encounter with Martin Luther King Jr. occurred in a place where most whites continued to fight to maintain their racial privilege—the exclusive Detroit suburb of Grosse Pointe. That these two civil rights icons would have their last encounter in a segregated Michigan suburb demonstrates both the breadth of their political lives and the national scope of the struggle. On March 14, three weeks before his assassination, King came to speak at Grosse Pointe South High School, and Parks and a friend went to hear him. The school board had debated for months about whether to allow the event to take place and agreed only after organizers took out an extra one-million-dollar insurance policy. Fearing an assassination attempt on King, the police chief sat on the civil rights leader's lap as they drove up to the school, and about two hundred right-wing anticommunist protesters demonstrated outside the building and periodically interrupted the speech. Parks later remembered, "There was a horrible mess when he tried to speak out there. They disrupted the meeting." In his speech, King reminded those gathered of the larger context of the riot and the racial structures that limited black freedom in Detroit and other supposedly liberal northern cities:

> But it is not enough for me to stand before you tonight and condemn riots. It would be morally irresponsible for me to do that without, at the same time, condemning the contingent, intolerable conditions that exist in our society. These conditions are the things that cause individuals to feel that they have no other alternative than to engage in violent rebellions to get attention. And I must say tonight that a riot is the language of the unheard. And what is it America has failed to hear? It has failed to hear that the plight of the [N]egro poor has worsened over the last twelve or fifteen years. It has failed to hear that the promises of freedom and justice have not been met. And it has failed to hear that large segments of white society are more concerned about tranquility and the status quo than about justice and humanity.[62]

Just three weeks later, King was gunned down in Memphis. Devastated by King's assassination, Parks joined many of her comrades to continue King's work to create the Poor People's Campaign. In June 1968, she journeyed to Washington, D.C., to take part in the Poor People's March on Washington with Coretta Scott King and Ralph Abernathy, speaking at the Solidarity Day rally. In August 1968, Parks was part of what the African American *Pittsburgh Courier* newspaper called a group of "militant blacks" at the Democratic National Convention in Chicago who refused to endorse any candidate, seeing both parties as undemocratic and uncommitted to black people's interests.[63]

Parks also worked to elect black candidates to lower-level offices. She supported Coleman Young's 1960 bid for the Detroit Common Council as well as George Crockett's successful 1966 campaign for the judgeship of the Wayne County Recorder's Court. She also backed Richard Austin's unsuccessful 1969 campaign to become the city's first black mayor and Young's successful effort four years later. In addition, Parks worked on behalf of Erma Henderson, who in 1972 became the first black woman elected to the Detroit City Council. According to Michigan state representative Fred Durhal, Parks was more than just a figurehead or a symbol in these efforts: "She was an active participant, not a sideline person."[64] Parks also helped on the mayoral campaigns of Carl Stokes in Cleveland and Richard Hatcher in Gary, Indiana.

An early opponent of U.S. involvement in Vietnam, Parks had initially supported Conyers's candidacy in part because of his opposition to the war and subsequently participated in numerous antiwar demonstrations. She attended the 1968 Black Power Convention in Philadelphia and the 1972 National Black Political Convention in Gary, Indiana, and supported the movement to provide African Americans with reparations for slavery.[65] She visited the Black Panther School and was active in the movement against South African apartheid, picketing outside the country's Washington embassy. She worked to support African Americans accused of crimes and imprisoned. An ardent opponent of the death penalty, she spoke out against it well into the 1990s.[66]

Why have observers overlooked the fullness of Rosa Parks's political life? Despite a wealth of new scholarship on movements in the North, Midwest, and West, the predominant view of the postwar freedom struggle is still indelibly southernized. The South is portrayed as a world distinct and separate, where racists proudly owned their beliefs and their violence and where a noble movement painstakingly and courageously built by ordinary black people emerged to challenge Jim Crow. This narrative, which Charles Payne has identified as highlighting "southern backwardness," is often contrasted with the liberalness of northern whites and the alienation of northern blacks, who are often portrayed as angry, rioting ghetto dwellers uninterested and unable to build movements like their southern counterparts.[67] Thus "blinded by a 'barbaric' South," in the words of historian Heather Ann Thompson, historians and others have overlooked the "polite" injustice of the North.[68] In his 1963 "Letter from a Birmingham Jail," King identified the "Negro's great stumbling block in his stride toward freedom [as] the white moderate who prefers order to justice, who believes he can set a timetable for another man's freedom."[69] Parks herself decried how often whites gave African Americans the "run around" in the years before the Montgomery Bus Boycott.[70] But the perils of southern (and northern) "moderation" find little place in understandings of how racial inequality was maintained. Moreover, the southern struggle has been reduced to a seat on a bus or at a lunch counter even though Parks and other activists foregrounded jobs, criminal justice, school desegregation, and real political power—in other words, the system of oppression rather than just its most visible manifestations.

Parks's description of the Detroit to which she moved—"the Northern promised land that wasn't"—offers a palpable reminder that racial inequality was a national condition, not a southern sickness.[71] While most biographical sketches of Parks seem to end with a version of "and then she moved to Detroit and worked for John Conyers and lived happily ever after," Detroit was not a vacation home for the Parks family. The racial inequality that characterized Montgomery—job and school segregation, police brutality, negligible protection for black people under the law, limited black political power—was also endemic in Detroit. Indeed many white Detroiters (like their compatriots in Montgomery) fought for their right to live in white communities, protect "their" neighborhood schools, and reserve the best jobs for white people—sometimes alongside their support of the southern civil rights struggle and while asserting their own supposed color blindness. Parks thus did not find "too much difference" in the unequal structures of Montgomery and Detroit.

The idea of the South and the movement unfolding there and its presumed difference from the North in part represents a strategic response by northern politicians, citizens, and journalists to discredit northern activists and movements. Amid a burgeoning southern movement that increasingly captured the interest of northern journalists, Parks and other northern activists struggled to focus national media attention on their movements. Constantly told "This is not the South," northern activists were regularly asked by political officials to prove the existence of racism and segregation in liberal northern cities. Portraying the race problem as a southern problem also fit within Cold War interests, as the United States sought to win over the Third World. Racial inequality was thus framed as an anachronism of the South—and the northern, midwestern, and western struggles for justice became hidden in plain sight.

Many southerners reacted angrily to this hypocrisy, seeing northern liberals as eager to criticize the South without being willing to examine, much less advocate change, in their own backyards. During the bus boycott, for example, Montgomery police commissioner Clyde Sellers declared, "The northern press wants to play up things going on in the South, but they don't want to publicize segregation in their own cities."[72] However strategic this deflection was, it contained an element of truth about northern double standards. Montgomery's main newspaper, the *Montgomery Advertiser*, which opposed the boycott, ran stories on segregated northern locales, including a piece on the Detroit suburb of Dearborn in which mayor Orville Hubbard boasted, "Negroes can't get in here. . . . These people are so anti-colored, much more than you in Alabama."[73]

Part of the difficulty of seeing Parks in the North stems from interviewers at the time. Despite the public attention Parks garnered over the years, most of it ignored her life in Detroit. In 1965, on the tenth anniversary of the boycott, for example, reporters descended on Parks in Detroit: she told them that she "would do it again." But then she added, "I can't say we like Detroit any better than Montgomery."[74] But no one probed that response. When interviewers in the late 1960s and 1970s asked her about contemporary race relations, they often focused on the South and almost never asked about the racial situation in Detroit or about housing segregation or President Richard Nixon's welfare programs or police brutality or the Vietnam War, despite her considerable attention to these matters. Though many of these oral histories took place in Conyers's Detroit office, interviewers asked few questions about Parks's new hometown or her work with the congressman and perspective on constituents' needs. When one of these interviewers asked about her decision to leave the South, Parks pushed back, "I don't know whether I could have been more effective as a worker for freedom in the South than I am here in Detroit. Really the same thing that has occurred in the South is existing here to a certain degree. We do have the same problems."[75]

The fable of Rosa Parks is so compelling because it exemplifies the heroic success of a grassroots struggle. Seeing Parks at events in the late 1960s, 1970s, and 1980s demonstrates the limits of those successes and the larger goals still unmet. "I have never been what you would call just an integrationist. I know I've been called that. . . . Integrating the buses wouldn't mean more equality. Even when there was segregation there was plenty of integration in the South, but it was for the benefit and convenience of the white person, not us." She sought to bring an end to "all forms of oppression against all those who are weak and oppressed."[76] Her political activities and associations in these later decades in Detroit thus illustrate the continuities and connections between the civil rights and Black Power movements, South and North. A set of political commitments that had run through her work for decades—self-defense, demands for more black history in school curricula, justice for black people in the criminal justice system, independent black political power, economic opportunities—intersected with key aspects of these new militancies. A longtime believer in a black united front, Rosa Parks joined with an emerging Black Power movement in Detroit and across the nation.

Yet the focus on Parks's respectability and the bright line often drawn between the civil rights and Black Power struggles has contributed to the lack of attention to her activities in these later decades. Conyers has attributed the omission of Parks's radicalism to the "discongruity" of it—"she had a heavy progressive streak about her that was uncharacteristic for a neat, religious, demure, church-going lady."[77] Indeed, standard notions of Black Power leave little room for the quiet militant. In the popular imagination, black militants do not speak softly, dress conservatively, attend church regularly, get nervous, or work behind the scenes. Yet Rosa Parks—and many other activists—possessed all those traits.

So what are the consequences of failing to see the northern half of her life? Parks is the American version of a national saint, but her sanctification is used to put the movement firmly in the past. To see her early political work in Montgomery in the decades before her arrest and then to follow her to Detroit and see her work over decades there forces us to see beyond the bus and demonstrates a broader national system of racial injustice.

Looking at Parks's lifetime of political work also takes us beyond the happy ending. The racial systems she left behind in Alabama had parallels in Michigan, and the southern movement had sister struggles in cities across the nation. From Detroit to Montgomery and beyond, that movement continued on long after 1965, 1975, and even 1985. Until her death in 2005, Parks continued to remind the nation that the struggle was not over and she was intent on joining those who carried it forward. Taking up the second half of her life thus fundamentally challenges a popular understanding of the period that frames the race problem as a southern anachronism and the movement as firmly over. As an elderly Rosa Parks doodled sometime in the 1990s, "The Struggle Continues. . . . The Struggle Continues."[78]

NOTES

This essay is adapted from Jeanne Theoharis, *The Rebellious Life of Mrs. Rosa Parks* (Boston: Beacon, 2015), which contains further detail on Parks's political life and work.

1. Rosa Parks, interview by Sidney Rogers, in *Daybreak of Freedom: The Montgomery Bus Boycott*, ed. Stewart Burns (Chapel Hill: University of North Carolina Press, 1997), 83.

2. The Parks statue was commissioned by an order of Congress, not by either Alabama or Michigan. Each state is allowed two statues: Alabama's statues are Helen Keller and Joseph Wheeler.

3. George Metcalf, *Black Profiles* (New York: McGraw-Hill, 1970), 259.

4. Rosa Parks, *Rosa Parks: My Story* (New York: Dial, 1992), 30.

5. Mary Rolinson, *Grassroots Garveyism* (Chapel Hill: University of North Carolina Press, 2007).

6. Rosa Parks Collection, Box 18, Folder 10, and Box 19, Folder 2, Manuscripts Division, Library of Congress, Washington, D.C.

7. Ibid., Box 18, Folder 9.

8. Ibid., Folder 10.

9. Ibid., Folder 11.

10. Ibid.

11. Ibid., Folder 9.

12. Parks, *My Story*; Rosa Parks, interview for *You Got to Move*, Lucy Massie Phenix Collection, Wisconsin Historical Society.

13. Stewart Burns, *To the Mountaintop: Martin Luther King's Sacred Mission to Save America, 1955–1968* (New York: HarperCollins, 2004), 18.

14. Parks, *My Story*, 63.

15. Douglas Brinkley, *Rosa Parks: A Life* (New York: Penguin, 2000), 40.

16. Lynne Olson, *Freedom's Daughters: The Unsung Heroines of the Civil Rights Movement from 1830–1970* (New York: Scribner, 2002), 97.

17. Extensive correspondence between Montgomery branch members and national office found in NAACP Papers, Box II: C4, Folder 2, Box II: C390, Folder 4, Library of Congress.

18. Rosa Parks, interview, George Metcalf Papers, Rosa Parks File, Box 2, File 7, Schomburg Center for Research on Black Culture, New York Public Library.

19. Brinkley, *Rosa Parks*, 60–61.

20. Danielle McGuire, *At the Dark End of the Street: Black Women, Rape, and Resistance—a New History of the Civil Rights Movement from Rosa Parks to the Rise of Black Power* (New York: Knopf, 2010).

21. Parks, *My Story*, 102.

22. Parks Collection, Box 18, Folders 9, 10.

23. Joe Azbell, *Montgomery Advertiser*, March 1, 1955.

24. Troy Thomas Jackson, "Born in Montgomery: Martin Luther King, Jr. and the Struggle for Civil Rights Montgomery" (PhD diss., University of Kentucky, 2006), 109.

25. Preston and Bonita Valien Papers, Box 3, Folder 12, Amistad Research Center, Tulane University.

26. Brinkley, *Rosa Parks*, 43.

27. Ibid., 104–6; Parks, *My Story*, 131.

28. Rosa Parks, interview, Black Women's Oral History Project, Schlesinger Library, Radcliffe Institute for Advanced Study, Radcliffe College; Rosa Parks, interview by *Newsforum* (video), 1990, Schomburg Center for Research on Black Culture.

29. The community distanced itself from Colvin before she became pregnant later in the summer. For more on Colvin's case, see Phillip Hoose, *Claudette Colvin: Twice toward Justice* (New York: Farrar, Straus, and Giroux, 2009).

30. Parks, *My Story*, 130; Brinkley, *Rosa Parks*, 103–4; Hoose, *Claudette Colvin*.

31. Parks interview, Metcalf Papers.

32. Parks Collection, Box 18, Folder 10.

33. Parks, *My Story*, 132.

34. Yia Eason, "Mrs. Rosa Parks: When She Sat Down the World Stood Up," *Chicago Tribune*, June 7, 1973.

35. Rosa Parks interview, Valien Papers, Box 4, Folder 13.

36. Parks, *My Story*, 141.

37. Ibid., 139–44.

38. For more on the WPC and its role in the boycott, see Jo Ann Gibson Robinson, *The Montgomery Bus Boycott and the Women Who Started It: The Memoir of Jo Ann Gibson Robinson* (Knoxville: University of Tennessee Press, 1987).

39. David Garrow, ed. *The Walking City: The Montgomery Bus Boycott, 1955–1956* (Brooklyn, N.Y.: Carlson, 1989), 562–63.

40. Brinkley, *Rosa Parks*, 128.

41. Rosa Parks, interview by Academy of Achievement, June 2, 1995, www.achievement.org (accessed August 1, 2016).

42. Parks, *My Story*, 149–55; Brinkley, *Rosa Parks*, 151–62.

43. Virginia and Clifford Durr, interview, Virginia Durr Papers, Schlesinger Library.

44. Brinkley, *Rosa Parks*, 155–61. The famous photograph of Parks being fingerprinted and her mugshot are often misattributed to her December 1, 1955, arrest, but they come from this arrest.

45. Parks was listed as the first plaintiff in the first draft of the case, but her name was removed when the case was filed. See NAACP Papers, Box V:27, Folder 9.

46. Anne Permaloff and Carl Grafton, *Political Power in Alabama* (Athens: University of Georgia Press, 2008), 45.

47. Rosa Parks, interview, Civil Rights Documentation Project, Moorland-Spingarn Center, Howard University.

48. General Baker, interview by author, October 21, 2009.

49. In July 1960, *Jet* magazine ran a heart-wrenching article, "The Troubles of Bus Boycott's Forgotten Woman," on the economic and health troubles Rosa Parks was facing in Detroit.

50. Parks interview, Civil Rights Documentation Project; Sylvia Dannett, *Profiles of Negro Womanhood* (Yonkers, N.Y.: Educational Heritage, 1966), 2:293.

51. Martin Luther King Jr., "Speech at the Great March on Detroit," http://kingencyclopedia .stanford.edu/encyclopedia/documentsentry/doc_speech_at_the_great_march_on_detroit.1.html (accessed August 1, 2016).

52. John Conyers, interview by author, March 11, 2011. This seat was created as a consequence of the U.S. Supreme Court's 1962 *Baker v. Carr* decision, which found urban areas to be severely underrepresented in the U.S. Congress and required the creation of new districts in cities across the country. This underrepresentation had dramatically limited black voting power in northern cities.

53. Letter, April 5, 1972, Rosa Parks Papers, Box 1, Folder 1-7, Walter Reuther Library, Wayne State University.

54. JoAnn Watson, Leon Atchison, and Larry Horwitz, interview by author, May 5, 2011.

55. Ed Vaughn, interview by author, September 10, 2010.

56. Chokwe Lumumba, interview by author, September 9, 2010.

57. Hasan Jeffries, *Bloody Lowndes: Civil Rights and Black Power in Alabama's Black Belt* (New York: New York University Press, 2009).

58. Dorothy Dewberry Aldridge, interview by author, October 24, 2010; Carol Schmidt, "Individualism a Luxury We Can No Longer Afford," *Michigan Chronicle*, October 8, 1966.

59. Earl Selby and Miriam Selby, *Odyssey: Journey through Black America* (New York: Putnam, 1971), 66.

60. Dan Aldridge, interview by author, October 24, 2010.

61. Martha Norman Noonan, interview by author, December 21, 2010.

62. Rosa Parks, interview by Steven Millner, in Garrow, ed., *Walking City*, 566; for the full text of the speech, audio recording, and accompanying press, see "Dr. Martin Luther King's 1968 Speech at Grosse Pointe High School," Grosse Pointe Historical Society website, http://www.gphistorical .org/mlk (accessed August 1, 2016).

63. "Black Militants 'Won't Back Any Presidential Candidate,'" *Pittsburgh Courier*, August 31, 1968.

64. Fred Durhal, interview by author, May 21, 2012.

65. Muhammad Ahmad, interview by author, January 7, 2011.

66. See Theoharis, *Rebellious Life*, chapter 7.

67. Charles Payne, *I've Got the Light of Freedom* (Berkeley: University of California Press, 1995).

68. Heather Ann Thompson, "Blinded by a 'Barbaric' South," in Matthew D. Lassiter and Joseph Crespino, eds., *The Myth of Southern Exceptionalism* (New York: Oxford University Press, 2010), 74–95.

69. Martin Luther King, "Letter from a Birmingham Jail," https://kinginstitute.stanford.edu /king-papers/documents/letter-birmingham-jail (accessed August 1, 2016).

70. Rosa Parks Collection, Box 18, Folder 10.

71. Brinkley, *Rosa Parks*, 67.

72. wcc Meeting Notes, Valien Papers, Box 4, Folder 1.

73. David Good, *Orvie: The Dictator of Dearborn* (Detroit: Wayne State University Press, 1989), 264.

74. "I'd Do It Again Says Rights Action Initiator," *Los Angeles Times*, December 16, 1965.

75. Selby and Selby, *Odyssey*, 66.

76. Ibid.

77. Brinkley, *Rosa Parks*, 189.

78. Parks Collection, Box 19, Folder 2.

Lurleen Burns Wallace

Making Her Way in Wallace Country

SUSAN YOUNGBLOOD ASHMORE

❀ ❀ ❀

Monday, January 16, 1967, turned out to be a bright, cold day that was perfect for the thousands of spectators celebrating the inauguration of Alabama's first woman governor. The largest parade in the state's history stretched ten miles and took five hours to pass the reviewing stand where the Wallace family stood, waving at each passing group. Confederate battle flags were everywhere, twenty-one bands played "Dixie" when they reached the viewing stand, and some of the ROTC groups marched proudly holding their bayonets at the ready.[1] After the parade, twenty thousand spectators moved to the capitol grounds to witness the swearing-in ceremony and listen to the new governor's inaugural address. With her husband by her side, Lurleen Burns Wallace stood on the star that marked the place where Jefferson Davis took his oath of office as president of the Confederate States of America. Placing her right hand on top of two Bibles—a personal one that George had inscribed "the Inaugural Bible of Lurleen Burns Wallace, governor of Alabama, January 16, 1967; wife of George Corley Wallace, governor of Alabama, 1963–1967," and the historic "Jefferson Davis Bible" that had been used for this occasion since 1853—she vowed, "I will faithfully and honestly discharge the duties of the office upon which I am about to enter to the best of my ability, so help me God."[2]

A lot had changed since her husband had stood on that spot four years earlier, which helps to explain why the day's events were marked defensively with Confederate symbols. Since 1963, events in Alabama had captured the nation's attention: George Wallace's attempt to block the integration of the University of Alabama by "standing in the schoolhouse door"; his picture on the cover of *Time* magazine after the bombing of Birmingham's Sixteenth Street Baptist Church, associating him with the death of four black girls; and the Alabama State Troopers' attack on marchers crossing Selma's Edmund Pettus Bridge.

LURLEEN BURNS WALLACE, C. 1965
Alabama Department of Archives and History, Montgomery.

George Wallace's defiance won him the allegiance of many white voters across the state but provoked a national feeling of shame that encouraged support for federal civil rights laws. The 1966 statewide elections were the first since the passage of the Voting Rights Act made black voters full citizens of Alabama.

This election also marked an important turning point in American conservative politics. Most obviously, the election of Lurleen Wallace as Alabama's governor kept her husband's political career alive after the Alabama Senate failed to pass a bill enabling voters to amend the state's constitution to allow the governor to serve consecutive terms. With Lurleen in office, George would have continued access to the state political apparatus, not only continuing his policies in the state but also supporting his 1968 presidential bid.[3]

Yet George Wallace's ambition often concealed the many ways that Lurleen brought a new voice into the political conversation both as a candidate and later as governor, pulling many Alabamians into the burgeoning conservative movement. Covering the day's events, *Atlanta Constitution* reporter Celestine Sibley fantasized that "Lurleen Wallace would assert her independence of George." "All the time he was using this pretty, seemingly mild little mother of four children to keep his hold on the state's reins," Sibley pointed out, "many people enjoyed the ironical thought that Lurleen, once in, would show him." Even though the new governor's inaugural address stayed true to her husband's politics, Sibley's hopes were not completely dashed. Reflecting on the entire inauguration day, Sibley saw what those close to Lurleen's campaign already knew: "The thing that convinced me that there is a lingering hope for the liberation of Lurleen is that she is obviously tough. Anybody who could stand for six hours and watch that inaugural parade the way she did ... plainly has physical stamina and a special kind of never-say-die mental strength." Atlanta's popular reporter was onto something, but Lurleen did not want liberation: she wanted respect. Tom Wicker reported that others in Montgomery did not "regard [Lurleen] as entirely a foil for [George's] ambition or as altogether submissive to his will." According to one local official, "Lurleen just might make a pretty good governor and I'll tell you why. She's got a warm feeling for people. She's going to want to do something for folks. She won't want to just sit there in the big office. And she'll work hard."[4]

Marriage to George Wallace and raising children while he chased his political dreams all over the state had not been easy for Lurleen Wallace. Even though equal rights feminists existed in 1966, she was not one of them. She chose a different path. Like many other working-class Alabama white women, full-time domesticity had been the ideal. When such domesticity turned out to be a frustrating mirage and a source of deep disappointment, Lurleen decided her best option was to make her husband's ambition her ambition. Being the only person who could keep his presidential hopes alive became a source of power for her in their marriage. She finally had something that he needed, and she used that leverage effectively. Her experiences in midcentury Alabama were typical of many women of her generation, which meant her campaign style resonated with voters across the state. She used her identity as a wife and mother to full effect and in the process became part of the political transformation of a Deep South state that distanced itself from the push for equality and moved instead to protect families from what many perceived to be an ever-more-powerful federal government. Lurleen found her own way in Wallace Country through the choices she made in her marriage, for her family, and most importantly for herself.[5]

The rise in George Wallace's popularity after he confronted federal officials trying to implement racial integration at the University of Alabama in June 1963 increased his desire to serve a second term. Gaining strong support in three presidential primaries in 1964 sealed this desire. And in the spring of 1965, as the nation watched events unfold across the Alabama Black Belt, eventually leading to a march from Selma to Montgomery and a federal law guaranteeing African Americans' voting rights, Wallace prepared to make his move. One major roadblock stood in his way: the Alabama Constitution did not allow governors to serve consecutive terms. Wallace started joking that he would have his wife run in his place. "He used to say to us 'I don't know if the people are ready for a lady governor' before he decided to run Lurleen," Oscar Harper told Wallace biographer Marshall Frady. "It was the way he said it . . . sort of funny." Wallace then approached his old friend, Glen Curlee, "What about feelin' the people's pulse" about Lurleen running for governor? Curlee then traveled "around the state and found that about four of every ten thought it was a good idea. . . . The others said 'They ain't gonna elect no woman.'" After a failed attempt to revise the Alabama Constitution, the lark turned serious.[6]

Lurleen Wallace's health initially complicated the governor's plan. In November 1965, she experienced abnormal bleeding and visited her gynecologist. He ran some tests and performed a biopsy on November 23 at St. Margaret's Hospital. Lurleen was alone in her hospital room when she learned that she had a cancerous tumor in her uterus. He prescribed radiation therapy followed six weeks later by a hysterectomy. In the days after her radiation treatment and before her surgery, Alabama's First Lady faced some hard truths about her husband's ambition and some cold realities about her determination to make her marriage work. Despite her impending surgery, the governor arranged a meeting between the First Lady and several of his aides at the capitol. "Formally, gingerly," Frady reported, the governor "had them propose" that Lurleen should run for governor. "She balked but only half-heartedly." She began to minimize her health condition, revealing a willingness to play along for their political future. Lurleen later met with Bob Ingram, a political reporter for the *Montgomery Advertiser*, and told him that she was still considering a run for the governor's office. She tried to reassure him that she was well: "If I was half as sick as some people think I've been all these years, I couldn't have set the pace that is required of the wife of a governor." As she awaited her operation, an old family friend revealed that questionable tissue had been discovered during her cesarean section in 1961, a diagnosis that George knew but Lurleen did not. Shocked, Lurleen confronted her husband and others she thought complicit in the cover-up, but George told her, "Now, honey, there was no point in you worrying about that." This attitude in some ways highlighted how the Wallace administration would try to minimize Alabamians' concerns about the health of the First Lady. Instead of acknowledging that she would have major surgery to remove a cancerous tumor, reports from the governor's office described her condition in vague terms and declared that she required only "minor surgery." On January 10, 1966, Lurleen Wallace underwent a two-hour surgery at St. Margaret's Hospital, with doctors declaring the operation successful. After two weeks of recovery in the hospital, she returned to the governor's mansion.[7]

While she recuperated, Lurleen contemplated running for office, and Alabama newspapers started weighing in. Grover C. Hall Jr., the editor of the *Montgomery Advertiser* and an early supporter of George Wallace in 1958, opposed the idea, which he found "bizarre." However, the *Advertiser*'s state editor, Stuart X. Stephenson, said Hall "saw the romance in it—like a kid with a new toy—a dime store girl seeking the highest office in the state." The governor's inner circle remained divided: some advisers doubted that Lurleen had a chance, while others thought that she could win. The deadline for filing approached, increasing the pressure to make a decision. Sometime in February, Catherine Steineker, the First Lady's assistant, remembered that the governor came to the mansion for lunch and told his wife, "I've decided we're *not* going to run. We're going to get out of all this pressure. . . . We're going back to Clayton when my term is up." But Lurleen had her own ideas: "Yes, George, we *will* run. I want to run. And I'll be disappointed if I can't." She chided him, "Now, George, if you want to sit up there in that Capitol and not help me campaign, well . . . okay. But I'm going to run."[8]

After the death of the Democratic front-runner, Ryan de Graffenreid, in an early February plane crash, George thought Lurleen's chances of winning seemed less daunting. He had little interest in policymaking and the finer points of governing, so her limited education and political experience did not matter to him. Only campaigning carried weight, and he would stand beside her the entire time. He was also basically a party of one, a Democrat only in the context of a Deep South state that he dominated, so her lack of engagement with the national Democratic Party was of no concern. What mattered was that she was a Wallace who could be trusted to maintain the status quo and would not steal too much of his limelight. Without fully acknowledging it, George had depended on Lurleen's resourcefulness since their early days together. Even as she recovered from major surgery, he had faith that she would come through for him again. And as her No. 1 adviser, he would still have access to the state plane, office staff, and kickbacks from contractors, all of which would prove useful for his 1968 presidential run.[9]

But why did Lurleen Wallace want the governorship? How would she benefit? Since 1946, when her husband first ran for the state legislature, she had learned that he needed politics the way other people needed oxygen. According to Wallace biographer Dan T. Carter, she recognized that if she did not run, her life with him might become more difficult because he could be unbearable outside the political fray. Others believed that her deep love for her husband played a key role in her decision. Frady noted that she doted on him when they were alone together, and she told Bill Jones, Wallace's press secretary, that she "did it for George." In addition, however, as her daughter, Peggy, pointed out after George Wallace's "stand in the schoolhouse door" in June 1963, Lurleen Wallace knew that the simple life she wanted was no longer possible. Publicly, she took pride in her husband's accomplishments and probably believed that he could turn the country around if he won the presidency. Frady, too, noticed George Wallace's political gifts: "I began to realize, that around Wallace there is that same air of limitless possibility, of excitement, of adventure, of incredible prospects—that same feeling that anything is possible." While Lurleen did not want to miss out on this presidential adventure, she also saw an opportunity for herself closer to home. As the campaign got under way and even after Alabamians elected her governor, the decision to run became a personal stand for herself in their marriage. By running, she shifted the balance of power in their relationship, and she did so not to satisfy her personal ambition to govern but to earn his respect. They had traveled down a long, hard road since their May 22, 1943, marriage in Tuscaloosa.[10]

Born on September 19, 1926, in Tuscaloosa County, Lurleen Burns met George Wallace in August 1942, when she was working behind the cosmetic counter at Scott's Five and Dime in her hometown. They felt an immediate attraction to each other. He liked her olive complexion and auburn hair; she liked his brown eyes and sense of humor. Wallace asked her for a date that afternoon. At first glance a sixteen-year-old dime-store clerk would not seem to have much in common with a twenty-three-year-old law school graduate, but both had faced struggles during the depression years and had ambitions for a better life. George's attention gave Lurleen plenty to daydream about. Her life had been on hold since she had completed her training at Tuscaloosa Business College, where she learned typing, shorthand, and bookkeeping. She was working at Scott's and planning to go to nursing school when she turned eighteen. She had spent most of her life in and around Tuscaloosa in the shadow of the University of Alabama; now she was dating an Alabama law school graduate who was about to be inducted into the military—he was going places. On many of their dates George shared his future plans, talking about his political ambitions—he dreamed of becoming Alabama's governor. "He was a pretty good catch," she told Marshall Frady in a 1966 interview, "don't you think?" Wallace proposed in late January 1943, and Lurleen accepted, hitching her wagon to his star and hoping for the best.[11]

The early years of their marriage passed in the whirlwind of the Second World War II, as they moved from base to base, living in makeshift housing and starting their family just as George left for the planned invasion of Japan. In the postwar years Lurleen proved her mettle while she tried to hold onto her domestic dreams no matter the circumstance. Her husband focused on his political ambitions, often at the expense of his family, which had grown to three children by 1951. In short order he won election to serve in the Alabama House and then as a judge on the Third District Circuit Court, always keeping his focus on the governorship. His soul found nourishment from campaigning rather than from making a meaningful life with his family. Sometimes he would go out of town without leaving Lurleen enough cash for groceries and living expenses, forcing her to borrow money from friends until he returned. Household chores that Lurleen could not do herself had to wait for her husband, and even then he would not do them properly. George Jr. remembered "a time when we had a hole in the floor in our den that needed repair. I suppose after he had heard it enough, he brought in a board, nails and a hammer, nailed the board to the floor, looked at Mother and said, 'Lurleen that hole is fixed.'" Lurleen's frustration with her husband's neglect at times boiled over into heated arguments. On two occasions, she borrowed a car from a friend, loaded the children inside, and drove around until she found George's poker game. She announced that they were his children, too, and left them with him. On other occasions George Jr.

remembered his parents arguing and then his mother taking the three children and driving across the state in the middle of the night to her parents' house in Greene County. She contemplated filing for divorce, but it was not really an option. She would have had to work full-time, probably in a low-wage job, and would have had difficulty caring for her young family at the same time. And a failed marriage would have ruined her husband's chances in Alabama's political world. After George entered the governor's race in 1957, Lurleen decided to join him toward the end of the campaign, stepping away from her domestic dreams and into his world. Her adjustment took some time and required fortitude: "I was frightened every time I got with a crowd," she said. "Most of the time I'd just sit in the car and wait for him." Although she chose to keep the marriage intact and ended the lost cause of competing with her husband's political mistress, she still had little to no control over the direction of their lives.[12] But by running for governor, Lurleen showed George that he could no longer take her for granted. In February 1966 she was literally the only person in the world who could keep his national political aspirations alive. If they worked as a team, she could hold his place in Alabama while he took his message beyond the state borders.

On February 24, 1966, surrounded by all the trappings available to a sitting governor, Lurleen Wallace announced her candidacy. She spoke from the podium in the Alabama House chamber to an audience packed with rowdy Wallace faithful from every county in the state. It was a family affair. As she delivered her three-sentence statement, her children swiveled around in leather chairs behind her, and her husband stood nearby, waiting to give a full-length speech after she finished. When Lurleen spoke her opening line, "Ladies and gentlemen, I *will* be a candidate for governor of Alabama," the room erupted in shouts and cheers. "My election would enable my husband to carry on his programs for the people of Alabama. We will continue the type of administration that has proved to be in the best interest of all the people of this State." With these words, she waded fully into the political rapids of Alabama politics. When the governor followed her to the podium, he made sure everyone knew the campaign's purpose: "If my wife is elected, we are frank and honest to say that I shall be by her side and shall make the policies and decisions affecting the next administration." The *New York Times* reported, "If Mrs. Wallace is elected, Mr. Wallace will be her No. 1 advisor at $1 a year."[13]

Critics responded to Lurleen Wallace's announcement by calling her a pawn, a puppet, and a stooge and by claiming that he had forced her to run for office. Her answer illustrated her own self-esteem: "Of all the untruths I've read and heard about myself, the thing that upsets me most is to hear someone say George made me run. I don't believe in people being dominated. And George certainly doesn't dominate me. He didn't force me into this." For thirty-eight years, she had made the most out of whatever life gave her; now would be no different.[14]

As the only female candidate for governor in the nation during a time of rapid social change, Wallace and her campaign staff had to walk a fine line to clarify her validity as a contender for Alabama's highest office. She had to be serious enough to be believable as the governor but not too serious that voters could imagine her exploiting the power of the office for her own ambitions. She needed to be feminine enough to maintain her appeal to voters but not too feminine that she appeared frivolous or sexy. The campaign framed Lurleen as a no-nonsense, down-to-earth wife and mother of four. In many interviews she spoke not only of her love of fishing, swimming, and skiing but also of how she enjoyed knitting and crocheting. "They say she's just as adept at baiting a hook," noted one Alabama newspaper, "as she is at serving as hostess in the governor's mansion." In many ways her gender became a magic coin that both Lurleen and George used to assure Alabama voters that the changes sweeping across the country could be stopped at the state's borders. Her role as a wife and mother was one side of this coin, providing a new way to legitimize the ongoing fight with the federal government over racial equality; her need for her "number one assistant" was the other side of the coin, keeping her subordinate and confirming George's role as the state's patriarch, guiding and protecting the southern traditions of state's rights and white supremacy that the Wallaces and their supporters held dear. Her candidacy was a godsend for those Alabamians who feared the future based on what they saw in the news: a nation rocked by urban riots in the North and West; antiwar protesters demonstrating against the country's fight in Vietnam; and calls for black power that federal voter registrars could make a reality in the Alabama Black Belt. Throughout the primary and general elections, political cartoonists, journalists, candidates, and constituents hoped to sway public opinion using Lurleen's gender to criticize and mock as well as to celebrate and affirm. As she found a way for herself during this un-usual campaign, finally gaining the respect she craved from her husband, she unwittingly contributed to the early development of a new political worldview that shifted the focus away from the push for equality and toward protecting families from the encroaching power of the federal government.[15]

Newspapers and magazines beyond Alabama took an immediate interest in Lurleen Wallace's run for governor, portraying her as detached, aloof, or out of her league and Alabama by extension as deserving of its pariah status. *Life* magazine's Shana Alexander piled on when she covered the National Governors Association Conference in Los Angeles that summer. Her article, "The Feminine Eye: On the Lookout for Lurleen," mocked Alabama as a real-life version of Al Capp's Dogpatch—"Who else but Daisy Mae would campaign on a promise to keep liquor out of the governor's mansion for the next four years? Or consider Lurleen's big campaign promise that if elected she will 'make my husband my number one assistant.' Shades of Sadie Hawkins Day!" Describing Alabama's First Lady as "small and rather mousy," the reporter painted all things Alabama as backward and out of style: "Mrs. Wallace is not an easy woman to spot in a crowd. . . . [I]n contrast to the finery of some other women she looked defiantly drab, a pea-hen in a tropical aviary." Alexander wondered what Wallace had been doing all week: Was she working on matters "gubernatorial with her future colleagues," or was she going to sightsee with the governor's wives? The answer—neither—highlighted Wallace's lack of political engagement. Instead of hobnobbing with other governors or their wives, Wallace had gone to visit Disneyland, the Movieland Wax Museum, Knott's Berry Farm, and Marineland. Oblivious to Alexander's expectations of a woman running for governor, Wallace came across as a naïf exploring a new world. Even when Alexander conceded that "Mrs. Wallace turned out to be a frail woman in a rough spot doing a good job," it was a backhanded compliment. In response to the journalist's statement that Wallace seemed more confident in person than she had on television in the spring, the First Lady provided the same sort of reassurance that she would have offered back home in Alabama: "It wasn't being governor that bothered me then. I knew I was fortunate enough to have an experienced man as my assistant. It was those TV cameras. You, know, I *still* don't like those cameras. But about being governor, I have no reservations about that at all."[16]

The scrutiny of the national press ultimately strengthened rather than damaged the First Lady's appeal among Wallace supporters. By 1966 the majority of white Alabamians had embraced a siege mentality that enabled George Wallace to use these insults as political fodder to garner support for his wife from those who also felt abused and misunderstood by the national press. Casting a vote for Lurleen offered residents of the state one way to express their outrage.[17]

Lurleen Wallace defined herself to the only audience that mattered to her as she and her husband sought votes across Alabama in the spring and fall of 1966. The audience at the campaign's kickoff rally, held in Montgomery's municipal auditorium on March 18, was the largest gathering she had ever addressed, and she set the tone for the remainder of the campaign. Playing to the crowd, she opened by stressing that Alabamians should not be ashamed: "My husband and I are proud of Alabama. We want to help keep our state on the upswing!" She used the words *we* and *our* seventeen times during her short address, joining herself to her husband's record and implying that they had always been a team.

And she reassured the crowd that her decision to run for governor was made "with enthusiasm and determination!" After highlighting all of her husband's accomplishments as governor, she used coded language to acknowledge her dismay with the federal government's enforcement of the new civil rights laws: "Our administration will continue to speak out over this country against the trends that threaten to destroy the local government [and] free enterprise system upon which it was founded." She closed by reminding listeners that George Wallace would be ever-present in a Lurleen Wallace administration: "I ask you to cast your vote for me on May 3. My pledge to you is that I will continue, with my husband's help, to provide the same kind of state government you have experienced in the last three years. We want to continue to Stand Up for Alabama!" The crowd's adulation carried Lurleen away from her frustrating days of sitting at home and raising children alone while her husband ignored his family. Others in the campaign observed that after her announcement even George was nicer to her. According to Glen Curlee, whereas previously when she called her husband at the capitol, he would ask, "What the hell you want? . . . I'm busy now . . . don't be bothern' me," now he was "talkin' sweet to her on the phone."[18]

The Wallaces usually campaigned as a couple as they crisscrossed the state, although they traveled in separate cars. They often would attend four or five rallies in one day, beginning at ten in the morning and wrapping up by eight at night. Closer to Election Day, the campaign began holding large outdoor rallies at night. George Wallace had begun holding these events outside during his 1962 campaign because, as Oscar Harper explained, "people come to hear you outside when they won't go inside" because they would have to dress up to do that. In small towns the crowd might number between fifty and one hundred; events in larger cities drew thousands. Wallace supporters came to rallies in their old pickup trucks and early model Chevrolets, Fords, and Pontiacs. The curious turned out in their overalls, work khakis, and business suits, in their housedresses, hair curlers, and Sunday best. Attendees were elderly, middle-aged, teenagers, and children. In Selma, several schoolteachers marched their elementary classes to the courthouse square, joining the crowd of more than five thousand that gathered to hear the Wallaces speak. Wallace bumper stickers could be seen on hat brims and football helmets and wrapped around little children's heads. Some people brought their own signs: some said simply, "Bibb for Wallace" or "We Want Wallace"; others parodied popular cigarette advertising with such slogans as "U.S. Wallace People Had Rather *FIGHT* Than Switch," "Come on Over to the L and G SIDE." Along Alabama's back roads, handmade signs nailed to telephone poles and fence posts warned, "This Is Wallace Country." They looked like "posted" signs trying to keep out change. Confederate symbols abounded at these events. In many of Alabama's small towns, the flat-bed trailer on wheels that the campaign used as a traveling stage parked near the courthouse square under the watchful gaze of the town's Confederate monu-ment; the Confederate battle flag flew at one end of the stage; and a country and western band played "Dixie" to signal the Wallaces to the stage. Someone usually marked the podium with a "Wallace Country" license plate that featured portraits of Lurleen and George on a background of the Southern Cross.[19]

Retail politics Alabama-style was the name of the campaign game. A local dignitary or politician—always male—would open the rally with some re-marks, peppering his talk with gendered language that reinforced Lurleen Wallace's proper place as a way to mitigate the fact that she sought Alabama's highest office. When Richard Beard of Trussville vouched for Lurleen's qualifi-cations, he introduced George and then said, "The lady who accompanies him is thoroughly familiar with the office which she seeks, and having been associated very closely with an outstanding administration of her husband, it is my plea-sure at this time to present to you the next governor of Alabama, Mrs. Lurleen Wallace, and also the next president of the United States, George C. Wallace." Like a warm-up act before the headliner appeared, Lurleen would tout the Wal-lace administration's local accomplishments—roads improved, bridges built, or junior colleges opened—before issuing dire warnings and reassuring the crowd that the Wallaces were paying close attention: in Trussville, for example, she an-nounced, "Our administration will continue to voice over the country the need for an awakening to the dangers of the trends that, unless checked, will destroy all local government, the property ownership system, and individual liberty and freedom." Then she pledged to continue what her husband had started so that they could "Stand Up for Alabama" before asking, "May I now present to you the man who will be my number one assistant, my husband and your governor, George C. Wallace." As the band played another round of "Dixie," Lurleen then took her place in a chair on the corner of the stage and listened attentively as her husband spoke. She admitted to a reporter in Talladega, "This type of speaking is new to me. . . . I don't pretend to be the speaker that the governor is. So, of course I don't speak as long." Lurleen's honesty drew people to her, and over the course of the campaign she rehearsed her speeches with her children and her friends and improved her speaking style. As crowds appeared to respond to her on the stump, her confidence grew.[20]

Once George Wallace took the stage, his thirty- to forty-five-minute speeches could tap into a full gamut of emotions: flattery, humor, fear, anger, and vio-lence. He talked to crowds as if they were his old friends, making them feel good about themselves. They were, he told them, "just as refined, and cultured, and intelligent, and righteous as people in any state of this union and don't you ever forget it." He would often mention how a national or Alabama big-city newspaper had insulted him, and then he would say, "You see what they are trying to do to us?," connecting those in the crowd to the slap in the face he received. In Fairfield he brought up the presence of reporters from "the *Newsweek* and the *Life* magazine and the national press": "They made fun of me, they made fun of you. . . . These big newspapers say you got to change your image. We don't gotta change any such thing." Sometimes he told jokes. He mentioned that Alexander had referred to Alabamians as "Dog-Patch folks, cause of the way we *dressed*. Well, I want to tell you something, the woman that wrote that article, I wisht you had seen what *she* was wearing!" He frequently brought up how Lurleen's opponents had insulted her and by extension all Alabama women and how he, in the tradition of southern patriarchy, would avenge those insults. After gubernatorial candidate Bob Gilchrist, who was also one of the state senators who had stopped the succession bill, declared that Governor Wallace had "wrapped himself in a skirt and bonnet" to stay in power, Wallace twisted those words into a form of violent language: "My opponents say they don't want no *skirt* for governor of Alabama. That's right—no *skirt*. Well, I want you to know, I resent that slur on the women of this state." In the general election, George indicted Lurleen's opponent, Republican Jim Martin, by similarly manipulating a familiar civil rights refrain: in the spring, Robert F. Kennedy had come "to Alabama to speak against my wife. That was a tough obstacle to overcome, but we finally overcame it." "Now," George told them, "the national Republicans have come to Alabama to try to beat my wife." He could have chosen different words that did not evoke violence against Lurleen, but he sought to arouse listeners by framing a vote for her as a vote to protect white womanhood. He closed this rally with more fighting words: "We, the people of Alabama, are going to hurt the leaders of both national parties. That is the point of it all. We are going to hurt the leaders in both of these national parties because they have hurt us enough all through the years."[21]

At all of these events and in official campaign publications, Lurleen and George presented themselves as a happy couple—an Alabama version of such political celebrities as the late John F. Kennedy and Jacqueline Kennedy. In the world of Alabama politics, Lurleen's composure and respectability contrasted with George's lowdown, defiant style, and through their differences they validated each other to a wide cross-section of Alabamians. After rallies, the Wallaces circulated through the crowds, shaking hands and engaging with people. Although George was known for never forgetting a person he met while on the hustings, Lurleen, too, would bend down to speak to a small child, lean close to make eye contact and hear an elderly woman's words, or hold a man's hand in both of hers as she listened attentively to him. Some people hugged Lurleen or put their arms around her shoulders or waist, expressing their feelings for her. Supporters could laugh, cheer, and ultimately vote for Lurleen as a way to defy the authority of their own state constitution, the national political parties, and especially the federal government, which had upended their racial world. Alabamians could delight in George's uncouth and violent ways and at the same time support his nice wife, who stayed in her place while she "helped" the people of Alabama have their say.[22]

Because this was the first statewide election after the passage of the Voting Rights Act had enfranchised significant numbers of African American voters, the Wallace campaign had to figure out alternative ways to maintain the southern tradition of white supremacy. They needed to reassure the denizens of Wallace Country without alienating the national audience that George would need to take his message beyond Alabama. In 1966, when the Wallaces discussed racial segregation, they claimed that they were not racists, and Lurleen told a journalist, "We believe in segregation but have at heart the interests of all the people. We feel the states should handle racial matters." The Wallaces maintained the long-standing rationalization that segregation did not equate to bigotry and was in the best interests of all the people. In this campaign, the familiar white supremacist vocabulary adopted a nascent right-wing narrative that cloaked its politics in the language of tradition, patriotism, God, and family, and other conservative forces across the country picked up this narrative as the decade progressed. The Wallaces named their approach the Alabama movement, signaling a clear contrast to the civil rights movement and hoping to garner recruits to Wallace's presidential run as a force to hold back change.[23]

In her own style, Lurleen Wallace lent credibility to this counterforce in the way she reasoned with those at a campaign rally just before Election Day, offering issues beyond race that could help Alabamians feel good about themselves: "When many sections of the country had been brainwashed into feeling that it is out of style to be patriotic, Alabama said, 'No, patriotism is still in style.' When many apparently thought that there is something wrong with prayer in the public schools, Alabama said, 'No, this nation was founded on a belief in God.' Otherwise, there would be no public schools." She upheld Alabama traditions as timeless, honorable American customs in no way in need of change. "When misguided young people in other sections burned their draft cards, the young people of Alabama said, 'no, our nation today deserved defense against any enemy just as in times past.' . . . Although they fought with modern weapons their courage was the same as the pioneer who carved this nation from the wilderness." All the examples she used bypassed what had made her husband famous: saying *no* to racial integration. Through speeches like this one, the First Lady provided a way for Alabamians, disgraced nationally for their violent and obstructionist response to the black freedom struggle, to be proud of themselves. "We intend to set the style," she promised. "Regardless of what may be the popular trend, Alabamians have the courage and the fortitude to lead the way, to set the example, to do what is right rather than try to do what is expected." Mocked and criticized as an out-of-date citizen of Dogpatch, she was the perfect vehicle for this message. "Alabama and Alabamians have always led in the defense of our native land," she reassured the crowd. "We have gladly taken whatever role was given us and we have stood every test." For her the people of Alabama had no need to alter their ways; instead, she urged the nation to look south and be inspired by Alabama's example. "We will again meet the challenge before us. We will not quit our beliefs for the sake of fleeting popularity. We will not sacrifice our principles for the praise of editors. We are with you in this fight, and you are with us." She turned the tables, widening the Wallace appeal by telling her voters that despite the prevailing national narrative, they could indeed claim loyalty to the nation.[24]

Ten candidates sought the Democratic nomination for governor in the May primary. Lurleen was listed on the ballot as Mrs. George C. Wallace, although female candidates for other offices were listed under their own names—Mrs. Agnes Baggett, Melba Till Allen, and Mabel Amos. The campaign sought to ensure that no one mistook Lurleen for anything other than the stand-in for George Wallace. She received 371,256 votes (52 percent of the total) and carried all but six counties—Bullock, Greene, Hale, Macon, Sumter, and Wilcox. Because she had taken an outright majority, no runoff was necessary, an outcome that she could not have imagined in February when she announced her candidacy. She was thrilled to have received 164,000 more votes than her husband got in 1962 and to have carried counties that had been troublesome for him— Jefferson, Madison, Etowah, Morgan, and Lauderdale (all in North Alabama). After winning the primary, she reassured supporters that if she were elected in November (a foregone conclusion in one-party Alabama), the dual role of governor and mother "would not create any problems." The Wallace team had made her a credible candidate in just a few months. Timing was also crucial to her success. The movement for women's liberation was only just beginning in 1966, but by 1970, when the next gubernatorial election took place, the advances made by second-wave feminism would have prevented a woman from running for governor as her husband's proxy. Lurleen also won because the Wallace campaign nurtured and utilized the state's siege mentality, convincing voters that the Wallaces would continue to "Stand Up" for Alabamians. The storm created by the Wallaces drowned out the messages of the other Democratic candidates, who never really had a chance in such a crowded field. Staying true to herself, Lurleen told a reporter after the grueling primary win, "I'm going to take a few days off and try to catch some fish—in Alabama, of course." These interludes of calm sustained her through the stress of her public life.[25]

The general election campaign kicked off in October with an enormous Birmingham rally attended by more than nine thousand people, with thousands more across the state watching on television or listening on the radio. The *Opelika News* declared that Lurleen Wallace looked much more "poised and confident" than she had during her primary appearances. For the general election she rolled out a new but no less feisty slogan: "There has been progress without compromise and accomplishment without surrender." The Wallaces' populism also continued unabated: "We are responsive only to one thing," Lurleen reminded the huge crowd, "the will of the people." As at primary rallies, the candidate spoke for about ten minutes before the governor took the podium for another thirty minutes. Lurleen continued to flatter voters by telling them that millions of people outside of Alabama "feel that we are honest, intelligent people, capable of running our own affairs without a lot of out-of-state advice." She focused on the federal government as the source of the state's problems, declaring that "determined Alabamians . . . will not be lulled to sleep by Washington promises of something for nothing." She issued dire warnings about taking money from the federal government since "many of these promises have a string attached which will eventually become a rope with a noose at the end." And she often closed by encouraging voters to make their voices heard.[26]

Lurleen Wallace won the general election in a landslide, winning nearly two-thirds of the vote and carrying sixty-five of the state's sixty-seven counties although Martin had received the endorsement of Alabama's big-city newspapers. His attacks on Lurleen Wallace's abilities had included full-page newspaper ads featuring his picture alongside hers and the headline, "The Real Choice: A Man or a Woman!" Voters clearly rejected this approach and accepted the Wallace scheme. Announced the *Alabama Journal* the following day, "Lurleen Did it . . . By George . . . 2 to 1."[27]

After only one day of relaxation, Lurleen started planning for the inauguration and her transition to governor. Over the next two months, she spent more than eight hours a day, five days a week, in her temporary office space, demonstrating that she did not intend to be a figurehead. She answered thousands of congratulatory letters—sometimes fifty in a day—fulfilled requests for autographed portraits, and met regularly with the inauguration planning committee. When she moved into the executive suite, Wallace made changes that stamped it as hers and bolstered her legitimacy as governor. Taken as a group, such seemingly small actions illustrate her determination to validate her new position within the state government—and within her marriage. When gendered gifts arrived, she put them to use. The Hermitage Association, for example, presented her with a rolling pin and stand made from a cedar tree at Andrew Jackson's historic home near Nashville, Tennessee. It was inscribed: "To be used with judiciousness and without discrimination, with discretion and complete authority." As an ordinary kitchen tool that unruly women had long used as a weapon, the gift carried great symbolism, evoking both femininity and power and giving her permission to govern on her terms. She placed it prominently on her desk in the governor's office, where her husband had once kept his humidor. She also displayed a poem encased in glass

> Woman may be small of frame
> with tiny feet that patter
> but when she puts one small foot down
> the shoe size doesn't matter.

But she was also careful not to go too far with these determined images: her office featured a "'Housewife' Touch"—a coffee percolator that she could use to provide refreshment for herself and visitors.[28]

Lurleen's duels with George became more direct after her election. That Christmas she gave her husband a ruffled tea apron, a gift that "startled" him, Ray Jenkins reported, "especially with all his top state officials standing around, but then he dutifully played his role and modeled the apron with mock chagrin while his colleagues grinned knowingly." She also teased that "George is going to be my highway beautification director," referring to Lady Bird Johnson's role in her husband's White House administration. According to Lurleen, George was "going to plant magnolia bushes." Lurleen had long since developed the skill, common among the marginalized and oppressed, of teasing others to disarm them while simultaneously asserting her position. As governor she continued in this playful but not too subtle way, claiming a new place for herself in her marriage. The morning of her first day in office, Lurleen chose to sit on the right side of the backseat of the car that would take the couple to the capitol. When George came out of the governor's mansion, a security officer remembered "from habit he went to the right rear door to get in, but when he opened the door, Gov. Lurleen was already sitting there." George laughed and said, "Oh, honey, I forgot.... You're governor now." She laughed, too, and told him, "Yes, George, I want you to realize that," but the underlying message was serious. George received another reminder when they arrived at the capitol and found that Lurleen occupied the executive suite, while his office was now in Room 101, with no title on the door. Though he had no choice but to acquiesce, George occasionally pushed back. Late in the afternoon, after the governor had gone home, George sometimes crossed the hall and made his phone calls from her desk, like a tomcat returning to his marked territory. At other times, George moved his shaving gear and other grooming materials into the private bathroom inside the executive suite; Lurleen simply had a member of her security detail pack up her husband's things and move them back to his private bathroom. The governor also did not hesitate to put her husband in his place in front of others. Once when he walked into a cabinet session that had already begun, she asked, "Can't it wait, George?," treating her husband just as he had treated her when she was First Lady. Though she laughed, such treatment no doubt rankled him.[29]

Newspaper articles, magazine essays, and later biographies have noted her behavior as evidence of her fun-loving, light-hearted personality. Though certainly true, such accounts overlook the evolving place of women in southern and American culture in the mid-1960s, an evolution that the 1964 passage of the Civil Rights Act made more obvious. In an effort to derail the bill's passage, Virginia congressman Howard K. Smith added sex to the categories of discrimination banned by the new law. Smith's tactic backfired, and the act passed with this provision, even though most politicians and members of the press found the idea ludicrous. Treating men and women differently seemed obvious and natural, and women's "innate" differences from men were desirable. Many Americans believed that women's work outside the home could only be thought of as secondary and therefore was not worthy of equal pay. Lurleen Wallace's efforts to claim legitimate space for herself and even poke fun at her husband's newly subordinate role reveal the subversive nature of her actions, especially in the personal sphere. Although she used this strategy primarily in her relationship with her husband, her refusal to be his subordinate was clear to anyone who visited her office or read about her in the press. By claiming—and demonstrating—that she could be both the governor and a wife and mother without any disruption, she highlighted her recognition that she was breaking some of the culture's accepted standards. Declared one Alabama newspaper headline, "This is Lurleen: Parent, Wife, Head of State." The accompanying article noted, "Gov. Lurleen B. Wallace, who has already said she will be an active governor, will have her hands full as she becomes a full-time $25,000-a-year government employee and remains a homemaker and mother." Mentioning her salary (a significant sum at the time) reminded readers that she had become the family breadwinner. The article went on to list all of her responsibilities as governor and to warn that she would have difficulty combining her duties to the state and to her family.[30] She turned this argument on its head, using her experience as a wife and mother to justify her service as Alabama's governor, and by the day of her inauguration, her supporters fully accepted that a no-nonsense, down-to-earth wife and mother of four could be their governor and even use her feminine role to defend the southern customs of state's rights and white supremacy under a new guise of tradition, God, and family.[31]

On that cold day in January 1967 Lurleen Wallace stood at the podium and confidently delivered her inaugural address. The first half of her speech justified Alabama's defiance as only a white mother could; she then moved on to explain her plans as governor, articulating her feminine responsibilities as a guardian of Alabama's families. "If there is any change in my administration," she clarified, "it will not be a change of policy or priorities, but rather one of attitude toward our programs. It will be an attitude reflecting an inner feeling of a wife and mother. I believe earnestly that the family is the vital unit of society, and that no nation may remain strong, unless it is founded on enduring family relationships as the source of its strength." Valuing families in this way enabled her to position them as more important than racial equality, an idea she never directly stated in the address but implied in almost every paragraph. If families were indeed timeless and everlasting, they could not and should not be altered, and thus they must be protected from federal interference. "As a wife and mother, as well as your Governor, I shall be inclined to examine programs, of each of our departments, from the standpoint of how they affect the family." She would focus on jobs "for the family breadwinner"—that is, the man of the household. She would "be intensely interested in rehabilitation, in adequate care for the sick, the elderly, and the handicapped; in strengthening local governments, schools, hospitals, and community facilities, upon which our families rely; and in providing personal security of the individual, his home and his family." She boldly reinforced the myths she had been raised to believe and support despite the struggles in her own marriage. Finally, she would turn the state's attention to its "overcrowded and understaffed" mental institutions, changing the subject from racial equality to a different disadvantaged group that Alabamians could feel good about helping. Displaying the sort of emotion that would have seemed weak in a man but that not only seemed appropriate for a woman but also conveyed her sincerity, she ended her address with tears in her eyes: "With God's help and guidance—and wise counsel to call upon, I shall make you a good Governor. I ask your prayers that I may serve you with honor and with grace, and that I shall not fail you in the trust that you have placed in me. May

God Bless the people of this great State and Nation." When she took her seat, her husband leaned over and whispered, "You were great!"[32]

She did as she promised. Her work as governor encompassed ceremonial duties including ribbon cuttings and plant dedications, and she continued her husband's stand against Lyndon Johnson's War on Poverty in the Alabama Black Belt. She also focused on key pieces of legislation that reflected her personal priorities and endeared her to many constituents: improving the state's mental health facilities and fighting federal guidelines for integrating the state's public schools. Both had lasting effects that outlived her, and each of these issues revealed something about Lurleen Wallace's fortitude and how she chose to spend her time as governor. In both cases, she used her gender to justify her actions as the guardian and defender of Alabama's families.[33]

In July 1967 another tumor was found on Lurleen Wallace's colon. For the next eleven months she traveled back and forth to the University of Texas M. D. Anderson Hospital and Tumor Clinic in Houston, undergoing surgery and receiving radiation treatments.[34]

Throughout the months of treatment, Wallace gained the respect of many Alabamians by the way she dealt with her illness. On September 17, 1967, the *Birmingham News* printed an interview with Wallace conducted by Anita Smith, who had visited the governor often when she was in the hospital. Under the front-page headline, "Exclusive: 'If I Have Cancer Again, I Want to Be Told,'" Lurleen candidly explained that she disapproved of her husband's paternalism in deciding that she should not be told about her medical condition six years earlier: "I don't want anything hidden from me about my condition." Moreover, she also thought that "it would have been unfair to the people had we tried to keep this a secret"; "once that decision was made, I knew we had no choice except for the truth to be told. I knew that even if the physicians found I had no more than a year to live, this is what would have had to be told." Such frankness regarding cancer was rare for 1967, as was her admission that she was frightened: "You know, this is life we're talking about. The first time someone tells you that you have cancer is bad enough. But the second time, it's so much worse." Her public forthrightness sent a message to other cancer patients regarding the need to advocate for themselves and push their doctors to be completely honest. The governor's willingness to disclose such personal information probably explains why many in Alabama continued to feel emotionally tied to Lurleen Wallace. The big-city newspapers covered every surgery, treatment, setback, and recuperation, and people responded with cards and letters. As she returned to the hospital in January 1968, the *Birmingham News* printed an editorial, "Prayers Go with Her," acknowledging that "Lurleen Wallace, perhaps more so than any

male governor could, has won a special place in the hearts of Alabamians. She
has never been considered a 'politician.' Alabamians still think of her more as a
wife, mother and woman than as governor."[35]

Lurleen Wallace was only forty-one when she died late on the night of May 7,
1968, surrounded by her family on the second floor of the governor's mansion. Her death sent the Wallace family into turmoil. After her funeral, they
moved out of the mansion and into a new house in Montgomery. Her youngest
children—Peggy (age eighteen), George Jr. (sixteen), and Janie Lee (seven)—
lost the most important person in their lives and faced a difficult future without her, while their father continued to campaign for president. Lurleen and
George's oldest daughter, Bobbi Jo Wallace Parsons, who was already married,
became a surrogate mother to her younger siblings—she cared for Janie Lee
and provided love and guidance, as evidenced by her signature on Peggy's and
George Jr.'s report cards after their mother's death. When Peggy left for college,
George Wallace's mother, too, stepped in to care for her grandson so that her
son could continue campaigning for the presidency.[36]

Although Lurleen Wallace served as governor for only seventeen months and
was ill for much of that time, she left her mark on both state and national politics. Her focus on Alabama's families contributed to the country's burgeoning
conservative movement, as did her husband's 1968 and 1972 presidential campaigns. Without her election as governor and the voice she added to Alabama's
political culture, his chances of becoming a national political figure would have
diminished greatly. From the last half of the 1960s through the 1970s, critics
painted liberalism as a moral threat that needed to be curtailed, especially in
the wake of the civil rights movement and as the women's liberation movement
pushed for government-financed child care, reproductive rights, and equal employment. The Wallaces' racial politics built a bridge that took many Alabamians
away from the Democratic Party of the New Deal and Great Society and toward
the Republican Party of the Religious Right and "limited government." Governor Lurleen Wallace provided a different role model for conservative women—
subordinate but not dominated, passionate but not bombastic, traditional but
not conventional—even though she became her family's breadwinner, relied
on others to care for her children, and was just the third woman in U.S. history elected governor of a state. By the time of her death, she had clearly made
her way in Wallace Country. Not every woman had the options available to
Lurleen—joining herself to her husband's political ambition and gaining self-
esteem and satisfaction from that choice. The civil rights laws she so vigorously
opposed eventually opened doors for African Americans and women across the

country, reforming employment, housing, health care, and education, enabling more people without connections to make their way for themselves.[37]

NOTES

This research project received funding from the Emory University Research Committee Humanities Grant in 2013–14. I am also grateful to Dixie Dysart for her generosity and hospitality as my home away from home in Montgomery.

1. Gene Roberts, "Wife of Wallace Succeeds Him: Alabama Negro Becomes Sheriff," *New York Times*, January 17, 1967; Celestine Sibley, "Lurleen Becomes Governor as 250,000 Cheer," *Atlanta Constitution*, January 17, 1967, both in Dan Carter Papers, MS 777, Box 6, Stuart A. Rose Manuscript, Archives, and Rare Book Library, Emory University; Wallace Photographs, SG 033873, Alabama Department of Archives and History (hereafter ADAH).

2. "Two Bibles," *Montgomery Advertiser*, January 17, 1967, SG 031280, ADAH; Gene Roberts, "Wife of Wallace Succeeds Him: Alabama Negro Becomes Sheriff," *New York Times*, January 17, 1967; Steve Ball Jr., "Lurleen Gets Oath as 'Bama Governor," *Atlanta Journal*, January 17, 1967; Celestine Sibley, "Lurleen Becomes Governor as 250,000 Cheer," *Atlanta Constitution*, January 17, 1967, Carter Papers, Box 6.

3. "Remarks Gov. George C. Wallace Inauguration Ceremonies of Gov. Lurleen Burns Wallace," January 16 1967, "Inaugural Address—Lurleen Vows Home Rule Fight," *South Magazine*, Lurleen Burns Wallace inauguration program, all in SG 031280, ADAH.

4. Celestine Sibley, "Her Parade Stamina Gives Hope for Liberation of Lurleen," *Atlanta Constitution*, January 18, 1967; Tom Wicker, "Lurleen Might Not Be Copy of George," *Birmingham News*, December 5, 1966; Jane Schermerhorn, "Many Alabamians Believe in Their Governor," *Detroit News*, [ca. December 1966], all in SG 031280, ADAH.

5. Robert O. Self, *All in the Family: The Realignment of American Democracy since the 1960s* (New York: Hill and Wang, 2012), 22–23, 104.

6. Marshall Frady, interview transcripts, 3C–5C, 10C–11C, 27C–28C, 72C–74C, Marshall Frady Papers, MSS 1099, Box 5, Stuart A. Rose Manuscript, Archives, and Rare Books Library, Emory University; Jeff Frederick, *Stand Up for Alabama: Governor George Wallace* (Tuscaloosa: University of Alabama Press, 2007), 132–33, 139, 161, 168–69; James Chisum, "Mrs. Wallace Is a Loser, Delegates Say," November 9, 1965, *Birmingham News*, Al Fox, "Wallace Sends up Trial Balloon: 'Succession'— Just Color Me Lurleen," *Birmingham News*, October 27, 1965, Bob Ingram, "Forecast:—No Senate Race, Lurleen for Governor," *Montgomery Advertiser*, October 27, 1965, all in Carter Papers, Box 6.

7. Anita Smith, *The Intimate Story of Lurleen Wallace: Her Crusade of Courage*, (Montgomery: Communications Unlimited, 1969), 8–9, 44–46; Marshall Frady, "Governor and Mister Wallace," *Atlantic Monthly*, 38, SG 031280, ADAH; Frederick, *Stand Up for Alabama*, 163–64; Anita Smith, "The Real Lurleen: The Steadying Force: A Mercurial Man's Placid Mate, Lurleen," *Birmingham News*, November 2, 1967, SG 031280, ADAH.

8. Frederick, *Stand Up for Alabama*, 165, 162; Bob Ingram, "Done in Twice by JP, Wallace Won't Forget It," *Montgomery Advertiser*, October 24, 1965, Carter Papers, Box 6; Smith, *Intimate Story*, 78–79; Frady, interview transcripts, 12C, 55C–57C, 64C, 72C–74C; M. W. Espy Jr. to George Wallace, February 1, 1966, SG 21951, ADAH; George Wallace Jr., *The Wallaces of Alabama: My Family* (Chicago: Follett, 1975), 89.

9. Frederick, *Stand Up for Alabama*, 165–66, 141, 134, 39, 33; "Air Crash Kills Candidate for Alabama Governor," *New York Times*, February 11, 1966, Hugh Sparrow, "A Point of View," *Birmingham News*, June 19, 1966, both in Carter Papers, Box 6; Frady, interview transcripts, 110C, 173A–174A.

10. Frederick, *Stand Up for Alabama*, 13, 165; Dan T. Carter, *The Politics of Rage: George Wallace, the Origins of the New Conservatism, and the Transformation of American Politics* (New York: Simon and Schuster, 1995), 280. Frady, interview transcripts, 15–16, 58, 130; Melissa Brown, "Wallace's Daughter Speaks about 50th Anniversary of Stand in the Schoolhouse Door," www.al.com, June 10, 2013; Michele Norris, "A Daughter's Struggle to Overcome a Legacy of Segregation," *National Public Radio*, June 11, 2013, http://www.npr.org/2013/06/11/190387908/a-daughters-struggle-to -overcome-a-legacy-of-segregation (accessed August 1, 2016).

11. *A Tribute to Lurleen B. Wallace*, WSFA-TV, May 7, 1968, SG 031280, ADAH; Frederick, *Stand Up for Alabama*, 11–12; Lurleen Wallace, interview by Marshall Frady, 1966, 13D, 1E–5E, Frady Papers, Box 5; Janean Mann, "Meet Lurleen Wallace No. 2: Young Lurleen Burns was a Tomboy," *Birmingham Post Herald*, November 1, 1966, Janean Mann, "Meet Lurleen Wallace . . . No. 3—High School Days Filled with Fun," *Birmingham Post Herald*, November 2, 1966, Janean Mann, "Meet Lurleen Wallace . . . No. 4—Since School, Lurleen Wallace Always Has Been Busy," *Birmingham Post Herald*, November 3, 1966, all in Carter Papers, Box 6; Notes on Lurleen Wallace's Life, SG 031280, ADAH; Frady, interview transcripts, 1E–5E, 13D; Frady, "Governor and Mister Wallace," 38–39.

12. Lurleen Wallace, interview, 13D, 1E–5E; Frederick, *Stand up for Alabama*, 13–16, 184; "Kindly Mother of Four Makes History Tuesday" (clipping) [ca. 1967], SG 031280, ADAH; Self, *All in the Family*, 103–4, 107, 110–11; Sim Thomas, interview by Marshall Frady, 82C–83C, Frady Papers, Box 5; George Wallace Jr., *Wallaces of Alabama*, 35–36, 42–43; George Wallace Jr., *Governor George Wallace: The Man You Never Knew* (Montgomery, Ala.: Wallace, 2011), 6–10; Frady, "Governor and Mister Wallace," 37; Royal Reynolds, interview by Marshall Frady, 8D; Vernon Merritt, interview by Marshall Frady, 196A; Gerald Wallace, interview by Marshall Frady, 100C; McDowell Lee, interview by Marshall Frady, 154A, 157A, all in Frady Papers, Box 5. Lee noted that there were rumors of the Wallaces' marriage troubles as early as 1954.

13. Smith, *Intimate Story*, 83; Frederick, *Stand Up for Alabama*, 168; "Statement by Mrs. George C. Wallace," February 24, 1966, SG 031280, ADAH; "Lurleen Wallace 1966 Campaign for Governor," You-Tube, https://youtube/OQjMOZg4nc4 (accessed August 1, 2016); Dan Dowe and Al Fox, "Makes It Official—Mrs. Wallace's Bonnet in Ring," *Birmingham News*, February 24, 1966, Roy Reed, "Gov. Wallace's Wife Enters Race to Succeed Him," *New York Times*, February 24, 1966, both in Carter Papers, Box 6.

14. Carter, *Politics of Rage*, 280; Frederick, *Stand Up for Alabama*, 165; Frady, interview transcripts, 15–16, 58, 130; "Wallace Spits on Constitution," *Tuscaloosa Graphic*, reprinted in *Montgomery Advertiser*, March 7, 1966, Hugh Sparrow, "Wallace Drive Starts Fast, Funds Asked," *Birmingham News*, February 27, 1966, Frances Lewine, "Top Political Women Criticize Lurleen," *Gadsden Times*, n.d., all in Carter Papers, Box 6; Smith, *Intimate Story*, 78–79.

15. Self, *All in the Family*, 4, 6–7, 13, 28–29, 32; Herman H. Ross to George C. Wallace, March 14, 1966, SG 030836, ADAH; Charles Gomillion, interview by Marshall Frady, 127–28, Frady Papers, Box 5; "Lurleen Still Knows Simple Joy of Fishing" (clipping), n.d., SG 031280, ADAH; "The Wallace Record: It Speaks for Itself," *Birmingham News*, April 24, 1966, SG 034459, ADAH; Marshall Frady, notes for manuscript, 5E, Frady Papers, Box 5.

16. Shana Alexander, "The Feminine Eye: On the Lookout for Lurleen," *Life*, July 22, 1966, 19.

17. Mrs. T. J. Potts to *Ladies' Home Journal*, September 20, 1966, Anna M. Gibson to Lucille Irwin Smylie, September 9, 1966, Shirley G. House to Mrs. Robert Smylie, August 30, 1966, all in

SG 030836, ADAH; James Free, "U.S. Provided Wallace with Help on 'Standing Up for Alabama,'" *Birmingham News*, May 5, 1966, Carter Papers, Box 6.

18. "Speech of Mrs. George C. Wallace State-Wide Campaign Kick-Off, Municipal Auditorium, Montgomery, Ala.," March 18, 1966, Anne Plott, "A Visit with Lurleen Wallace," *Talladega County's Daily Home*, March 24, 1966, both in SG 031280, ADAH; Rally Photograph in "The Wallace Record: It Speaks for Itself," *Birmingham News*, April 24, 1966, SG 0304459, ADAH; Frady, interview transcripts, 81C; Kate Harris, "'All Those Numbers Belong to Mama,' Wallace Tyke Learns," *Birmingham News*, November 9, 1966, Carter Papers, Box 6; Jamie Wallace, "Large Crowd Hears Wallaces in Selma Appearance," *Selma Times Journal*, reprinted in "The Wallace Record," *Birmingham News*, April 24, 1966, SG 034459, ADAH. Curlee told Wallace "he'd better start sleepin' with that woman." Wallace responded: "Wouldn't it be a helluva note if she run me off?"

19. Frederick, *Stand Up for Alabama*, 174, 176–77; Note Regarding July 1966 *Esquire* Magazine, SG 031280, ADAH; George Wallace Jr., *Wallaces of Alabama*, 92–93; Frady, interview transcripts, 3, 76C; Peter Goldman, "Alabama's New Era: The Negro Votes," *Newsweek*, May 16, 1966, 26–27, Frady Papers, Box 3; Photo Contact Sheets from 1966 Campaign, SG 033629, ADAH; "The Great Debate: Governor Hopefuls Gang Up on Wallace," *Birmingham News*, March 30, 1966, Carter Papers, Box 6.

20. Frederick, *Stand up for Alabama*, 171, 175–76; Lurleen B. Wallace speech 1966 campaign, critique of Wallace's speaking style, unidentified newspaper clipping, [1966], Anne Plott, "A Visit with Lurleen Wallace," *Talladega County's Daily Home*, March 24, 1966, all in SG 031280, ADAH; Smith, *Intimate Story*, 84–85; George Wallace Jr., *Wallaces of Alabama*, 92–93.

21. George C. Wallace, campaign speeches, 1966, SG 031280, ADAH; Frady, interview transcripts, 18–19; Frady, "Governor and Mister Wallace," 36; Goldman, "Alabama's New Era," 26–27; Pete Daniel, *Lost Revolutions: The South in the 1950s* (Chapel Hill: University of North Carolina Press, 2000), 91, 93, 114. Daniel describes "lowdown culture" as including working-class rural southerners who flouted respectability, defied authority, and were proud of being rude, uncouth, and violent. George Wallace's campaign style tapped into this culture. Robert Kennedy's speech was not about Lurleen Wallace. Before he gave his address as the keynote to Emphasis66, RFK made a passing joke: "I hear people saying I'm making these speeches around the country to further my campaign for the presidency. But I'll tell you one thing, my wife is not running for president." This drew loud applause. Tilford notes, "Kennedy then leaned over the podium, looked at his wife in the front row and asked, impishly, 'Or are you?' Again, the applause thundered" (Earl H. Tilford, *Turning the Tide: The University of Alabama in the 1960s* [Tuscaloosa: University of Alabama Press, 2014], 91).

22. "The Wallace Record: It Speaks for Itself," *Birmingham News*, April 24, 1966, SG 034459, ADAH.

23. Janis Hawk, "Lurleen Wallace Pointing Toward 'Community Property' for Governorship" (clipping), March 17, 1966, George Wallace, speech, 1966, both in SG 031280, ADAH; Al Fox, "Wallace Takes Over at Rally for Wife," *Birmingham News*, March 5, 1966, Carter Papers, Box 6; Frady, interview transcripts, 4–5, 24, 30. George Wallace also refused to become a Republican because of what he saw as the party's obsession with the dollar (Seymore Trammell, interview by Dan T. Carter, January 11, 1988, 22–23, Carter Papers, Box 9). According to Seymore Trammell, racial issues formed the core of Wallace's campaign as a way to reach out to ordinary whites who did not like black people. Publicly, however, he maintained a focus on state's rights: "The liberal crowd, or pointy heads; it all means the same thing."

24. Lurleen B. Wallace, speech, [ca. November 1966], SG 031280, ADAH.

25. Sample Ballot, 1966, "Lurleen Wins Easily in Alabama," *Miami News*, May 4, 1966, both in SG 030836, ADAH; Goldman, "Alabama's New Era," 28; Bob Ingram, "N. Alabama Vote Big Factor in Win," *Montgomery Advertiser*, May 5, 1966; Al Fox, "Negro Vote Badly Split: Overwhelm Op-

ponents Wallace Win Easily, Face Martin in Fall," *Birmingham News*, May 4, 1966, Kate Harris, "'All Those Numbers Belong to Mama,' Wallace Tyke Learns," *Birmingham News*, November 9, 1966, all in Carter Papers, Box 6; Frederick, *Stand Up for Alabama*, 169–79; "After May 3" (clipping), SG 031280, ADAH; "Commencement Address—Judson College, Marion, Alabama," April 16, 1967, SG 031280, ADAH.

26. Wilbur L. Blackmon, "Still a 'Love Affair,'" *Opelika Daily News*, October 3, 1966, SG 030836, ADAH; Wallace Campaign Press Release, n.d., Mrs. George C. Wallace, speech, Alabaster, Ala., November 1, 1966, both in SG 031280, ADAH.

27. "Thousands Attend Wallace Nite Here," *Clayton Record*, [ca. November 6, 1966], Joel P. Smith, "Keep Your Eyes on Lurleen Wallace," *Eufaula Tribune*, [ca. November 1966], both in SG 031280, ADAH; Frady, interview transcripts, 55–56; Frederick, *Stand Up for Alabama*, 178; "Elect Jim Martin," *Birmingham News*, November 7, 1966, Carter Papers, Box 6; Carter, *Politics of Rage*, 290–92; Jane Margold, "Madame Governor: Lurleen Wallace Is the Chief Executive of Alabama, but Her Predecessor-Husband Is Never Far Away," *Boston-Herald Sunday Magazine*, March 19, 1967, "Lurleen Did It . . . ," *Alabama Journal*, November 9, 1966, both in SG 031280, ADAH.

28. George Wallace Jr., *Wallaces of Alabama*, 99; Tom Wicker, "Lurleen Might Not Be a Copy of George," *Birmingham News*, December 5, 1966, Dan Dowe, "Mrs. Wallace Keeps Busy: Being Governor-Elect Takes Time, Too," *Birmingham News*, December 29, 1966, Jane Margold, "Madame Governor: Lurleen Wallace Is the Chief Executive of Alabama, but Her Predecessor-Husband Is Never Far Away," *Boston Herald Sunday Magazine*, March 19, 1967; Al Fox, "Fresh Coffee Aroma: Lurleen's Office Has 'Housewife' Touch," *Birmingham News*, [ca. January 1967], all in SG 031280, ADAH; Natalie Zemon Davis, *Society and Culture in Early Modern Europe* (1965; Stanford: Stanford University Press, 1975), 140, 144–45, 147. In her essay "Women on Top," Davis discusses unruly women and ways they subverted the presumed natural inferiority of women.

29. Ray Jenkins, "A Woman May Be Small of Frame . . . but . . . ," *Birmingham News*, January 1, 1967, Carter Papers, Box 6; Frederick, *Stand Up for Alabama*, 178, 181; Smith, *Intimate Story*, 94; Press Secretary, typed clipping, n.d., SG 031280, ADAH; Frady, "Governor and Mister Wallace," 38; Jules Loh, "Lurleen May Be More Than Mere Figurehead," *Montgomery Advertiser-Journal*, February 19, 1967, Carter Papers, Box 6; George Wallace Jr., *Wallaces of Alabama*, 104; "'Where's My $1?' Chief Adviser Asks," *Birmingham News*, [ca. January 1967], SG 031280, ADAH.

30. Self, *All in the Family*, 25–26, 105; A. C. Spectorsky to Lurleen Wallace, January 1967, SG 030836, ADAH; "This Is Lurleen: Parent, Wife, Head of State" (clipping), [ca. January 1967], SG 031280, ADAH. Her salary would be the equivalent of $179,715 in 2015 dollars.

31. Davis, *Society and Culture*, 147. Stephanie McCurry, *Confederate Reckoning: Power and Politics in the Civil War South* (Cambridge: Harvard University Press, 2012), 175, 179, 197. Both Davis and McCurry provide examples of women using the moral economy to justify their unruly behavior in an effort to protect traditional rights against change. Lurleen Wallace's actions were not viewed as unruly, but a woman governor in 1967 could be seen as out of her proper place. By couching her position as governor in her roles as wife and mother, she had license to speak out against federal intervention to support racial integration, which was still part of her moral universe even though much of the nation no longer agreed. See Jason Morgan Ward, *Defending White Democracy: The Making of a Segregationist Movement and the Remaking of Racial Politics, 1936–1965* (Chapel Hill: University of North Carolina Press, 2011), 84–86, 88.

32. Lurleen Wallace, inaugural address, January 16, 1967, SG 034376, ADAH; Smith, *Intimate Story*, 86–87.

33. "Stars and Bars Still in Breeze," *Alabama Journal*, September 1, 1967, Carter Papers, Box 6;

Susan Youngblood Ashmore, *Carry It On: The War on Poverty and the Civil Rights Movement in Alabama, 1964–1972* (Athens: University of Georgia Press, 2008), 229.

34. Smith, *Intimate Story*, 4–5, 34–35, 102–3; George Wallace Jr., *Wallaces of Alabama*, 11, 108–9, 115; Carter, *Politics of Rage*.

35. Anita Smith, "Exclusive: 'If I Have Cancer, Again, I Want to Be Told,' Says Governor Wallace," *Birmingham News*, September 17, 1967, Anita Smith, "The Real Lurleen: Tenseness All Around, She Smiles Within," *Birmingham News*, October 30, 1967, Rex Thomas, "Reports to Hospital Today: Lurleen Faces Cancer Fight Calmly," [ca. January 1968], "Prayers Go with Her," *Birmingham News*, January 6, 1968, "Prayers," *Andalusia Star-News*, January 11, 1968, all in SG 031280, ADAH.

36. "Wallaces Leaving Mansion" (clipping), May 17, 1968, typed clipping about Wallace's death, "'Stand Up for America' Wallace Backers Urged," *Houston Post*, January 12, 1968, all in SG 031280, ADAH; Joy Brooks to Mrs. Mark Kennedy, March 14, 1983, Lee Wallace, report card, St. James School, 1967–68, George Wallace Jr., report card, Lanier High School, 1967–68, George Wallace campaign schedule, March 3–5, 1968, all in SG 034459, ADAH; Joy Williams, "Soft-Spoken—Wallace Kids Stir Sympathy," *Birmingham News*, October 27, 1968, Carter Papers, Box 9.

37. Self, *All in the Family*, 7–8, 277, 303. Self explains George Wallace's significance on national politics. Wallace popularized a brand of southern populism that appealed to "the 'little guy,' who does his best to be a breadwinner and live up to the obligations of manhood, while others—hippies, feminists, welfare recipients, intellectuals—do no real work and use the state for experiments in social engineering." With no grassroots organizations to promote such views, they remained the province of what Self calls "Wallace-style demagoguery from above."

Harper Lee

To Kill a Mockingbird *and "A Good Woman's Words"*

NANCY GRISHAM ANDERSON

In July 1960, few people would have imagined the phenomenal success ahead for Harper Lee's first novel, *To Kill a Mockingbird*. However, Lee's childhood friend, Truman Capote, might have been among those who did: in a 1959 letter, he wrote: "Yes, it is true that Nelle Lee is publishing a book. I did not see Nelle last winter, but the previous year she showed me as much of the book as she'd written, and I like it very much. She has real talent."[1] Even that praise, however, does not hint at the novel's continuing success more than half a century after its publication. The author's upbringing in a small, rural town in South Alabama certainly gave no hint of the fame to come.

Nelle Harper Lee—known as "Nelle" to her friends—was born on April 28, 1926, the youngest of four children of lawyer Amasa Coleman (A. C.) Lee and Frances Cunningham Finch Lee.[2] Her two sisters were fifteen and ten years her senior; at six years older, her brother, Edwin, was close enough to be a playmate on occasion but also left his baby sister behind to pursue other entertainment. Between 1928 and 1933, Capote spent summers with relatives who lived next door to the Lees and became Nelle's primary playmate. The two were kindred spirits, and in a 1964 interview, she recalled, "We had to use our own devices in our play, for our entertainment. We didn't have much money. . . . We didn't have toys, nothing was done for us, so the result was that we lived in our imagination most of the time. We devised things; we were readers, and we would transfer everything we had seen on the printed page to the backyard in the form of high drama."[3] Scout; her brother, Jem; and their playmate, Dill, devised many of the same things in *To Kill a Mockingbird*.

Nelle attended Monroe County's public schools, graduating from Monroe County High School in 1944. One teacher in particular, Gladys Watson, who

HARPER LEE, 2007

Courtesy of the *Montgomery Advertiser*.

taught Nelle English from her sophomore through senior years, served as a mentor. Nelle's oldest sister, Alice, had attended Montgomery's Huntingdon College for one year before dropping out when the stock market crashed, and Nelle followed in those footsteps, spending the 1944–45 academic year there before transferring to the University of Alabama to study law. While at the university, she wrote for its literary publications and newspaper and edited the school's humor magazine, *Rammer-Jammer*, in 1946–47. In the summer of 1948 she briefly attended Oxford University in England before returning to and then leaving the University of Alabama in 1949, one term short of a degree.

Lee then moved to New York to become a writer. After a brief stint working in a bookstore, she became an airline reservation agent, spending her evenings and nights writing. Weeks and months extended into years as she wrote short stories, revised them, and began transforming one of them into a novel that she tentatively titled *Go Set a Watchman*.[4]

About this time, good friends gave Lee a generous gift that allowed her to quit her job and devote herself full time to writing. As she wrote in "Christmas to Me," a personal essay published in *McCall's* magazine in 1961, the friends "wanted to show their faith in me the best way they knew how. Whether I ever sold a line was immaterial. They wanted to give me a full, fair chance to learn my craft, free from the harassments of a regular job. Would I accept their gift? There were no strings at all. Please accept, with their love."[5] Finally able to devote her full attention to her writing, every few weeks she submitted between fifty and one hundred pages to her agent, Maurice Crain, who sent out a draft to potential publishers. J. B. Lippincott offered Harper Lee a contract, and editor Tay Hohoff became the guiding force of the novel. By the end of February 1957, Hohoff had a complete draft of the story, which told of a summer visit by twenty-six-year-old Jean Louise "Scout" Finch to her childhood home. The astute Hohoff apparently saw potential in the protagonist's memories of her childhood escapades and encouraged Lee to write that story instead. After two years of revisions, *Go Set a Watchman* became *To Kill a Mockingbird*, and the novel went into production in 1959.[6]

In November 1959, while her novel was in design and printing, Lee accompanied Capote on a trip to Holcomb, Kansas, to research the murders of the four members of the Clutter family. Lee was crucial to Capote's investigation, gaining the trust of the stunned and terrified residents of the small town and interviewing residents and law enforcement officers. Lee took more than one hundred pages of detailed, single-spaced typed notes (with handwritten marginal comments). They open with an intriguing dedication:

> These Notes Are Dedicated To The Author of
> The Fire and The Flame
> and the
> Small Person
> Who So
> Manfully Endured
> Him.[7]

Capote acknowledged his friend's assistance with part of the dedication to *In Cold Blood*—"For Jack Dunphy and Harper Lee / With My Love and Gratitude"—but did not mention her contributions in the acknowledgments, although on other occasions he called her his "assistant researchist."[8] Serialized in the *New Yorker* beginning in September 1965 and published as a book in 1966, *In Cold Blood* has variously been called a "nonfiction novel" and "creative nonfiction," and it is a classic in its own right. The friendship between Lee and Capote apparently dissolved soon after the publication of *In Cold Blood*, though neither of them ever explained why. One theory is that Lee was saddened by Capote's decline into drugs and alcohol and wanted to distance herself. Another is that she was hurt by her friend's failure to acknowledge her contributions to his work with more than a dedication shared with his partner.

Soon after she returned from Kansas to New York, Lee became caught up in a whirlwind of activities associated with the release of *To Kill a Mockingbird*, which officially appeared on July 11, 1960. Lee admitted that the setting for the novel "was my childhood" but always insisted that the narrative is fiction rather than autobiography.[9] Set in fictional Maycomb, which was based on Monroeville, the story follows Scout, Jem, and Dill from the summer of 1932, as Scout readies for her first year of school, through the evening of Halloween 1935. The children's lives revolve around two major small-town concerns: the mysterious Arthur "Boo" Radley, secluded in a dark house in the neighborhood, and the trial of Tom Robinson, an African American farmhand accused of raping a nineteen-year-old white girl, Mayella Ewell, who lives with her father, Robert E. Lee "Bob" Ewell, and her seven younger siblings near the town's dump. Scout's and Jem's father, Atticus Finch, has accepted an appointment as Robinson's defense attorney, despite the racist sentiments of many of the townspeople.

Initial reviews did not find greatness in this first novel by a previously unknown southern writer, although Roy Newquist wrote in 1964 that "high praise was almost unanimous, both for the excellence of the book itself and for the welcome draught of fresh air that seemed to come with it."[10] Some of the early reviews praised the realistic characters, powerful storytelling, and subtle, complex point of view.[11] *Commonweal* proclaimed it "the find of the year."[12] Other reviews offered mixed or more negative assessments, citing stereotypical characters, problems with the viewpoint, and the failure of the two plot lines to come together. Granville Hicks criticized Lee's handling of point of view but praised her creation of Atticus as "a notable portrait of a Southern liberal."[13] Phoebe Adams condemned Lee's handling of point of view but concluded that the novel was "pleasant, undemanding reading."[14] In a 1966 study of Pulitzer Prize–winning novels, W. J. Stuckey declared that *Mockingbird* possessed "fatal flaws": the two plot lines do not merge, the point of view does not work, and the characters, especially Tom Robinson, are unrealistic.[15]

As several reviewers noted, the coming-of-age story appears to be told through the deceptively simple point of view of the child, Scout. However, the words are actually those of an older, more reflective Jean Louise, who is remembering how she and Jem grew from childhood innocence to an adult understanding of the world. The trial and the "bogeyman" down the street teach them a more realistic—and sadder—view of their neighbors and their society. Throughout the narrative, Lee carefully reminds readers that Scout's story is being remembered, using such phrases as "when enough years had gone by," "until many years later," and "in later years." Atticus teaches the children by example and explains his actions to be sure they understand: do not kill mockingbirds because they do no harm and bring songs to our world; learn to look at things from other people's perspectives; courage is not facing the world with a gun but taking on a losing task and completing it. The Finches' neighbor, Miss Maudie, explains that Atticus has taken on the losing task of defending Tom because communities must have "some men . . . who were born to do our unpleasant jobs for us."[16]

Lee also saw the novel as a "love story"—the love between a father and his children and the love of small-town life. In 1964, Lee explained, "I would like . . . to do one thing, and I've never spoken much about it because it's such a personal thing. I would like to leave some record of the kind of life that existed in a very small world. I hope to do this in several novels—to chronicle something that seems to be very quickly going down the drain. This is small-town middle-class southern life, as opposed to the Gothic, as opposed to *Tobacco Road*, as opposed to plantation life. . . . I would simply like to put down all I know about this [rich society] because I believe there is something universal in this little world, something decent to be said about it and something to lament in its passing."[17] This personal goal of Lee's also became a concern of the 1962 movie adaptation of the novel, as the film's art director, Henry Bumstead, described: "Monroeville is a beautiful little town of about 2500 inhabitants. It's small in size, but large in southern character. . . . Most of the houses are of wood, one story, and set up on brick piles. Almost every house has a porch and a swing hanging from the rafters. Believe me, it's a much more relaxed life than we live in Hollywood. . . . I have also visited the old courthouse square and the interior of the courtroom Nelle wrote about. I can't tell you how thrilled I am by the architecture and the little touch that will add to our sets."[18]

To achieve the goal of capturing small-town life in south-central Alabama in the 1930s, Lee had to pay close attention to history, politics, and sociology. Her characters struggle with the hardships of the depression and the harsh realities of Jim Crow laws. Lee was, of course, a child in a small town in Alabama during these years and knew these realities firsthand. Furthermore, as the daughter of a respected small-town lawyer, Lee would have been acquainted with the classes that Jem so precisely explains to his sister: "You know something, Scout? I've got it all figured out, now. I've thought about it a lot lately and I've got it figured out. There's four kinds of folks in the world. There's the ordinary kind like us and the neighbors, there's the kind like the Cunninghams out in the woods, the kind like the Ewells down at the dump, and the Negroes."[19] As an intelligent, intellectually curious person growing up in a lawyer's household, Lee would also have been aware of the notorious trials of the Scottsboro Boys and Walter Lett, who were black men accused of raping white women. Lee did not, however, directly base Tom's trial on a specific case.

To Kill a Mockingbird is much more than a simple coming-of-age story or a love story. It contains a richness, and perceptive readers find new depth each time they open the book. Not only does Lee capture the depression-era hardships that cut across all levels of society, but Tom's trial offers a way to study segregation in small-town life. The children are confused by the various reactions to Atticus's defense of Tom, which range from respect for taking on a difficult case to anger that he is seriously trying to defend a black man. The children are puzzled by racial prejudice on the part of people they have known all their lives and are stunned when the jury finds Tom guilty even though their father has proved beyond a doubt that the man is innocent. Jem in particular is seriously disillusioned by these adult actions.

Though the novel explores the issue of race in the 1930s, its release in 1960 also places it at the heart of the civil rights movement, which picked up steam after the U.S. Supreme Court's 1954 *Brown v. Board of Education* decision and the 1955–56 Montgomery Bus Boycott. *Mockingbird*'s publication occurred less than six months after students at North Carolina A & T had staged the first civil rights sit-in and ten months before Freedom Riders arrived in Alabama and were beaten by Klansmen in Anniston and Birmingham. The film version opened at Birmingham's Melba Theater on April 3, 1963, just as the Southern Christian Leadership Conference was turning up the heat with a boycott intended to force the city's businesses to integrate; exactly one month later, the country would be shocked by images of Birmingham officials turning police dogs and fire hoses on children demonstrating for civil rights. As novelist Mark Childress, who was born in Monroeville in 1957, reflected on the thirtieth anniversary of *Mockingbird*'s publication, "The amount of change [in the racial climate] that has taken place is remarkable. . . . *To Kill a Mockingbird* had a lot to do with that in the same way that *Uncle Tom's Cabin* woke people up to injustice 100 years earlier."[20] Lawyers embraced *To Kill a Mockingbird*, with analyses of the character of Atticus Finch appearing in law reviews all over the country and attorney and radio talk show host Mike Papantonio publishing *In Search of Atticus Finch: A Motivational Book for Lawyers*.[21] Attorneys often explain their choice of profession by saying, "I wanted to be Atticus Finch," or "I read *To Kill a Mockingbird* and was inspired to be a lawyer." In 1997 the Alabama Bar Association dedicated a monument to Atticus Finch on the grounds of the old courthouse in Monroeville, the only such honor the organization has ever granted to a fictional character.

The academic world took some time before it began to consider *To Kill a Mockingbird* a legitimate subject for scholarship. The attitude began to change in 1974, when an Indian scholar, R. A. Dave, published one of the first full-length articles on the novel: "*To Kill a Mockingbird*: Harper Lee's Tragic Vision."[22] Subsequent volumes have included Claudia Durst Johnson's *To Kill a Mockingbird: Threatening Boundaries* and several collections of critical essays, with scholars focusing on the novel's themes and viewpoint and on changing views of Atticus. Other authors have explored the novel's symbolism; its treatment of such phenomena as coming of age, race, gender issues, the law, religion, and small-town southern life during the depression; its Gothicism; its place in southern literature; and its role in using literature to teach moral values.[23] When asked what the novel is about, scholars, teachers, and students give a wide variety of answers: hope, tolerance, courage, race, life's lessons, and, perhaps most inclusive, "America." Many readers would agree with historian and critic Wayne Flynt that the novel is significant because it says something about the fabric of the United States: "Ironically, a novel written by a woman from Monroeville in Alabama's Black Belt has become the primary literary instrument worldwide for teaching values of racial justice, tolerance for people different from ourselves, and the need for moral courage in the face of community prejudice and ostracism."[24]

Though reviewers did not immediately realize that *Mockingbird* was a classic, readers reacted differently, keeping the book on best-seller lists for eighty-eight weeks. If Harper Lee was serious when she told an interviewer that she hoped for the novel's "quick and merciful death at the hands of the reviewers," her hopes were quickly dashed.[25] The book received the 1961 Pulitzer Prize for Fiction; the 1961 Brotherhood Award of the National Conference of Christians and Jews; and the 1961 Alabama Library Association Award. It was a Literary Guild selection, a *Reader's Digest* condensed book selection, and an alternate Book of the Month Club selection. After more than a half century in print, it continues to sell nearly a million copies each year around the world. The more than three dozen translations bear such titles as *The Story of Maycomb City* (Chinese), *Who Disturbs the Nightingale* (German), *The Blackbird Does Not Quarrel* (Hungarian), *To Kill a Parrot* (Korean), *The Sun Is for* Everyone (Portuguese), and *The Darkness beyond the Shrubbery* (Italian). A 1991 survey by the Library of Congress declared that *Mockingbird* ranked second behind the Bible in making a difference in the lives of individuals, and in 1999 American librarians named it the best novel of the twentieth century. It was chosen for One Book, One Chicago, a community reading program, and has become one of the most popular selections of the Big Read, the community reading initiative sponsored by the National Endowment for the Arts. Surveys from the National Council of the Teachers of English indicate that the novel is assigned reading in more than 70 percent of public high schools throughout the United States. Lee's honors have included the 2002 Alabama Humanities Award, the 2007 Presidential Medal of Freedom, presented by President George W. Bush, and the 2010 National Medal of Arts, presented by President Barack Obama.

Despite its widespread appeal, *To Kill a Mockingbird*, like many other literary classics, has also raised some objections, and various individuals and groups have attempted to keep it out of classrooms or off library shelves. In 1968 the National Education Association reported that it trailed only *Little Black Sambo* in generating complaints from private organizations. The American Library Association listed it among the top one hundred books banned between 1990 and 2000. Critics of the book have cited its racist language (the word *nigger* appears forty-eight times), racial stereotyping, discussion of rape, and profanity (*damn* and *whore lady*). The school board in Hanover County, Virginia, banned the book as "immoral literature" in 1966, with the controversy playing out over several weeks and receiving detailed coverage in the *Richmond News Leader* and *Richmond Times-Dispatch*. Lee herself weighed in with a letter to the editor and a contribution to a fund "to enroll the Hanover County School Board in any first grade of its choice" in an effort to stamp out illiteracy among its members.[26]

During the early 1960s, Lee faced tremendous demands for appearances and interviews, and she was involved in the movie production. She conferred with Horton Foote, who adapted the novel for the screen; entertained Bumstead and the movie's star, Gregory Peck, in Monroeville; and visited the set during filming. But Lee disliked the spotlight and soon began to withdraw from public life. Though she was frequently described as "a recluse" or "reclusive," *private* was probably a more appropriate term. She maintained a circle of friends and family and would make unannounced appearances at library activities, luncheons, or presentations, particularly in her hometown. She also began dividing her time between Monroeville and Manhattan, where she found some anonymity and a respite from the visitors who came to Monroeville in hopes of obtaining an autograph or asking her about "The Book," as she came to call it.

Before Lee ceased giving interviews, she was constantly asked about when she would release another book. Though at various times she was reported to be working on another novel and in the early 1980s she conducted research for a true-crime work about a series of murders in Alexander City, Alabama, nothing was published. Then on February 3, 2015, HarperCollins announced that the original manuscript for *Go Set a Watchman* had been found and would be published the following July. Most of those who had known of the long-ago existence of a manuscript by that title had believed that it was either a rough draft or a working title for *To Kill a Mockingbird*. With its rediscovery and publication, however, readers learned that although it gave rise to *Mockingbird*, *Watchman* was also a separate novel set in Maycomb, Alabama, in 1956, when Jean Louise makes her annual two-week trip home from New York to see her father. The novel focuses more on the lives of Maycomb's middle class and on the racial tensions of the South in the mid-1950s. By the time *Watchman* was published, Lee was in poor health, and critics and friends questioned whether she was mentally competent to approve its release. Statements issued in Lee's name by the publisher and by her attorney did little to quell the controversy, with critics decrying publication as "fraud" and as "one of the epic money grabs in the modern history of American publishing."[27] The state agencies that investigated elder abuse and financial fraud found no evidence and dismissed the charges. Family members and close friends refuted the claims of diminished mental capacity, explaining that Lee's compromised vision and hearing could be misinterpreted as diminished mental capacity. Thus, the controversial novel was released with no editing or revising of the text by Lee. Reviewers were less than enthusiastic, describing the book as at best raw and unpolished and often in less charitable terms. Nevertheless, it became an instant best seller.[28]

Harper Lee's only other published work was a handful of short selections: "Dewey Had Important Part in Solving Brutal Murders" (1960), "Christmas to Me" (1961), "Love—In Other Words" (1961), "When Children Discover America" (1965), "Truman Capote" (1966), and "Romance and High Adventure" (1985).[29] Lee also describes her love of reading in an open letter to Oprah Winfrey that was published in *O, the Oprah Magazine* (2006).[30] The letter tells how words came into her life when she was a child and evokes Scout's description of learning to read while sitting in Atticus's lap as he reads law books and newspapers.

In 2013, Davis Raines and Frye Gaillard wrote a song, "Mockingbird," that captures the novel's richness and complexity and pays tribute to its power and universality. The lyrics, underscored by a plaintive melody, immortalize the pain and the sorrow and the hope found in "a good woman's words":

> I heard an old, old story
> One of trouble and a trial
> It was all laid out before me
> Through the eyes of a child
> It was a story of sin
> And a man of his word
> The color of skin
> And the song of a bird.
>
> It's just an old, old story
> One of heartbreak and of fear
> I see it still before me
> In places far and near
> In a good woman's words
> A man of inspiration
> And the song of a bird
>
> It all keeps happening
> Again and again
> We're still living
> With the same old sins
> But the story lives
> And the mockingbird sings
> Of truth and beauty
> And life's precious things.
>
> REFRAIN:
> Mockingbird, mockingbird
> It's the sweetest song
> We've ever heard
> Lifts us up beyond the hate
> And the hurt
> Listen to the mockingbird.[31]

Lee died on February 19, 2016, in Monroeville.

NOTES

1. Truman Capote to Mary Ida Carter, July 9, 1959, Monroe County Museum.

2. Harper Lee did not approve the writing of any biographies, but facts about her life are available in a number of books and encyclopedia entries: Nancy Grisham Anderson, "Harper Lee," in *Encyclopedia of Alabama*, http://www.encyclopediaofalabama.org/face/Article.jsp?id=h-1126 (accessed July 30, 2016); Kerry Madden, *Harper Lee (Up Close)* (New York: Viking, 2009); Charles Shields, *Mockingbird: A Portrait of Harper Lee* (New York: Holt, 2007); Charles Shields, *I Am Scout: The Biography of Harper Lee* (New York: Holt, 2008); Charles J. Shields, *Mockingbird: A Portrait of Harper Lee from Scout to Go Set a Watchman* (New York: Henry Holt, 2016).

3. Roy Newquist, "Harper Lee," in *Counterpoint* (Chicago: Rand McNally, 1964), 407.

4. Shields, *Mockingbird* (2016), 73–101.

5. Harper Lee, "Christmas to Me," *McCall's*, December 1961, 63.

6. Shields, *Mockingbird* (2016), 87–92, 99–101; Gaby Wood, "Harper Lee: The Inside Story of the Greatest Comeback in Literature," *The Telegraph*, February 10, 2016, http://www.telegraph.co.uk/books/go-set-a-watchman/the-curious-case-of-harper-lee/ (accessed September 18, 2016).

7. "In Cold Blood, Typescript Notes," Truman Capote Papers, Box 7, Folder 1, New York Public Library.

8. Jackie Sheckler Finch, "To Save a Mockingbird," in *It Happened in Alabama: Remarkable Events That Shaped History* (Guilford, Conn.: Globe Pequot, 2011), 92.

9. Newquist, "Harper Lee," 407.

10. Ibid., 404.

11. "*To Kill a Mockingbird* Is a Wonderful First Novel," *Time*, August 1, 1960, 70; R. W. Henderson, "To Kill a Mockingbird," *Library Journal*, May 15, 1960, 1937; Richard Sullivan, review of *To Kill a Mockingbird*, *Chicago Sunday Tribune*, July 17, 1960.

12. L. R. Ward, review of *To Kill a Mockingbird*, *Commonweal*, December 9, 1960, 28.

13. Granville Hicks, "Three at the Outset," *Saturday Review*, July 23, 1960, 15.

14. Phoebe Adams, "Summer Reading," *Atlantic*, August 1960, 98.

15. W. J. Stuckey, *The Pulitzer Prize Novels: A Critical Backward Look* (Norman: University of Oklahoma Press, 1966), 194.

16. Harper Lee, *To Kill a Mockingbird* (Philadelphia: Lippincott, 1960), 227–28.

17. Newquist, "Harper Lee," 412.

18. Henry Bumstead to Alan Pakula, November 1961, Monroe County Museum.

19. Lee, *To Kill a Mockingbird*, 239.

20. Mark Mayfield, "Listening to 'Mockingbird': 1960 Book Aided Change in the South," *USA Today*, November 5, 1990.

21. Mike Papantonio, *In Search of Atticus Finch: A Motivational Book for Lawyers* (Pensacola, Fla.: Seville Square, 1996). Law journals that published articles on Atticus include the *University of Pittsburgh Law Review* (1981), *Mercer Law Review* (1982), *Mississippi Law Journal* (1990), *Journal of Legal Education* (1990), *Legal Times* (1992), and *New Jersey Law Journal* (1997).

22. R. A. Dave, "*To Kill a Mockingbird*: Harper Lee's Tragic Vision," in M. K. Naik, ed., *Indian Studies in American Fiction* (Dharwar: Karnatak University and Macmillan Company of India, 1974), 311–24.

23. Claudia Durst Johnson, *To Kill a Mockingbird: Threatening Boundaries* (New York: Twayne, 1994); Alice Hall Petry, ed., *On Harper Lee: Essays and Reflections* (Knoxville: University of Ten-

nessee Press, 2008); Donald Noble, ed., *Critical Insights: To Kill a Mockingbird* (Pasadena, Calif.: Salem, 2009); Michel J. Meyer, ed., *Harper Lee's To Kill a Mockingbird: New Essays* (Lanham, Md.: Scarecrow, 2010).

24. Wayne Flynt, "*To Kill a Mockingbird*," in *Encyclopedia of Alabama*, http://www .encyclopediaofalabama.org/face/Article.jsp?id=h-1140 (accessed July 30, 2016).

25. Newquist, "Harper Lee," 405.

26. The letters to the editor, including the concluding letter by Harper Lee, from the *News Leader* and *Times-Dispatch* are printed in Claudia Durst Johnson, "A Censorship Attempt in Hanover, Virginia, 1966," in Harold Bloom, ed., *Modern Critical Interpretations: To Kill a Mockingbird* (Philadelphia: Chelsea House, 1999), 23–28, and in "*To Kill a Mockingbird* and Censorship," in Terry O'Neill, ed., *Readings on To Kill a Mockingbird* (San Diego: Greenhaven, 2000), 84–91.

27. Joe Nocera, "The Harper Lee 'Go Set a Watchman' Fraud," *New York Times*, July 24, 2015.

28. William Grimes, "Harper Lee, Author of 'To Kill a Mockingbird,' Dies at 89," *New York Times*, February 19, 2016.

29. Lee, "Christmas to Me," 63; Harper Lee, "Love—In Other Words," *Vogue*, April 15, 1961, 64–65; Harper Lee, "When Children Discover America," *McCall's* August 1965, 76–79; Harper Lee, "Romance and High Adventure," in Jerry Elijah Brown, ed., *Clearings in the Thicket: An Alabama Humanities Reader* (Macon, Ga.: Mercer University Press, 1985), 13–20. Lee first presented "Romance and High Adventure" at the 1983 Eufaula History and Heritage Festival, an appearance arranged by her sister, Louise Lee Connor, a Eufaula resident. In 2017, Charles J. Shields identified two previously published but unsigned works by Lee: "Dewey Had Important Part in Solving Brutal Murders," *Grapevine*, March 1960; "Truman Capote," *Book-of-the-Month-Club News*, January 1966.

30. Harper Lee, "Dear Oprah," *O: The Oprah Magazine*, July 2006, 151–53.

31. Davis Raines and Frye Gaillard, "Mockingbird" (Big Front Porch Productions, 2013).

Contributors

NANCY GRISHAM ANDERSON holds a bachelor's degree from Millsaps College and a graduate degree from the University of Virginia. Prior to her retirement in 2015, she taught southern and American literature and writing courses at Auburn University at Montgomery. Her publications include works on Zelda Fitzgerald, Richard Marius, Lella Warren, and Harper Lee, and she has taught extensively on *To Kill a Mockingbird*. She currently serves as a distinguished outreach fellow for Auburn University at Montgomery Outreach.

SUSAN YOUNGBLOOD ASHMORE is a professor of history at Oxford College of Emory University. She holds a doctorate in American history from Auburn University. She is the author of *Carry It On: The War on Poverty and the Civil Rights Movement in Alabama, 1964–1972* (2008), which won the 2009 Willie Lee Rose Prize from the Southern Association for Women Historians and the 2009 Frances Butler Simkins Prize from the Southern Historical Association.

LISA LINDQUIST DORR is an associate professor of history and an associate dean in the College of Arts and Sciences at the University of Alabama. She is the author of *White Women, Rape, and the Power of Race in Virginia, 1900–1960* (2004) and is currently completing a book on the smuggling of liquor from Cuba to the southern U.S. coast during Prohibition.

HARRIET E. AMOS DOSS is an associate professor of history at the University of Alabama at Birmingham. She holds a bachelor's degree from Agnes Scott College and master's and doctoral degrees from Emory University. She is the author of *Cotton City: Urban Development in Antebellum Mobile* (1985, 2001); the introduction to the 1994 edition of James Benson Sellers, *Slavery in Alabama*; and articles in such journals as the *Alabama Review* and *Gulf South Historical Review*.

WAYNE FLYNT is a community activist and professor emeritus of history at Auburn University. He is the author of fourteen books, including *Poor but Proud: Alabama's Poor Whites* (1989), nominated for the Pulitzer Prize and winner of the Lillian Smith Award from the Southern Regional Council; *Alabama in the Twentieth Century* (2004), winner of the 2004 Anne B. and James B. McMillan Prize; and *Mockingbird Songs: My Friendship with Harper Lee* (2017).

CAROLINE GEBHARD is a professor of English at Tuskegee University and holds a doctorate in English from the University of Virginia. She and Barbara McCaskill are coauthors of *Postbellum, Pre-Harlem: African American Literature and Culture, 1877–1919* (2006), and she, Katherine Adams, and Sandra Zagarell served as coeditors of a special 2016 issue of *Legacy: A Journal of American Women Writers* focusing on Alice Dunbar-Nelson.

STACI GLOVER holds a master's degree from the University of Alabama at Birmingham, where she is currently an adjunct instructor in the history department. She also serves as the director of the Brookside History Museum. Her publications include *Coal Mining in Jefferson County* (2011) and "When Only the Heavens Wept: Death at Banner Mines" (2012). Her research interests include the history of Alabama's working class, coal miners and their communities, and immigrants in Jefferson County, Alabama.

SHARONY GREEN is an assistant professor of history at the University of Alabama. She holds a doctorate in history from the University of Illinois and is the author of *Remember Me to Miss Louisa: Hidden Black-White Intimacies in Antebellum America* (2015). Her research interests include race, gender, urban history, and transnationalism.

SHEENA HARRIS is an assistant professor of history at Tuskegee University, where she also serves as the interim director of Student Engagement Initiatives and coordinator of the University-Wide Honors Program. She holds bachelor's and master's degrees from Florida A&M University and a doctorate from the University of Memphis. She has published works on women during slavery and contributed a chapter to *Real Sister: Stereotypes, Respectability, and Black Women in Reality TV*. She is currently completing a monograph on Margaret Murray Washington.

CHRISTOPHER D. HAVEMAN is an assistant professor of history at the University of West Alabama. He is the author of *Rivers of Sand: Creek Indian Emigration, Relocation, and Ethnic Cleansing in the American South* (2016).

KIMBERLY D. HILL is an assistant professor of African American history at the University of Texas at Dallas. She holds a bachelor's degree from the University of Texas at Austin and a doctorate from the University of North Carolina at Chapel Hill. She contributed a chapter to *Faith and Slavery in the Presbyterian Diaspora* (2016) and is currently researching a book on early twentieth-century black Presbyterian missionaries and industrial education.

TINA JONES holds a doctorate in American literature from the University of Southern Mississippi. She is a professor of English at the University of West Alabama, where she also serves as the executive director of economic development and research. She and Joe Taylor coedited *Belles' Letters: Contemporary Fiction by Alabama Women* (1999). She serves on the boards of directors for the Sumter County Fine Arts Council, Friends of the Alabama Department of Archives and History, Alabama Folklife Association, and Black Belt Treasures.

JENNY M. LUKE holds bachelor's and master's degrees from the University of Texas at Arlington, where she was named a University Scholar and received the 2012 Wolfskill Award for Excellence in Master's Studies in History. Her work on African American nurse-midwives won her the 2013 W. Curtis Worthington Jr. Graduate Prize from the Waring Library at the Medical University of South Carolina. She is currently pursuing research on African American childbirth traditions and midwifery.

REBECCA CAWOOD MCINTYRE is coordinator of the History and Reading Initiative at Middle Tennessee State University. She holds a doctorate from the University of Alabama and is the author of *Souvenirs of the Old South: Northern Tourism and Southern Mythology* (2011) as well as several articles on tourism and women's history in the South. She is currently exploring the intersection of public memory, tourism, and the civil rights movement.

REBECCA S. MONTGOMERY holds master's and doctoral degrees from the University of Missouri-Columbia. She has published *The Politics of Education in the New South: Women and Reform in Georgia, 1890–1930* (2006) as well as essays on farm women and agricultural careers. She is currently working on a biography of Celeste Parrish.

PAUL M. PRUITT JR. is special collections librarian at the Bounds Law Library at the University of Alabama. He holds a bachelor's degree from Auburn University, a master's degree in library science from the University of Alabama, and a doctorate in history from the College of William and Mary. He is author of *Taming Alabama: Lawyers and Reformers, 1804–1929* (2010) and editor of *New Field, New Corn: Essays in Alabama Legal History* (2015).

SUSAN E. REYNOLDS holds master's and doctoral degrees from the University of Alabama and currently serves as the associate editor of *Alabama Heritage*. She is the author of "Augusta Evans Wilson: Writer, Rebel, and Family Woman" (2011) and "William Augustus Bowles: Adventurous Rogue of the Old Southwest" (2012). She also contributed a chapter to *Harry Potter's World Wide Influence* (2009).

MARLENE HUNT RIKARD is a professor emeritus of history at Samford University, where she taught for thirty-seven years, initiated the course on the history of American women, and served as director of the London Studies Program. She holds a bachelor's degree from Auburn University, a master's degree from Samford University, and a doctorate from the University of Alabama. She has published works on the welfare capitalism programs of the Tennessee Coal, Iron, and Railroad Company as well as biographical articles and essays on business leaders of the Alabama steel industry, Alabama women in the Civil War, and Alabama artist Roderick Dempster MacKenzie.

PATRICIA SULLIVAN is a professor of history at the University of South Carolina, where she specializes in modern U.S. history with an emphasis on African Americans, race relations, and the civil rights movement. Her works include *Days of Hope: Race and Democracy in the New Deal Era* (1996), *Freedom Writer: Virginia Foster Durr, Letters from the Civil Rights Years* (2006), and *Lift Every Voice: The NAACP and the Making of the Civil Rights Movement* (2009). She and Waldo Martin Jr. are coeditors of *Civil Rights in the United States* (2000) and of the John Hope Franklin Series in African American History and Culture, published by the University of North Carolina Press. She is currently completing a book that invites a reconsideration of twentieth-century African American civil rights struggles.

JEANNE THEOHARIS is the Distinguished Professor of Political Science at Brooklyn College of the City University of New York. She has published numerous books and articles on the civil rights and Black Power movements, the politics of race and education, and social welfare and civil rights in post-9/11 America. She is also the author of *The Rebellious Life of Mrs. Rosa Parks* (2013), which won a 2014 NAACP Image Award and the Letitia Woods Brown Award from the Association of Black Women Historians.

Index

Italicized page numbers refer to tables and illustrations.

CPSIA information can be obtained
` www.ICGtesting.com
₁ited in the USA
.VHW042336241120
672602LV00003B/94